COPLAND

Copland

1900 THROUGH 1942

by AARON COPLAND

and VIVIAN PERLIS

St. Martin's / Marek

NEW YORK

Frontispiece photograph by Victor Kraft.

Designed by Cynthia Krupat

Copland, Aaron, 1900–
Copland.

Includes index.

1. Copland, Aaron, 1900–   . 2. Composers—United
States—Biography.   I. Perlis, Vivian.   II. Title.
ML410.C756A3   1984   780'.92'4 [B]   84-11703
ISBN 0-312-16962-0

FIRST EDITION

10 9 8 7 6 5 4 3 2 1

To the memory of my parents

Sarah and Harris Copland

AARON COPLAND

For my mother, Frances Goldberger,

and my late father, Charles Goldberger

VIVIAN PERLIS

Contents

A Note to the Reader

For better or worse, I have lived a composer's life, which might be described as an occupation of putting small black notes on ruled lines. To a composer, music is a kind of language. Behind the written score, even behind the various sounds they make when played, is a language of the emotions. The composer has it in his power to make music speak of many things: tender, harsh and lively, consoling and challenging things. Composers hope that their art will speak of all these things for them, since they are generally reluctant to talk about themselves.

Nevertheless, I think that I always intended to write an autobiography. My idea was not to present a personal memoir so much as to tell the story of American music as I experienced it in my lifetime. Toward this purpose, I saved letters, kept diaries when traveling abroad, and jotted down anecdotes about people and events, in much the same way as I had collected musical fragments with an eye toward their use. When I stopped composing in the early seventies, I thought the time had come for setting down my story. But a whole new conducting career had opened up for me, so the time was not right after all for staying at home with my scores and files.

In 1975 and 1976 Vivian Perlis tape-recorded a series of interviews with me for preservation in her oral history project in American music at Yale University. We met many times, with the aid of scores and recordings to refresh my memory. One day—lo and behold—there were two large volumes of the interview transcripts, looking amazingly like a draft for an autobiography. From then on, our collaboration was a natural one. Without it, my book would have remained no more than an intention, rather than becoming a reality. Together, we edited transcripts and added segments from my earlier writings. Vivian wrote connecting passages in the form of historical interludes to set the time and place, and an introduction about my family background. A considerable amount of work went into searching through my papers and other sources of written materials. The final result is the first volume of my autobiography, covering the years of my coming of age as a composer; the second volume is in preparation.

I have no answer to the question of whether knowledge of an artist's life is necessary for the enjoyment and understanding of his art; it has always seemed to me impossible to separate the two. I find that the following passage, written for my first book on music, still holds true: "What after all, do we listen for when we listen to a composer? He need not tell us a story like the novelist; he need not 'copy' nature like a sculptor; his work need have no immediate practical function like the architect's drawing. What is it that he gives us, then? Only one answer seems possible to me: He gives us himself."

Aaron Copland

Acknowledgments

A book of this kind owes much to many who have generously assisted at various points along the way. First and foremost are the few who have been central to the project from the start, helping in uncountable ways, perhaps most essentially by the continuity of their support, understanding, and enthusiasm. Naming them here cannot be adequate; however, we hope that Sanford Perlis, Janice Fournier, and David Walker will comprehend the range and depth of our gratitude. We want to thank also in a special way Minna Lederman Daniel, Ellis J. Freedman, and William Schuman for valuable advice, expert counsel, and loyal friendship.

We appreciate the spirit of generosity and participation from those who contributed interviews and thank them for permission to include information, and in some cases, to quote interviews directly in this volume: Betty Randolph Bean, Arthur Berger, Rosamond Bernier, Leonard Bernstein, Nadia Boulanger, Paul Bowles, Henry Brant, Henry Leland Clarke, Harold Clurman, John Colman, Irving M. Copeland, Milton Copland, Minna Lederman Daniel, Agnes de Mille, Edwin Denby, David Diamond, Martha Dreiblatt, John Duke, Lehman Engel, Eliot Feld, Vivian Fine, Ross Lee Finney, Robert Fizdale, Lukas Foss, Madeleine Friedman, Selma Gordon Furman, Alberto Ginastera, Leopold Godowsky II, Hans Heinsheimer, Bernard Herrmann, John Kirkpatrick, Lincoln Kirstein, John Kober, Mary Lescaze, Robert Lewis, Eugene Loring, Marcelle de Manziarly, Felice Copland Marlin, Arnold Mittenthal, Jerome Moross, Ruth Page, Robert Palmer, Claire R. Reis, Earl Robinson, William Schuman, Charles Seeger, Roger Sessions, Harold Shapero, Elie Siegmeister, Leo Smit, Gerald Sykes, Virgil Thomson, and Harold Uris.

The preparation of a manuscript is a collaborative activity. In this, William Owen and R. Allen Lott have had important roles as dedicated and persevering researchers, and Susanne Fusso and Kay Welch as patient and careful readers and typists. Robert Lantz and Joy Harris have always been available to smooth the way as our manuscript evolved into a book.

In the forefront of that complex procedure has been Richard Marek, our editor and publisher, who has shown extraordinary devotion and resolution throughout, as has his expert staff at St. Martin's/Marek, among them Erika Goldman and Amelie Littell. The challenge of designing a book that incorporates such extensive visual matter has been met with artistry and creativity by Cynthia Krupat. We want to thank the late Victor Kraft, among the numerous photographers who preserved many precious moments on film and allowed us to reproduce them.

We are grateful to the music publishing firm of Boosey & Hawkes, particularly to Stuart Pope and Sylvia Goldstein, and to the Library of Congress Music Division, where Donald J. Leavitt and his colleagues were cooperative in supplying our needs, as were the Music and Dance Collections of the Lincoln Center Library for the Performing Arts, the Beinecke Rare Book Library, the Music Library, and Oral History, American Music of Yale University. Several music organizations and societies were informative and helpful: the American Music Center, the American Composers Alliance, the Berkshire Music Center, the Koussevitzky Foundation, the MacDowell Colony, the National Academy and Institute of Arts and Letters, and the Corporation of Yaddo.

Assistance came from varied sources in many ways. While we cannot describe every contribution here, we remember and are thankful for each one: Ann Adelman, Gillian Anderson, William Austin, Milton Babbitt, Victor Basso, Jack Beeson, Howard Boatwright, Alan Boehmer, Caitriona Bolster, Margaret Brenman-Gibson, Leonard Burkat, Anita Burroughs, Victor Cardell, Gilbert Chase, Chris Cole, Edward T. Cone, William Conroy, Robert Cornell, Annette Dieudonné, David King Dunaway, Verna Fine, Gail French, John Gallagher, Steven Gilbert, Francis L. Grameny, Johanna Harris, Richard Jackson, Robert Kimball, George Maynard, Donald Mitchell, Roberta Mittenthal, Paul Moor, Luther Noss, Ana Chávez Ortiz, Geraldine Ostrove, Peter Pears, Andrew Pincus, Phillip Ramey, Ned Rorem, Allen Sapp, Carleton Sprague Smith, and Julia Smith.

Aaron Copland and Vivian Perlis

COPLAND

Introduction
The Mittenthals and
the Coplands

In the world of music, "Aaron" means only one person. But in the Copland family, the name was not so inclusive. A younger cousin, Aaron Levine, lived with the Coplands for several years, so there were "Little Aaron" and "Big Aaron" in the house. Both boys had been named after their grandfather, Aaron Mittenthal. It is tempting to consider whether Aaron Copland had more in common with his maternal grandfather than a name. As young men, both left home to better themselves in a foreign country: in the 1920s, Aaron Copland set out from Brooklyn to further his musical education in France; many years earlier, Aaron Mittenthal left a small village on the border of Russia and Poland in search of freedom and security in America. His wife, Bertha, and four children were to follow later. The youngest of them, Sarah, would become the mother of Aaron Copland.

The Mittenthal side of the family is large and geographically widespread, but they have taken care to trace the family genealogy and to pass down stories and information from one generation to the next. It is said that Joseph Ben Ezra was the founder of the Mittenthal clan. He took the name in the 1850s when the Government of Lithuania decreed that the Jewish populace adopt surnames.[1] In English, *Mittenthal* means "midvale" or "between valley and fields," and this name was chosen because it described the countryside of Vishtinets[2] where Joseph lived with his wife, Bessie.

Three generations of Mittenthal girls have delighted in the story of Bessie's "liberation." It seems that her parents had signed a marriage contract in the traditional custom without the bride seeing the groom, and gifts were exchanged to bind the contract. When Bessie saw the man she was to marry, she refused to go through with the wedding. His family sued. At the court hearing, when the judge asked why she would not honor the contract, Bessie stood up and said, "Look at me—now, look at him!" Bessie was tall and attractive, and the groom was short and unimpressive. Bessie won the case, and the contract was broken. Then came the favorite part of the story—it turned out that Bessie had been in love with a young man named Joseph Mittenthal all the time!

Joseph and Bessie were married and had many children. The eldest was Aaron (nicknamed Archie), and next came Ephraim. These two emigrated to America first; the six younger children followed.[3] When Joseph and Bessie grew old, they came to America (between 1875 and 1880) to see all their children for one last time. They visited in New York, Texas, Peoria, and small towns where their children had settled, before returning to Russia. Then they sold their belongings and moved to Palestine. Prior to the 1948 war, family members who traveled to Israel could visit their graves in the old cemetery in Jerusalem, but more recently, relatives have been unable to locate the Mittenthal tombstone.

It was after the American Civil War, about 1868, and before the first massive relocation of Russian Jews to America,[4] when Aaron and Ephraim Mittenthal reached New York City. With bits of information and recommendations from cousins who had preceded them, the brothers headed west and south out of New York. Aaron settled first in Chillicothe, Illinois, while Ephraim continued on to Texas. They sold dry goods off their wagons or opened small stores wherever they settled. They were Yankee peddlers, but with a difference—these were Yiddish Yankee peddlers. Settlers came from miles around just to see what a Jew looked like. When

H. S. Mittenthal store moving from Panhandle City to Amarillo, Texas, 1889.
(H. S. was Hyman, son of Ephraim.)

their customers were Indians, verbal exchanges must have been a unique mix of Yiddish, English, and Indian. After Aaron Mittenthal established himself in Chillicothe, he sent for Bertha, known as "Boshie," and the four children. Sarah was then six or seven, young enough so that she grew up with no trace of a foreign accent. The family lived in Chillicothe for about two years, where a fifth child was born. Then they moved on to Peoria, opened another store, and had another baby. Sarah and the older children attended public school in Peoria before the family moved to Texas.

In 1874 and 1875, when Aaron Mittenthal moved across the plains in his wagon, Dallas was a small town. But he settled first in the smaller village of Ladonia and then either in Graham or Jefferson before joining Ephraim in Dallas to open A. & E. Mittenthal, a large wholesale and retail dry-goods store.[5] There, two more children were born.[6] Aaron Mittenthal was well known in Dallas for two reasons: he was a Jew, and he hired Jesse James' brother, Frank, to work in his store. Frank James was a drawing card, but it is said that he took off with the store's profits. This may have been the reason Aaron Mittenthal pulled up stakes and returned to New York in 1881.

Aaron Copland's mother, Sarah Mittenthal, born in Russia, grew up in Illinois and Texas, where cowboys and Indians were a natural part of her life. Perhaps this is at least a partial answer to that question so often asked the composer: "How could a Jewish boy, born and raised in Brooklyn, write 'cowboy' music?" Sarah was nineteen when she came to New York City with her parents and younger siblings. (The older sisters and a brother were established by then in Texas, in Waxahachie and Dallas, and stayed on there.) The family lived first on East Broadway, and then at 413 East 122nd Street. Nathan, the youngest child (there were nine in all), was born there. New York became family headquarters. Mittenthals came to visit in summers from California, Texas, Illinois, Atlanta, and other places south and west "to get away from the heat." On Friday evenings, Sabbath dinners at Boshie and Aaron Mittenthal's apartment, 939 Longwood Avenue in the Bronx, were in the Jewish tradition. Although the family has not been a religious one in the orthodox sense, they have always been proud of their heritage. Jewish holidays and Sabbath dinners served as occasions to bring the family together. Boshie continued in these customs after her husband died in 1896, before Aaron Copland was born.[7] Grandmother Mittenthal was part of the fabric of Aaron Copland's young life, as she was for others of his generation, among them a cousin who remembers her well:

Selma Gordon Furman[8]

I adored Aaron's Grandmother, "Tanta Boshie." She had great warmth and understanding. My part of the family lived in Atlanta and Charlotte, N.C., and she and I carried on a correspondence all during the winter months. She wrote to me in Yiddish, and I had to find someone to translate for me. We had many trips to New York to visit my mother's four sisters, and I remember the lovely times on Friday nights. Sometimes the children and mothers were away at the beach in Jersey or Long Island, and the men would all come to Grandmother's for Friday night supper—Abe, college-educated and the patriarch of the family, Sam, who lived in Texas and was a charmer, and Ben Brin, a grandson. After supper, the men did the dishes. They all adored their grandmother and took great care with her. I knew only one of her daughters—cousin Sarah, Aaron's mother.

Sarah Mittenthal was not a pretty girl. She was rather tall and very thin, a look not in style in those days. Aaron Copland clearly resembles his mother. She is described as having been somewhat reserved and formal, but with a sweet and warm nature beneath the surface. The Mittenthals consider these traits part of their Southern background. They were brought up not to shout, raise voices, or lose tempers. Copland's quiet manner is called "that Southern charm" by his mother's family. Mittenthal family members were amused by a television tribute for Copland's eightieth birthday, in which Leonard Bernstein, while rehearsing the National Symphony Orchestra in *Lincoln Portrait* with Aaron as narrator, told the players that if they didn't play more softly, Copland would have to shout to be heard. The composer's rejoinder was typical—"I'm not a shouter."

Music was part of Sarah's upbringing—she took piano lessons, as did her sister Lillian, and it is said that she accompanied herself as she sang the popular songs of the day. Copland does not remember his mother singing or playing the piano, but his niece, Felice Copland Marlin, recalls: "Grandma sang a song to me when I was very young about hanging Jeff Davis to a sour apple tree,"[9] and family legend has it that it was Sarah's singing of "I'll Await My Love" at a social gathering that proved irresistible to the young and dapper Harris Copland.

Harris Morris Copland, Aaron's father, was born on 15 July 1860 in

4

Shavli,[10] a part of Russia that was then Lithuania. The family name, spelled in Russian, would have been Koplan, or in English, Kaplan. Harris was the eldest of eight children of a furrier, Sussman Alexander Kaplan, and his wife, Frieda Leahe. Had it not been for the long history of intolerance that spread over Europe from Poland in the northwest to Armenia in the southeast, the father of Aaron Copland would never have come to America. But Harris, like so many young European Jewish boys faced with military conscription, felt the lure of the land of freedom and opportunity. These immigrants crossed the borders illegally—north to Amsterdam or by foot through Germany and then by sea to England or Scotland. Young Harris Kaplan went first to Glasgow and then to Manchester, where he took menial jobs to earn passage for the crossing.

Harris arrived at New York Harbor in 1877, at a time when millions of homeless and penniless Russians were making a mass exodus from Europe. He was a boy of seventeen; somehow, between Russia and America, his name became Copland.[11] Young Harris was not running away from home,

Sarah Mittenthal, c. 1885.

Harris M. Copland, c. 1890.

The Copland family at the wedding of Harris' sister Sadie to H. H. Uris, 1899. Top row: the wedding couple between Harris' brothers Abe (left) and Alfred (right); center row (left to right): Harris' sister Becky Abrams, Hyman Abrams, Aaron's grandmother Frieda Kaplan, his brother Leon, Harris M. Copland, Sarah Copland, Aaron's brother Ralph; bottom row: Elsie Abrams, Aaron's sisters Laurine and Josephine.

nor did he intend more than a temporary absence from his family. Like many other Jewish immigrant families, the young men came first to earn enough money so that parents and younger children could follow. Some families never saw their sons again, but Harris Copland was determined to bring the entire family to America from Russia. A cousin in Brooklyn helped get him started by supplying a pushcart and a place to live. Harris was plucky and resourceful. Before long he was able to bring over his brothers and sisters one at a time, and then his parents[12] and three younger sisters. Harris helped his brothers, Abe and Alfred, to establish businesses in Brooklyn. When his sister Sadie came over, she lived in Harris's home and was married from there, and another sister, Fanny, worked in his store until she too was married. Later generations of Coplands have been puzzled at the Yiddish newspapers still in their parents' homes, but there was little extra money for school, and certainly not for the women in the fam-

6

ily. Many of the immigrant generation never learned to read or write in English.

Harris M. Copland was lively, outgoing, and good-looking. He has been described as being "all business," and it is no wonder, considering the intense competition in retail merchandising, and the work hours that stretched from nine to nine every day plus a half-day on Sunday. Later in life, Harris Copland found a second topic of conversation—his son, the famous composer. He would carry newspaper clippings in his vest pocket ready to show at a moment's notice. At family gatherings, knowing relatives would quickly move away from Harris as he reached for the reviews, but the unsuspecting were cornered and bombarded with stories of Aaron's most recent successes. "What?" Harris would exclaim in his Russian accent, "You never heard of the famous Russian conductor who is playing Aaron's music?" And the name "Koussevitzky" would fairly explode from him to the bewilderment of the captive audience.

Sarah Mittenthal and Harris Copland were married on 25 October 1885 in Pythagoras Hall on Canal Street. For the first few years of their marriage they lived in an apartment in the neighborhood near Washington Avenue and Dean Street where they were to settle. Ralph, their first child, was born there. This was an ordinary middle-class neighborhood with only a few other Jewish families among the predominantly Irish and Italian residents. Stationery from "H. M. Copland's Department Store" in the twenties gives the date of establishment as 1884; therefore, Harris must have had a store a year earlier and for several years after his marriage, before renting the property on the northwest corner of Washington Avenue and Dean Street from Sebastian Vollmuth, a baker, in 1890.[13] Under the terms of Copland's lease with Vollmuth, he acquired "a five-year tenure [for 626 and 628 Washington Avenue] at the yearly rate or sum of $560. . . ." It was not until 1897 that Harris acquired 630 and 632 Washington Avenue, where Vollmuth put up a new building for occupancy by Copland.

In this expanded building, Aaron Copland was born. The house was above and to the side of the store, with three floors and a private entryway. On the first floor were the kitchen, dining room, and maid's room. The parlor and master bedroom were on the second floor, and the children's rooms on the third. There was little distinctive about the house, though a curio cabinet with a silver spoon collection sat in the dining room and a Steinway upright piano—"The glory of the household"—in the parlor.[14] The store was a typical dry-goods establishment of the times. There was a shoe section, a toy department, household items, and clothing, such as handkerchiefs and underwear. According to reports, "Corsets and ribbons were big." Vollmuth, being the neighborhood baker, specified in the 1897 lease that Copland "may underlet the whole or any part of the premises for any business except a bakery or for the sale of bread and cake." Subsequent leasing agreements were executed between the two. When the store expanded and prospered, Harris acquired 771 and 773 Dean Street in 1907. From 1906 on, Copland's Department Store had a telephone; Aaron recalls the number to this day—Prospect 4666—and a horse and wagon were kept at the local livery. The Coplands were considered people of standing in the neighborhood, and the store was a source of pride to Sarah and Harris, who both worked there with a dozen employees. Quite recently, in April of 1980, Aaron Copland received a letter from a stranger, one John Gallagher:

> My mother and father lived at 745 Dean Street, Brooklyn, in a small row family house, a few doors short of Underhill Avenue. My mother and her mother, and indeed the whole family knew your father well. They were frequent customers at "Coplands" on Washington Ave. My mother used to relate to me how kind your father was. As an example—evidently Copland's would have some sort of a surprise sale. When the announcement was made all the customers would rush over to the counter. Your father would say, "Make room for Mrs. Gallagher. She has a large family." And he would hand goods over the heads of others to my grandmother. . . . I thought you might be interested in knowing how highly regarded your father was from some persons who knew him so well, the Gallaghers, your old neighbors from the dusty but lovely past in Brooklyn. . . . I remember one time standing at the front basement window in my mother's house. A young boy was walking past the door. He was dressed in black and had a black case under his arm. My mother said, "That's young Aaron Copland. He's studying music in New York. . . ."

In 1898, when Harris's sister Sadie married Harris H. Uris, Grandmother Kaplan came over from Europe for a visit, and soon afterward she came back for good with her husband and the three youngest girls. Harris H. Uris was known as "H.H." in the family, while Harris M. Copland was called "H.M." Sadie and H.H. lived in New York and often entertained the Brooklyn Coplands on Sunday afternoons at home or at a favorite restaurant, Pabst's, on 125th Street. The children were impressed with Sarah's unusual habit of drinking a glass of beer in the evening. When old enough, the Uris and Mittenthal youngsters traveled to Brooklyn by streetcar to "help out" at Copland's. They were always paid for their ser-

Aaron's grandmother Frieda Kaplan (1844–1916) and grandfather Sussman Alexander Kaplan (1838–1918) with their three youngest daughters (left to right): Lillian, Rose, and Fanny, 1899.

vices. They all remember that on Christmas night, after the store closed, all unsold toys were distributed among the children.[15] But Christmas was not a religious holiday—the celebration was one of relief that the most demanding work time of the year was over. Jewish high holy days were observed, but the regular Saturday Sabbath could not be celebrated, since Saturday was the busiest day of the week and stores were open until nine as on weeknights. "Somehow," according to Aaron Copland, "religion had to accommodate itself to the business of living, especially in neighborhoods such as ours that were not Jewish in character."

There were four or five Copland stores at various times in Brooklyn during the first decades of the century. Harris' was the largest and most successful. Another Copland's at 1794 Fulton Street was run by Fanny and her husband, Arthur Abrams. Smaller than Harris', it ran for the longest period, from 1909 to 1933. A trolley ride between stores cost five cents, and Fanny's son, Irving, recalls the trip to pick up orders made jointly or to deliver merchandise: "Aaron at age sixteen took the streetcar in the other direction to our place to teach my sister Ruth piano."[16] After Fanny Abrams became a young widow, she ran the store and supported her three children alone. Abe Copeland operated a third store. Aaron's Uncle Abe chose this spelling, perhaps because his wife, Etta, thought it more distinguished. The result is that Aaron Copland has both Copeland and Copland relatives. Uncle Alfred Copland also acquired stores, first in Brooklyn and later in the Bronx. Alfred married Helen, a sister of Harris Uris, further tying the relationship between the two families.

It was while Aaron was in Paris that his parents sold the store. They had been considering retirement, and after the store was broken into and robbed, their decision was made. Aaron responded to this news (11 July 1921): "I have just received your letter about the robbery and the selling out. . . . I don't suppose there's much hope of recovering the goods. Still don't understand what you will do with the store if you do sell out, because the lease doesn't expire till May. . . ." Aaron heard from home that they planned a big sale. He wrote (15 July 1921): "When do you expect to be out for good?" And (27 January 1922): "The news about your intentions to sell out both businesses[17] was very thrilling but you don't give many details. What are your plans afterwards? How long do you intend to live on Washington Ave. after May 31st? How about your trip to Texas and California? What does Pop intend to occupy himself with (since one can't play pinochle *all* day long). . . ." (15 March 1922): "I was very tickled to hear that being out of the store agrees with you so well. And I was quite astounded to hear you asking my advice as to a trip to Europe. . . ." (Aaron discouraged this, advising Texas and California instead.)

On 29 June 1923 Harris sublet his interests in 626–32 Washington Avenue as well as 771 and 773 Dean Street. It is not known precisely where Sarah and Harris were living when Aaron returned from Paris in 1924. They rented an apartment briefly on Prospect Place. It was not until 1926 that the name of Harris M. Copland reappeared in the telephone directory at 1745 Caton Avenue; there it remained until 1929. Although Harris had acquired a building at 1176 President Street in October of 1923, the mortgages were not secured until 1928. Sarah and Harris moved into the apartment on the ground floor and rented out those above. It was a peaceful and quiet neighborhood, and Sarah and Harris Copland might have lived there comfortably in semi-retirement had it not been for the Depression. Rents collapsed and Harris lost his savings and had trouble paying off the mortgages. After many years as a successful businessman and head of the Copland family, he was forced to borrow money from his relatives. In 1935 or 1936 Harris and his son Leon went into a "job lot" shoe business together in Manhattan.

Sarah and Harris did not discuss their financial troubles with Aaron. They were a devoted couple, and in 1935 the entire family gathered to help celebrate their fiftieth wedding anniversary. In 1937 the *Brooklyn Daily Eagle* carried an article and picture captioned: "Married 52 years, the Coplands still enjoy going out together. Climax of happiness in their wedded life is acclaim their son has won as a composer." All seven brothers and sisters of Harris Copland died in their middle years. Sarah passed

Sarah and Harris Copland in front of Copland's Department Store during the final sale before their retirement, 1922.

away 17 July 1944 at the age of eighty-three, and Harris less than a year later, 12 February 1945 at eighty-six.

Aaron Copland, the composer, was different from the rest of the family. There had been no artists on either side, Mittenthal or Copland, nor did any follow. Although Copland's life and interests were to lead him far from the family, he never rejected or forgot them. From generations back, when relatives helped each other settle in America, the unwritten rule was for family to help family. Harris Copland had felt that responsibility when he left home as a boy. And after the Uris brothers became financially successful, they quietly and generously came to the aid of the "artist" member of the family when he was an unknown and struggling composer.

Aaron Copland, in his turn, has been helpful and welcoming to family whenever and wherever he could be. A cousin, Arnold Mittenthal, remembers that Aaron played at his Bar Mitzvah party on a piano that had keys missing, and that later, Aaron wrote from Paris to advise him on his education. Cousin Madeleine Uris Friedman recalls that when she and her husband came to Paris, Aaron met them at the boat and guided them through the city.[18] For many years, at innumerable concerts and receptions, Copland, on spotting a relative, could be seen throwing up his hands in a characteristic gesture and exclaiming, "What? You here! You came all that way just to see me?" Requests from family are always acknowledged with graciousness, from signing photographs to conducting home town orchestras. (In the 1980–81 concert season, Dallas, Las Vegas, and San Diego were added to Copland's full schedule in order to please relatives anxious to show off the celebrity of the family.) Aaron was the youngest of five. Since his brothers and sisters have all died, he takes special pleasure in the many Mittenthal and Copland nieces, nephews, and cousins, and they find in him a great source of pride and joy.

Brooklyn

1 9 0 0 - 1 9 2 1

For a long time I harbored the pleasant notion that I was a child of the twentieth century, having been born on 14 November 1900. But some authorities claim that the twentieth century began on 1 January 1901. I calculate therefore that I spent my first forty-eight days in the nineteenth century—an alarming thought! Unlike some creative artists, I have no memory of a lonely childhood. It seems to me I was always surrounded by people. Certainly, at birth, I must have been stared at in my crib by my four considerably older siblings: Ralph, twelve, Leon, ten, Laurine, eight, and Josephine, seven. I might have been stared at more by my father and mother if they hadn't been so preoccupied with the management of the source of our livelihood: a fair-sized department store located at the corner of Washington Avenue and Dean Street in Brooklyn, New York.

I mention the store right off because it provided the central core of our lives. It most certainly proved to be influential in the shaping of my formative years. I grew up in the midst of a larger world than would have been supplied by a mere "home." The store's "help"—as our dozen or more employees were called—and the customers themselves provided me, at times, with a wide audience at a tender age. And the family as audience was ever present, for we lived above one section of the store, being the sole occupants on three floors of a red brick tenement-style building. I hasten to add that this seemed luxurious living to me at the time, partly because I always had my own bedroom, and partly because we always had domestic help and plenty to eat. I remember comparatively little surveillance as far as growing up was concerned—everyone was too busy with his own affairs. Moreover, my guess is that by the time I came along, my parents had expended a large measure of their guiding instincts on the four older children, so that I had a sense of being on my own from an early age.

The daily routine at the store was demanding. Saturdays and Sale Days were particularly exhausting, and Christmas was the busiest time of all. I distinctly remember "helping out" in the toy department (after school hours, of course). In retrospect, it occurs to me that I was selling toys to other children at an age when I might well have been playing with the toys myself. In any event, I was always paid for working in the store—an excellent way of feeding a child's ego. In my teens I bought music with my store money. I occasionally acted as relief cashier when the regular employee was off duty. The cashier's perch was a balcony area near the ceiling from which one could survey most of the premises. Cash and sales checks arrived with a bang via a system of wired "trolley cars," which gave the post a certain dramatic punch. But most important was the responsibility and trust that the job implied. Artists have usually been thought to be nitwits in the handling of money. No one has ever accused me of that particular failing.

Both my parents were members of large families, my father being the oldest of eight children and my mother one of nine. All of my fifteen uncles and aunts were either born in the United States or brought here from abroad. Even a child could sort them out, if only because of the way they spoke—with or without a foreign accent. (I mention this detail because it may have had something to do with my later stressing the need for a specifically American speech in our serious music.) On Sundays we generally visited relations in Manhattan or the Bronx, where Grandma Mittenthal lived with her youngest son, Nathan, who never married. I particularly recall visits to our affluent branch, the Uris family, at their roomy apartment on upper Madison Avenue. When spring came, the family went on outings down Ocean Avenue to Brighton Beach in our horse and buggy (the same horse that pulled the delivery wagon on weekdays). By 1914 or thereabouts, we bought our first automobile. One felt like an absolute plutocrat riding around the neighborhood in that new gray Chalmers. Now on Sundays or holidays we were able to travel as far away as Arverne or Rockaway Beach. My older brothers Ralph and Leon drove, of course, but it was when my lively sister Laurine took the wheel that all heads turned to stare at the sight of a girl driving a car. I learned to drive the Chalmers from Laurine when I was about sixteen.

In a brief autobiographical sketch, written in 1939 at the invitation of the *Magazine of Art*,[1] I began: "I was born on a street in Brooklyn that can only be described as drab. . . ." To my surprise, the idea of a composer of so-called serious music being born on a drab street seems to have caught the fancy of many a commentator. But that was the way Washington Avenue seemed in retrospect, long after I had left it. To any boy living there it would have seemed like an ordinary Brooklyn street. There were our neighbors Vollmuth the baker, Peper the painter, Levy the butcher, the candy store man across the street from our house, the large grocery store down the block (no chain stores yet), and, of course, the corner saloon with its occasional neighborhood drunks. Culture could hardly be said to be a familiar word on our street, yet it wasn't entirely absent from the area. A ten-minute walk up Washington Avenue brings you to Eastern Parkway where you will find the Brooklyn Museum. (It was there, aged ten, that I suffered my first "cultural" shock at the sight of a nude statue.) Ten minutes in the opposite direction from our house was the Brooklyn Academy of Music, where I heard my first symphony concert when I was sixteen. How pleasant it is to be able to point out that both the museum and the academy continue to fulfill their cultural mission on their respective sites three quarters of a century later.

Family life in the Copland household might be characterized as lively and industrious; there was little dawdling. My father, Harris Copland, was a strong figure in the eyes of both his family and his employees. Father was justifiably proud of what he had accomplished in the business world. But above all, he never let us forget that it was America that had made all this possible. A longtime member of the local Democratic Club, he voted a straight Democrat ticket at every election. Moreover, he depended on the club for his principal diversion: playing pinochle on many an evening with

In the family automobile, c. 1916 (left to right): Dorothy and Ralph Copland, Sarah Copland, Abe Copland, Harris Copland, Charlie Marcus, and Laurine Copland Marcus.

17

his fellow members. Once in a while he took me on an outing. I recall especially going together to the Lafayette Baths in Manhattan, topped off with an evening at Minsky's Burlesque!

Of my parents, I was closer to my mother. She might best be described as everything a maternal parent should be. She was affectionate, and a very nice mother to have. More sensitive than my father, she had profited by the experience of bringing up the four older children, and by a seven-year hiatus before I came along. I don't know if our family doctor brought us all into the world, but Mother had great confidence when one of us was sick that all would be well once Dr. Dower arrived. Fortunately for us, she could always be depended upon to act as sympathetic intermediary when my father—referred to as "The Boss" by everyone—had to be swayed. Mother led a busy, fruitful, and sometimes hectic life between overseeing the household and aiding my father in the store. If ever she was depressed or irritable, she managed to hide it well. I can only conclude that I must have inherited some of my own comparative evenness of temperament from my mother.

Because of Mother's involvement in the store, we always had a maid-of-all-work to take charge of household affairs. I remember best Lily Coombs, a native of Barbados, who stayed with us longest and left the deepest impression. Of a calm disposition, she had a gift for intuiting the underlying motives of those around her. I was a favorite of hers, and took her seriously when she would prophesy, as she did more than once: "Mr. Aaron, someday you're goin' to be swingin' in circles!" As one way of showing my appreciation for her many kindnesses, I took it upon myself to teach her daughter Ena how to play the piano. When I was in Paris in the twenties, I wrote home about a soirée at Mademoiselle Nadia Boulanger's apartment attended by many famous musicians: "Tell Lil I am finally swingin' in circles!"

Another "servant girl" I particularly remember was Tessie Tevyovitch, from Hungary. It was she who was delegated to accompany me on my annual one-day spree to the Amusement Park at Coney Island. What the family never knew was that Tessie had prearranged a rendezvous with a boyfriend at the end of the Coney Island trolley line. That left me free to go off on my own for a glorious day of hair-raising rides, sideshow visits, and hot dog interludes. At the appointed time we met again at the trolley car barn for the ride home, during which, with a far-off gaze, she seemed to be lending only half an ear to my excited recital of the daring exploits of my day.

Sometime before I was born, my parents had enrolled as members of Brooklyn's oldest synagogue, Baith Israel Anshei-Emes, situated at Kane and Court Streets in downtown Brooklyn.[2] On high holy days you weren't supposed to ride, and it took us about forty-five minutes to walk there. By the time I was almost thirteen and being readied with Hebrew lessons for my Bar Mitzvah, my father had been president of the synagogue for several years. By curious coincidence our rabbi, Israel Goldfarb, was himself a composer of liturgical music and the possessor of a fine baritone voice. Rabbi Goldfarb[3] was a sensitive human being and an effective leader of his congregation. The part of my Bar Mitzvah I recall most vividly was the banquet—it actually took place in the store! Relations came from near and far. The merchandise was moved away and an area cleared where we could set up tables. Religious observance in the Copland family was mostly a matter of conventional participation rather than a deep commitment to other-worldly experience. Despite this, one very solemn moment remains vivid in my memory: on Yom Kippur, the Day of Atonement, the elder graybeards of the congregation stretched themselves out prone in the aisles of the synagogue and prayed for forgiveness of man's evil ways. In a lighter vein, it was the small dance bands at Jewish weddings and parties that fascinated me.

School life had begun in the usual way at age six when I was taken by my mother to be registered at Public School No. 111 at Vanderbilt Avenue and Sterling Place. Our school was situated in the midst of a "nice" neighborhood—that is to say, Sterling Place boasted rows of upper-middle-class houses with brownstone fronts. But the trouble was that in walking there I had to pass through a few blocks near St. Patrick's Catholic School on Dean Street, and that was always "dangerous territory." A Jewish boy had to watch out for himself. For whatever reason, I recall the tough trip to school, but I seem to have blotted out the eight years of grammar school attendance—teachers, fellow pupils, and all. I did my homework, moved ahead each term in the usual way, and graduated from P.S. 9 in 1914. What left a deeper impression were the summers I spent at boys' camp between 1910 and 1913. Camp Carey was situated on the shores of Lake Carey, not far from Wilkes-Barre in the mountains of Pennsylvania. It was there that I learned to swim (the guy in charge would throw me in and yell, "Swim, you son of a gun, swim!"), to row a boat, and to play tennis. The last was the only sport I was ever any good at. What I remember with special nostalgia, however, were the overnight hikes we used to take along the banks of the Susquehanna River. I can still hear the wail of the engine whistles of the seemingly endless freight trains on the opposite bank, jangling their way toward Chicago as we slept out under blankets on the low cliffs above the river. Many years later, in 1976, I was giving a concert in Harrisburg and saw views of what I remembered of the Susquehanna, and I stood outside to listen for those sounds I had heard as a boy. One other aspect of summer camp life I still remember with considerable pleasure. Though my record at sports was nothing to write home about, I can recall the satisfaction of being looked up to by the other boys when decisions had to be made. By my third summer at Camp Carey, "What does Aaron think?" became a familiar phrase.

My Uncle Alfred played the violin, but I don't recall hearing him or even seeing him with his instrument. Whatever music we heard at home was supplied either by my oldest brother, Ralph (violin), or my sister, Laurine (piano). Ralph studied with Heinrich Schradieck, a German violinist of some reputation, while Laurine had her lessons with Mrs. Schradieck. Ralph and Laurine played duets at home—mostly potpourris from operas—but their top accomplishment was a fair rendition of the Mendelssohn *Violin Concerto*. Ralph was more serious about his music than Laurine. Her piano studies were for the purpose of accompanying herself and the rest of us. I clearly recall ragtime and selections from popular shows of the day being played in the evenings at home. One song, "The Pink Lady," made a memorable impression. Music-making at home took on a glow that the development of the phonograph tended to dissipate. The only phonograph I knew about was at the home of my Mittenthal cousins at 41 Convent Avenue in the Bronx, and there I would sit for hours with my ear to the horn listening to popular records. Laurine, or "La," always the lively one, was a good dancer. She and Josephine tried out their latest dance steps on me. I learned them rather easily, and have enjoyed dancing ever since I was a boy.

Laurine traveled to Manhattan for singing lessons at the Metropolitan Opera School. She had access to a seat in a box at the old Met, and whenever she attended a performance, she always brought back a libretto and program for my delectation. These served their purpose when I turned seventeen or eighteen and joined the ranks of standees for performances of *Carmen* or *Tristan* at the Met. My brothers and my sister Josephine claimed that they first became aware of my showing an interest in music when I began hanging about the piano whenever Laurine was practicing, much to her annoyance. If Laurine was fifteen years old, I was seven. I used to think that my first attempts at "composition" dated from my elev-

Top: Aaron with Josephine, 1909.
Right: Aaron at age six.
Above: Aaron at age two.

enth year, but this notion was dispelled when Ralph's wife, Dorothy, whom I had known as a child, produced a letter of mine postmarked "Brooklyn, N.Y., April 19, 1909." Apparently I had been ill and Dorothy had sent me a present. In my thank-you letter, I am astonished to read the following passage:

> Mother said I should tell you in this letter that you
> made me very happy this morning when I received your
> cherry. I even made up a song with your name in it.
>   I will be very pleased to sing it for you the
> next time I come down, which I hope will be very soon.
> With best love to everyone from all, I remain,
>
>   Your sweetheart,
>   Aaron
>
> These for yourself
> X X X X X X X X X X X X X X X

The letter is proof-positive that I was beginning to make up songs at age eight and a half. The first written-down notes that have survived consist of about seven measures for chorus and piano, composed when I was about eleven. At the top of the page stands the rather ambitious title: "Music for opera, *Zenatello*, Act I." Also, when I was eleven, I persuaded Laurine to start me off on piano lessons, and at about this time I decided to re-set *Cavalleria Rusticana*. Laurine must have brought home the libretto. Having no music paper, I drew a six-line staff and got as far as the offstage women's chorus at the start of the opera, about two pages, before giving up. I must have realized even then that opera was tough going. At about fourteen, I composed part of a song, "Lola," and copied out music by others that I could not afford to buy. These feeble attempts are rather alarming to look at now. I was so naive that I didn't even know how to connect the notes! But before long, Laurine decided she had taught me everything she knew, and it was time for me to find a real piano teacher.

Mr. Leopold Wolfsohn was giving lessons to the Uris children. His claim to distinction in our minds was that he was a teacher from Manhattan who spent one day a week in Brooklyn, giving lessons in a rented studio in the old Pouch Mansion at 345 Clinton Avenue. It took some convincing for my parents to agree to my piano studies—after all, they had paid for lessons for their other kids without remarkable results. But they finally agreed. It was typical that no one in the family accompanied me when I went to arrange for lessons with Mr. Wolfsohn. My parents always had a kind of basic confidence in me—"If he thinks he can do it, let him do it." Fortunately for me, Wolfsohn was a competent instructor, with a well-organized teaching method. He used the Hanon book of exercises[4] and was responsible for my debut as concert pianist, when after studying with him for three years he invited me to take part in his annual student concert held in the spacious auditorium of the Wanamaker Department Store in downtown Manhattan.

It was ironic that my debut should have taken place in a store, of all places. The year was 1917, and the piece I was to perform was the *Polonaise in B* by Paderewski. The one memory that comes to mind in connection with my debut is that as I approached the stage to make my entrance, Mr. Wolfsohn suddenly began boxing my ears and head, exclaiming excitedly: "Don't be nervous, don't be nervous!" I was taken completely by surprise and couldn't imagine what had come over him. Later, he explained that this was a well-tried expedient for taking a student's mind off his stage fright. Despite this contretemps, I think I acquitted myself well enough. In any event, I don't believe I ever really seriously entertained the idea of embarking on a career as a concert pianist.

Zenatello, an opera, composed at about age eleven.

My piano debut was not my first public performance. As a child I recited poems, particularly one that was called "How Would You Like to Be a Dog?" That was spoken with great emotion. I sang in public too, before my voice changed. I was in the Glee Club at Boys' High on Marcy Avenue, where I was enrolled during the years of piano study with Mr. Wolfsohn. Here again, as in grammar school, despite four years of attendance before graduation in June of 1918, I recall very little of daily school life. I do remember that there was not much in the way of musical stimulation. Our teacher, Mr. Flint, was a joke—or so the students thought—and not an entertaining one. The Latin teacher, when moved to call upon me, always did so by expressively reciting a line from *Julius Caesar*: "Yond Cassius has a lean and hungry look. He thinks too much." An apt description, no doubt, because I was undeniably tall and skinny for my age.

My fellow students made a more lasting impression on me than our instructors, perhaps because I still have the photograph of our graduating class. That helps to bring many of them to mind, especially Bob Gordon, Daniel Burns, Gus Feldman, and Frank Carroll. My marks were fairly good, but if I distinguished myself musically in any way it has left no trace. Again, it was the summers away from home that played a significant role in my development. After Camp Carey, the summer of 1915 was spent at a YMHA camp. The first half of the summer of 1916 was occupied berry-picking in Marlboro, New York, to help the war effort by taking the place of men who were drafted. I went with a small group from Boys' High, picked all day, and slept in the hay in the farmer's barn at night.

By August I must have needed a rest, for the family decided to send me off to spend a few weeks at the Fairmont Hotel in Tannersville, New York. This was the gathering place for well-known Jewish literary people. There I became friendly with a niece of the original owner of the hotel, Martha ("Marty") Dreiblatt. We were chums. I taught her how to canoe, and we played tennis together. At the weekly Saturday dances we were both happy to have someone to dance with, and later when we returned to Brooklyn, we occasionally went out dancing or to a show at the Orpheum vaudeville theater.[5] It was also my good fortune to meet Aaron Schaffer at the Fairmont that summer of 1916. He was my senior by seven years, a young intellectual, the son of a respected rabbi in Baltimore, and himself a student at Johns Hopkins University concentrating on French and French literature. Best of all, he was a music lover, who liked nothing better than to have me play the pieces I was studying and beginning to write. After that summer when Schaffer occasionally came to New York from Baltimore, he and Marty Dreiblatt and I would get together, and I would play my latest musical discoveries for them. (Again, there was "Big Aaron" and "Little Aaron," but this time the roles were reversed.)

The summer of 1917 was divided between more berry-picking and a job as a runner for a Wall Street brokerage firm. That job consisted of delivering stocks and bonds to other firms in the area—not too onerous except that the summer heat made it hard on the feet. Nevertheless I went back to Wall Street for a second summer in 1918, but this time I was promoted to an inside job. I looked forward to the lunch periods that year because I had come upon a basement bookstore that sold second-hand books in French. It was there that I invested in my first French book, a battered copy of Alphonse Daudet's play *Sappho*.

As near as I can calculate, it must have been during the winter of 1915–16 when I was just fifteen that I came to the daring decision to spend my life as a musician. It was so startling an idea that I dared not share it with anyone. By this time my brother Ralph was at Columbia University, studying to become a lawyer even though he was not at all of the right temperament to be a successful one. My other brother Leon followed Pa into the store. But a musician? Music is so uncertain, so few reach the top, and how does one support a family on so shaky a basis? And where did you get such an idea anyway? I asked myself all these things if only because I realized I would hear them from my father sooner or later. But deep down I knew that reasonableness had nothing to do with it. The urge toward spending a life in music was irresistible.

It wasn't quite clear to me as yet what aspect of music I would concentrate on. I seem to remember drifting off from what was meant to be piano practice into improvising music of my own. When I was fifteen I composed a waltz—unfinished, but the written part makes sense. I was a mere novice, but some inner conviction led me to think that someday I might achieve my fondest hopes. In Aaron Schaffer I had a kindred artistic spirit with whom I could share my yearnings and ambitions. My first letter to him was written on the train home after the summer's vacation of 1916. My letters to him are lost, but something of their tone can be surmised from a reply Schaffer mailed me soon after he returned to Baltimore:

> If I have stimulated you just the slightest bit towards continuing in the ennobling work for which you seem now so well fitted, I feel that I have accomplished something worth while and that my vacation was anything but a failure. You say that your heart is full of high ideals and great ambitions. I need not tell you that I, too, have certain definite aims which might seem, to the average

man, either incomprehensible or useless. . . . Young men with aesthetic qualities and aspirations have always had, and have today more than ever, a terrific
battle to fight against the dogged "horse-sense" (a word I almost detest) of the
everyday, work-a-day world. So that when I urge you to be firm in your resolution to enter one of the most glorious professions in the gift of God and not be
deterred by the carping of small-minded people, I am only strengthening myself
for the same task. . . .

This was heady stuff for a youngster of sixteen! Schaffer's attitude encouraged me to believe that it was not a foolhardy ambition, this idea of
mine to adopt music as a profession. We continued to correspond. My
new friend advised me about literature, his own field, and at about this
time I began to read voraciously, adding French literature to the Horatio
Alger and Mark Twain I was already familiar with. I sat on the "stoop" in
front of the store reading while the kids in the neighborhood played street
games. No one seemed to think it strange.

It was at Boys' High that I came to know an aspiring young Brooklyn
organist named John Kober. We met in the Glee Club. Aaron Schaffer
could feed the higher reaches of my artistic aspirations, but John was right
there in Brooklyn to share musical experiences by playing four-hand piano
arrangements of the symphonic repertoire with me. We familiarized ourselves with the classic literature at a time when these pieces were not yet
available on recordings. In a letter to John on 11 October 1917 I wrote:
"The four hours was real enjoyment, playing duets together at my sister's
home. The slick piano is still there."[6] The music was borrowed from the
Montague Street branch of the Brooklyn Public Library. In other letters of
1917 I wrote about seeing *Boris Godunov* at the Metropolitan Opera and
hearing Percy Grainger play Grieg's *Piano Concerto*. And after hearing
Tchaikovsky's *Symphony No. 6*, I wrote: "Could you get the Pathétique
for four-hands through your library? I heard the Philharmonic play it and I
am sure I can now show you some beauties in it that we missed. It is perfectly ravishing. Need I say more? . . ." I arranged to meet John for a concert (18 October 1917): "I also have the program and in the musical
literature that I have are included some of the numbers. These include
Beethoven's Sonata Op. 110, the Brahms Intermezzo, and the Chopin
Valse and the Ballade in G minor. I also have the original song from which
Liszt derived the 'On Wings of Song.' It is a song by Mendelssohn and I
sing it often. . . "[7] At the end of the year: "I have 4 piano pieces by my
teacher [Rubin Goldmark] that I want you to hear. And this confiden-
tially, I have just composed a song that I have not been able to sing to any-

one yet, so you will be the first victim.[8] The words, written by a Belgian poet are in my opinion very stirring. . . ."

In 1916 I was still lacking a finished composition. I sent for a mail-order harmony course, but when I could not complete a *Capriccio* for violin and piano in 1916, I realized that in order to develop I needed a real teacher of harmony and counterpoint. Once again, my parents were good enough to agree to pay for lessons if I found the teacher. Not knowing any harmony teachers myself, I naturally asked Mr. Wolfsohn if he could recommend someone. He did—Rubin Goldmark, whose studio was at 140 West 87th Street in Manhattan. I telephoned for an appointment and at the agreed time approached the brownstone house with a certain trepidation. As I mounted the outdoor steps I noticed a sign in the first-floor window that read: Dr. Goldmark. That's reassuring, I thought to myself; if he earned a doctorate in music, he *must* be good. The maid who answered the doorbell ushered me into an anteroom and said that Dr. Goldmark would see me shortly. I waited as patiently as I could—so much depended on this visit. After what seemed like a long time, the double doors finally opened and a portly gentleman motioned to me to enter. When we were seated he said, "Well, what's the matter with you?" "Nothing," I replied. "I just want to study harmony." "In that case," he said, "you want to see my brother Rubin on the third floor."

Rubin Goldmark, as it turned out, proved to be an excellent teacher in the fundamentals of musical composition. He was born in New York and came from a musical family—his uncle, Karl Goldmark, was the famous Austro-Hungarian composer of operas in mid-nineteenth-century Vienna. Rubin Goldmark had studied composition at the Vienna Conservatory, and later in New York with Dvořák. The lessons he gave were clearly presented and stayed close to the subject under discussion. He used Richter's *Manual of Harmony* and *Modern Harmony in Its Theory and Practice* by Foote and Spalding.[9] Goldmark had a dry wit, and had earned a well-deserved reputation as after-dinner speaker at musical gatherings. If a student made a real boner, he was invited by Goldmark, with a twinkle in his eye, to become a member of his "Schlemiel" Club. I studied with him for four years, from the winter of 1917 to the spring of 1921. The one drawback—a serious one from my standpoint—was that he had little if any sympathy for the advanced musical idioms of the day, and frankly admitted the fact. I remember seeing on his piano in 1921 a copy of Charles Ives' extraordinary *"Concord" Sonata.*[10] I immediately asked if I could borrow the music, but Goldmark said, "You stay away from it. I don't want you to be contaminated by stuff like that." I didn't see the piece again, actually, until ten years had gone by. Moreover, I never remember his discussing the subject of nationalism or folklorism, and he certainly never suggested them to me as possible influences. Other talented musicians, George Gershwin, Leopold Godowsky II, and Frederick Jacobi studied with Goldmark during my time with him, but I had little contact with them. I don't believe I met Gershwin then, and I saw Jacobi and Godowsky only a few times.[11] I suffered from a sense of musical isolation during those years. Nevertheless, I have always been grateful to Goldmark for the solid basic training he was able to impart,[12] and which accounted, I believe, for the high regard in which he was held. When the Juilliard School of Music was founded in 1924, he was named head of the Department of Composition.

After my initial winter of study we both agreed that I might do well to find a new piano teacher. My own idea was that I had absorbed about as much as I could from Mr. Wolfsohn. Goldmark advised a New York pianist named Victor Wittgenstein. I spent two winters as his student, hoping to gain some insight into the performance of a more contemporary piano repertoire, without any memorable results. Wittgenstein considered me to be something of a musical radical, and in that sense, perhaps, too much for him to handle. In any event, I moved on from Wittgenstein to a well-known piano pedagogue, Clarence Adler, and remained with him from the winter of 1919 to the spring of 1921. Mr. Adler was a cultivated and sensitive musician with broad tastes, known for the beautiful tone he drew from the instrument. From time to time his pupils gathered at his studio to perform for their friends and for one another. At one such occasion, I played the Ravel *Sonatine*. The piece was considered so unconventional as to need explanatory remarks from me. It was my first talk about a musical "modernist." Without being aware of it, I was embarking here for the first time on the role of musical commentator, which has afforded me pleasure and income ever since.

These same four years, from the fall of 1917 to the spring of 1921, represented much more to me than the study of piano, harmony, counterpoint, and form. What made them truly stimulating was the sense I had of uncovering a whole cultural world outside the field of music that I gradually became aware of in my growing-up years. This sense of discovery was doubly exhilarating because, for the most part, I found it out for myself. It was at the Brooklyn Public Library on Montague Street that I made my acquaintance with Sigmund Freud, Havelock Ellis, Romain Rolland's *Jean Christophe*, and Walt Whitman's *I Hear America Singing*. Reading became a passion second only to music. Along with this came a broadening of my musical horizons. I can still recall the thrill of coming upon racks of music scores in the dingy upstairs corner room at the library. And what was equally surprising was the fact that music scores, like the books downstairs, could be borrowed for study at home. I learned to orchestrate by borrowing scores from the library. When I knew I was going to hear something performed, I imagined what it would sound like, took the score to the concert, and followed it to see whether it matched what I thought I was going to hear. The difficulty was that they used to turn down the lights very often, so that you couldn't see. I remember an embarrassing incident when I was looking forward enormously to hearing *Pelléas et Mélisande* for the first time, and I think it was the Chicago Opera Company that came to the Brooklyn Academy of Music with a one-shot guest performance of this "odd" work. I got myself all prepared in my seat up in the gallery with a little searchlight and the score—the piano-vocal score actually, because the other one would have been way out of my price range—and I waited till all the lights went out and then quietly turned my light on. Well, I hadn't gotten beyond two pages when an usher dashed up and said, "Turn that light out, you dope! Turn that light out!", and my whole plan collapsed. That must have been around 1918.

Further exploration in Manhattan uncovered another unusually good music collection for borrowing at the 58th Street branch of the New York Public Library, under the aegis of Miss Dorothy Lawton. She was thought to be a crotchety old character by some borrowers, but to me she couldn't have been more kind, pointing out her latest acquisitions, and on occasion putting them aside until I appeared, as she knew I would be looking for the most recent arrivals of contemporary music. These were war years and printed scores were difficult to acquire, not being exported in quantity from Europe. I found a music store on Livingston Street in Brooklyn where to my delight I could occasionally discover a piano piece by Debussy or Ravel. But my particular passion in those days was Alexander Scriabin, whose scores were practically unobtainable. That fact made them doubly cherishable. Suddenly to come upon a copy of his *Vers la flamme* (1914) or the *Tenth Sonata* (1913) was an unbelievable stroke of good fortune.

During 1918, Aaron Schaffer sent me a book of poems he had published[13] (he was by then on the faculty of Johns Hopkins), and I set three of them to music: "A Summer Vacation," "Night," and "My Heart Is in the East." "Big Aaron" had written (23 May 1918) to suggest that we

"Night," an early song set to a poem by Aaron Schaffer.

by a foun —

stains play
a night bird

L.H. L.H.
mark the bass
mf mf

pp

cres f f
sings its tune - ful lay — Full of the nights vast joy and ache

8va ppp bbp

in the slowest time
a low wind sighs thro' ghost - ly trees
which shiv - er
ppp sfp p
sfp ppp

cres f p
in the danc - ing breeze
mf

Begun July 1, 1918 Marlboro N.Y.
Finished Dec 16, 1918 Brooklyn N.Y.

publish a volume of *lieder* together—"A splendid, foolhardy notion?" As much as Schaffer influenced my thinking in those impressionable years, he admitted to being musically conservative. Of the first of the songs I sent, he wrote, "Too much and too sudden variety? The last song captivated the entire household. Sudden changes of key and occasional discords à la Debussy and Ravel." That letter was signed "Yours in the love of poetry and music." And in June 1918, "The next thing you know we will be collaborating on an epoch-making American opera. You are blessed with a rare gift."

When Schaffer left to study at the Sorbonne in 1919, I was eager to hear about artistic life in Paris. He described his adventures at the opera and theater. From my side I wrote about what meager contemporary musical events I could find in New York. One was a recital by Leo Ornstein, considered *the* radical "futurist" composer, whose *Danse sauvage* was stirring up so much controversy. I can't say I knew the names of more than a handful of other contemporary American composers at the time. John Alden Carpenter and Charles Griffes stood out. I read about them and other new composers in the pages of *The Dial, the* literary avant-garde monthly of that period (published from 1880 to 1929). Their music commentator was Paul Rosenfeld, and he was considered the one to read for the most recent developments. Rosenfeld's prose style may have been too lush at times, but the important thing was that he wrote perceptively about controversial figures such as Schoenberg, Stravinsky, Ornstein, Mahler, and Sibelius.

This was also the period when I began extending my musical horizons by attending more concerts. Earlier, I had gone with Mother to hear John McCormack sing at the old Hippodrome on Sixth Avenue and 43rd Street, and Jascha Heifetz play at Carnegie Hall. The pinnacle was reached when I attended a Paderewski piano recital in a darkened hall, his head effulgent in a glow of golden hair. I went to hear Walter Damrosch and his New York Symphony performing Brahms and Wagner at Aeolian Hall in Manhattan on Sunday afternoons, or to the Boston Symphony, who came to Brooklyn on Friday nights for a series of five concerts each year. During the season of 1918–19, the French composer Henri Rabaud was at the head of the orchestra. He was an especially intriguing figure to me because his opera *Marouf* had been successfully produced only a few years before at the Opéra Comique. I attended one of his Brooklyn Academy concerts with the Boston Symphony and during the course of it determined to go backstage at the end of the performance to see a real composer-conductor close up, and perhaps shake his hand. As the final chord sounded, I hurried outside to the stage entrance, but the attendant wouldn't let me in. I waited where I was until the great man emerged. At the least, I thought, I could shake his hand as he passed. But when the moment came and Maître Rabaud appeared, I lost courage and let him pass without a word or a handshake. Perhaps that explains why I tend to be kind to young aspirants who show up at the green room door after I have conducted one of my own concerts.

I decided not to go to college after high school, but to devote myself entirely to the study of music. Aaron Schaffer was concerned about my plans, for he wrote: "Do not go even temporarily into theater playing! Hold on to youthful ideals!" In the winter that followed graduation, I looked for a part-time job as a pianist in order to spare myself the embarrassment of depending on my parents for pocket and concert money. I noticed an advertisement in the *Brooklyn Daily Eagle* that the Finnish Socialist Hall in our borough needed a pianist to play for dances two nights a week in a trio consisting of violin, clarinet, and piano. I applied and landed the job; as it turned out, there were two unexpected by-products. I made my first contact with what seemed to me then to be "radical" politics, and I gained a new friend in the clarinet player, Arne Vainio. Vainio was a young intellectual who played clarinet and cello and liked to talk about books, politics, music, and poetry. He introduced me to a socialist newspaper, *The Call.*[14] It wasn't long before we were exploring the cello and piano literature together, especially the Beethoven cello sonatas. This stimulated me to write two pieces myself, thereby learning the importance of testing one's work in live performance.[15] Interspersed were discussions of socialism as a political philosophy and of Eugene V. Debs, the American Party's leader. All this, remember, was close to the events of the 1917 Russian Revolution. Coming as I did from a thoroughly bourgeois environment, I found Vainio and his contact with Finnish socialism fascinating. But there was little sympathy for radical politics at home. My father had too vivid a memory of Russian oppression to believe that any theory of socialistic government could possibly establish itself in so backward a country as Russia. Aaron Schaffer, who was a staunch Zionist, considered my friendship with Vainio downright dangerous. He was convinced that my new friend was not only radical but anti-Semitic.

As an offshoot of my job as pianist at the Finnish Socialist Hall, I looked for similar employment during the summers of 1919 and 1920 in what came to be known as the Borscht Belt of the Catskill Mountains. In July

Above: A sketch page showing part [of] *Tone Poem,* 1918, above a draft for *Waltz Caprice.*

Left: Detail of high school graduation photograph, Copland center.

1919 I was employed at the White Sulphur Springs Hotel in White Sulphur Springs, New York, and in August at the Breezy Hill Hotel in Fleischmanns, New York. During July I met and played with Sidney Roof, violinist (later to become a medical doctor), and at one or the other hotel I made the acquaintance of Miss Minnie Rutenberg, aspiring pianist, who had considerable interest in my early piano pieces. The summer of 1920 was spent working as pianist at Schoharie Mansion in Elka Park, Green County, New York. But by that time my mind was elsewhere; I was dreaming of nothing less than Paris, France. Aaron Schaffer was in Paris for nine months of graduate study at the Sorbonne. "If only you could come to Paris with me," he wrote. "Wouldn't we be two happy Bohemians!"

I began to plan to join my friend in June 1920, but it turned out that Rubin Goldmark thought otherwise. In his mind the sonata form was the pinnacle of our work together, and I had yet to write a fully completed four-movement sonata. He considered especially the first-movement sonata-allegro form the key to all future composition, and would not allow me to leave town without it! Reluctantly, I allowed myself to be persuaded to delay departure for a year—until June 1921. And when, finally, I went to France, Goldmark wrote to remind me (26 August 1921): "I hope you will make some more progress in the Sonata form. Don't get to despise this, even if you should fall into the hands of some radicals. There is no preparation like it—if you once master it—for doing anything you like afterwards. . . ."

I had read in the magazine *Musical America* of a plan by the French government to establish a summer school for American musicians in the Palace of Fontainebleau, a short distance from Paris. This was said to be a gesture of appreciation to America for its friendship during World War I. I was in such a rush to enroll that I was the first student to sign up and be accepted. Actually, I was one out of nine awarded scholarships. My parents were less than enthusiastic, but it was known that any well-educated musician had to have the European experience. In the past, that had meant Germany, but since the war, the focus for the arts had shifted to France. Schaffer had returned from Paris by now and taken a position at the University of Texas. When I wrote to him about Fontainebleau, he responded in December 1920: ". . . Need I tell you my answer? You know well what it will be! Cherish the ideals you have formed and carry them away with you. . . ." I must have bombarded Schaffer with questions that he handled as best he could, about passport, hotels, bookstores, plays, restaurants, and so on. And then he wrote: "Well, old pal, if you are leaving June 9, I am afraid we shall not see each other again for a long time. I sincerely wish for you the finest success. Be sure to write me often and keep me posted on the happenings in the *Ville-Lumière*. . . ."[16]

The winter of 1920–21 in New York before leaving for France was a busy one. I was intent on reading as many books in French as I could lay my hands on; I played quantities of French music borrowed from the Brooklyn Public Library, alone, and with John Kober; and I attended as many concerts as I could afford. I had composed a *Prelude* for violin and piano in November of 1919; in February of 1921 I decided to try another. They seem to me to be somewhat in the style of César Franck. I had written several early songs in addition to the three settings of poems by Schaffer.[17] These were in the style of Debussy, who I thought was "hot stuff" before Scriabin and then Stravinsky took his place in my mind as the foremost modern composer. During my last months at home, I composed two songs that seem to me to show the beginnings of a musical personality, at least in terms of rhythmic feeling, frequent meter changes, and sense of form. "Pastorale" was set to a text from the Kafiristan translated by E. Powys Mathers. Its brief two pages are dated 4–12 April 1921. This and "Old Poem," dated 1920, with a text translated from the Chinese by Arthur Whaley, I took with me to France; they were performed several times during my first year abroad.

Most of my early music was for solo piano.[18] I composed sonnets and dedicated them to my friends, and my *Waltz Caprice* was a big number. It was six pages long and a show-off work, rather Lisztian and grandiose and more of a virtuoso piece than anything I had composed up to then. The *Sonata* was dutifully finished for Goldmark before I left, and went with me to France together with a few more interesting freely written pieces. The first two of my *Trois Esquisses*[19] were composed before leaving—"Amertume" on my twentieth birthday, 14 November 1920, and "Pensif" on 8 January 1921. The third, "Jazzy," must have been in my mind or sketched out the spring before I left for France, but it was not put to paper until Paris, 3 November 1921.

One short piano piece that was composed before leaving Brooklyn proved to be more important to my career than I could possibly have imagined at the time. *Scherzo Humoristique: Le Chat et la Souris* (*The Cat and the Mouse*) was written after a poem by La Fontaine, "Le Chat et la Souris." Considering its modern harmonies and unconventional rhythms, I decided not to show it to Goldmark. On 12 May, shortly before my de-

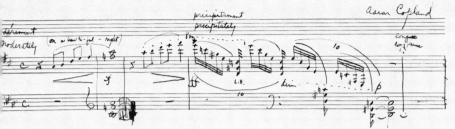

Above: Manuscript page, *The Cat and the Mouse*, 1920.
Right: Copland at age twenty.

parture, Goldmark's composition students honored him with a dinner party at the Restaurant Esplanade at 305 West End Avenue. As part of the after-dinner festivities, it was announced that we would hear several different harmonizations of a chorale, without identifying the authors. Example number three bristled with irritating dissonances. Without hesitation, Mr. Goldmark pointed an accusatory finger at me. "*You* are the culprit!" It was a joke, of course, and we all laughed. But I have remembered it after these many years since it stamped me as the "modernist" member of the class.

The news of my upcoming European venture soon spread to the outer reaches of the family. Before long I heard from my cousin, Elsie Abrams, that her husband, Dr. Morris Clurman, had a younger brother of about my age who was planning to spend a year in Paris as a student of French civilization at the Sorbonne. We arranged to meet at Brentano's bookstore in New York. We liked each other at that first encounter and agreed that it would be economically advantageous and less lonely if we shared an apartment in Paris. I was to arrive in France first, so I offered to locate suitable quarters. The shy young man's name was Harold Clurman. Our friendship started then and lasted for sixty years, until his death in 1980.

À Bord de "FRANCE"
June 1921

le _____ 191

Wednesday — 9 A.M.
(June 15, 1921)

Well, to-day is our last day on the water, and Heavens! It was all very nice, but —! [Yes]terday, the sea was at its roughest, and after [ha]ving decided I would never be sea sick again [I] felt it worse than ever. The worst part of it [w]as that I had promised to play a solo, and also [ac]company a fiddler at a concert in the first [cl]ass. In spite of feeling punk, I played the solo. I was the only one in a room of 400 people that [ha]d no dress clothes on. Even if I had had them I [wou]ld not have been well enough to change into them. [I a]m enclosing the program. Ask Ralph to tell you [wh]o Irene Bordoni is (she was on the program me.) [I] had the exquisite honor of being congratulated [on] my playing by the captain of the ship, who is like [a k]ing here! So much for that.

Fontainebleau

Summer 1921

A Bord de "France"
le Fri. June 10, 1921
9:05 A.M.

Dear Ma & Pa,—

I have decided to write you a little every day and so give you an idea of life on board this boat. After I left the deck for the first time, I looked over some of the numerous presents showered upon me. Harry Brin gave me a fancy book about France, Arnold a swell wallet, and Charlie a brand new camera with plenty of films, so that you shall get plenty of pictures. I got on deck again just in time to wave good-bye to the Statue of Liberty. By that time, dinner was ready. It was very nice and I ate my share. Then I started looking for my deck chair, but I haven't found it yet. We just sit down in any chair until someone puts us out. It seems there aren't enough chairs to go around and I have been advised to get my money back. But, of course, you are anxious to know whether I am sea sick. Everyone agrees that they never saw the seas calmer, but nevertheless, I feel none too sure of myself. You know how it feels to be in the dentist's chair when he is drilling your teeth for 8 minutes. Well, the throbbing of the ship does the same to my stomach, only this is for 8 days! However, I have had no spells or mishaps and so I feel the worst is yet to come. I feel fairly perfect when I stay on deck, it is only when I go below that the foolish feeling comes on me. You can well believe that I fly down those stairs and up again as fast as my long legs can carry me. To my great surprise, I slept quite well last night.

It seems that the fourth fellow missed the boat. So we have a little spare room in that dinky little place. But even if it were a palace, you couldn't get me to *stay* down there! I have met the other two fellows and some more of the students going to Fontainebleau but I haven't felt the need for company yet, and so have been rather by myself, looking out at the sea and resting. The piano is also below deck and so out of the question. I have begun reading my French book, but feel that I can learn more by listening in on some French conversations. There are a great many Frenchmen on board, and I make it a point to speak French to the stewards and waiters, even tho they don't understand me.

Saturday: noon

Today I feel fine. The sea is like a lake and so I am just beginning to enjoy the trip. Let's hope it stays this way. This morning I and a violinist got a pass to get into the first class and played there for an hour. It certainly was a relief to get something to do. Until now the time dragged terribly, but now that I can eat and move off the deck I think things will go better. There is to be a dance this evening to help break up the monotony and then, of course, I read a great deal—I am continuing now, after having eaten my dinner. We had some soup, some omelettes with potatoes inside, some mutton chops and french fried potatoes and coffee. I also ate the whole business for the first time since Thursday noon. They also serve white and red wine at meals. I don't like the white stuff, but the red wine tastes like poor port wine. I am getting used to it. I am very lucky in being seated next to three French people, who always converse in French. One is an old priest, another a painter, and a young woman who has attended college in America. They are very nice to me and always encourage me when I try to splash some French.

Sunday: 6 P.M.

One more day gone, and still nothing but water, water everywhere. On board ship Sunday is exactly like every other day. Last night there was a very dense fog and the fog horn kept on blowing every 2 minutes. It was quite dangerous since we were right in the iceberg zone, but by tonight we shall be out of the way of those unnecessary affairs, they tell me. I have gotten thoroughly accustomed to the movement of the ship and have not been at all sick since Friday, nor do I expect to be in the future. You can just imagine how glad I am. I also sleep and eat well. Tell Lil they serve everything in a peculiar manner. Breakfast is opposite—first coffee, then eggs, and *finish* with oatmeal! At dinner if we have, say, green peas, they always serve them separately, and never with the meat. And then there is always the wine which everyone drinks like water, and it is little more than that. But best of all at meals are the three French people who have taken me under their care and teach me French while eating. They roar at my funny mistakes, and I learn by leaps and jumps. I spend a great deal of time with one of them, the painter, who is a man of about 30 and has been giving me the most valuable information about Paris, a fellow who reminds me of Aaron Schaffer sometimes.

Monday: 6 P.M.

I don't expect to add much to-day. Everything is about the same. Altho the sea is rougher to-day than it has been, I feel just as if I were at 628. To kill some time I took a bath to-day and so spent my first franc for soap! After putting 3 cakes in my trunk, I find that they do not supply any soap on the ship. Also, I forgot to tell you that there were handkerchiefs in my valise.

Wednesday: 9 A.M.

Well, to-day is our last day on the water, thank heavens! It was all very nice, *but—!* Yesterday, the sea was at its roughest, and after having decided I would never be sea sick again, I felt it worse than ever. The worst part of it was that I had promised to play a solo, and also accompany a fiddler at a concert in the first class. In spite of feeling punk, I played the solo, tho I was the only one in a room of 400 people that had no dress clothes on. Even if I had had them, I would not have been well enough to change into them. I am enclosing the program.[1] Ask Ralph to tell you who Irene Bordoni is (she was on the programme). I had the exquisite honor of being congratulated on my playing by the Captain of the ship, who is like a king here. So much for that.

We expect to arrive at Havre sometime during the night, and leave for Paris about 7 A.M. to-morrow morning. I expect, then, to go to a hotel that my friend the painter has assured me is fine. I'll mail this letter today in order that it may go off as soon as we land and write you again from Paris. You may write to me as soon as you get this letter in care of the school at Fontainebleau (Viola has the address), since by the time it gets there I will be there also. At any rate, I may send you a cablegram from Paris, as I imagine you must be anxious to hear from me by now. Well, you need never worry. If anything extraordinary should happen (like my giving a concert in Paris) why, I will cablegram to you immediately.

It is impossible for me to name everyone to whom I send my love, but spread it around generally, to yourselves, the folks, Lil and Ena and the girls in the store.

Yours for Paris,
Aaron

P.S. Give my special thanks to La and Charlie who lavished on me book, candy, shirts and camera. To-day I expect to drop Arnold and Uncle Sam a card, tip the waiter and steward. Now that the trip is almost over I can say that altho France may be a Paradise, it is H-- to get there. Anyway (at times)! (Save my letters as I have decided not to bother with a diary.)

T he painter was Marcel Duchamp. This meant nothing to me, despite the fact that in 1913, at the New York Armory Show, he had sent the art world into a tizzy with his *Nude Descending a Staircase*. Duchamp took a dim view of me trying to learn anything of importance about music, and especially the music of our time, at Fontainebleau. "Well," I said, "you're probably right, but what am I to do? Since I know absolutely no one in France, it seems like a good idea to spend two and a half months with fellow American music students in a French musical environment such as the school provides."

"Wrong—you are mistaken," said Duchamp. "It will be a waste of your time. You would do better to take your chances in Paris."

Duchamp was right, of course, except that he didn't know of the presence at Fontainebleau of a teacher named Nadia Boulanger. But then, neither did I. I was very impressed by Duchamp on the morning of our debarkation. We were due to land at eight. By six all the passengers, as was only natural after eight days at sea, were hanging over the rail, gazing rapturously as the coast of France slowly emerged from the fog, dim on the horizon. All the passengers, that is, except Duchamp. I still see him vividly, pipe in mouth, reclining in his deck chair, oblivous of his fellow passengers, intent on the solution of some tough chess problem. I was terribly impressed by his independence of mind.

Imagine my naiveté—arriving in Paris in the middle of June without a hotel reservation! Duchamp had recommended the Hôtel Voltaire on the Quai Voltaire, and he drove there with me in a taxi, but we were told that it was full. I then headed for the Hôtel Savoy on the rue Vaugirard where Aaron Schaffer had stayed. Fortunately, they had a vacancy. The rest of that day was spent walking endlessly about town. I was the typical American tourist, impressed at how *foreign* everything seemed. The streets, the taxis, the sidewalk cafés, the spoken sound of the language—so different from my high school French—all produced a certain hectic ambiance not unlike New York's East Side ghetto neighborhoods. While walking about the streets of Paris on that first day, I noticed on the billboards that there was to be a premiere performance of a new ballet by Darius Milhaud, *Les Mariés de la tour Eiffel,* performed by the Ballet Suédois at the Théâtre des Champs Elysées the night of 19 June. Of course, I decided to go. It was a show put on by Cocteau and a group of composers called *Les Six.* The program included an overture by Georges Auric and new works by Germaine Tailleferre, Arthur Honegger, and Francis Poulenc. The audience was shocked by the modernity of the music and the fanciful nature of the production; they whistled and hooted each time the curtain descended. I recall seeing Milhaud take a bow from the stage to mixed applause and hisses. It was the perfect way to spend one of my first nights in Paris—to get right into the action, where controversial music and dance were happening.

Exciting as this first taste of Paris was, I soon wanted to get to work and found it difficult not to have a piano. The best I could do was to go to the American Women's Club to use theirs at odd hours, and I wrote home that I was ready to leave for Fontainebleau. It seems to me, rereading those first letters from France, that I must have been at least a little homesick. I reminded the folks several times to send my magazines, *The Dial* and *Musical America,* "and be sure to keep me well supplied with letters as this is a very, very long way from home." I made a habit of writing every Sunday and sending a financial report at the end of each month. I wrote to

44

Aaron Schaffer about Cocteau and *Les Six,* but my letters to Ma and Pa tended to be more prosaic—about food and finances:

> . . . Now that I can understand the menus better, I am not forced to order only omelettes. . . . They never serve butter with meals anywhere, and always charge extra for it if you ask for it. They have no pies at all, and if you ask for coffee they always serve it black, no milk. Then if you are eating dinner, the waiter asks you what kind of wine you want, and if you say no wine, he looks at you as if you were drunk! . . . I find that I can eat my 3 meals a day for a little less than $1.50 including tips, wine and not stinging myself.

During my first week in Paris I saw Duchamp twice again, and he treated me to a show and dinner. On the evening of 24 July before leaving for Fontainebleau, I wrote home: "How silly Prohibition seems from Paris! All the saloons are wide open, with women standing at the bar like the men. And, don't forget this—I have never yet seen anyone drunk in Paris! Everytime I take a glass of beer here, I think of you. . . . It seems strange to think that when I am getting in bed here at 12 o'clock, you are having supper in New York. It's a funny world anyway. Affectionately, Aaron."

Fontainebleau
June 25th, 1921

Dear Ma & Pa,

At last I am in Fontainebleau! Everything has turned out splendidly. There was an autobus at the station to meet us, and we had dinner at the Palace. It certainly is a marvellous place, all surrounded by forests and woods, which are open to the public during the day. The conservatory rooms are on the ground floor, the girls live upstairs, and the boys live with French families around the town. I am living in a room for myself which I like *very* much. It is as big as our parlor, with 3 windows bigger than ours, is nicely furnished, has running water, and the nicest old lady to take care of me, who speaks French only, so that I am forced to learn by talking to her. I have already hired a piano (at about $5.00 a month). The house is on a very quiet street, about a 10 minute walk from the Palace, where we all eat our meals. The dinner was very good, so I don't think we'll have any trouble on that point. My trunk is going to be sent here tonight. You have no idea how good it is to feel that I am settled, at last.

To-morrow, a great all day affair is being prepared as the formal opening of the school. All the high muck-a-mucks will be here, there are to be concerts, speeches and fireworks. I really can't see why they make so much fuss. The school is really to begin on Monday. All the pupils are not here yet, as one of the boats is late.

I have been playing on one of the baby grands at the Palace all afternoon,

Aaron with his landlady at 195 rue St. Merry, Fontainebleau, July 1921.

and enjoyed myself immensely, after not having any piano for over 2 weeks. I have decided to study piano here also for 220 francs, (about $20) a month extra. If I don't think I'm getting my money's worth, I'll quit after a month. The piano teacher, Isadore Philipp, is very famous, and known all over Europe and America, and I think it is certainly worth the money.[2]

The town of Fontainebleau itself is very sleepy, but tries very hard to be up-to-date. They have one or two movies even. And by the way, in the Paris moving picture houses, I noticed that they advertised only American pictures, with Charles Ray and Norma Talmadge and Charlie Chaplin. I already noticed that there are a great many tourists who come here daily, to see the Palace and the Forest. And I must say, they are worth coming to see. Someday soon, I shall take my camera and get some pictures to send you.

Now I must get back to the Palace to eat supper. In the mornings I must be up at seven, so it will be a case of early to bed, early to rise. There is nothing to do here at night, anyway.

Well, I'm sure you'll be glad to hear I am so nicely settled. Love to all.

Affectionately,
Aaron

Walter Damrosch was the American founder of the school at Fontaine-bleau. The director in France was Francis Casadesus (the uncle of Robert and Jules, who was then about my age and who became my friend during that summer). Saint-Saëns held the honorary position of general director. In later years, Fontainebleau attracted some very fine students, among them pianists Beveridge Webster, who enrolled as a teenager in 1922, and John Kirkpatrick, who was there for several summers in the twenties. But the student body that first summer of 1921 at Fontainebleau was not my dream of what a student body might be. The degree of scholarly interest was rather mild, I would say. The Americans were there partly because the school was in France, and to some, it was a pleasant way of spending a vacation in a foreign land. But after all, I also went there because I was concerned about going to France all alone, not knowing a living soul. Most of the ninety-one students like myself had never been to France, and we thought of it as an easy way of making contact with French culture, especially musical culture. But the students were friendly and called me "George" because of the fame of the pianist and Debussy specialist George Copeland. It was, as Duchamp had warned, a rather conventional school, except for the presence there of Nadia Boulanger.

Whatever reservations I had about the school, I had none about Fontainebleau itself. In fact, I fell in love with the quiet town and everything connected with it. I took great pleasure in walking in the beautiful gardens and in renting a bicycle and riding with other students through the countryside and through the Forest, coming into small ancient villages that seemed very quaint to me, considering my Brooklyn background. I was impressed with being served "real, live champagne" on Bastille Day, and with the library at the Palace. I wrote home about the forty thousand volumes of books there, all marked with a gold-leaf "N" for Napoleon, who had lived in the Palace. "It sure does give me a thrill to walk into that marvellous room (It's a block long and all decorated in gold like a ball room). They have all sorts of old books in English and French and if it wasn't for the fact that we can only go in once a week, I would never get out of there." My rented piano had arrived early in the summer. "My piano is an awful tin can," I wrote home. "I do some work on it. There are no pianos in France to compare with the Steinway. America is ahead in that, anyway."

The composition teacher was Paul Vidal, at that time about sixty years of age, who had served in that capacity for many years at the Paris Conservatoire. I had considerable difficulty understanding the French patois he spoke, but in any event it was clear from the outset that he had little or no sympathy for the contemporary musical idiom. In that respect he was not very different from Rubin Goldmark. In the midst of our studies, Maître Vidal took off for three weeks of vacation and we were assigned to his assistant, André Bloch. As it turned out, Monsieur Bloch spoke some English and displayed a certain understanding for the harmonic idiom of the day. I played *The Cat and the Mouse* for him, and a few songs that he seemed to like. Under Bloch's guidance I practiced setting songs to French words, and Jules Casadesus and I translated "Old Poem" (the title was first "Mélodie chinoise"; later, "Vieux Poème"). I worked on arrangements, such as a reduction of Brahms' *Second Symphony* for violin, cello, and piano. But in retrospect I can't say that the summer's compositional work was anything more than routine.[3]

During the course of that summer, we met for a few times for conducting lessons with Albert Wolff, a well-known *chef d'orchestre* at the Opéra Comique. I had been given a choice between piano instruction and conducting lessons and had chosen the latter. I wrote home to report: "I have had my first conducting lesson and enjoyed it immensely. If ever the opportunity to conduct presents itself, I won't be so green at it. . . . You ought to see me conducting an imaginary orchestra, waving my arms wildly in the air, making faces at empty chairs!" I found myself seated at meals next to a talented and charming harp student, Djina Ostrowska, and a young composer from Cleveland named G. Herbert Elwell. It wasn't long before we became good friends. (In later years Elwell served as longtime music critic for the Cleveland *Plain Dealer*.)

Djina Ostrowska was older than the rest of us, and had come to study with the French harp virtuoso, Marcel Grandjany, who was a member of the faculty at the Paris Conservatoire. (In the thirties Ostrowska became second harpist with the New York Philharmonic, the only woman in the orchestra at that time.) It was she who first began talking to me about Nadia Boulanger, enthusing about a harmony teacher at the school. I had had several years of harmony, so, of course, I wasn't interested in further harmonic studies. It was old stuff to me. I had worked on harmony, counterpoint, and composition with Rubin Goldmark for four years. It's perfectly possible that I might never have had any contact with Nadia Boulanger at the Fontainebleau school if it were not for the enthusiasm of Ostrowska, urging me to visit Mademoiselle's harmony class. "Just go and see the way she does it." I said to her, "I've had three years of harmony. I'm not interested in harmony classes." But she repeatedly urged, "Just go

Manuscript page, "Old Poem," with words in English and French, 1921.

Nadia Boulanger surrounded by students at Fontainebleau (left to right):
Zo Elliott, Harrison Kerr, Copland, Melville Smith.

and see the way she does it." So I allowed myself to be persuaded.

I no longer recall what Mademoiselle Boulanger was doing that day, harmonically speaking, that was so striking, although I remember that the subject was *Boris Godunov.* Her sense of involvement in the whole subject of harmony made it more lively than I ever thought it could be. She created a kind of excitement about the subject, emphasizing how it was, after all, the fundamental basis of our music, when one really thought about it. I suspected that first day that I had found my composition teacher. Later in the summer, I was rather surprised and flattered when Mademoiselle invited me with a group of her students to come to the other side of Paris for tea at her summer home in Gargenville. It felt like special attention. So I went, and that day I made the decision to study with her after returning to Paris in the fall.

By the end of July I was playing the short piano pieces that I had brought along to France with me at school concerts. I wrote home (3 August): "Sad to say, my composition made quite a hit; I say it is sad, because I can't get over the idea that if a thing is popular it can't be good." (Needless to add, I was to change that opinion!) By the end of the second month at Fontainebleau, I decided to give up my rented piano. "I have banged all the guts out of it by this time, and will thereby save about $5." By then, I had access to decent pianos in the Palace.

Harold Clurman wrote during the summer urging me to find our apartment in Paris. After a few unsuccessful and exhausting trips into the city, I began to fear that the idea might be impossible. Clurman was to sail on 14 September. His arrival was to coincide with the closing concert of the school in Paris on the twenty-third. That was to be a repeat of one at the Fontainebleau Theatre on the twenty-first, when my "Old Poem" was sung by a Miss MacAllister, and I played several piano pieces. I wrote home: "The last one is based on two jazz melodies and ought to make the old professors sit up and take notice."[4]

One of the pieces was *The Cat and the Mouse,* and the most amazing thing happened during intermission of the Fontainebleau concert. Monsieur Jacques Durand, the music publisher of Debussy, came backstage and asked me to come to see him in Paris about publishing the piece. I wrote home (27 September):

Let me try to calmly explain to you what this means. In the first place Durand & Son is the biggest music publishing firm in Paris, which means the world. To finally see my music printed means more to me than any debut in Carnegie Hall ever could. . . . Don't expect me to make any fortunes out of my compositions. Composing is not a business, but a luxury, which you are so good as to allow me to afford. . . . I received a long letter from Mr. Goldmark. What would he have to say to all this!

The last week of Fontainebleau, at the end of September, was filled with excitement after the somewhat lazy and quiet summer. For one thing, just a few days before Clurman arrived, and after despairing that it would ever happen, I found an apartment. I was overjoyed because it was big enough for both of us, although by any standards modest. It was on the fourth floor at 207 Boulevard Raspail, near the Latin Quarter, exactly where I wanted to be. The rent was about $25 a month, to be split between us. After tipping and bribing the right people, I recall coming out on the street and having a wild desire to run up to every stranger I met and howl the marvelous news. I wrote home: "Please don't pronounce *Raspail* like Raspale, but like this—Raspighy to rhyme with skiey. . . . *Now* you need never worry. I shall take care of Harold and he shall take care of me. . . ."

That same week, the students at the school were "treated" to a free tour of the battlefields. This was a sobering experience in the midst of gala preparations for the closing festivities of Fontainebleau. It was terribly disturbing to see the city of Rheims in ruins and to be shown trenches, forests, barbed-wire entanglements, and cemeteries with black crosses. About this experience I wrote to Ma and Pa: "To think that man can be such a beast. One thing is sure—I am absolutely inoculated against war fever, for all time to come, and not if everybody on earth stood on their heads, would I fight in any army for any cause. I'd go to prison first. If everyone did the same there would be no war. . . ."

The apartment and the upcoming concerts quickly took my mind off such matters. It was my first opportunity to wear the tuxedo I had sent over in my trunk. To the outfit I added a hat bought in Paris for 25 francs. "It's very French and makes me look like the giraffe I am. . . ." Clurman arrived, and I met him on the evening of the Paris concert.[5] Harold used to remind me that I was introduced to the audience that evening by the ancient organist and composer Charles Widor as "un jeune compositeur américain de tendences modernes."[6] The program included songs and four piano pieces[7] played by myself. Both "graduation" concerts (Fontainebleau and Paris) were well attended and gala, with newspaper announcements in advance and champagne receptions afterward. Not wanting the folks at home to think I was getting too fancy, I wrote: "Don't think I've forgotten Washington Ave. I shall certainly think of you all eating those enormous dinners on Rosh-hashona and groan at the thought of missing the marvellous cakes after the fasting is over on Yom-kippur. . . ."

The day after the Paris concert, Clurman and I returned to Fontainebleau together. Since we could not move into our Paris flat until 1 October, Clurman stayed with friends in Paris while I remained at the Palace at Fontainebleau at the invitation of Jules Casadesus. I was given a room with a good piano and had to pay only for my meals. I walked in the beautiful gardens in the evenings and "felt the presence of Napoleon's ghost." Although Duchamp had not been mistaken about Fontainebleau, it had been a special place for me in many ways. I sent the clippings from the French newspapers home, translating each for the folks, and the diploma, warning them not to bother to frame it. Then I began to pack my trunk for Paris.

Oct 11, 1921.
207 Bd. Raspail
Paris.

Dear Ma + Pa, —

I really ought to be sending you a cablegram with this wonderful news, but I was afraid it would scare you. Just think, I have just sold my _first_ composition. Let me catch my breadth and tell you the whole story. I wrote you that M. Durand, the biggest publisher in Paris, had promised to publish a piece of mine called "the Cat and the Mouse" after he had heard me play it at Fontainebleau. Well, I have just been to see him at his office here and have sold him the piece outright for 500 francs.

Paris

1921-1924

Verso: The first page of a letter from Copland to his parents.
Opposite: Copland, 1921.

If there was anything wrong with being twenty in the twenties, it is being eighty in the eighties. From a musical standpoint it was a marvelous time to be alive. In exploring the artistic climate of our times, it would be difficult to exaggerate the importance of the decade 1920 to 1929. I can speak with some authority on the period because I had what might be called a front seat. As I lived in Paris as a student for three years, from 1921 to 1924, I am able to give an eyewitness account of those interesting and fascinating years. Of course the twenties are famous! No other decade rivals their appeal. The sheer glamour of the period exerts a magic spell. The very word "modern" was exciting. The air was charged with talk of new tendencies, and the password was originality—anything was possible. Every young artist wanted to do something unheard of, something nobody had done before. Tradition was nothing; innovation everything. The publicized twenties are easy to laugh at. It was the period of the jazz age, of what Americans called the "flappers," and the time of Prohibition. We laughed then too, at all those more grotesque aspects of the twenties—the atmosphere was somewhat hysterical. But the real twenties that concerned the artist were full of activity and vitality. We profited by this sense of new things happening.

The end of each war seems to bring to artists, as well as the rest of the world, a sense of relief and renewal. The end of World War I was very different from that of the end of the war in the forties. We were left with no anxiety complex. The German Kaiser was really finished at the end of World War I. In most of Europe and America money and art patrons were plentiful, and there was the conviction that nothing but prosperity and good times lay ahead. I have often thought that all our preoccupations in music since then may be traced back to that period. Nothing really new, with the possible exception of electronic and computer music, has happened since. That is to say, nothing that did not have its origins during the twenties. There seemed a wealth of new voices from all parts of Europe,

North and South America. Among them were two dominant musical personalities who would profoundly influence twentieth-century musical thinking: Stravinsky and Schoenberg, or, if you prefer, Schoenberg and Stravinsky. Each represented a distinct aesthetic, a different manner of composing, and a quite different way of thinking about the whole problem of the composer's art.

Paris, of course, was the center of this renewed excitement in the arts. Arriving at twenty on French soil, my expectations were dangerously high, but I was not to be disappointed. Paris was filled with cosmopolitan artists from all over the world, many of whom had settled there as expatriates. It was the time of Tristan Tzara and Dada; the time of André Breton and surrealism; it was when we first heard the names of James Joyce and Gertrude Stein, T. S. Eliot and Ezra Pound, and also of the French writers Marcel Proust and André Gide. The painters were enormously active, with Picasso taking centerstage and interesting figures like Georges Braque and Max Ernst working in Paris at that time. All kinds of artistic activities were bursting around me, and I was determined to take it all in as fast as possible.

Perhaps my three student years in France are so vivid in my memory because they had such enormous influence on my future career. Man has not yet devised a method for measuring influences on an artist—influences can be direct or indirect, positive or negative, sharp or subtle. All this notwithstanding, it was in France in the early twenties that I reached my majority, that my ideas came of age, and it was there I came to know those who were to be the major and continuing influences in my life. I speak of Nadia Boulanger, my teacher, and Serge Koussevitzky, the great Russian conductor. I cannot imagine what my career would have been without them. And of course, Harold Clurman. We were together constantly during the Paris years.

Harold Clurman[1]

When I look back, it was a crummy apartment. Furnished, but not well. The bed developed bedbugs, and we had to have it fumigated. Aaron tended to be very economical. He had a great sense of the value of the dollar, which I have not. I told him, when he sold his first piece of music outright to that French publisher, that it was the only bad business deal I ever saw him make. He sold it for about 500 francs, and at that time $40 *or thereabouts seemed like a fortune to him. I tended always to want to eat more luxuriously than Aaron. And I always used to complain, "I don't understand why your bill comes to less than mine." Well, it was simple. I liked to eat better and more. I was always wanting to go to more expensive places; he to less expensive ones. But we never had a real quarrel—not in all the time we've known each other. We each paid for our own meals very carefully in Paris. He would do the adding 'cause I couldn't add. He was at that time in every way much more used to dealing with the world. We both got money from home—about $20 or $25 a week. It was enough to keep us going and we had money for concerts, plays, and books too.*

I was very, very shy in those years—a fact that seems to astonish all who have known me since. Aaron was the same as now—careful, judicious, balanced. I, on the other hand, was impetuous and absolutely impractical. I'm not too practical now either. You see, Aaron was brought up by a father who was a businessman and I by a father who was at the same time a doctor and a dreamer. I can get very assertive and just yell at the top of my voice. Aaron never expressed himself that way. But when he would say very quietly, "I don't like it" about something, it was just as strong as when I yelled. He was able to find a word, one word maybe, and that's why he writes well. Finding what he's saying adequate to what he means. One of the reasons we couldn't quarrel is because I have such faith in his judgment. Anyway, he never says something is no good, only, "I don't care for it." How can you argue with that?

I would spend the days at the Sorbonne or the American Library while Aaron was in the apartment, composing and practicing. I heard certain pieces over and over again. We had lunch and dinner together every day. I'd meet Aaron after his classes with Boulanger. The first thing I'd say was, "What did you learn today?" And as nearly as he could describe it to a layman without technical knowledge of music, he would tell me what he learned. And you know he had a faculty that stood him in good stead as a teacher—making complicated matters clear. He would ask me about my classes and what I was reading. We didn't speak very much to anybody else, since we had established a great friendship and we discussed everything together. In the evenings, I took him to the theater or he took me to concerts. We were very serious about the arts, but we had a lot of fun too, going around to places like Sylvia Beach's bookstore and catching glimpses of famous writers like Hemingway, Joyce, and Pound, and seeing the composers and poets in the cafés and restaurants. When people ask, "What was Joyce like?", or Pound, or Satie, I have to laugh, thinking of us two

greenhorn kids. Twenty years old we were! We were pretty well read and knew what was happening, but we didn't know anybody. We kept comparing French culture to what we didn't have at home, wondering why Americans were not as interested in the arts. In our youthful enthusiasm we talked about changing things around.

I had been to college and read a lot. Aaron respected that. He still does. One day he said, "Who is Caligula?" I told him, and he said, "That's the advantage of going to college. You know who Caligula is." Even nowadays when he is on a college campus he always says, "You know, I missed this," and he feels nostalgic about something he never had. But he made up for it. He was a good reader. Sometimes I went with Aaron to Boulanger's place when she had those teas with all the musicians, and her outspoken Russian mother was pouring tea. Aaron was pleased that Boulanger thought me intelligent. She would say, "Tell me, young friend of Copland, you who read everything . . ." Well, I had to read a lot and to work hard to become a good writer, if I am a good writer. Aaron helped me not only learn music, but with my own writing. He'd say, "This is not bad, but what do you need this passage for?" If he didn't like something, he'd always say so. One time he said, "You know, I really learned a lot from what you wrote, but it's so badly written!" That was in 1927. And it was badly written. Later on when I got better, he'd say, "That's a good article. That's a very good article. But this whole passage is wrong." His sense of fitness, which he has in the writing of music, extended to literature. I always remember his compliments to me because he doesn't give them out injudiciously even to his best friends. Things he knew when he was twenty-one

Opposite: Copland with friends in Paris (left to right): Herbert Elwell, Copland, Clurman, Eyvind Hesselberg.
Left: On the reverse of this snapshot Copland wrote to his parents: "This is my gorgeous tin pan at 207."

took me till I was forty to know. He said I was a late developer. Aaron knew what he wanted to be when he was fourteen, and I didn't ever know what I wanted to be. In Paris already he was composing mature pieces. I wasn't mature enough to wipe my nose. I still am not sure which I am—critic, writer, director, ladies man, or teacher! I just say I am Harold Clurman. But Aaron always knew. I don't know how he achieved it. It's like a talent for music or mathematics, that enormous balance.

Our second apartment in Paris we rented in the fall of 1922, after I had gone home for the summer and Aaron had spent a few months in Berlin. It was in a private house on the Villa d'Alesia. A very nice lady who had been a singer ran it, and it was nicely located on the Left Bank. When we first saw it, Aaron said, "This is going to be too expensive." But it wasn't so expensive, and it was the most pleasant place we lived in together. Aaron's main work with Boulanger that year was the writing of a ballet. We saw a film together, called Nosferatu, *with vampires and graveyards and other gruesome things. Aaron wanted a libretto based on that, so I worked on it. That's why he dedicated Grohg to me. I wasn't a libretto writer, and it was a young effort by both of us. Later, Aaron dedicated his book* Copland On Music[2] *to me, and I dedicated* All People Are Famous[3] *to Aaron, since he's on almost every page.*

You ask me if Aaron ever got angry or resentful. He doesn't take time out for that. Even at the time of the McCarthy hearings, which was one thing he really felt passionately against, he only expressed his anger very briefly. When we returned together from France in 1924, and he had no money and had to play at summer hotels, he didn't seem to mind too much. He took everything in his stride. He is a man who knows about acceptance, not in the sense that others do, but a kind of metaphysical acceptance. I get stirred up and very angry and hurt about certain things, but Aaron's indignation is intellectual and unviolently expressed. Through the years I joked that he was not a dramatic character, because he didn't change much. He just got better. He got more mature. He got more knowledge. He got more experience. But his basic character never changed. Once I remember him talking about a fear of being isolated in his old age. I could see he was moved by it, but he said it just once. When I had trouble in my private life, I could talk about it and would repeat myself and repeat myself and become a big bore. Aaron was never that way.

Was he ambitious, you ask? His ambition was to be a great man for himself. The only ambition I ever heard him remark on was, "I want to be remembered." We were open with each other. I would confess personal things to him, but there was nothing for him to confess. His life was not complex. He was always just what you see, not a crazy romantic fella like me. I have such a big admiration for him as a person. To me he's a great man.

After three years in Paris, we sailed home and never lived together after that. We conducted our private lives separately, but we saw a great deal of each other and always kept in touch. When Stella [Adler] and I were married, Aaron got along with her. She liked him, and he liked her. He was too smart ever to interfere when I was unhappy. But I always poured my troubles out to him, including the Group Theatre and money problems. What bothered me, I had to take money from him for a while when I needed it desperately. He got Guggenheims right away, and my affluence came not until much later. And as I said, he knew how to save money, which I never did.

Aaron was around the Group Theatre a lot, since he was my friend, and also the conception of the Group interested him. We both knew when we returned from Europe in 1924 that we wanted to be spokesmen of our generation in American arts. I tried to do it through the Group, and Aaron tried with his Copland–Sessions Concerts and other efforts. My involvement in the Group was more political than Aaron's. I was moving pretty far to the left. Aaron was not political, but he liked the idea of sharing creative efforts and ideas. That stirred him. He was sociable, and he liked to fit in. Maybe that's why some of his music is popular. He didn't have to push to become popular. Whenever someone would ask why he wrote a *particular kind of music, he'd answer, "It came out that way." It was just normal for him.*

Aaron is my composer in the sense that he is part of the world I inhabit. I can understand why Nietzsche was made for Wagner. In the theater I would say that Odets was closest to the way I feel—he has a certain sense of America all through his work which is part of my sense of America and part of my experience with life. As Odets is my playwright, Copland is my composer. His world is parallel with mine.

I lost no time after settling into our Paris apartment in going to see M. Durand about the publication of *Le Chat et la Souris*. A contract for 500 francs[4] was offered and I was delighted to sign it. It may not have been a good business deal in the long run, but it seemed wonderful to me in 1921. I felt that at least a start had been made toward a career as a professional composer; best of all, I could write home that I actually was to get *paid* for my music. I ended that letter (11 October): "So, we have a composer in the Copland family it seems. Who says there are no more miracles!" The proofs were promised in a few weeks, and I planned to send copies of my first published piece to the States before my twenty-first birthday. I began to think about how I would spend the 500 francs. But as the weeks stretched into months, and 1921 became 1922, I learned my first lesson in regard to publication dates. Never again would I announce such an event in advance! Pop had already placed an order for twenty-five copies of *The Cat and the Mouse*; what he planned to do with them was a complete mystery.

The time had come to continue my studies. On 26 October I went to 36 rue Ballu[5] to talk to Nadia Boulanger about composition lessons. As the small shaky elevator lifted me to her fourth-floor apartment, I began to have second thoughts. I knew of no other American who had ever studied advanced composition with her. In fact, I had never heard of any composer who had studied with a woman. History, for some unexplained reasons, had not yet produced a great woman composer. How was this going to sound to the folks back home? Standing alone in Mademoiselle Boulanger's imposing presence—the long dark skirt, pince-nez glasses—I was conscious of the stark differences between us: a gawky twenty-year-old from Brooklyn and the self-assured "older woman" who regularly dined with the intellectual Parisian heroes. She glanced at the sonata written for Goldmark and then asked to hear one of my other compositions. I played a short piece rooted in the jazz idiom, so modern that Goldmark earlier had confessed he didn't know what to say about it. Mademoiselle, as all her students called her, simply said, "Yes. Come. We will start tomorrow."

So began the decisive musical experience of my life, for Nadia Boulanger turned out to be one of the great music teachers of her time.[6] I wrote home: "Now be prepared for a surprise. My teacher is not as you suppose—a man, but a woman of about 40 [she was actually 34], one of the best known musicians in France, a teacher of harmony at the Paris Conservatoire. . . . She understands the kind of modern music I like to write, so that she was the teacher I was looking for. It has been all arranged and I have a lesson on Saturday morning of each week. . . ." To soften the surprise, I added: ". . . she charges only 60 frcs. (about $4.20) a lesson, which compared with the $6.00 I paid Goldmark is not so expensive. . . ."

Two other Americans found Mademoiselle at about the same time— Melville Smith and Virgil Thomson. They came to Boulanger for organ lessons, and Virgil for counterpoint as well. I believe that I was the first to study advanced composition with her. Many years later, Virgil wrote that every town in the United States could boast two things: a five-and-ten-cent store and a Boulanger student. As it turned out, he was not far from the truth. Over the years, Mademoiselle taught a host of gifted young men and women, composers and conductors of contemporary music, teachers, writers, and performers. Twentieth-century music was nurtured in her old-fashioned salon. "The composition of music cannot be taught," she used to say—then went ahead and taught it anyway. She knew everything about music—what came before Bach, Stravinsky's latest works, what came after Stravinsky, and everything in between. Technical skills—counterpoint, orchestration, sight-reading—were second nature to her. She believed in strict discipline and she worked hard herself. She might say to a student, "Come at seven," and one would not know whether to arrive in the morning or evening—both were in the range of her work day. She was profoundly committed to music. In her eyes, one *had* to be wholly committed. Technical mastery was to be rigorously pursued and absorbed, and essentials implanted early. There wasn't anything she couldn't do in a technical sense—read all the various music clefs with ease, play orchestral scores at the piano—all those things that are desirable for a young musician to know, she was able to do easily. She knew that unerring musicianship had to become a reflex so that the mind could be free for the art of composition. "To study music, we must learn the rules," she would say. "To create music, we must forget them." And then she might quote Stra-

Nadia Boulanger at the organ in her apartment, 36 rue Ballu, Paris, 1922.

vinsky, "If everything would be permitted to me, I would feel lost in this abyss of freedom."

No one ever came to a Boulanger class late more than once; her disapproval could be annihilating. Nor was her praise lavishly given. When Mademoiselle called something good, it was a red-letter day. She never missed student concerts and could be seen applauding with the rest of the audience, but the next day she would enumerate every flaw in the performance. She could look at a score and "hear" the music in her head, understanding at once what the composer was attempting. Mademoiselle could always find the weak spot in a piece you suspected was weak, but had hoped she would not notice. She could also tell you *why* it was weak. Her critical facility was unerring. Known to be difficult with those she considered untalented, she felt it her duty to be brutally honest and uncompromising. There must have been some unhappy scenes in that studio at times! I must say that I never witnessed that side of Boulanger's nature, although I do recall having to read torturously through Mahler orchestra scores at the piano with Mademoiselle insisting I go on to the end without stopping, no matter how slowly; this was a routine requirement of her score-reading classes.

But it was wonderful for me to find a teacher with such openness of mind, while at the same time she held firm ideas of right and wrong in musical matters. The confidence she had in my talents and her belief in me were at the very least flattering and more—they were crucial to my development at this time of my career. Mademoiselle had the sensitivity of the finest musician and the matchless gift of conveying her understanding with such enthusiasm that it made me try harder, which was all she really wanted. Having divined the depth of talent with which each of her students was endowed, she simply proposed to develop it to the full. She had an unusual method of rating her students: the poorest ones were taught on Monday. On each successive day in the week the quality improved, so that by Saturday she was teaching her best students. Then, in each category, she put the poorest students earliest each day, so everyone knew that those who came late on Saturday were Mademoiselle's favorites. I do not know exactly how she taught others; some must have sat at the organ that dominated the far end of the spacious living room of that legendary apartment. For my lessons, we both sat at one of the grand pianos, and at her command, I would prop my most recent composition on the music stand and play it for her. She did not lecture, but she would ask, over and over, "What do you *hear?*" And constantly searching my own heart and mind, I would play on, ending the hour exhausted, exhilarated.

It might not seem so at first, but perhaps it was an advantage that Nadia Boulanger was not herself a regularly practicing composer. Teaching came first for her; it was not something she *had* to do in order to free herself for something else. To what extent Mademoiselle had serious ambitions as a composer has never been entirely established. Born 16 September 1887 as Nadia Juliette Boulanger, she came from a musical milieu. Her father, Ernest Boulanger, was a composer and singing teacher at the Paris Conservatoire, and her mother, formerly the Princess Mychetsky, had been his pupil. Nadia had a few short pieces published and had aided the pianist Raoul Pugno in the orchestration of an opera. Mainly she was credited with the training of her gifted younger sister, Lili, who won the first Prix de Rome ever accorded a woman composer. Lili fell ill and died at the age of twenty-four in 1918, and Nadia mourned her the rest of her life. She told me that her dedication to teaching was in Lili's memory and therefore a sacred trust.

64

Mademoiselle was a very devout Catholic. Her students would sometimes joke that if you wrote a work with religious words for her, you were made. But Nadia considered personal beliefs a private matter. In all the time I knew her, I never recall any remark or discussion about religion. A biographer has accused Boulanger of anti-Semitism, and then to cover any conflicting opinion, such as my own, the writer claimed: "Her self-control was so remarkable that apparently none of her Jewish students ever noticed any tinge of anti-Semitism in her behavior."[7] Nadia's strength and self-control were indeed admirable, but being without family, she relied on her friends in times of personal need and support. She and I became close friends, and there were other Jewish students who were Nadia's friends. It is impossible that one of us would not have noticed anti-Semitism in her behavior. Especially during the war years, we were very much aware of such things. I feel certain that anti-Semitism was not part of Nadia Boulanger's personality. I also find puzzling the descriptions of Nadia as masculine and dour. I must assume that they come from persons who saw her only in later years. As a young woman, she gave off a kind of reserved warmth, and there was an old-fashioned womanliness about her that was charming. She wore low-heeled, "sensible" shoes, long black skirts, and glasses, but these seemed to contrast pleasantly with her bright intelligence and lively temperament. In later years, as she became smaller and thinner, Nadia was quasi-nunlike in appearance. Her voice was distinctive—it was very low and remained extraordinarily resonant throughout her long life.[8]

It soon became clear that the teaching aspect of our relationship was not the only valuable thing for me. One must not forget that Mademoiselle's intelligence went beyond the subject of music. She was a superior person, knowledgeable about literature and other arts. Altogether, you had the warmth of her personality, the extensive musical knowledge, and a first-class intellect. The feeling in her Paris studio was of being at the center of what was going on in the artistic life of Paris. You weren't merely studying an art that happened in the past. It was all alive, and being created around you. It was not at all unusual to find the latest score of Stravinsky on her piano, still in manuscript, or those of Albert Roussel, Milhaud, or Honegger. I discovered Mahler through Mademoiselle. How she got on to him I don't know, but she had the score for *Das Lied von der Erde* in 1922, and we pored over it together—especially the orchestration. On Wednesday afternoons she held class meetings for her students, *déchiffrage* classes, where new works were read at the piano by some bright student. They would be discussed and enthused about, or dismissed. At other times we

Mademoiselle Boulanger with students, 1923 (left to right): Eyvind Hesselberg, unidentified, Robert Delaney, unidentified, Copland, Mario Braggioti, Melville Smith, unidentified, and Armand Marquint.

sang Monteverdi and Gesualdo madrigals, which were virtually unperformed at that time. Also, the latest literary and artistic works were examined: Kafka, Mann, Gide, Pound. Those Wednesday afternoons became an institution. After two hours or more of music, tea and cakes were served. The musical greats came to Mademoiselle's Wednesday teas—pianists, singers, and composers—as well as students and journalists. I met Stravinsky there, Milhaud, Poulenc, and Roussel. I saw Ravel and Villa-Lobos, and on one occasion I shook hands with Saint-Saëns. He played the piano and he played well, though he was in his eighties. I came to know Nadia's French students: Jean Françaix, Annette Dieudonné, and Marcelle de Manziarly.[9] Nadia's mother always presided over the tea table, her hand shaking, but never spilling a drop. I never heard Nadia boast about her mother being of the aristocracy as has been stated in some writings

66

about her. Madame was an ebullient type who seemed to take pleasure in shocking visitors with her outspoken language. She was very much in evidence and at times younger in behavior than her daughter. Nadia was quite proper, while her mother was rather Rabelaisian at times; their roles often seemed oddly reversed to me.

When I first knew Nadia, she was already teaching harmony at the Paris Conservatoire (later she became professor of composition); she also taught organ and counterpoint at the Ecole Normale de Musique, and in summers she drove twice a week from her home in Gargenville to teach at Fontainebleau. She was second organist at the Church of the Madeleine and served on several important boards, among them the score-reading and program committees for the Société Musique des Indépendants (SMI),[10] which sponsored contests of contemporary music for little-known and unpublished composers. It was not long after our lessons began that Mademoiselle suggested a performance of my music at a December SMI concert. My songs, "Pastorale" and "Old Poem," were sung by the American tenor Charles Hubbard with Boulanger at the piano. That was my first experience of hearing my music performed by others while I sat in the audience. The concert was favorably reviewed the next day in the Paris *Herald*. Later that season, on 10 January 1922, Hubbard performed the songs again in a recital at the Salle des Agriculteurs.

I can still remember the eagerness of Nadia's curiosity concerning my rhythms in these early works, particularly the jazz-derived ones. Before long we were exploring polyrhythmic devices together—their difficulty of execution intrigued her. Mademoiselle was confident that I could write in larger forms. Within a short time she was able to extract from a composer of two-page songs and three-page piano pieces a full-sized ballet lasting over thirty minutes. At the period when I was her pupil, Boulanger had one all-embracing principle, namely, the desirability of aiming first and foremost at the creation of what she called "la grande ligne" in music. Much was included in that phrase: the sense of forward motion, of flow and continuity in the musical discourse; the feeling for inevitability, for the creating of an entire piece that could be thought of as a functioning entity. Boulanger had an acute sense of contrast and balance. Her teaching, I suppose, was French in that she stressed clarity of conception, textures, and elegance in proportion. Much has happened in music since those years, and perhaps Boulanger's theories seem outdated; but in the early twenties her musical ideas and her confidence in my ability to apply them meant a great deal to my development as a composer.

Nadia Boulanger[11]

A very long time ago Copland was my student. To let him develop was my great concern. One could tell his talent immediately. The great gift is a demonstration of God. More the student is gifted, more you must be careful not to invade his self. But I hope that I did never disturb him, because then is no more to be a teacher, is to be a tyrant. And it brings nothing. He must learn to write well, read well, understand, see, pay attention, have memory trained—every obligation he has, many obligations. But he must never spoil his personality. The teacher must respect the personality of the student, and the student must submit to what makes life possible: order, rigor, and freedom. If Copland would ask of me, "Is this what you want?" I would say, "I want nothing. I want to answer your questions; I will know what you think about, what you talk about." Since 1921 we are not one year without connection. He is such a faithful human being, and today as warm as when he was a youngster. What is fascinating is to see youngsters develop—to have seen the beginning of Copland with a sense of proportion (already an accomplishment itself), and then his long development. I adore seeing the progress of the very gifted or the small progress—but some change, if only the student is ready to express himself.

I am not interested people to know what I do or do not. I am interested in the student—to bring people to be themselves, and at the same time, know how to conform to the limits that he may find freedom. We can establish logically all the degrees of education—grammar, calculation, numbers—all that we can. But the real value is not in our hands. I have earned my living since seventeen, but there are things you penetrate only rather late in life, because more you go in life, more you touch the real expression. It is the life of the spirit that counts, but we are not in a society for that. No, it is a life of money, and you cannot avoid it. Everybody is obliged to earn his bread. I have had to earn my living in teaching, and it offends me today as it did when I started in 1904. What has been given me to think is so deep, so authentical, that I am grateful. I can explain the grammar of music, I can make a youngster see if he has any kind of gift— not to become great, but to be a little more himself, a little better, a little more understanding.

My mother was Russian; I adored her. I received much help from her, much affection from my family, my teachers, my students. My mother was not a musician, but her principle was "Have you done all what you

Copland and Boulanger, 1976.

could?" But we are so lazy! I confess that I suffer very much not to talk Russian. If for ten years I learned one word a week, I would talk Russian. Have I done it? No. I have worked very much in my life, but would I have died because I learned one word a week? I can't believe it! The greatest influence on my life was the one of my sister Lili. When she was born, I had the impression I had been honored by a responsibility that I must guide, protect her. She was six years younger than I. Very soon she was such an unbelievable personality that she became my guide. She was so pure and inaccessible to any kind of temptation. She led her life in the memory of our father, who died when Lili was six years old. She knew she was to become a composer. When she was already so sick, she said to me, "Be aware when your students will be near you, they will have the age when I quit you." She knew she was to die. I believe she was then already a great composer.

Generation after generation have come to me since Copland, and still talented American youngsters come. Yes, they have a certain characteristic. Also, my Japanese students. I say to them, "Don't forget you are Japanese. Remain Japanese. Then know that we exist. Feel at home in Europe. But do not lose your quality." I will have this summer two Korean students, and with them I say the same. But on the very high level, everything is either good or not good. Now, I am tired beyond words and I am sick. I never pay attention to my health, but now I have been stopped. I am glad to have the boys around me. One is fourteen years only! I forget completely when I am with them. Now tonight I write my lesson to prepare for Fontainebleau tomorrow, where I am terrified and delighted to see what I must do. I was happy to talk to you about Copland, but I cannot explain love, I cannot explain music, I cannot explain art. I feel it, but I can only explain the means employed to do what we do.

It must have been cause for profound satisfaction for Nadia that she guided the musical destiny of so many of this century's fine composers: in France, Marcelle de Manziarly, Jean Françaix, and Igor Markevitch; in England, Lennox Berkeley; in America, Walter Piston, Roy Harris, Marc Blitzstein, David Diamond, Elliott Carter, Irving Fine, Harold Shapero, Louise Talma, Arthur Berger, Easley Blackwood, and others, many of whom came to Nadia through my recommendation. We were called the "Boulangerie." I have lost track, if I ever knew, how that got started, but Nadia used the term herself in a letter to me as early as 1925. Honors and awards were bestowed on Nadia Boulanger during her lifetime, but we have no reward in this country commensurate with her contribution to our musical development. I am certain that she had the reward she most coveted—the deep affection and respect of her many pupils. Even those who were critical of her had respect for her profound musical knowledge and devotion to her art and to her students. She wanted them to do well, not out of vanity for herself, but out of the depth of her caring for them. Of course, Boulanger's insistence on discipline and reliance on traditional formulae was not right for everyone. Roy Harris said that except for the strongest musicians it was dangerous to study with Boulanger, because her *own* personality and talents were so strong.

My relationship with her began in 1921 as student to teacher and grew into an enduring friendship. She always helped me in every way she possibly could, and we were never out of touch with each other for long. Even now, I think of Nadia as still there in that legendary apartment on the rue Ballu where she lived for over seventy years. From my very first lessons, I sensed something special there. I soon realized that I was going to need more than one year abroad, and I convinced my parents to let me stay another year in Paris and then yet another—three in all to study with her and to absorb the unique artistic atmosphere of the times.

Very much on the scene in Paris in the early twenties was a group of composers of diverse talents who realized that they could more easily get heard as a unit than individually; they were first named *Les Six* by the critic Henri Collet. The group represented new attitudes in music and the spirit of the period. They signified the absolute end of the Germanic Brahmsian and Wagnerian approach—the one that seemed to say you had to listen to music in a very solemn and sacrosanct manner with your eyes closed and your head in your hands. They were not long-haired romantic genius types. These six, five men and one woman, were what we would call "regular guys." Francis Poulenc and Georges Auric were young, lively, full of temperament, and to me, very *French*. Poulenc had a charming personal gift that he knew very well how to use. There is something about his pieces that always brings to mind the joyful period in which they were written. Germaine Tailleferre was a beautiful girl who wrote a kind of post-impressionist music, and Louis Durey seemed to be standing around at the time; his early music sounded modern, but for some reason, he seceded from the group in 1923 and was not heard of again.

The two most striking composers of *Les Six* were Arthur Honegger and Darius Milhaud. Honegger was of Swiss background and closer to German music than the others. It was Milhaud who interested me most.[12] I was amazed at his verve and wit, the ease with which he turned out reams of music, and his confident and outspoken manner. When other people were thinking, "Down with Wagner!" he was the one who *yelled* "Down with Wagner!" He and other members of the group taunted the critics, who fought back, giving *Les Six* a great deal of notoriety and publicity.[13] Erik Satie was their musical godfather. He had a program for French music: it had to be anti-German, anti-grandiose, anti-impressionist, and even anti-impressive. Virgil Thomson, longtime admirer of Satie, has written, ". . . during an acquaintance with it of more than forty years his music has never ceased to be rewarding. People take to Satie or they don't. . . ."[14] Virgil took to him, as did others who seized on Satie's aesthetic to announce themselves free of romanticism and impressionism once and for all. I saw Satie occasionally in a restaurant in Paris. He was always alone and invariably ate with his face in his plate, casting quick glances from right to left as if he feared somebody might snatch the food away from him. He really was what the French call "un caractère." He was thought of as part mascot, part jester, part primitive, and part sage. If Satie was the spiritual godfather of *Les Six*, Jean Cocteau was their literary spokesman. His well-known pamphlet *Le Coq et l'harlequin* had in it all the shibboleths of the new day. He coined the phrase, "une musique de tous les jours," and *Les Six* insisted on that kind of music—the everyday kind that you listened to with your eyes wide open.

By far the most dynamic musical presence in France was a Russian. I still retain a vivid memory of the first time I laid eyes on Igor Stravinsky. I was walking down the rue Saint-Honoré one day in the fall of 1921 when suddenly I spied a short man approaching from the opposite direction. "Oh Lord," I thought, "that looks like Stravinsky in the flesh." I was much too overawed to dream of speaking with him, but as soon as he passed, I found myself wheeling around and following after him as if drawn by a magnet. It was a reflex action, inspired by admiration for the leading creative spirit of the new decade. I didn't tag after him for long, because I felt embarrassed at the naiveté of my behavior, but the memory of that spontaneous need to pay homage has remained with me for more than half a century. Years later I told him of my first live view of him, and we both had a good laugh about it. It was soon after that incident that I actually *did* meet Stravinsky in Paris at one of Mademoiselle's Wednesday afternoon classes, and I was one of the dozen or more students who stood about in awe of the Master's presence. More than once during those early years we had the privilege of examining Stravinsky's most recently completed work, even before performance and publication. Because of his close friendship with Boulanger (aided by the fact that her mother was of Russian origin), his latest opus found its way onto her piano rack. Even so, Mademoiselle always referred to him as "Mr. Stravinsky." One of her favorite students, Jean Françaix, said: "Nadia had two polestars, God and Stravinsky. Of course, no one had any objection to the first. The trouble with the second was that he was her close friend *and* the world's greatest living composer, so she tended to lead her students toward the Stravinsky style. . . ." It was the period of his anti-string pieces, and we examined the scores of the *Symphonies of Wind Instruments,* the *Octet,* and the *Concerto for Pianoforte and Wind Instruments.* I was fascinated to see these works in which he dispensed with strings in order to create just the kind of dry sound he was after.

For me there was no doubt that Stravinsky was the most exciting musical creator on the scene. He was the hero of my student days, and I was relieved to hear at one of Boulanger's classes that he composed at the piano as I had always done. Heading the list of Stravinsky's gifts was his rhythmic virtuosity. The ballets, *Firebird, Petrushka,* and the *Rite of Spring,* had such rhythmic power and unspoiled vigor. There was also much to learn from Stravinsky's bold use of dissonance and his unusual instrumental combinations that projected sharply defined colors so different from the luminous, soft lines of French impressionism. I was particularly struck by the strong Russian element in his music. He borrowed freely from folk materials, and I have no doubt that this strongly influenced me to try to find a way to a distinctively American music. It was easy to see a parallel between Stravinsky's powerful Slavic rhythmic drive and our American sense of rhythmic ingenuity. The most important thing for me, though, was that Stravinsky proved it was possible for a twentieth-century composer to create his own tradition.

Several of the new Stravinsky works were heard for the first time at the orchestral concerts organized and conducted by Serge Koussevitzky. The "Concerts Koussevitzky" took place at the Paris Opera House each spring and fall between 1920 and 1924 and attracted an international audience of the musical elite. I went to every one and sat high up in the gallery along with the other students. It was my first introduction to Koussevitzky, the conductor who would become so important to my own career. Those concerts were a unique opportunity to hear premieres and performances of contemporary works, among them the neoclassic compositions of Stravinsky that we had discussed in Boulanger's classes. These were not works one fell in love with on first hearing. Their dry sonorities and classically oriented tunes lacked surface charm. When I heard the premiere performance of the *Octet* at a Koussevitzky concert in the fall of 1923, it was a reverse shocker, even after seeing the score at Boulanger's. Its neoclassicism was a curious about-face on Stravinsky's part and indicated a surprising development that nobody could have predicted. Here was Stravinsky—who had created a neoprimitive style that everyone agreed was one of the most original in modern music—now, without any explanation, presenting a piece to the public that bore no resemblance to the style with which he had become identified! We could not have known then, in the early twenties, that Stravinsky was to persist in this neoclassic style, and that it would have so great an influence, not only in Europe, but all over the world. As always with Stravinsky, it was the power of his musical personality that carried one along. This was especially true of the *Piano Concerto* when, as at its first performance with the composer himself as soloist, he played his instrument in a markedly dry and relentless fashion; one was aware of an inner drive that was both irresistible and unforgettable.

After Paris, I would see Stravinsky occasionally at concerts and dinner parties. I recall one evening in about 1930, my friend Mary Lescaze sat me down for dinner between Stravinsky and the violinist Sam Dushkin.

Olga Samaroff was at that party also. I tried to imagine what questions I might put to the great composer that posterity would like to have answered. But the evening went by without my thinking of a single one, even though I had written an article on his *Oedipus Rex* for the *New Republic* in 1928.[15]

In Hollywood during the early forties, Stravinsky was full of praise for the film *The City*. He told me that "the score was wonderful." George Antheil and I were invited to Vera and Igor Stravinsky's home in March of 1943. He was very cordial. After dinner we played off-the- air recordings of his music. I had been reading Alfred Kazin's *On Native Grounds* (1942), and it prompted me to write the following to Arthur Berger (10 April 1943): "I've come to the conclusion that Stravinsky is the Henry James of composers. Same 'exile' psychology, same exquisite perfection, same hold on certain temperaments, same lack of immediacy of contact with the world around him. . . ."[16] Another dinner at the Stravinsky home on 6 January 1949 must have impressed me, because I jotted down the following in a notebook: "Conversation included: bowing with Sol Babitz, violinist; he to talk to Victor Co. for me as conductor; anti-conductor talk; stories by others of Nadia B. elicited no comment; presentation of 'Mass' and 'Mavra'; disappointment with Ansermet for 'Mass' performance; his devotion to opera; advice as to libretto; delight with 'L'Elisir' and da Ponte Memoires; Theodore Strav's book mentioned." For another dinner with the Stravinskys in California on 19 May 1957, the composer picked me up at the Bel Air Hotel. He had been ill, and during the previous winter had looked very weary. But now he seemed to have his old vitality back, except that it was difficult to understand his speech, which was mumbled at times. But he still had his old interest in good food and the best wine. Young Robert Craft and Lawrence Morton were at that dinner, and there was a great deal of talk about Boulez and Gesualdo led by Craft, who was very friendly to me. He had unbounded admiration for Boulez and called him "the empire-builder." It was clear that Stravinsky listened carefully to Craft and reflected his enthusiasms, except for Messiaen, whom Stravinsky said categorically he did not like.

In 1959 (1 September) Stravinsky wrote to me about a performance of *Les Noces* planned for 20 December at Town Hall: "I would consider it a pleasure and an honor if you would consent to be one of the four pianists taking part in this presentation. I have never conducted *Les Noces* before, and it has always been my wish that it be performed by four of my esteemed colleagues."[17] Even then, at seventy-seven, Stravinsky communicated to his performers that same rhythmic impulse the entire world has come to recognize as uniquely his own.

Stravinsky and I corresponded occasionally through the years; we sent birthday greetings and developed an informal way with each other. Once in a while, I sent him a score. About my *Clarinet Concerto* he wrote (14 August 1950): "I want to tell you how much I love your *Clarinet Concerto* and how glad I have been to receive it from you. . . ." Yet even after we began to address each other as "Cher ami," I never completely lost that awe I felt for Igor Stravinsky from the time I was a young student in Paris.

Clurman and I often went to concerts, ballets, and plays where we saw other young American students, among them, Melville Smith and Virgil Thomson. Virgil says that he never saw our "pad" in Paris,[18] but I seem to recall that he visited us. In any case, Virgil was more at home with the French crowd led by Cocteau, who frequented Le Boeuf sur le toit, a bar named after a Milhaud score. Although jazz was featured there, we Americans were more likely to be found around the cafés of Montparnasse and the Left Bank: Le Dôme, La Coupole, or Les Deux Magots. We got to know George Antheil after he came to Paris from Berlin in 1923.[19] Antheil lived with his little Hungarian wife, Boskie, in a tiny room above Shakespeare and Company, Sylvia Beach's famous bookstore at 12 rue de l'Odéon. He was much admired by Ezra Pound and James Joyce. I recall a concert in 1923 where Antheil played, and Ezra Pound, with his striking red beard much in evidence, passionately turned pages.

For me, the bookshops were even more attractive than the cafés, for it was there one might see the great artistic and literary figures of the twenties. I never went to Shakespeare and Company without a sense of excitement. For one thing, it helped me to keep in touch with what was going on back home in literature; for another, it was one of the centers where things were happening. Hemingway was around, a big presence with a surprisingly squeaky voice, and Joyce came there almost every evening at six o'clock to pick up proof sheets of *Ulysses*, which Miss Beach was publishing. One day I got up the nerve to approach him with a question about the source of some music in *Ulysses*, and he answered politely that it was a song his mother had sung when he was a boy. I bought a first edition of *Ulysses* from Miss Beach's and, unfortunately, sold it later for $40. For French books, we went across the street to La Maison des Amis des Livres, presided over by Adrienne Monnier, Sylvia Beach's partner and friend. I familiarized myself with the monthly *La Nouvelle Revue Française*, which featured French writers such as Gide and Proust, and I occasionally saw these figures at the bookshops. Harold and I felt that we were living in a very civilized atmosphere. There was much more than music going on, and we were well aware of it. In an effort to become even more a part of it all, I signed up for free classes twice a week in French literature and history at the Collège de France at the Sorbonne.

Before my twenty-first birthday on 14 November 1921, I received an avalanche of greetings from home, including a rare letter directly from Pa. I answered: "I begin to understand that half the fun in accomplishing anything is to be able to share it with others. . . . It is very nice of you to ask me what I would like for my 21st birthday. Don't you think you have already given me quite enough for a couple of birthdays?" At the end of November, I wrote: "I must tell you how very well satisfied I am with my composition teacher. She is the exact sort of instructor I needed, and knows every musician of any importance in France." On 1 December Charles Hubbard sang my two songs (with Boulanger at the piano) at an SMI concert, and on the fifteenth the student quartet written at Fontainebleau was played as a competition piece for an invited audience. I sent the program home with a letter:

> I have been meeting some of the Fontainebleau students at various concerts and they all seem to be much more excited about it than I am. You understand there is only one other contestant, a Mr. [Stanley] Avery, a man of about 40, who is now in Minneapolis, so that the whole burden of the affair rests on my shoulders. By which I mean to say, that to my great disgust, I fear *I* am to be the center of attraction on Thursday. . . .

In my next letter I enclosed the favorable review from the *Herald* along with my own less enthusiastic description of the results:

> I need only make clear that neither I nor Mr. Avery got the "Prix de Paris" (a fancy name for a mere diploma). For reasons best known to the jury of judges, the prize was not given to anyone and we both got honorary mentions. Anyway I'm glad the whole business is over, since I never took any interest in it from the start. Understand that I am not at all disappointed, and that I did not need 10 judges to tell me my quartet was rotten; I knew it myself. . . .[20]

Ma and Pa wanted me to continue my piano studies, probably thinking that I would have a better chance of making a living as a performer than as a composer. (I had not as yet told them that I had no intention of being a concert pianist.) In mid-December I chose Ricardo Viñes for my teacher. He was a well-known Spanish pianist who lived in Paris and played the contemporary French and Spanish repertoires. I had some idea that we need not study in the usual way—our lessons were to be a special kind of thing. Viñes, I believed, had the key to the performance of contemporary piano literature; he had introduced several works of Debussy and Ravel to the public and was known to be one of the first to understand them. Viñes was a modest man who didn't say much, and our lessons were somewhat of a disappointment; there weren't many, and they ended when the pianist went on tour in the spring.

Meanwhile Paris was preparing for Christmas. On all the streets and boulevards were hundreds of little extra wooden shops where everything imaginable was sold. It looked like New York's Hester Street on a grand scale. I bought winter gloves and wrote home describing how the "Yiddisher Frenchman" rubbed his hands together just as I had seen merchants do on Canal Street. I thought about the family in Brooklyn, knowing it was the last Christmas for Copland's Department Store, but there was little time for nostalgia. I was preparing to leave for London on 20 December. Since Harold had decided not to go with me, I got in touch with Herbert Elwell, who had left Fontainebleau abruptly during the previous summer to live in London, and he offered to meet me at the Victoria station. After recovering from the Channel crossing—for three hours I was even more seasick than on the Atlantic—I had a fine time seeing the sights in London. There were few concerts or operas due to the Christmas season, but Elwell and I went to the ballet, and saw *The Beggar's Opera* together. When the time came to go back to Paris, I faced the return crossing with cotton in my ears, lemon in one pocket, and Mother Somebody's Pills in the other.

I am told that I began to be known that winter in Paris as "that talented young American composer." If so, it was due to Boulanger's interest in me, and the contract with Durand (I was still waiting for that piece!). At home, my family made sure that the local newspapers reported on my activities regularly, and one Sunday in December, the *Standard Union* ran an article accompanied with pictures. My response was: "I really don't know what to say about all this free advertising. . . . I suppose it's all right, and I hope you are all getting a lot of fun out of it, but I want to warn you that I'm exactly the same tall, lanky lux who left America seven months ago." A student of Goldmark wrote that my old teacher was as proud of me "as a mother hen," and Alma Harwood, a patroness of music in New

York, met Goldmark at a concert where he jokingly remarked that I got more for my piece from Durand than he had ever gotten for one of his. *That* story made the rounds. In my weekly letter home I wrote: "It's sad since it shows how much serious music is worth in dollars and cents in America. But at the same time one must remember that most composers in America get royalties while most composers in Europe sell their music outright. But the long and the short of it is that there is no money to be made in composition either way. Therefore, one makes a living some other way (teaching, accompanying, concertizing and so forth)." My big news was non-musical: "I regret to announce that I have sat the seat of my pants out! The pants of the suit that was new when I left home. When Harold made the discovery I was astounded to think of all the water that must have flown under the Manhattan Bridge since last I went over it with those pants *absolutely new!*" We were often cold in our apartment that winter. Harold would pray for warm weather so that we could be comfortable without using gas. We dreaded the arrival of the gas bill and held our breath each time it came, before looking at the amount.

All Mademoiselle's pupils wrote, among other things, motets and a passacaglia. *Four Motets,* written under her instruction in 1921, were settings of biblical texts for an a cappella chorus of mixed voices. Mademoiselle had them sung in class several times, and both she and Melville Smith directed performances of the *Motets* at Fontainebleau in 1924. I think of these works as student pieces that show some influence of Moussorgsky, whom I admired. Mademoiselle conducted the *Motets* again in Paris in 1937,[21] and they have recently been dug out and performed at Columbia University.[22] I agreed to the publication of the *Four Motets* with mixed emotions. While they have a certain curiosity value—perhaps people want to know what I was doing as a student—the style is not yet really mine.[23] The *Passacaglia* is a more mature work, reflecting Boulanger's insistence on disciplined writing. In my treatment of an eight-bar theme in G-sharp with eight variations, there is an emphasis on architectural structure. Perhaps because of this, the work appeared cold to some critics when it was first heard, but Mademoiselle recognized the underlying emotion in it right away. The *Passacaglia* is dedicated to her. I am told that it is not an easy piece to play. The last two variations build to such a climax that in places it was necessary to use three staves.

The *Passacaglia* was first performed in January 1923 by Daniel Ericourt at an SMI concert in Paris. I attempted an arrangement of the *Passacaglia* for orchestra in 1923 and reached the double bar, but the ending is only

PARIS March 21, 1922

Dear Ma & Pa,—

_I_ have decided not to wait for your letter, but to write right away in order to tell you the great news. I have signed a contract with Monsieur Senart, the publisher who is going to bring out 2 of my compositions !!! First a piano piece (longer than the "Cat and Mouse") called a "Passacaglia" and then a song for voice and piano entitled "an Old Poem". This, you must agree is a most gorgeous piece of luck which fell out of a clear sky.

The first page of a letter home, 1922.

Proof page of *The Cat and the Mouse* with corrections and marginalia by Boulanger.

outlined and not complete.[24] Evidently, I decided not to finish the orchestral version—or perhaps I was only practicing orchestration. Melville Smith transcribed the *Passacaglia* for organ. He performed it, but died before the edition was ready for publication. (In 1981, the organist William Owen completed Melville's work and played the organ transcription in New York.) In 1931 I was pleasantly surprised when the choreographer Helen Tamiris asked to use the *Passacaglia* for a ballet, *Olympus Americanus*, set in six parts in ancient Greece, which was first performed on 3 February that year.

I finally received *Le Chat et la Souris* from Durand in February 1922. I promptly sent copies home and to Aaron Schaffer, who asked a piano student in Texas to study and play it for him, and I mailed a copy each to my teachers Clarence Adler and Rubin Goldmark. Goldmark wrote (16 May 1922): "I think it very good—clever, musicianly and not too extreme for my tastes." Mademoiselle had written to the publisher, Maurice Senart, about my compositions, and he responded by inviting me to play for him. I arrived at the firm's offices on 7 March, and to my surprise found a committee of seven men, the entire board of Senart publishers, gathered to judge my works. I performed the *Passacaglia* and accompanied myself in three songs on the worst piano I had ever played. Everyone was very polite, and when I finished, Senart said he would let me know by mail whether they would publish anything. He kept my compositions and then kept me waiting nervously for the decision. Eventually, the pieces were accepted. This time I would not be selling the compositions outright, but on a royalty basis of 10 percent on each copy for the first thousand and 15 percent on the second thousand. I was delighted to be published again, even though I feared that I would not make anything on "Old Poem," because I had to pay the poet $5 for the rights. I sensed that without Mademoiselle's influence these publications would not have come about. As with *The Cat and the Mouse*, she helped me prepare the works for publication.

During the winter I made plans to go to Italy for three weeks in the spring. I began to study Italian to learn the essentials. Harold was going to Berlin over Easter, and since we did not want to leave the apartment untended for long, I decided to leave for Italy by the end of March. Melville Smith went with me; he knew some Italian, and it was more fun than going alone. Melville was an enthusiastic type, even though relentlessly self-effacing. We left for Milan on 26 March. It was a twenty-four-hour train trip and in second class there were no sleeping cars, but my first glimpse of the Alps and the Italian lakes made up for any discomfort. We settled into the Grand Hotel Metropole in Milan, walked everywhere, went to La Scala twice, and then left for Rome. At the Hotel Lugano Pension Fleurie we paid 55 lire a day, or about $2.75, for a room with three full meals with lots of spaghetti. Through Boulanger's contacts, I met two young American musicians who were on scholarship, and I thought that I might follow in their footsteps in order to return to Rome someday. After four days in Florence, we came back to Paris. It was altogether a wonderful trip, and I hastened to explain to the folks that the Italians in Italy were very different from those around Washington Avenue in Brooklyn.

Harold was in Berlin when I got back to Paris, and I missed him. We had really become inseparable friends. I stayed quietly at home with my music and books, and wrote to the family:

> I wonder if you ever realize what a large part the reading of books on all imaginable subjects plays in my existence. I read not to learn anything, but from the pure love of it. Had I gone to college, I should be graduating this year, but I never regret not having done so. Of course, there are plenty of people who must see you with a college diploma to make them believe you are educated, but I feel my extensive reading has done a great deal to make up for any geometry or chemistry they teach one there. I often think, in planning ahead, that rather than teach or concertize to make a living, I should greatly prefer to write on musical subjects. I intend to make an attempt at writing some short articles this summer and sending them to musical papers at home and see what happens.

When Harold returned from Berlin, we had only one month left before he was to sail home for the summer. Harold had been homesick during the gray wintry months, but when the weather changed, he was sorry that he was not going to Germany as I had decided to do that summer. I had only five lessons left with Mademoiselle and wanted to make the most of them. She thought it was time for me to attempt an orchestral work, so I began to search for an idea, and when I showed her a few piano sketches (one was a dance, *Petite Valse*), Mademoiselle suggested that I try to build them into a ballet. Everyone wanted to write ballets due to the enormous popularity and influence of the Diaghilev, Nijinsky, and Stravinsky ballets.[25] I planned to work on the sketches during the summer months in Berlin. While I grappled with the problem of what to do with my belongings (especially all the music), I thought about the changes at home. It's curious that one can sometimes see America more clearly from across the ocean than when living right inside it. I became sentimental about Brooklyn while in Paris in a way that I could never have done while living there. I tried to picture the store closed and the household on Washington Avenue disbanded. What had happened to all the help? And Lil, who had taken special care of me?[26] Ralph and Dorothy had a baby girl I had never seen. And Grandma died that spring. "Dear Ma and Pa," I wrote once again, "It is needless for me to tell you how very deeply moved I was to hear of Grandma's death. I will remember the time I went to the Bronx to say goodbye to her, and something seemed to tell me then that I was seeing her for the last time."

I wrote to Goldmark and Adler for letters of introduction to musicians in Germany, since they had both studied there. Goldmark sent letters to Artur Schnabel in Berlin and to a cousin in Vienna who was a music critic. My plan was to spend the summer of 1922 in Berlin and perhaps the following one in Vienna in order to make contact with German and Austrian musical life. I had been aware for some time of Schoenberg, Berg, and Webern, and I thought, to be fair, I should get a sense of the German side of things. I had no clear idea *how* to get in touch with German musical life, since I knew no one in Berlin at the time. But I took a room in the modest house of a Frau Jurges at BruckenAllee and began to explore the city. My sense of isolation grew, partly because the only German I knew was from the Yiddish I had heard at home.

I cannot say that I got a great deal out of my two months in Berlin. For one thing, it was a politically unstable time. The German mark had collapsed, and every time I changed a dollar, I got more marks. Finally you had to bring a valise to take it all home from the bank. Each day I woke up richer than the day before. I was sitting pretty, but it couldn't go on, and nobody knew what was going to happen next. I just didn't feel good about Berlin. Everyone was getting more prosperous each day, but it was very grim. I called on Schnabel, and he was cordial enough, but depressed about the conditions in Germany, and I did not see him again. I met Kurt Weill—we were both twenty-two years old. He was in an even more precarious position than I, since he didn't have any foreign money to exchange. Weill was studying with Ferruccio Busoni, and he had the idea that he wanted to write a new kind of opera, one that would be closer to contemporary life and preoccupations. Within a few years, his *Three-penny Opera*, so cynical and strangely moving, would present the perfect image of that hopeless and stressful time in Berlin. The concert scene was virtually nonexistent in the summer, but I heard a performance of Mahler's *Das Lied von der Erde* conducted by Bruno Walter that carried me away, and some operas. I was impressed with *Der Freischütz* and Franz Schreker's *Der Schatzgräber*, and it excited my curiosity to hear

Schoenberg's *Pierrot lunaire* in Germany, since I had just had my introduction to that unusual work before leaving Paris.

My first letter to Nadia Boulanger was sent from Berlin that summer.[27] It surprises me now to be reminded that I had ever considered spending my second year abroad in Germany. When I wrote to Boulanger asking to return to study with her, she responded: "I am anxious to see the new parts of the ballet whose beginning pleases me so much." She asked me to buy some music for her—Schoenberg's *Traité d'harmonie*, and "anything else that's new and seems interesting to you." I found all except the Schoenberg, and on my own I bought for her "among quelque chose de nouveau, Béla Bartók's *Improvisations* [on Hungarian Folksongs] op. 20 for piano, an exquisite little work, and also Egon Wellesz' *Quatuor à cordes* that I find very interesting. . . ." I decided to carry the music back with me instead of sending it. I was lonely in Berlin and impatient to return to Paris; 10 October couldn't come soon enough to please me.

Harold and I often saw foreign films in Paris. One evening in the fall of 1922, we went to see the popular German horror film *Nosferatu*. It was about a vampire magician with the power to make corpses come to life. I was still searching for a story for my ballet, and by the time we reached home that night, I decided that this bizarre tale would be the basis for my ballet. Harold had never written a scenario, but he was eager to try. At first we called it *Le Nécromancien*. The title *Grohg* was chosen later. This ballet became the most ambitious undertaking of my Paris years—I had no choreographer, commission, or contact with a major ballet company. Nevertheless, I wrote this for the big time: a one-act, thirty-five-minute ballet for full pit orchestra plus piano. The opening section, "Cortège macabre," calls for four coffins to be displayed before Grohg, a magician. Three dances follow: one by one, the magician brings to life the corpses of an adolescent, an opium eater, and a streetwalker.[28] The magician's passions get the better of him, he attempts to embrace the girl, and she slaps him. He loses control, the corpses rise and jeer, and Grohg hurls the girl at them. The ballet ends with a return of the "Cortège" as the magician drags the coffins offstage.[29] In addition to these characters, an elaborate retinue of "servitors" dance around the coffins. There was a taste for the bizarre at the time, and if *Grohg* sounds morbid and excessive, the music was meant to be fantastic rather than ghastly. Also, the need for gruesome effects gave me an excuse for using "modern" rhythms and dissonances. In spite of the grotesque nature of the work, Mademoiselle encouraged me. She was taken with my use of polyrhythms and was the first to point out that I had

The adolescent
pees' (GROH in)
for the first time.

Above: Manuscript page from the
ballet *Grohg.*
Right: Copland with Harold Clurman, Paris, 1921.

a rhythmic sense that differed from that of the Europeans. She was fascinated with trying to play independent rhythms herself, and I remember sitting together at the piano, with me poking away at one rhythm while she played another.

Until *Grohg*, I had written only short piano pieces using jazz-derived rhythms. Now I was translating those techniques into a larger framework. On one polyrhythmic section of "Cortège," I wrote the following note: "to le chef d'orchestre: N.B. To facilitate the task of the conductor, a common bar line has been retained in this polyrhythmic section. The small notes indicate the precise rhythm desired." In the Finale, an allegro vivo, I let loose with alternating 5/4, 3/4, and 3/8 measures. *Grohg* as a youthful work had its shortcomings, but it foreshadowed my preoccupation with experiments in jazz for the next few years and was the forerunner of my later ballets. In 1924 before I left Paris, Mademoiselle and I played *Grohg* for piano four-hands at a farewell party at her rue Ballu apartment. I revised the ballet in 1932 but did not release it for publication. *Grohg* has never been choreographed or staged. I arranged the introductory "Cortège macabre" as a separate work; it thereby became my earliest orchestral piece.[30] Other usable material from *Grohg* went into the *Dance Symphony*.[31]

Soon after I returned to the States, I submitted *Cortège macabre to Howard Hanson in Rochester, who chose it and six others from forty-eight pieces submitted to the Eastman Philharmonia for the first of the American Composers Concerts. The date was* 2 May 1925, and the occasion received national attention. (These annual concerts became the Festival of American Music in 1930; they were important in introducing works by many young composers through the years.) After *Cortège* was performed again in New York in 1927 by a different orchestra, I decided to withdraw it from my catalogue. In 1971 Hanson asked to conduct *Cortège* once more in a concert marking the last Festival of American Music; I agreed, thinking if Hanson liked it, there must be something good about it!

In 1922 though, the important thing was that the ballet was my chance to work on orchestration with Boulanger. While still in Brooklyn, I had made attempts to reorchestrate standard works, and I wrote songs in several versions with various instrumental accompaniments. (One song, "Alone," I arranged for voice and piano with viola, and in another version for voice and orchestra.)[32] In Boulanger's instrumental class I wrote seven short studies for instruments with piano: flute, oboe, clarinet, bassoon, horn, trumpet, and trombone. While these early efforts were instructive, I had had no formal studies in orchestration before working on *Grohg* with Boulanger.

Many of my evenings in Paris were spent composing. I have always found night hours agreeable for working. The stillness and tranquillity seem to me conducive to composing music. There is something romantic about the night time with its peaceful uninterrupted hours that is appropriate for a slow worker like myself—I have never dashed anything off in a burst of inspiration, even when very young. I tend to work carefully, put things aside, and then take them up again for a fresh look. Because I spend a lot of time and care with a work, once it's done, it's *done*. I rarely make changes or feel dissatisfied with a finished work. I have only occasionally, as in the case of *Grohg*, made revisions or recalled a piece. I try to make relatively certain that I am satisfied before letting a work go out into the world. In Paris my composing hours often extended into the early morning hours, since the days were filled with classes, practicing, and other practical matters. In my second year abroad, I began to feel more at home. I wrote to my cousin, Arnold Mittenthal, who was about to enter Yale College (10 February 1923):

> . . . The Paris I live in today is very different for me than the Paris of my first weeks. Many things—language, customs, morals which seemed impossibly strange then, I now take for granted. That doesn't mean that I have adopted the Gallic attitude toward "l'amour," but I certainly understand all these things better than when I arrived. After all, I suppose if one lived here long enough, Paris could become as commonplace as Brooklyn. Luckily, I have not arrived at that state yet. The awful smell in the subways, the marvellous pastry shops, a walk on the boulevard, the astounding lack of bathtubs in France, the very atmospheric Café de la Rotunde, those painted things who "once were women,"—all these aspects of Parisian life and many more still strike me as quaint and European. . . .

Determined to experience as much of this quaint and European flavor as possible while still abroad, I traveled again in the spring, this time to Bruges and then Brussels, where the wonderful organ recitals at the Conservatoire Royal were most impressive.

In my catalogue under "Chamber Music" can be found *Two Pieces—Lento Molto and Rondino for String Quartet.*[33] The *Rondino* was written in the spring of 1923 in Paris as the second part of an "Hommage à Fauré." (Gabriel Fauré was Boulanger's favorite composer, and I soon shared her admiration for him.) Preceding the *Rondino* had been an arrangement for string quartet of the *Prélude IX* from Fauré's *Préludes pour piano* (op. 103). The *Rondino* was based on the letters of Fauré's name. Mixed with his influence can be heard a hint of American jazz and a bit of mild polytonality. *Rondino* was my first completed work for string quartet. Mademoiselle got together a professional quartet to read through it one Wednesday afternoon. Nadia often did this for students, and the hearing of one's imagined instrumentation did more toward the learning of instrumentation and orchestration than many hours of spoken instruction.

The first performance of "Hommage à Fauré" took place in September 1924 at Fontainebleau. The old master, Fauré, was then seventy-eight and within a few months of his death. I came to admire his classic sense of order. It is strange that the musical public outside of France has never been convinced of his special charms, the delicacy, reserve, imperturbable calm—qualities that are not easily exportable. One of my first published articles was: "Gabriel Fauré, a Neglected Master."[34] My arrangement of Fauré's *Prélude* was appropriate to the occasion in 1924. In 1928 it was replaced by *Lento Molto*, which, when paired with *Rondino*, became *Two Pieces for String Quartet*.

Harold and I left for Vienna in June 1923. As Goldmark had indicated, Vienna was very different from Berlin, and the summer was rewarding and enjoyable. We found rooms with a Frau Steinhof and explored the delights of the city. Mademoiselle wrote reminding me to work on the ballet and again commissioning me to buy music for her, "for hundred or hundred and twenty francs . . . to be curious of music for a price, but no more, pleases me infinitely." Wanting her to know how much her teaching meant to me, I wrote (25 July 1923): "I might get really sentimental about the rue Ballu and all that it has meant and still means to me. . . . Not being romantic, I mustn't get 'sentimental' about anything, must I? But I am sure you will understand what I feel I owe you after two years of work, just as you understood the emotion in my apparently cold *Passacaglia*. . . ."

I had improved my German enough by then to read through some German literature, and I looked at a lot of music—Bruckner, Reger, and Mahler. Reading through a violin sonata (op. 72) by Reger, I was surprised to find it so good that I wanted to familiarize myself further with his work. But I was not so much impressed with Bruckner. About five hours a day was spent on the ballet and on an assignment for a chamber music piece for clarinet and flute that Boulanger had given her students as a task for

Summer 1923

My Dear Copland,

Just few lines to send you this letter — to tell you how much I hope you have a good time there, in this city where are so much reason of artistic atmosphere.

We are quite here, but - - - Fontainebleau is a true regular interruption. I like it better than it disturbes me and it evering thing well.

Dont forget your ballet, your quatuor, the concours, . . . but profite of your freedom —

Sincerly and affectionately
N Boulanger

bei Frau Steinhof
IX Hörlgasse 4, Vienne,
July 28, 1923

Dear Mademoiselle Boulanger, —

Nothing of very great importance has happened to me since I left Paris. But I want to write you at least a few words so that you may have no cause for thinking that I have forgotten you. No! I most certainly haven't forgotten you. In fact, if I liked I might get really sentimental about the Rue Ballu and all that it has meant and still means to me. Mais, après tout, vous le savez aussi bien que moi, et puis — n'est-ce pas, c'est vous qui a dit 'Copland n'est pas romantique du tout'!) Not being romantic, I musn't get 'sentimental' about anything, must I? But I am sure you will understand what I feel I owe

ove: Letter from Boulanger to *pland,* 1923 (the date is in *pland's* hand).
ght: Letter from Copland to *ulanger* from Vienna, July 1923.

the summer. I was determined to do as much as possible on both works before leaving for Salzburg with Clurman at the beginning of August, for the First Festival of the International Society for Contemporary Music (ISCM). I wrote to Boulanger, "Six successive evenings of modern music should prove a big enough feast for even so insatiable a gourmand as myself. . . ."

We were thrilled to be there with so many of the world's leading composers. It was a stimulating experience and one of the checkpoints in time when the place of my own country's music on the international scene became clear to me. I knew then that I wanted to see American music represented with more important offerings than the modest Emerson Whithorne piece that alone was American. I reported on the festival to Boulanger, relating that Stravinsky and Ravel were still the most popular composers, and that Milhaud, Poulenc, and Honegger were not very well received. I was excited ("le plus frappé") on hearing Hindemith, Krenek, and Hába, and reported that Hindemith was the most played and talked about. Personally, I found the quartets of Ernst Krenek and Alois Hába the most interesting. One day while in my hotel room, mystifying sounds came from the room adjoining mine. I could not imagine what was going on. At the evening concert I realized that it had been the musicians rehearsing Hába's quarter-tone quartet. When I returned to Vienna from the Salzburg festival, I used quarter tones in the viola solo linking the slow movement of *Grohg* to the Finale.

In Vienna that summer I listened to jazz in the bars, and hearing it in a fresh context heightened my interest in its potential. I began to consider that jazz rhythms might be the way to make an American-sounding music. The Finale of *Grohg* reflects these ideas. I returned to Paris with additional pages for the ballet and a brand new piece. I had been playing around with some ideas for the flute and clarinet assignment when I came upon a poem by the seventeenth-century English poet Richard Barnefield. "As It Fell Upon a Day" had the simplicity and tenderness that moved me to attempt to evoke that poignant expression musically. I got the idea to add a voice part to Boulanger's assignment. The imitative counterpoint between the two instruments in the introduction would satisfy my teacher's request. The harmonies that seem to evoke an early English flavor were suggested by the nature of the text. I am often asked about "modal" writing in connection with "As It Fell. . . ." I can only say that I never learned all about the modes—major and minor were the only modes my generation were taught! If the music sounds modal it is because I wanted to come close to the expression of the poetry. The SMI was once again responsible for a premiere. "As It Fell . . ." was played first under their auspices in the Salle Pleyel on 6 February 1924. Ada MacLeish, wife of the poet Archibald MacLeish, was the soprano soloist. The reviewer for *Le Ménestrel* called "As It Fell . . ." the best piece on a program that included works by Leo Sowerby, Jean Deré, and Roussel. This song has been performed often and is usually well received.[35] I recall particularly an all-Copland concert in New York in 1935, perhaps because of the performers—Ethel and Otto Luening and Robert McBride.

In October 1923 Clurman and I moved into our third apartment in Paris at 66 Boulevard Pasteur. A mulatto family were the landlords, and I will never forget the distinguished gentleman of the household, a judge in the French court, asking us politely if we held any racial prejudices. Harold and I were horrified to realize that Americans had the reputation for such bigotry abroad. Soon after we were settled in that fall, I met Mme Geneviève Butez, who invited me to play chamber music with a small group of accomplished amateur string players. We read through the classics, and occasionally I brought along a contemporary piece and got kidded about being a modernist. We became good friends. The quartet gave a farewell party for me when I left Paris in the spring of 1924, and they all wrote to me after I returned to the States.

The "Concerts Koussevitzky" continued to be highlights on the musical scene that season. Maestro outdid himself with unusual programs in both the fall and spring. Only in the atmosphere of Paris in the twenties could an orchestral series like that have taken place, and with such expectation and popularity. We heard Honegger's *Pacific 231* and Prokofiev's *Sept, ils sont sept* in premieres, and Koussevitzky presented an all-Stravinsky program with the composer as soloist in the first performance of his *Piano Concerto*. Koussevitzky's four years of conducting this series in Paris were to end that spring. The announcement came that the famous Russian conductor would lead the Boston Symphony Orchestra the following season. It seemed unbelievable to us. Would he play such ultra-modern music in Boston? When Mademoiselle saw the announcement in the papers, she said, "We must go and visit him." She was on cordial terms with Koussevitzky and took it for granted that he would want to meet a young composer from the country he was about to visit for the first time.

The Koussevitzky house in Paris seemed very grand to me. Under my arm I carried my only orchestral score, *Cortège macabre*. Maestro asked me to play it. Prokofiev was visiting that day (perhaps Dr. Koussevitzky had invited him to see Boulanger) and much to my discomfort, he stood directly behind me at the piano while I played—I wanted to do my selling job alone. When I had finished and before anyone could say anything, Prokofiev blurted out, "Too much bassi ostinati." But Dr. Koussevitzky promised to conduct the piece with the Boston Symphony Orchestra during his first season. And, knowing that Boulanger planned to be in the States at the invitation of Walter Damrosch, Koussevitzky suggested that she appear with the Boston Symphony as organ soloist in a new orchestral work that I would compose.[36] "*You* vill write an organ concerto, Mademoiselle Boulanger vill *play* it and *I* vill conduct!" Koussevitzky pronounced in no uncertain terms. Mademoiselle agreed, but when we left, I exclaimed, "Do you *really* think I can do it?" (I had never heard a note of my own orchestration or written anything for the organ. Moreover, the organ was not a favorite instrument of mine.) She pointed her finger at me. "*You* can do it." And when Mademoiselle said, "*You* can do it," that was the end of the discussion.

I can only assume that Koussevitzky trusted Boulanger's faith in me and that he wanted a new American work with her as soloist. Whatever the reasons, I had misgivings, and it was only my teacher's confidence that gave me the courage to go on. Boulanger must have written immediately to Damrosch, for the next thing I knew, a big unwritten composition for organ and orchestra was scheduled for performance in the 1924–25 season by both Walter Damrosch with the New York Symphony and Serge Koussevitzky with the Boston Symphony Orchestra. Two major performances were at stake. It was very tempting, but *very* scary. I was confident that if I wrote music that could be played on an organ, Mademoiselle would advise me as to the appropriate organ registrations needed. I would only have to indicate to her what effect I was hoping to obtain. Looking back, I realize how lucky I was, first to have found Boulanger, and then Koussevitzky at just the perfect time for any of this to happen. In a personal way I was pleased, for it meant that my connections with Paris would not be cut off suddenly. I would be constantly in touch with Boulanger about the music, and within a few months she and Koussevitzky would be in America.

Interlude I

What was the state of the arts in America during the years Copland was in France? Little could compare with the ferment of Paris or Vienna, but the explosion of experimentation and innovation abroad had been so strong that its shock waves reached New York and reverberated across the country. In the visual arts as early as 1913, the Armory Show had heralded the arrival of modern art; in literature by the early twenties, Hemingway, Joyce, and Lawrence were being read by those who considered themselves the American avant garde. But music lagged behind. Contemporary works were programmed only occasionally, giving rise to snickers, giggles, or downright sarcasm from audiences and critics. Arnold Schoenberg's name was familiar among the cognoscenti, but not his music; Charles Ives was not known at all, although by 1920 he had virtually finished composing; and Leo Ornstein, the "futurist" composer, was shocking audiences with performances of his unusual early pieces. It was Igor Stravinsky whose popularity abroad was reflected most strongly on the New York concert scene. The critic Pitts Sanborn wrote, "Inevitably the New York music season of 1923–24 will go down in history as the Stravinsky season. . . ."[1]

Characteristically, the first societies to champion the cause of modern music in America were led by foreigners. In 1920 E. Robert Schmitz, a French concert pianist, founded and directed an international society based in New York that was first called the Franco-American Musical Society, and later Pro-Musica, Inc. It became an influential force in introducing audiences to living composers and little-known music. By 1930 Pro-Musica had established over forty chapters in the States and abroad. American composers were not ignored by Pro-Musica, but its primary objective was to bring European musicians to the United States. The International Composers' Guild (ICG) was obviously international in scope.[2] Founded by Edgard Varèse in 1921 with a small group in Greenwich Village, the ICG ran into difficulties by the end of its second season after several of its leading members had a falling out with Varèse. Claire R. Reis, composers Lazare Saminsky and Louis Gruenberg, and the patroness Alma Wertheim left to form a new society in 1923, the League of Composers. The divorce was not a friendly one, and reasons for it have been disputed through the years by both sides.[3] Varèse and his colleagues, particularly Carlos Salzedo and Carl Ruggles, managed to keep the ICG alive until after its 1926–27 season. During this period, New York had the advantage of two groups in competition, both presenting modern music programs.

Copland was still in Paris during the League's first season of 1923–24. Claire Reis, executive director, and Minna Lederman, editor of *Modern Music*, subsequently brought the League and the publication into positions of prominence. Of course, in the overall musical picture, modern music played a small role. There was very little opportunity for the performance of American contemporary symphonic music until later, when Koussevitzky and Stokowski began to schedule works regularly. As for publication opportunities, only a few of the older established men such as Daniel Gregory Mason, Horatio Parker, and Rubin Goldmark had music in print. For young composers, there was no outlet whatsoever until Henry Cowell's bold experiment of publishing American works in *New Music Editions* began in 1927,[4] and only a very few young Americans were known well enough abroad to have an occasional piece published by one of the big houses. The few existing teaching positions were invariably filled by the older generation of conservative composers. There were no government or foundation grants, competitions, prizes, or commissions for financial remuneration. On the positive side, however, were the wealthy patrons and patronesses who occasionally made it possible for a promising young artist to experience financial freedom for a limited time.

In June 1924 Copland and Clurman sailed home from France. Copland recalls nothing of the return trip, although the crossing to France three years earlier is vivid in his memory. According to Clurman, Aaron was seasick and both were anxious to get home; neither had seriously considered becoming an expatriate. But Aaron had become a Francophile, and in less than two years he would return to France, and then twice again before the end of the decade. Copland's French had become fluent; but even so he knew what it took for a foreigner to be accepted by the French, and he never felt completely at home there. Moreover, there was an "affirm America" movement under way, spearheaded by young writers Waldo Frank and Edmund Wilson. It was catching on fast, and Aaron and Harold felt its pull.

Copland had gone to Europe to learn how to compose, and had "found" America while viewing it from abroad. He saw European composers take up American jazz and thought that if composers like Debussy and Ravel, Stravinsky and Milhaud could use ragtime and jazz rhythms, the way might be open for American composers. Perhaps, he thought, here finally was music an American might write better than a European. While Copland was in Paris, only a few composers at home had toyed with a polite form of jazz—John Alden Carpenter in the ballets *Krazy Kat* and *Skyscrapers*, and Louis Gruenberg with *The Daniel Jazz*. None made the impact of Stravinsky's *Ragtime for Eleven Instruments* and *Piano Rag Music*, or Darius Milhaud's *Création du monde*, which caused a sensation when premiered in Paris in 1923. (Milhaud had the temerity to lecture Americans on jazz when he visited the States in 1920–21.) The only American piece that came close to the notoriety of Milhaud's was Gershwin's *Rhapsody in Blue*, commissioned by Paul Whiteman and first played on Lincoln's Birthday in 1924 in a concert called, "An Experiment in Modern Music." Jazz was considered a new discovery, as though it had just happened on the scene in time for white composers to use its lively and danceable rhythms in their concert music. Composers made forays to Harlem to hear the way real jazz was played at the Apollo and Small's Paradise, and they suddenly began to talk about "riffs," "blue notes," and "breaks." The terms "Afro-American" and "black" were not yet in use, nor was there any perception of jazz as an indigenous Afro-American art. "Negroes" played jazz in nightclubs, but most of them could not read music, and therefore jazz was only art when incorporated into rhapsodies, symphonies, and ballets by white concert composers. Even then, the issue was hotly debated. Nevertheless, for a brief time it seemed possible that our popular and concert musics, so hopelessly divided, might have found a way of blending. High society went slumming in Harlem to hear jazz in the clubs, and on one memorable evening in the season before Copland returned to America, the League of Composers sponsored a concert in which the adventurous singer, Eva Gauthier, in formal black introduced George Gershwin in top hat and tails for a mixed program of popular and art songs at Aeolian Hall. Only black Americans puzzled over all this, including the question of how a bandleader with the incredible name of Whiteman had come to be called "The King of Jazz."

Copland was not to enter the mainstream of musical activities in New York immediately. First, he had to fulfill the commission to compose a major symphonic work with organ solo for performances in the upcoming season. Aaron contemplated the changes in his life: never again would he live at home; his student days were over; and he would have to find a job that would allow time to compose. How he would support himself he had no idea, nor did he have any more notion in 1924 of how a composer gets started in America than when he left Brooklyn in 1921. As Copland and Clurman stepped off the gangplank of the *France*, they solemnly shook hands and turned to greet the Mittenthals, Coplands, Urises, and Clurmans who had come to welcome the young men home from their European adventures. Then they went their separate but inseparable ways, each to achieve in his own art what he had dreamed and talked about in Paris.

After a few weeks of family reunions and kidding from brother Leon about being "Frenchified," Aaron got to the urgent business of finding a job. He looked up an old friend, Abraham Ginsburg, a violinist with whom he had played chamber music years before. Abe offered him a job as pianist in a trio at a resort hotel in Milford, Pennsylvania, for the summer, and Aaron was delighted to find a way of working in music in a place that promised quiet and time to compose. The manager of the Hotel Colonial, Signore C. Lauritano, had dabbled in music. Business was slow, so the boss stood over the trio at lunch, dinner, and for dancing in the evenings, making their lives miserable and giving them "hell" for their interpretations of popular Italian opera. Aaron rented a movie theater, and there he worked every morning at the piano in the musty, dark house. He managed to make a final ink draft of the *Cortège macabre* before the young lady who played piano for the movies in the evenings heard him and insisted that he stop banging on her piano.

Progress was slow on the symphony. Mademoiselle wrote impatiently from her summer home, "Les Maisonettes," in Gargenville, "Give me quickly news of the brain child. . . ." Copland responded, thanking his teacher for preparing five of his works for performance at Fontainebleau and informing her that in mid-August he was resigning his job as pianist of the Hotel Colonial's music trio because it was impossible to make headway on the "sinfonietta." (At various times the piece was called concerto, sinfonietta, symphony.) Copland fled to Laurine's home in Brooklyn at 557 East 12th Street for the use of her good piano, and there set to work full time. He reported to Boulanger:

Let me tell you how far it is advanced—for several reasons I have decided to make it in three movements instead of four. The first will be a short andante (the andante I wrote in May), then the scherzo, and lastly will come the most important movement with which I originally thought I would begin the work. It will take about twenty minutes altogether. (Honegger's first violin sonata has three movements arranged something like that.) So far I have completely finished only the first movement, which is also orchestrated. But the other two movements are, pour ainsi dire, finished—that is, they are clear in my mind, but I must still write them down and orchestrate them and fill in the details. If I sent it to you by October 1st, you will still have two full months to prepare it. It goes without saying that any corrections you make, I approve of a priori.

Aaron and Harold met often. When Melville Smith returned from Paris, they sat him down and made him talk for hours about all that had happened since their departure. While finishing the first draft of the symphony in October, Aaron moved into his first small studio in Manhattan at 135 West 74th Street. Excitedly he sent out cards with his address, announcing his availability for teaching and stating: "Recently back from Paris." But not a single response ever came in. This was, at the least, disheartening. His confidence was restored, however, when Mademoiselle wrote her reactions to the *Organ Symphony:* "I can't tell you my joy—the work is so brilliant, so full of music. . . . I must at once thank you profoundly for the dedication to which, I assure you, I attach a value that surpasses in everything obvious questions. . . . This to me is truly a genuine pride of an artist and the real joy of a friend. . . ."

From this time on, New York City became Copland's home base. Travel would satisfy his thirst for a wide range of experience, but the pull back to New York was strong. Even later, when Copland moved to the countryside, he was never far from the city. But wherever he lived, the center of interest was always the room with the piano. A house without one felt bare. (Once, when in Tangier, an instrument that only mildly resembled a piano arrived across the backs of two sturdy mules. Copland would not have stayed without it.) Travel would never be pure vacation, but always stimulated by some sort of musical assignment. Wherever he would find himself—Paris, Mexico, South America, Moscow, Japan, Israel, or Hollywood—Copland would channel his energies and talents to the work at hand. The ability to take music wherever and however he found it would communicate itself to performers. This accounts, at least in part, for Copland's enormous popularity; he would never expect a high school band or South American orchestra to play like the New York Philharmonic.

Returning from a trip, Copland's first activity was always to catch up with musical events at home. After settling into his small studio in 1924, it did not take long to appraise the current musical scene and to become part of it. In Paris Aaron Copland had made a splash as a promising newcomer. But when he moved to New York in the fall of 1924, the name Copland was not known—not until January 1925, when a big new work for organ and orchestra by a twenty-four-year-old American was premiered by the New York Symphony Orchestra.

Oct. 6, 1925
135 W. 74th St.
New York City, N.Y.

Mr. Koussevitzky,

Mrs. Reis has ... me to inform you that the ... e of Composers has accepted ... ew work for chamber orchestra ... ic for the Theatre") for performance ... 28th of November. I should like to ... you the score immediately, but ... your permission, I shall first ... the parts copied, which will ... a few weeks. I hope you will ... o objections if I come to Boston ... n the rehearsals; and perhaps ... or two before they begin, you will ... me to give you an idea of the ... at the piano, as we did ... winter with the 'Symphony'. ... Since I have mentioned the ... phony", I shall take the

liberty of pointing out that if you intend to repeat that work, it will be necessary to find another organist, as Mademoiselle Boulanger will not be in America this season. I should be glad to send the organ part to whomever you may select.

Also, I want you to know that I have a new score for large orchestra ("Three Dances") that I am keeping for you and the Boston Symphony. The parts are almost ready, I only await your pleasure in the matter.

I sincerely trust that my new works may not be unworthy to have expended on them the genius of your baton.

With kindest regards to Madame Koussevitzky, I am,

yours devotedly
Aaron Copland

New York

1924-1926

Verso: Letter to Serge Koussevitzky, 1925.
Opposite: Copland outside Koussevitzky's house, Boston, 1926.

How I got through the first few months, I really don't know. I had met the American composer Marion Bauer in Paris the season before, and she recommended me to the League of Composers. It was the start of their second season, and they were initiating a series devoted to "The musical youngsters of America, England, and the Continent." I was invited to audition for the board at Claire Reis' apartment. I accompanied myself singing the "Old Poem" and played a few piano pieces. The *Passacaglia* and *The Cat and the Mouse* were accepted for the League's first "Young Composers' Concert." Led for years by Marion Bauer, this series often served to introduce compositions by unknown American composers. The first program, held at the Anderson Galleries in November 1924, presented the critic Olin Downes introducing works by George Antheil, Mario Castelnuovo-Tedesco, Alois Hába, Richard Hammond, Ernst Krenek, Bernard Rogers, Alexander Steinert, and myself. It was my first public presentation in New York—not a very impressive debut, but the pieces were well received, and when Paul Rosenfeld called me the next day to tell me he liked my music, I could not have been more surprised than if the President of the United States had called. To me, an okay from the critic of *The Dial* seemed better than approval from *The New York Times.*

Paul Rosenfeld is rather unjustly forgotten nowadays.[1] He was not a newspaper critic in the usual sense and never wrote in a journalistic style. His prose was richly expressive, sometimes even too much so, with occasional sentences in a language all his own. Paul had the unusual ability of being able to write about all of the arts. Anyone interested in new music in the twenties, of course, read him regularly. What made Paul so special was not so much what he said or how he said it, but his complete involvement in the music he was criticizing. The American scene in particular was a consuming interest—he believed passionately in the emergence of an important school of contemporary American composers. Paul was one of the first critics to write perceptively about Ives, Ornstein, Varèse, Ruggles, Cowell, Harris, and Sessions. Rosenfeld's description of my appearance at that first League concert has been quoted often: "A slim, beglassed, shy and still self-assured young fellow with the aspect of a benevolent and scholastic grasshopper. . . ."[2] Rosenfeld lived a bachelor life surrounded by the latest books. He invited me to dinners at his apartment on Irving Place with the most interesting people in the avant-garde literary, music, and art worlds. Among the writers I enjoyed meeting there were Hart Crane, Lewis Mumford, Waldo Frank, e.e. cummings, and Edmund Wilson. I seem to remember that Rosenfeld introduced me to Minna Lederman soon after I returned from Paris. Minna was the brand-new editor of the brand-new magazine *The League of Composers' Review* (soon to become better known as *Modern Music*). Paul became interested in promoting my career and was well aware that I would be in need of financial assistance. I kept him informed about the *Organ Symphony*, and he promised to keep me in mind should a wealthy patron or patroness appear on the scene.

Sections of the *Symphony* were sent off to Nadia as soon as they were composed. Although my student days were over, it was important for me at that time to have such a highly practiced eye look at my work and make suggestions. And, of course, I was relying heavily on Nadia for correcting the organ part and providing registrations. Mademoiselle wrote in October:

> I am sailing December 27, playing in New York January 11—Engles [George, manager of the orchestra] has asked me for my program—I can ask him to be patient for a bit—but will you be ready and what title? When shall I have the music? Will the orchestra parts be ready? There is no more time to lose—above all, don't be too complicated—one cannot rehearse very much and orchestras are not ready to handle certain problems properly.
>
> How much pleasure our little parties will give me—I hope to remain a while in New York since I play there the eleventh, I have my first lecture there the nineteenth—and I hope to have a little freedom—it will be necessary to work, it is true, for your organs are different from ours—and I shall have to give some lessons probably, without counting the appearances in society! . . .

Nadia never expressed doubt about the *Symphony* as a whole, but after I sent the completed score, she wrote again suggesting I compose an alternate ending in case the one I had written didn't work when we got together with the orchestra. Also, she feared that the tempo in the Scherzo was too fast and might lead to "confusion." I accepted some of her suggestions, but decided to take my chances with the ending and with the tempo of the Scherzo.

Walter Damrosch, conductor of the New York Symphony Orchestra, would never have accepted my *Organ Symphony* if I had presented it to him cold. I was just a brash young man from Brooklyn as far as he was concerned, who for some strange reason had attracted Boulanger's attention. He greatly admired her, and if she wanted to perform the piece, well, of course, he agreed. He probably said "Sure," without any idea of what I was going to present to him. I had no idea what Damrosch or his musicians thought of my composition. Undoubtedly, from their standpoint, it was "far out." I have a vivid memory of the first rehearsal, because of all times, I was late due to an unexplained delay on the subway. I was really in a panic, thinking that I was going to miss the entire rehearsal. I dashed from Times Square to Aeolian Hall on 43rd Street near Sixth Avenue. I was in such a hurry to get into the hall that instead of going around the block to the stage entrance, I yanked open the front door of the main hall—suddenly, I got a blast of my own orchestration!

It was a moment I shall never forget. It was the Scherzo movement, very brilliant, brassy, and glamorous-sounding. I had orchestrated the piece for large orchestra: triple woodwinds, full brass, and an array of percussion requiring five players in addition to the timpanist. I was absolutely overwhelmed to hear my own orchestration for the very first time. It sounded so *glorious* to me, so much grander than I could possibly have imagined. Had I arrived at the beginning of the rehearsal, it might not have been quite so impressive, since the symphony begins quietly with a first movement Prelude, rather short and reflective and not much like a traditional symphonic first movement.

All three movements are loosely connected by an unobtrusive recurring theme that becomes more significant as the piece proceeds. The first big climax is in the Scherzo, a movement designed to maintain a strong drive all the way through. This second movement interested Boulanger and Koussevitzky most, because of its rhythmic experimentation, irregular note groupings, and uneven accents. The Scherzo was my idea of what could be done to adapt the raw material of jazz. I was not yet using jazz openly and directly; nevertheless, if you listen to the Scherzo even now, you hear rhythms that would not have been there if I had not been born and raised in Brooklyn.[3] The final movement of the *Symphony* is a modified sonata form, resembling a traditional symphonic first movement.

The *Symphony for Organ and Orchestra* had its premiere as planned on 11 January 1925 with the New York Symphony Orchestra conducted by Walter Damrosch at Aeolian Hall. This was Nadia Boulanger's American debut, and she was very warmly received by the press and audience. Perhaps Nadia had planned the order of the program, for my piece was placed prominently, second from the end, and after the audience had been won over. At its conclusion, there was considerable applause, and when Mr. Damrosch pointed to the upper box where I was seated, I rose to bow. As things quieted down, Mr. Damrosch advanced to the footlights and to everyone's surprise, addressed the audience. "Ladies and gentlemen," he began, "I am sure you will agree that if a gifted young man can write a symphony like this at twenty-three"—and here he paused dramatically, leaving the audience to expect a proclamation of a new musical genius— then continued, "within five years he will be ready to commit murder!"

It was a joke, of course, and I laughed along with the audience; but it was also Damrosch's way of smoothing the ruffled feathers of his conservative Sunday afternoon ladies faced with modern American music. For years after, whenever I met Damrosch, he said apologetically, "Copland, you understood what I meant by that remark?" Far more important to me was that Mademoiselle found the music worthwhile. She was intrigued with certain rhythmic aspects of it, and it pleased me to know that when she asked Virgil Thomson his opinion of the *Organ Symphony*, he said, "I wept when I heard it." Nadia asked, "But why did you weep?" Virgil replied, "Because I had not written it myself!" More recently, Virgil added: "The piece that opened the whole door to me was that *Organ Symphony* of Aaron's. I thought that it was the voice of America in our generation. It spoke in the same way that Kerouac did thirty years later. . . ."[4]

The day after the premiere, a news article proclaimed, "Young Composer to Commit Murder!" But Lawrence Gilman, the open-minded critic of the *Herald Tribune*, quipped:

> Copland does not strike me as one of the murderous kind. . . . The real murderers of music are the unimaginative standpatters among composers. . . . There are pages in Mr. Copland's symphony which have bite and power, both rhythmical and harmonic. . . . Mr. Copland, even though he does present us with some second-hand Stravinsky—his second movement is redolent of *Petroushka*—even though he suggests to us in his first movement a kind of Prospect Park Schoenberg, is nevertheless, on the whole, working out his own musical destiny in his own way, and we shall follow his pursuit of it with lively interest. . . .

Others were not so kind. The *Standard Union* writer commented, "To the names of Cowell, Ruggles and Varèse (potential volcanoes, all three) must now be added that of a new and seething crater, Aaron Copland, of

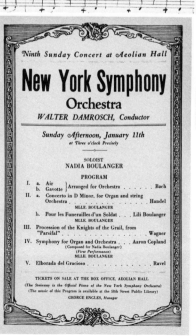

Above: Manuscript page of the Second Movement *Scherzo* from the *Symphony for Organ and Orchestra.* *Right:* Program from the premiere of Copland's *Symphony for Organ and Orchestra,* Aeolian Hall, 1925.

Brooklyn." But no one was indifferent, even the conservative W. J. Henderson of the *New York Sun*: "The real defect of the symphony is its undisguised search of thrills. This is a pity, for the work discloses the existence of a real talent. . . ." Paul Rosenfeld, writing in a characteristic lush prose, was positively rhapsodic.

Harold Clurman and I escorted Nadia around New York City, showing her the sights. The Great White Way was particularly impressive in those days. Her reaction amused us: "It is *extraordinaire*, but not very *raffinated!*" The Boston performance of the *Organ Symphony* was not far off. Koussevitzky invited me to come up a week in advance to go over the score. Damrosch and Koussevitzky had both taken my composition on Boulanger's word, but the difference between the two conductors was striking. I was astounded at the attention Koussevitzky gave to the work. He created an atmosphere that implied there was nothing else of importance on the program; my piece was to be the main event of the symphony week. It was quite an amazing experience for a young unknown composer to have the Boston Symphony Orchestra and its famous conductor at his disposal.

I've never seen anything like Koussevitzky's enthusiasm for new music before or since. He showed the same adventurous spirit in Boston as in Paris, and I had the good fortune to be the first American composer on the scene as Dr. Koussevitzky began his musical life in Boston. Others would have similar experiences, William Schuman and Leonard Bernstein among them. We would be invited to spend an entire week at the Koussevitzky home in Boston with the Maestro and his gracious wife Natalie. There, each evening, after orchestra rehearsals during the day, we would go over the score at the piano, working on difficult rhythms that sometimes did not come naturally to Koussevitzky. He was interested in these rhythmic experiments, and even if they made conducting the music more difficult, he was willing to work them out. I'm sure he knew in advance that his rather conservative audience was not likely to enjoy a composition based on jazz materials and avant-garde harmonies, but he was excited to be part of the movement for modern music.

There was an unforgettable occurrence during Boulanger's performance of the *Organ Symphony* in Boston. An organ key got stuck and would not release. While the orchestra kept playing, the tone grew stronger, filling the hall with a loud and insistent sound. Koussevitzky stopped the orchestra. Nobody was playing, but the organ tone continued, becoming more and more unbearable. Mademoiselle motioned to Koussevitzky—some-

thing had to be done immediately! Suddenly, Nadia left the stage, while Koussevitzky remained on the podium, looking as dignified as usual. In a few moments, the tone ceased. The silence was deafening! The audience applauded as Nadia returned to proceed with the performance. If it had been an uncomfortable moment for audience and performers, imagine the poor composer! The whole episode probably lasted no more than two minutes, but to me it had seemed like hours.

After Boulanger, organists who played the *Organ Symphony* included Melville Smith, who made an organ and piano arrangement of it that has been published, and E. Power Biggs, who recorded the piece with Bernstein and the New York Philharmonic. In December 1982 William Owen was the soloist when I conducted the New Haven Symphony Orchestra in Woolsey Hall where there is a large and wonderful-sounding instrument. I was reminded of a difficulty inherent in music for this combination when Bill Owen informed me that the delay between depressing the key and the actual sound can be as long as a full second. This means that the organist must anticipate the conductor's beat by just that much time if organ and orchestra are to play together. This delay factor is not the only drawback in composing works for organ and orchestra. Not every concert hall has an organ, and the composer limits himself seriously in performance possibilities. Practical considerations, therefore, dictated a version of the piece without organ. It was not that I was dissatisfied with the original, and I am still delighted when the piece is performed with organ and orchestra.

In the summer of 1926, when I was staying in Guéthary, a Basque village in France, I tried out an arrangement of the Scherzo without organ, using an amateur orchestra. Fritz Reiner conducted it in this form with the Philadelphia Orchestra at Carnegie Hall on 4 and 5 November 1927. Reiner considered the work "very American." I decided to rescore the entire symphony; the result was a revised version that became my *First Symphony*. In it, the organ part is replaced with additional orchestration—woodwinds in lyrical passages, and piano elsewhere. Additional brass add necessary punch to sections that depended on massive organ chords, such as the closing bars of the Finale. The *First Symphony* was premiered in Berlin with the Berlin Symphony Orchestra conducted by Ernest Ansermet in 1931. Later on, I arranged the *Prelude* from the *Symphony* as a separate piece for chamber orchestra.[5]

In a tribute to Koussevitzky in 1944 on the occasion of his twentieth anniversary with the Boston Symphony Orchestra (BSO), I wrote, "The story of Serge Koussevitzky and the American composer will someday take on the character of a legend."[6] And so it has. Everyone who knew him has stories about "Koussie." (I doubt anyone ever called him that to his face, and I sometimes wondered if he knew how often and how hilariously his expressions and speech were imitated.) Koussevitzky was a unique combination—awesome as a musician, dignified and elegant as a man—but unintentionally funny when he spoke English. Part of the Koussevitzky legend has to do with the Maestro's strong support of new music, and his outspokenness in his reactions to it. If he didn't like a piece, he would say so in no uncertain terms. Some other conductor might perform a new work if Koussevitzky turned it down, but the special atmosphere that surrounded a Koussevitzky premiere would be lacking. But if he liked a work, he liked it wholeheartedly, and that meant a performance by the BSO, every young American composer's dream.

There are still players in the orchestra today who worked under Koussevitzky, and they too have their special stories about him. All agree that he was a benevolent despot. Whatever the piece, no matter how the orchestra felt about it, Koussevitzky would demand the same attention as for a recognized masterpiece. He would say to the orchestra, "The next Beethoven vill from Colorado come!" He felt responsible, as musical leader of the community, for convincing both orchestra and public of the value of the new music which he accepted for performance.

Koussevitzky's programs in Boston were planned so that the major portion of rehearsal time could be devoted to a new work, and when he invited composers to rehearsals, usually Thursday mornings, the orchestra members were on special guard—they knew the Maestro would be particularly demanding. He had the kind of authority over his men that no longer exists in American orchestras. One likes to think that it was his enthusiasm for the music that caught on to the players, but if not, his hold on them was so secure that we as composers felt supported by the entire BSO as well as its conductor. It is not by chance that during the twenty-five years of Koussevitzky's leadership, from 1924 to 1949, American symphonic music came of age. During that time he gave the first performance of sixty-six American pieces. Moreover, once a work was performed, it was often repeated several times, even on the heels of adverse comment. Recently, in 1981, a Sunday *New York Times* article summed up that year's musical activities. The title was "Is There Life After Premieres for New Music?" The answers were overwhelmingly negative.[7] It would not please Koussevitzky to know that he set no precedent by his custom of keeping contemporary works in the repertoire. Koussevitzky's profound commitment to contemporary music extended to the economic and physical well-being of each composer. He felt personally responsible for us. I recall being surprised to discover that in the late twenties Koussevitzky had spoken privately to Claire Reis, asking her not to urge me to join the board of the League of Composers because it might infringe on my composing time. He could never accustom himself to the fact that in a country as rich as ours, composers could not devote themselves full time to writing music. He had a reverential attitude toward the act of composing that seemed positively romantic, even though it was often directed toward twentieth-century music.

Koussevitzky was determined to support his ideas with more than talk. In 1942 he established a foundation in honor of his wife, Natalie, who died that year. The Koussevitzky Foundation's basic aim is to assist composers. I was on the board of the foundation for many years, and I recall Koussevitzky, at one of the earliest meetings, making a plea for a composers' fund to be started by musicians, who would donate one dollar each, because, as he said, "We musicians must be first to stand by the composer because we owe him most. . . ."[8] The Koussevitzky Foundation awarded many scholarships to gifted students of the Berkshire Music Center; it has aided composers and commissioned new works. In addition, it is a continuing tribute to Serge Koussevitzky, friend of the American composer. He was certainly a friend to me—in fact, Koussevitzky's support was crucial to my development as a composer. When the *Symphony for Organ and Orchestra* caused a furor in the Boston papers and was called "ultra-modern," Koussevitzky was unfazed. After all, he pointed out, if everybody loved it from the start, there would be no challenge. He promptly invited me to write another work for the Boston Symphony Orchestra to be premiered the following season. His confidence in me seemed unshakeable, perhaps because it was part of an unswerving belief in the creative musical force of our times. Sometime later I discovered that Koussevitzky was somewhat of a frustrated composer himself; I am convinced that this must have accounted for his deep understanding for what it means to write music.

After the performances of the *Organ Symphony*, Paul Rosenfeld discussed my financial problems with Minna Lederman, and they worked out a sketchy little plan. Several affluent women known to both of them were invited to her parents' house, and I came there to play my piano pieces for them. After I left, a collection was taken, but the amount was so small that Minna said to Paul, "Now you must go to Alma." Alma Wertheim, the daughter of Ambassador Morgenthau and a wealthy patron of the arts, had

June 5, 1944

Mr. Aaron Copland
New York City

Dear Aaron,

My heart is full to the brim with gratitude for the Testimonial Dinner you gave on May 16th 1944, in celebration of my twenty years in America.

My life is enriched by the memories of this evening. From now on, May 16th will always be a red letter day in my calendar - a holiday, an anniversary, a day of rejoycing. For it has brought close to me the priceless gift of your friendship, the warmth and wealth of your heart.

To that gladness, I can only add that I am richly rewarded for the faith I have always held in you.

Yours
Serge Koussevitzky

Top: Copland and Koussevitzky at Tanglewood, at the conclusion of 'Quiet City," 3 August 1941.
Right: Letter from Koussevitzky to Copland, 1944.
Bottom: Copland and Koussevitzky at Tanglewood in the forties.

me come twice to play for her. After some consideration she gave me a check for $1,000. I don't know how, without that, I would have managed in the year that followed while I was composing *Music for the Theatre*.

Minna Lederman Daniel[9]

I was at the concert when Damrosch made his splashy statement. The piece didn't seem to me in any way shocking. But it's true, from that very moment Aaron became a public figure. His parents were present and I was struck by the resemblance to his mother. She was slender, tall, had blue eyes and a kindly expression. Something of that look is in Copland's face too, but it's a little misleading, I think. It's partly due to his thick eyeglasses. He's not all so benevolent. He's really a little sharper than that.

When he first came to my parents' house, it was for help to get him survival money for the rest of the year. He now had a commission from the League for a new piece—and commissions in those days were seldom for money, mostly they were promises for public performance. I remember how he looked. Even then he had an extraordinary presence. Being young myself, I didn't think of him so much as a young man. The image of Stravinsky came to me immediately because the face had a similar irregularity of features, although it was not at all so composed and balanced as Stravinsky's. His clothes were very catch-as-catch-can, hanging loosely around him. Though of a very much better quality today, they often give the same casually-put-together air.

Aaron when young was sensitive about his appearance but I never could understand why. For artists and photographers he was always the perfect subject, the face one could never forget—after Stravinsky's, THE face. All in all he had, as the cartoonist Al Frueh said, a triangular look. A long, lean body gave the perfect balance to his impressive beaked head. Even then there was an air of unstudied elegance about him. A hawk, yet not predatory. Not what you would call good-looking—something much better, more striking.

Aaron wrote his first piece for me for the January 1925 issue of the Review. From then on, he became my unofficial associate. Although he did not join the League's board until almost a decade later, he had an immediate effect on the magazine. In a talk we had soon after that article appeared, he asked: "Why do you have all these Europeans write everything? There are plenty of Americans, and young ones too, who can do just as well." And to prove that, he soon introduced me to many of the composers of his generation who, writing for Modern Music, *became famous as composer-critics, a new departure in America. He brought Sessions, Piston, Harris, to me and soon afterwards Thomson, Bowles, McPhee, Nancarrow, Carter. Aaron developed a household interest in the magazine. He seemed to belong to it. He wanted to make it the voice of the American composer. Of course it never was quite that. The international presence remained very strong. But he did his best to give the journal a contemporary, made-in-America quality. In the immediately following years, he met so many people here and abroad that he became a great, vital contact for us. All at once he seemed to know everyone. There was especially Koussevitzky, who proved a tremendous resource not only for Aaron's own advancement but for others of his own period. Aaron could introduce people, and his words, no matter how offhand, were given consideration—though as he recently pointed out to me, Koussevitzky had his own predilections and made his own decisions. Aaron seemed to radiate influence. I never considered this a calculated effect or that, as has sometimes been alleged, he was trying to build a power base. The scene that grew up around him was, more simply, a consequence of his very open personality. He had a very real desire—no, more than that—a need for the companionship of colleagues. His concern for their development was as great as if it were part of his own.*

When Aaron traveled through Latin America as a United States ambassador of goodwill, he sent travel letters back to Modern Music. *When he went to Hollywood, he wrote about what that was like. As one of the first serious composers working for radio, he described that process. And when the magazine developed columns, he took on the leading one, "mostly because I wanted to get those scores and records for free." His criticism was always commonsensical, his style precise and matter of fact, and his sermons as brief as possible—a great asset for a magazine whose space was limited. To Aaron, I would always say, "Tell what you're doing." To Roger, "What's on your mind?" And to Virgil, "What's going on in places?" Aaron was very good on a one-to-one basis; he never seemed to enjoy conferences with a lot of people. Things should be done simply, he thought. There were certainly, until even the closing years of the magazine, no conflicts between us. I profited greatly by his ideas and by his worldwide connections, and I think he found it agreeable to have a place where he could set down, with little restraint, in easy prose, his latest thoughts on his latest experiences.*

I've been Aaron's companion many times when he seemed eager to avoid making a fracas. He hated stirring up a fuss over anything. That's how he was, and that's how he still is today. He likes things to go along agreeably—anything to avoid a quarrel. Aaron can lose his temper but it's known that he's never done so in public. Virgil seems to think that Aaron always planned to be cool to avoid controversy, but I don't see him just that way. Aaron knows what he wants and what's important to him. He has a self-preserving sense of not wasting himself. His coolness, his apparent imperviousness to insult and injury is deep and instinctive, a mode of self-protection. It has kept him going all his life, and it seems to me that it still operates. Situations that might have shattered others seem never to have even affected him. For better or for worse he appears immune to criticism. From Koussevitzky and Bernstein he might take suggestions leading to a better performance of his music; from Menotti, whose theater skills he greatly admires, he might follow advice about restructuring The Tender Land. But about his methods of composing, I don't think anyone since the early student days with Boulanger has had any great effect on him. Aaron was always confident that his was the right way at least for him and, moreover, that for him things seldom took the wrong turn. Indeed he was not only successful but fortunate. He never put his faith in someone else's promises. His slogan was always do it yourself, yet helpful things outside his control did seem always to happen. He was apparently the right man, at the right time, in the right place. Today he has a modest way of crediting all this to luck.

Copland's long-held mission has been to fulfill himself as a composer—he wanted, first and last, to compose. Well, that's enough mission for anybody. Then also he had a commitment, a deep, long-lasting one from his early youth, to the specific American situation. Nothing has persuaded him to deviate from that. The speedy recognition of him as a leader was not the result of composing the most advanced music. When he first came on the scene there were Varèse and Cowell and other more avant-garde figures already active, many of them getting a hearing at the concerts of the International Composers' Guild. But Copland was what we now call charismatic. And also he had a tremendous curiosity about new music. He would go to more kinds of things than you can imagine. The only other composer anything like that was Elliott Carter in the thirties and early forties. Copland, for three decades, pursued a continuously active interest in what was new, and he took it upon himself to get new music—of course the new music that appealed to him—into public view.

Aaron's speaking is best when brief and to the point, and I for one feel this way about his music, too. The works I prize most are those that show the bare bones, what he himself calls the "hard-bitten" pieces, the Piano Variations, Statements, *and* Short Symphony, *all written about 1930, and a few of the more daring works of the mid-sixties. Aaron admires those of his colleagues who have written eight, ten, or twelve symphonies, but he himself has experimented intensely with smaller and more restricted forms that project his individual self with great success.* Night Thoughts, *for piano, written as late as 1972, makes an appeal almost as personal and poignant as his early trio,* Vitebsk.

I have known Aaron for a very long time. One forms basic conceptions about people which are hard to get rid of. Then one day you wake up and see that there have been changes. Some things about Aaron have stayed the same. He's austere in his style of living and simple in his tastes, with little demand for luxury. As he has grown older there is a greater demand for the comforts of home.

The great change that has overtaken Aaron is entirely natural; it is due to the end of his composing life. He can be philosophical about this because, I suspect, he feels he has fulfilled himself. His whole being was centered on writing music, writing especially at night. A real night owl. One can picture him with the skies dark and the house dark, and only a light in his study, working it out for himself and out of himself. Now that's over. In recent years he has been projected into public view as a conductor, meeting hundreds of people everywhere—but that's all quite impersonal. He's charming, he's radiant, he smiles when admirers come up and ask for his autograph. This external life seemed for a time to take the place of everything before. But now, more and more, when he comes home from out there, he seeks tranquillity and rest, no longer to work but to recharge himself. He still likes everything about him to be merry, he still has no use for sad stories, and no time to waste on regrets or mistakes. He remains assured and confident. But there was always a modesty about Copland, an attitude of not taking success for granted. That's a lingering trait. Famous the world over, more than comfortably well off, there is still for him a modicum of wonder about it all. Virgil once said to me, "You treat Aaron like a prince." "Well," I said, "he's certainly not imperial. But in his manner, in his way of dealing with the world, yes indeed he is a prince."

During the winter of 1925 my article on Antheil appeared in *Modern Music*, and I wrote a piece for *Musical America* on the value of European study to American composers. In it I made a plea for the establishment of an American National Conservatory.[10] The *Times* printed a lengthy letter I wrote in defense of Mahler, who had been maligned by the critics after Mengelberg conducted his *Second Symphony*[11] in New York. Nadia had put me in touch with Gerald Reynolds, conductor of the Women's University Glee Club in New York, who commissioned me to write two choruses to be performed in the spring. For the first, "The House on the Hill," I chose a text by the American poet Edwin Arlington Robinson, "Children of the Night" of 1897. It is for female voices a cappella and opens with a wordless vocalise divided between two groups of singers. An unusual aspect of the score is the lack of common bar lines; instead, each of the four parts has vertical lines to indicate the stresses of certain words. Its feeling is deliberately simple and meant to reflect the melancholy expression of the abandoned house in the poem: "'They are all gone away, the house is shut and still. . . .'" The second chorus, "An Immorality," to a text by Ezra Pound from "Lustra" of 1916, is in an entirely different mood. Written for soprano, chorus, and piano, this chorus is complex and lively with snappy, syncopated rhythms. I had incorporated jazz polyrhythms into *Grohg* and the *Organ Symphony*, but "An Immorality" was my first real jazz piece.[12] It seemed natural for the piano part to be given the difficult rhythms, and I made sure to play it myself at its first performance. When Schirmer in Boston published the choruses in 1926, I wrote to a young composer friend, Israel Citkowitz, "E. C. Schirmer now possesses the signal honor of being the first gentleman to print my music in America. We poor American composers—no conductors and no publishers and no nothing."

My studio was modest and I lived simply, but it did not take long for Mrs. Wertheim's gift to disappear. Some bright soul established the Guggenheim Foundation[13] just when I needed it most. When the foundation's adviser, Thomas Whitney Surette, requested recommendations, Boulanger, Damrosch, and Koussevitzky wrote on my behalf.[14] If Mr. Surette did not have much feeling for contemporary music, he was a great admirer of Nadia and had respect for her judgments. I believe that she was in great part responsible for my receiving the first Guggenheim Fellowship in music. The amount was $2,500 to be used during the academic year 1925–26, and to be spent in whatever way I saw fit. I was delighted when the fellowship was renewed the following year. It meant I did not have to face the difficult problem of how to make a living until 1927.

The competition between the International Composers' Guild (ICG) and the League of Composers was such that a composer could not be allied with both. Since the League had presented my music first in New York, I could have no connection with the ICG. Varèse led his small group of supporters, principally the harpist Carlos Salzedo and American composer Carl Ruggles. These three seemed incongruous to me—Varèse and Salzedo so very French and Ruggles a salty New Englander. Ruggles was suspicious of audiences, fearing popularity might compromise the innovative nature of the group's activities. On the other hand, the League was aiming for larger audiences and more financial support. Claire Reis, executive director, was able to put the League on secure financial footing by gathering support from wealthy music lovers and patrons. Claire had extraordinary organizational ability and a great deal of personal charm. She was genuinely devoted to composers and determined to have the League run primarily by them, but she was smart enough to use outside expertise when needed.

The success of the League for so many years was due in great part to Claire's leadership. When she heard that Stokowski was to conduct two concerts for the ICG in the 1925–26 season, off she went to Boston to get Koussevitzky for the League. The League had commissioned me to compose a chamber orchestra piece. Claire, knowing of my recent association with Koussevitzky, asked him to conduct my newly commissioned work with members of the Boston Symphony in New York in the fall. The Maestro was delighted when I presented him with the idea; he simply repeated what he had already told me—that he was willing to play anything I gave him for the next season. I wrote to Nadia: "At first, I thought of setting part of Rimbaud's 'Saison en Enfer,' but I have changed my mind, and now I think I will write a series of pieces to be called 'Incidental Music for an Imaginary Drama.' I think that is a better idea. I even have a few themes already." These ideas would become my *Music for the Theatre.*

I needed a quiet place out of the city where I could work on the new piece during the summer months. Again, Paul Rosenfeld came to my aid by suggesting the MacDowell Colony in Peterborough, New Hampshire.

In 1906 the American composer and pianist Edward MacDowell had expressed the wish to found a center where artists in various fields could live and work without interruption, exchanging ideas with one another in a tranquil country setting. Mrs. MacDowell—Marian—also a pianist, had purchased a summer place in Peterborough, New Hampshire, in 1896, where the couple spent their summers. "Hillcrest," as the place was called, seemed a perfect setting for an artist colony. In 1907, a year before the composer's death, Mrs. MacDowell established the Colony, and it was she who was responsible for everything—funding, administration, and maintenance—in order to make her husband's dream a reality. At first, Hillcrest was used as the main building, and studios for housing the artists were modeled after the Log Cabin, built for MacDowell's own use during his lifetime. Marian MacDowell gave her personal attention to every detail. I recall her delivering lunches and leaving them quietly on the porch each day so that work hours would be uninterrupted. Studios were gradually added over the years until there were twenty-eight. A library, residence halls, and Colony Hall were also added, where in the evenings guests were expected to appear for dinner and conversation. Hundreds of acres of beautiful woodlands have been kept undisturbed. The MacDowell Colony offers a unique environment that combines the isolation needed for creative effort with a relaxed atmosphere for exchanging ideas with other artists. Each studio is equipped with just what is needed, but no more than necessary for one's particular art: a cot, an easy chair, a good reading light, and for musicians, always a well-tuned piano. The studios are isolated from each other and differ in architecture; each seems to have sprung up accidentally from whatever had been in its spot previously. There is the Irving Fine cottage (named after a colleague who had stayed at the Colony) and the Monday Music studio. Writers use Veltin cottage and painters love Alexander for its space and good light. I no longer recall the name of my first studio, but I can picture it clearly in my mind's eye. (I know that I used Chapman and Phi Beta studios through the years, among others.)

At the Colony in 1925 I met Louis and Jean Starr Untermeyer, Eleanor Wylie, William Rose Benet, sculptress Tennessee Anderson (she sculpted a head of me that summer), and composer Henry F. Gilbert from Boston. Gilbert was an unusual man of almost sixty who had written symphonic works incorporating Negro and Indian themes. He wrote articles and was interested in the subject of American music, but he was very much a loner and kept to himself. I shall always remember the amazement on the face of old Henry F. on hearing from me that one of our major symphony orchestras had paid an American composer for the performance rights to his first composition. Gilbert exclaimed, "What? Just like Richard Strauss?"

Another composer at MacDowell that summer was young and very lively and got to know everyone right off. He was just a few years my senior and had an impressive natural musical talent. His name was Roy Harris.

There was a freshness and homey quality about Roy at that time. He didn't seem at all like a composer—more like a farmer who had taken it into his head suddenly to become a composer of concert music. Roy had a simple charm and a winning personality when I first knew him. It was fun to have another young composer to talk things over with. When he told me that he needed a teacher, I suggested Boulanger, and a year later Roy was in Paris studying with her.

The atmosphere of tranquillity and seclusion at the MacDowell Colony, without total isolation from other artists, was perfect for me. I stayed at the Colony eight times in all, and later became active on the board of the MacDowell Association, serving as president for several years in the sixties. But as a young composer in 1925, I could not have foreseen that I would receive the MacDowell Colony Medal of Honor in 1961, an award given once a year to an artist of the Colony's choice. Only one thing was on my mind that first summer—a new orchestral work for Koussevitzky to premiere next season.

Certain musical works seem to have careers of their own, independent of those of their authors. For several years after it was written, conductors programmed *Music for the Theatre* more frequently than any other piece of mine. I suspect that this was partly because of the jazz content in several of the movements. It may be difficult to imagine today that the very idea of jazz in a concert hall was piquant in the twenties, but it seems that any piece based on jazz was assured of a mild *succès de scandale*. European composers thought of jazz as an exotic novelty; it was no surprise when Milhaud announced in 1927 that there was not a single young composer in Europe interested in jazz anymore. I was intrigued with jazz rhythms, not for superficial effects, but for use in larger forms, with unconventional harmonies. My aim was to write a work that would be recognizably American within a serious musical idiom. Jazz offered American composers a native product from which to explore rhythm; for whatever the definition of jazz, it must be agreed that it is essentially rhythmic in character. Perhaps jazz was, as Virgil put it, "Copland's one wild oat,"[15] but *Music for the Theatre* and the *Piano Concerto* were characteristic of my musical thinking at the time. And long after the fad of concert jazz faded, the influence of jazz would be felt in the development of polyrhythms. In a 1927 article, "Jazz Structure and Influence," I addressed these issues, concluding: "It [jazz] may be the substance not only of the American composer's fox trots and Charlestons, but of his lullabies and nocturnes."[16]

Music for the Theatre, composed mostly at the MacDowell Colony, was completed in September 1925 on Lake Placid at the summer camp of my former piano teacher, Clarence Adler. Adler had a shack built especially for me up the mountain and named it "The Clouds." He described my visit: "I have listened (at some distance, of course) to Copland in the throes of composition, and it is something to hear! He bangs and hammers at the piano, at the same time singing in shrill, dissonant tones."[17] In New York at the beginning of October, I received a letter inviting me to stay with the Koussevitzkys again for a week before the premiere. "Bring everything you have written in the past months," wrote Koussevitzky. So I arrived in Boston with *Three Dances* (excerpts from *Grohg*) and the new suite.

Music for the Theatre was written with no specific play in mind. It had started with musical ideas that might have been combined as incidental music to a play were the right one at hand. The music seemed to suggest a certain theatrical atmosphere, so I chose the title after developing the ideas into five short movements: The "Prologue" has a certain brashness about it that was typical of my age and the times. It begins rather suddenly with a trumpet solo, followed by a tenderly lyrical passage leading into an allegro mid-section with obvious jazz influence before a return to the lyrical material. (I am told that this resembles the nursery tune "Three Blind Mice," but there was no conscious intention on my part of quoting it.) "Dance," short and jazzy, quotes the familiar popular tune "East Side, West Side";[18] "Interlude," a kind of song without words, is built on a lyric theme repeated three times with slight changes. "Burlesque," best described by its title, emphasizes another characteristic of the twenties—the love of grotesquerie achieved by a liberal use of harmonic dissonance. It was partly inspired by the popular comedienne Fanny Brice. The "Epilogue" incorporates material from the first and third movements and recaptures the quiet mood of the "Prologue." *Music for the Theatre* is scored for small orchestra and is dedicated to Serge Koussevitzky. The challenging jazz rhythms caused the Maestro even more trouble than the *Organ Symphony*. Koussevitzky really knew nothing about American popular music or jazz—these idioms were not in his Russian bones, so to speak. So it was a matter of familiarizing himself with typically American rhythmic materials. To this end, we spent every evening before the concert in his studio going over the score together.

Koussevitzky decided to program *Music for the Theatre* after Mozart's Overture to *The Magic Flute* and Beethoven's *Fourth Symphony*, and before Wagner's *Prelude and Love-Death* from *Tristan and Isolde*. Boston audiences are brought up not to protest publicly when greatly shocked in the concert hall. Therefore, the reception of my new piece at its premiere, 20 November 1925, seemed to be of mild surprise and amusement. But the following day, Warren Storey Smith wrote in the Boston *Post:* "*Music for the Theatre* is a sort of super jazz. . . . The conductor exploded a tonal bombshell that left in its wake a mingling of surprise, perplexity, indignation and enthusiasm." On the other hand, the conservative H. T. Parker ended a lengthy review in the Boston *Evening Transcript* that compared me to Gershwin: ". . . a young modernist ready and unashamed with melodic invention; a young American composer neither repressing nor sentimentalizing poetic mood. Wonders are still possible; even Brooklyn may give them birth." And the venerable Philip Hale called me "a young composer of indisputable talent . . . with a great gift of imagination. . . ." Of jazz in the concert hall, Hale asked, "Why should not one movement in a suite be symbolic of American life as it now is?"

The trustees of the Boston Symphony voted their approval for the Maestro to appear in the concert in New York sponsored by the League of Composers. After conducting a full orchestra at Carnegie Hall in the afternoon of 28 November, Koussevitzky led a chamber orchestra made up of Boston Symphony players that evening at Town Hall in an all-modern program. Four Europeans were included—Alexandre Tansman, Prokofiev, Honegger, and Ravel—and one American. The critics in New York were extremely unsympathetic. One commented that Koussevitzky smiled throughout the concert as though he was in on a secret that nobody else knew. Samuel Chotzinoff of the *New York World* described the concert as "One of the League's evening comedies," and he called me "the cherished Scion of the League." But it was Olin Downes of the *Times* who was most scathing: "We do not care if a long time elapses before we listen again to *Music for the Theatre.*" A considerable time did elapse before Downes heard the piece again. Seven years later he wrote, "In 1925 when first heard, this music impressed the writer as ultra modern to the point of affectation. Today he feels that this is music of genuine inspiration and feeling, music composed and not merely invented, that it has a personal color, fancy and, in the best moments, emotion—the work of a young composer finding himself, with something real and not merely derivative to say. . . ."[19] Downes even included *Music for the Theatre* in his lecture-recital series of 1934.

This turnaround by a noted critic reminded me early in my career not to

Above: Manuscript, first page from the arrangement for piano–four hands of *Music for the Theatre*, including instructions in German for a ballet that has never been produced. *Left:* Program, *Music for the Theatre*, 1925.

take reviews too seriously. I never left a concert hall or read a writeup and felt hurt because I wasn't being understood. I was, on the contrary, rather brazen about it, thinking, "Those dumbbells, they'll see, just give them time." I didn't have any sense of "Oh well, if they think it's awful, it must be awful"—there was none of that. Reviews bothered me only when they upset my parents. After the reception of *Music for the Theatre* in New York, my father, who knew nothing about music, remarked: "After all, these fellows get *paid* for their opinions. They must know *something* about music!" But I composed out of real conviction. It never occurred to me to think that everybody was going to love my music right away. I realized I was using a contemporary musical language that most audiences were not accustomed to hearing. And actually, there was a lot of fun in bucking the tide and feeling part of the avant garde out there fighting new battles. That feeling was very much part of the excitement of the times.

Walter Damrosch conducted a concert each season called "Modern Music—Pleasant and Unpleasant." I don't know into which category *Music for the Theatre* fell, but Damrosch included it in his 1926 program. Since Dr. Damrosch had never made any secret of his antipathy to modern music, I was surprised and rather flattered at his conducting this piece; moreover, he invited me to play the piano part. During one rehearsal he stopped the orchestra abruptly on an astringent chord that disturbed him and turning to me asked, "*Must* that chord be that way?" I stood my ground with all the temerity of youth and firmly replied, "Yes, Dr. Damrosch, that's the way that chord must be."

Braving the wrath of the critical fraternity, Koussevitzky continued to schedule *Music for the Theatre.* He brought it back to New York only a few months after the premiere—this time as a regular part of a Boston Symphony program at Carnegie Hall and the Brooklyn Academy of Music (7 January 1926). Members of the board of directors of the Academy of Music came backstage during intermission to protest the playing of such ultra-modern stuff. "But gentlemen," Koussevitzky said, "Copland is one of *your* boys. I played it here in Brooklyn to do honor to *your* city." The representatives from Brooklyn said, "Moreover, we hired the *entire* Boston Symphony Orchestra, and there were only twenty-four musicians on stage!" "Gentlemen, have patience and you shall be satisfied. The next piece, *Alpine Symphony* by Richard Strauss, uses an orchestra of over a hundred players. They vill all be busy. You shall have your money's worth!" Koussevitzky continued to program my suite—a Paris performance stands out in my mind, because of an incident that involved the well-known French composer Florent Schmitt. It was May 1926 and Koussevitzky's first concert in Paris since he had left for Boston. He led an orchestra of French musicians, brought together for the occasion, at the Théâtre National de l'Opéra. I was in Paris, and Koussevitzky invited me to play the piano part. After the concert Schmitt came to me backstage and remarked, "See here, Monsieur Copland, what is the meaning of this? If you Americans begin now to export music instead of merely to import music, where will we poor French composers be?"

In 1933 Koussevitzky introduced *Music for the Theatre* at the Coolidge Auditorium in Washington, marking my debut at the Library of Congress; and in 1938 at Tanglewood, my first piece to be performed at the Berkshire Music Festival. Stokowski conducted the composition in 1932 with the Philadelphia Orchestra. In 1933 Serge Prokofiev wrote from Paris (2 October): "My dear Copland, I received a letter from Moscow, that the performance of your *Music for Theatre* [sic] is announced for this fall. . . ." I never heard whether it was played in Russia, but many other performances have taken place through the years, right up to 1980 when the suite was included in a twelve-hour eightieth birthday celebration at Symphony Space in New York City called "Wall-to-Wall Copland."

Several choreographers have found the rhythmic aspects of *Music for the Theatre* appealing.[20] The first recording was made in 1941, conducted by Howard Hanson with the Rochester Symphony on the Victor label; Leonard Bernstein recorded it for CBS with the New York Philharmonic in 1965.

I had dreamed of representing American music on the international scene, but had not expected to do so as early as 1927. It was announced that two American works had been chosen to be played at the ISCM Festival in Frankfurt in the summer: Henry Gilbert's *The Dance in Place Congo* and *Music for the Theatre*. I played the piano part myself, and it amused me to watch those honest German musicians struggling with jazz rhythms for the first time in their lives! During intermissions at rehearsals the men gathered around the piano to get first-hand advice on how to manage the new American rhythms. Imagine—a young American teaching the Germans *anything* about music!

Music for the Theatre and my other compositions of this "jazz period" *sounded* American; they could not have been written by a European. That is precisely what I intended at the time, just as I consciously hoped to forward the cause of contemporary American music by my activities and writings. If I was a leader in contemporary music, I was a follower of the modern movement in the other arts. As early as 1916, a group of writers began publishing *The Seven Arts,* a magazine conceived to promote their ideas.[21] Waldo Frank's book of 1919, *Our America,*[22] challenged writers to bring America into the modern art movement. Alfred Stieglitz was the unofficial leader of this group. His gallery was the hang-out for younger artists such as photographer Paul Strand, painters John Marin and Georgia O'Keeffe (later Stieglitz's wife), Waldo Frank and other writers I met at Paul Rosenfeld's apartment.[23] They were all aware that music lagged behind the other arts, and they took it for granted that I, as the contemporary composer among them, would do something about the situation. I thought of myself as involved in their movement and instinctively felt part of a "school." I knew that it would take a combined effort if America were to find an artistic voice of its own. In the twenties American composers had few outlets for making themselves known to each other and to the rest of the world. As a start toward alleviating this condition, I wrote a rather bold article for *Modern Music* naming seventeen promising composers between the ages of twenty-three and thirty-three. This may have been daring, but at least it pointed out the fact of our existence. I stated: "In America our new composers have been left to shift for themselves. . . . Perhaps hearing about them may induce someone to let us really *hear* them. . . ."[24]

I was convinced that it was important for American composers to hold their own in Europe as well as at home. At that time, recognition abroad was still an important credential. Since Nadia was planning an all-American program to be sponsored by the SMI and Koussevitzky was to conduct *Music for the Theatre,* I decided to return to Europe, so I left with Clurman at the end of March 1926. Once in Paris, we took rooms on our old street, this time chez Mme Simoneau, at 59 Boulevard Pasteur, and renewed old acquaintances: Nadia and her mother, Annette Dieudonné and Marcelle de Manziarly, Virgil Thomson, George Antheil, and Herbert Elwell. Teddy (Theodore) Chanler, Douglas Moore, and Walter Piston were also in Paris, and I met Roger Sessions for the first time that spring at one of Mademoiselle's afternoon teas.

I was uncertain about completing two new pieces for violin and piano for Nadia's concert, so I suggested that the *Rondino* be substituted. I thought that it could be played by the quartet performing Antheil's work. But Antheil did not like the idea, perhaps because he was paying the quartet's expenses, so I was spurred on to finish two new pieces, *Nocturne* and

A group of composers with the singer Ada T. MacLeish in Boulanger's apartment before a Paris concert of all-American music, spring 1926 (left to right): Herbert Elwell, Copland, MacLeish, Walter Piston, and Virgil Thomson.

Ukelele Serenade, after all. I invited the American violinist, Samuel Dushkin, to play the pieces with me. The program included six premieres. All the young Americans except Antheil were, or had been, Boulanger students. The audience was a distinguished one, since the SMI and Nadia had influential followings in the Parisian art world—even James Joyce made a rare appearance!

Two Pieces for Violin and Piano is about eight minutes in duration. The first piece, *Nocturne,* is slow and in the manner of a blues. It is dedicated to Israel Citkowitz, a promising young composer who was studying with me in New York. The second, *Ukelele Serenade,* dedicated to Samuel Dushkin, is an allegro vivo. It begins with quarter tones meant to achieve a blues effect, while arpeggiated chords in the right hand of the piano part simulate a ukelele sound. Later in the piece, the roles are reversed, with pizzicato quadruple violin stoppings representing the ukelele. The bar lines for the two instruments do not necessarily coincide.

The American premiere of *Two Pieces* took place at a League concert with works by five other young Americans on 13 February 1927: Randall Thompson, Teddy Chanler, Evelyn Berkman, Ruth Crawford, and Marc Blitzstein. Nadia promptly sent my new pieces to Schott & Sons. After I returned home, she wrote, "Strecker takes the two pieces with *joy....* I will speak with Sam [Dushkin] for some fingering perhaps but of course will not even consider any changes—naturally you will receive proofs (is it the word?). I advise you to write immediately to Willy Strecker in accepting—and perhaps say you are glad to be in his active, living business." Nadia suggested I submit other works—"Strike the iron while it is hot."

Antheil had become known as the *enfant terrible* of young American composers. Before Harold and I left Paris, everyone was discussing his *Ballet mécanique,* which was to be premiered on 19 June 1926. In a letter to Israel Citkowitz, I described this unusual event:

> The scene is a beautiful theatre off the Champs-Elysées, filled with an audience of more than 2,000 people among whom one can distinguish James Joyce, Serge Koussevitzky, Ezra Pound, Darius Milhaud, Nadia Boulanger, Marcel Duchamp, Alfred Knopf, Boris de Schloezer etc., etc., each and every one buzzing with the excitement and expectation of hearing for the first time anywhere a program which contained—oh marvel of marvels—your only true rival— George Antheil! who proceeded to outsack the "Sacre" with the aid of a Playela and amplifiers, ventilators, buzzers and other what-not . . . brought forth the usual near-riot so everyone went home content. . . . I am in all honesty bound to repeat my unshakeable conviction—the boy is a genius. Need I add that he has yet to write a work which shows it. If he keeps on exactly as he has started the sum total of all his genius will be exactly nothing. Voilà!

When *Ballet mécanique* was given its New York premiere the following April, Antheil invited me to be one of ten pianists on stage. The work created as much of a sensation in New York as it had in Paris.[25]

In 1926 Harold and I left Paris for Zurich to attend the Fourth Annual ISCM Festival, which I was to cover for *Modern Music.*[26] A more adventurous spirit had prevailed at earlier festivals; not only were there few new names, but the music that was performed was not of great interest. Schoenberg's *Wind Quintet* was a failure except with his closest supporters. Anton von Webern, who was present, complained to the critics, "One has no more reason to expect to appreciate this *Quintet* on a single hearing than to understand Kant after a cursory perusal." Webern's own *Five Orchestral Pieces* was the only work I was really taken with, and it had been written in 1913! As usual, the music was either French or German. I found Hindemith's *Concerto for Orchestra* (op. 38) to have "extraordinary vigor and exuberance." We left Zurich with the impression that the music had been secondary; the three-day festival served more as an international meeting place for composers, musicians, and publishers. This in itself was valuable. While in Zurich, I played *Music for the Theatre* on the piano for the Universal Edition representatives with the hope of getting something else in print, but nothing came of it.

Harold and I traveled on to Munich for a week's visit, and Harold told me that he could feel something like Nazism in the air even then, as early as 1926.[27] How we came to find a wonderful little villa for the summer in

Manuscript page from the *Concerto for Piano and Orchestra*.

the Basses Pyrenées I no longer recall, but it was exactly what we wanted. The village of Guéthary is built on the hills that rise from the sea, a half-hour away from Biarritz in one direction, with Spain close by on the other side. I worked steadily on my *Piano Concerto*. We dipped into the sea in front of our Villa Cendrillon whenever relaxation was needed. But by

128

mid-August, Harold was impatient to return to the New York theater scene. I stayed on alone until 1 October and returned to New York with the *Concerto* almost finished and with two short pieces put together from discarded materials, *Blues 1 and 2*.[28]

I moved to 223 West 78th Street, a slightly larger studio. This was hardly the movie version of what a musician's living quarters should be—a large room in an old-fashioned brownstone house on a quiet uptown street, very plainly furnished. A grand piano was set between the two windows and a big easy chair in front of the fireplace. I preferred being alone when composing, but I enjoyed company for the tedious business of copying orchestral parts. Gerald Sykes, a young writer whom I had met in 1925 through Paul Rosenfeld, often came to the studio while I was checking parts for the *Piano Concerto*. Gerald, Harold Clurman, and I became the best of friends. Israel Citkowitz also came over in the evenings. While I sat in the one chair under the only good light, Israel would stretch out on the cot and work on something of his own. After midnight, we would have tea and talk, before he went back out into the wintry nights to his own place.

Roy Harris had gone off to France with his wife and $1,800 given him by Alma Wertheim to subsidize his studies abroad. Roy's letters to me date from the summer of 1925 at MacDowell. They always seemed much like Roy—bigger than life, with a sprawling, open, western feeling. (Roy often teased me about not having been further west than Ithaca.) While I was abroad, Roy wrote asking that I speak to Nadia on his behalf: ". . . and tell her I want to study canon and fugue, form and orchestration, learn to play piano, read scores—and if possible conduct. I want to study and learn to speak a language of music." Even before meeting Nadia, Roy was writing instructions that made me suspect he would have some adjustments to make: "Aaron, will you try to make it clear to Mademoiselle Boulanger that I abominate Ravel and Milhaud and Debussy—and am not moved by Honegger. . . . The people out West are looking toward me to make Viking—'yea-saying' music. . . ." About my own music, Roy wrote:

> Am sorry you are writing a piano concerto—I think it is the wrong step—too much of music is lost in personalities—and concertos are largely a matter of personalities—even if you play them yourself—you are hindering the serious development of music. . . . I wish that you would write a choral symphony. . . . Jazz is on its way out. Beware for that new piano concerto which so many Copland enthusiasts are waiting for—don't disappoint us with jazz. . . .

The *Piano Concerto* was the last of my works to make explicit use of jazz materials. I have often described myself as a "work-a-year" man—1926 was the year of the *Concerto*. During this period, I was often critically paired with Gershwin. His *Rhapsody in Blue* was a kind of jazz piano concerto, and it was less than two years old when I wrote *Music for the Theatre*. It seems curious that Gershwin and I had so little contact, but the *Rhapsody* had been introduced by Paul Whiteman and his band, a very different milieu than Koussevitzky and the BSO. Gershwin came from Tin Pan Alley and Broadway musicals, while my only connection with the theater was through Clurman—and that meant serious drama. In those days, the lines were more sharply drawn between popular and classical musics. In many ways Gershwin and I had much in common—both from Brooklyn, we had studied with Rubin Goldmark during the same time and were pianists and composers of music that incorporated indigenous American sounds. But even after Damrosch commissioned Gershwin's *Concerto in F* for performance in the same season as Koussevitzky premiered my *Music for the Theatre*, Gershwin and I had no contact. We *must* have been aware of each other, but until the Hollywood years in the thirties, we moved in very different circles. On one occasion, when we were finally face to face at some party, with the opportunity for conversation, we found nothing to say to each other! I had always enjoyed popular music and admired those who could perform and compose in the lighter vein, but my talents clearly did not lie in that direction. I have no idea today whether Gershwin's *Concerto* of 1925 influenced me toward composing a piano concerto the following year. I doubt it. Koussevitzky had said, "If you write a piano concerto, you can play it yourself," and that temptation was too great to pass up.

I took the score of the *Piano Concerto* to Koussevitzky, he approved it and set to work rehearsing the orchestra on the difficult rhythms and instrumentation. The *Concerto* is scored for large orchestra with alto and soprano saxophones and extra percussion, such as tam-tam, Chinese drums, woodblock, and xylophone. At least I did not have to worry about a pianist; I could play the part myself from memory without practicing it, since it was so fresh in my mind. (Practicing piano was a musical activity I have always disliked intensely.) The *Concerto* is to be played without interruption, but it is actually written in two contrasting sections, linked together thematically. The first is slow and lyrical; the second fast and rhythmic. Two basic jazz moods are incorporated in each section—the slow blues and the snappy number. The melodic material of the first movement is taken from a traditional blues, one also used by Gershwin at about the same time in his *Prelude No. 2* for piano. The second movement is a modified sonata form, without a recapitulation. A short cadenza sounds like an improvised break, but is not—probably because I was not good at improvisation myself. The rhythms presented in this section were considered extremely difficult. Before the Finale, the first movement material is recalled, followed by a brief Coda. I considered the *Concerto* essentially dramatic in character. As I explained in an interview at the time of the premiere: "The piano is as the main character in a play, carrying on a dialogue with the orchestra and conversing with the other instruments."

My primary aim was to explore new avenues in the area of polyrhythms. I was also experimenting with shifting beats by introducing a variety of highly unorthodox and frequently changing rhythms—7/8, 5/8, 9/8, 1/8, etc., that made the music polymetric—the use of different time signatures one after the other. The challenge was to do these complex vertical and horizontal experiments and still retain a transparent and lucid texture and a feeling of spontaneity and natural flow. If I felt I had gone to the extreme of where jazz could take me, the audiences and critics in Boston all thought I had gone *too* far. One critic actually accused Koussevitzky of being a malicious foreigner who wanted to show how bad American music was! Another, Penfield Roberts of the Boston *Globe*, wrote (29 January 1927): "No music heard at these concerts in the past 15 years has created so great a sensation. The audience forgot its manners, exchanging scathing verbal comments, and giggled nervously. . . ."

My mother and father had come to Boston for the premiere. I was delighted with Ma when she said that her proudest moment was when I played my *Piano Concerto* in Boston that night. The only criticism that really bothered Pa was the headline in the Boston *Post*: COPLAND'S LATEST IS POOR STUFF. After all, Pa had been a storekeeper long enough to know the meaning of "poor stuff"! In the program notes, I indicated that the *Concerto* was not programmatic; nevertheless, the *Post*'s reviewer claimed, "With no effort at all the listener visualizes a jazz dance hall next door to a poultry yard. . . ." Philip Hale, learned arbiter of American mores in music and drama, set the tone of condemnation in his review in the *Herald*: "Copland's *Piano Concerto* shows a shocking lack of taste, of proportion . . . the piano is struck by fingers apparently directed at random." H. T. Parker, the most proper Bostonian of the lot, wrote in the *Evening Transcript* about "the ogre with that terrible Concerto." He published a special editorial to explain his dislike further: "The Copland *Piano Concerto* is a harrowing horror from beginning to end. . . . There is nothing in it that resembles music except that it contains noise. . . ." When complaints reached Parker's desk accusing Messrs. Koussevitzky and Copland of poking fun at America, Parker found himself in the curious position of championing our right to be heard!

With the assistance of Nicolas Slonimsky, then Koussevitzky's assistant, I presented a pre-concert lecture, sponsored by the orchestra, at the Boston Public Library. But familiarizing the audience with the program in advance did not seem to win any admirers. After I left Boston, "Kolya," as we called Slonimsky, with his playful sense of humor (not appreciated by Madame Koussevitzky, who thought him disrespectful) sent me the worst reviews (March 1927): "Enclosed you will find a usual Parkerian grimace at you. . . . You are not forgotten in Boston, and Parker untiringly continues to titillate public minds by mentioning, now and again, your notorious name."

The Boston Symphony gave the first New York performance of the *Piano Concerto* at Carnegie Hall on 3 February 1927. For once, New York was more tolerant than Boston, although Lawrence Gilman in the *Herald Tribune* was the only influential voice in either city to welcome the work: ". . . music of impressive austerity, of true character, music bold in outline and of singular character. . . ." Koussevitzky decided not to take my new piece to Brooklyn (to him, "the provinces"), but the Brooklyn reviewers came to New York. What a pleasant surprise it was to read Edward Cushing in the *Brooklyn Daily Eagle* (6 February 1927): "The Concerto was, all things considered, the most excellent of symphonic jazz expressions, Mr. Copland has quite outdone Mr. Gershwin and Mr. Carpenter. . . . There is more than jazz in the Concerto. . . ." Alma Wertheim, to whom the *Concerto* is dedicated, threw a gala party after the New York premiere in honor of Madame and Maestro Koussevitzky and myself.

The following summer I accepted an invitation to perform the *Piano Concerto* at the Hollywood Bowl, welcoming the opportunity to go west for the first time. There at rehearsals the musicians actually hissed. The conductor, Albert Coates, was distraught: "Boys! Boys, please!" he pleaded, pointing to me at the piano. "He's one of *us!*" The Los Angeles *Times* reported (21 July 1928): "Bowl stirred up a frenzy. . . . Fans greet sophisticated jazz with derision . . . catcalls, hisses, laughs and applause follow pianist. . . ." At about the same time, John Kirkpatrick arranged a two-piano version of the *Concerto*. I offered it to the Cos Cob Press, and since they were in a hurry for it, I simply took it for granted that John would like the idea and would get paid what was coming to him; but I miscalculated. John, who was in Paris studying with Boulanger, wrote that I should not have gone ahead without him. I answered (9 April 1929):

> You are absolutely right of course in saying that I had no "right" in arranging for publication without consulting you. Of course if you were a complete stranger to me I shouldn't have done this—but taking a friend's liberty and not expecting you to be fleeced I said go ahead. My mind worked in this fashion: John will want his arrangement published—at best there isn't a large sum of money involved—apparently John doesn't depend on his arrangements for a source of income—ergo, the main thing is to have the arrangement published. It was because of this, that I wrote you in the airy, non-business-like tone I did . . . the proofs are already finished and I have already corrected them—even before your letters came—so that I must throw myself on your good will and ask that no matter what happens you arrange the matter amicably. . . .

The problem was soon resolved with no further difficulty between us.

A composer sends a piece of music into the world much as a parent sends a child—tending to it for a time until it must go off on its own, and then, to some extent, what happens is out of the creator's hands. After playing the *Concerto* myself in six places in fourteen years (Boston, New York, Hollywood, New York's Stadium Concerts, Mexico, and Chile), the piece was not heard again in this country for sixteen years. During that hiatus it retained its reputation as a shocker, an illusion that was shattered when Leonard Bernstein revived the work with the New York City Symphony at the City Center (21–22 October 1946). Leo Smit was at the keyboard. Juxtaposed with the D Major *Concerto* of Haydn, the *Piano Concerto* seemed anything but shocking, and no one could imagine why audiences in 1927 had walked out on it. After the 1946 revival, the *Concerto* was called "a relic of Le Jazz hot," "the nostalgic ghost of Paris's left bank," and "the best roar from the roaring twenties." It recalled a time when anything seemed possible, when we young modernists thought the musical millennium around the corner. Lenny and Leo handled the rhythmic complexities of the *Concerto* with ease. Leo is a far better pianist than I—I had played the work like a composer, while he was a dazzling performer with enormous vitality and yet he kept everything absolutely clean and precise.

Leo played the *Concerto* again in 1953, this time under Charles Munch with the Boston Symphony. When a French pianist, scheduled to do a concerto, canceled at the last moment, Leonard Burkat, then Dr. Munch's assistant, suggested my *Concerto* as a replacement. (Munch had played some of my music in Europe and he liked Leo, who had performed the

Alexei Haieff *Concerto* with the BSO the previous year.) So on 16 October 1953 the once notorious "Jazz Concerto" came back home to Boston, where it had been born in 1927. Leo garnered rave reviews, while Munch's conducting was called "rectangular." (After all, one would not expect the jazz rhythms to be in *his* bones any more than Koussevitzky's.) Dr. Munch evidently liked the *Concerto*, taking it to Brooklyn and to Tanglewood in the summer of 1954.

I had not performed it myself in years when Lenny invited me to do it in a concert (9 January 1964) meant to examine the "jazz trend," part of a series of avant-garde orchestra concerts he was presenting at the Philharmonic. My *Concerto* was juxtaposed with more recent experiments by composers Larry Austin, John Cage, Stefan Wolpe, Earle Brown, Morton Feldman, and Pierre Boulez. The modern works were interspersed with standard repertory. How Lenny got away with it, I don't know, since the New York Philharmonic players are not fond of playing modern music. Leonard Burkat, by then head of CBS Masterworks, heard the performance and suggested we record it. I also played the piece under Alfred Wallenstein at one of the "Concerts in the Parks" in the Sheep Meadow in New York (24 August 1965).

The three musicians most closely connected with the *Concerto*— Lenny, Leo, and myself—had a reunion at my eightieth birthday concert at Kennedy Center in Washington. Lenny conducted *Lincoln Portrait*, which I narrated, and Leo played the *Piano Concerto* with the National Symphony Orchestra under my baton. During rehearsal, Lenny came on stage to give advice and assistance, and afterward, Lenny and Leo were full of reminiscences of 1946.

Jazz played a big role in the twenties. But I had been observing the scene around me and sensed it was about to change. Moreover, I realized that jazz might have its best treatment from those who had a talent for improvisation. I sensed its limitations, intended to make a change, and made no secret of the fact. In the Los Angeles *News*, an interviewer reported (20 July 1928): "Copland to Abandon Jazz in Future Compositions. The young composer of the jazz concerto which has made him internationally famous, and which is to be played at the Hollywood Bowl on Friday night, feels that this composition has exhausted all of the possibilities of the theme for him. His concerto is the culmination of a great many compositions written with a jazz theme; now he will search new fields for inspiration."[29]

Interlude II

When an artist adopts a new style, the reaction is likely to be one of surprise, even anger, as if to say, "How dare you make a sudden change when I have become accustomed to the way you were?" A radical change poses all sorts of questions. What is responsible? What turmoil, what extension into another region of the artistic territory occasioned such a turn in the road? The fact is that abrupt turnarounds are usually not so precipitous or so novel as they seem. With Copland, ideas leading away from a jazz-oriented music to a more abstract style had been in the back of his mind for some time. This new style did not spring suddenly from nowhere—and when it did appear, it incorporated sounds that were unmistakably Copland.

A period of assessment and exploration followed the *Piano Concerto;* the few pieces composed during that time were either experimental or transitional. They functioned as a bridge from the old to the new, very much the way a musical interlude connects familiar passages to new material, preparing the listener for a change. During this transitional period, Copland maintained a vigorous schedule of teaching, writing, lecturing, and promoting of concerts. These activities soon established him as the dominant figure in the American contemporary musical world. Several composers—Virgil Thomson, Roger Sessions, and Leo Ornstein—found it either necessary or desirable to remove themselves from New York, but Copland was never comfortable away from it for long; on the contrary, he preferred to observe and reflect on the active and changing scene around him, an extraordinary one in the years preceding the Wall Street crash of 1929.

Historians have called 1927 a turning point in the development of civilization: national radio networks, underwater tunnels, and international radio-telephone services were established; Lindbergh flew across the Atlantic, affirming the wonder and power of progress and technology. In music, Jerome Kern's *Showboat* was an enormous success on Broadway, Duke Ellington opened to "white only" audiences at the Cotton Club in

Harlem, and George Antheil's *Ballet mécanique* shocked an audience in Carnegie Hall. The League of Composers was gaining strength under the effective leadership of Claire Reis; and the Pro-Musica Society, led by E. Robert Schmitz, was arranging for composers Kodály, Bartók, and Ravel to come to America for the first time in 1928.

Since musical performances were virtually nonexistent during summer months, Copland arranged with Minna Lederman to cover two German music festivals for *Modern Music.* Most of the spring and summer of 1927 was spent in Germany. But first a visit to Nadia and other friends in Paris, before traveling with Roy Harris to the ISCM Festival in Frankfurt to hear *Music for the Theatre* performed for an international audience on the Fourth of July. Then on to the Festival of German Chamber Music in Baden-Baden, where Copland met Hanns Eisler and saw Kurt Weill, who was on hand to supervise the premiere of *Mahagonny.* It was Alban Berg's *Lyric Suite* that most impressed Copland at the festival. He wrote, "Berg is now forty-two and it is foolish to continue discussing him merely as a Schoenberg pupil. The similarities between his own style and that of his teacher are only superficial. In reality their natures are opposed. Berg, unlike Schoenberg, being essentially naive, with a warm, emotional, Tristanesque personality. The *Lyric Suite* seems to me to be one of the best works written for string quartet in recent years."[1]

For the remainder of the summer, Copland lived in Königstein, Germany, partly because of a passing acquaintance with members of the wealthy Seligman family in New York who had relatives there, but mostly to be where he could compose without distractions. Königstein was still occupied by the British. Soldiers and military installations were much in evidence, and Copland felt unsettled and uncomfortable there. He composed only one short "Song," later retitled "Poet's Song," to a text by e.e. cummings. Based on a tone row, the work was an early experiment with serialism. It is a difficult piece that reflects the direction of Copland's musical thinking at that time.

Copland was relieved to leave Germany at the end of the summer for a visit to Nadia's country home in Gargenville. Israel Citkowitz and Roy Harris were there (Harris had taken rooms in the small town of Juziers close by). Other Americans were by now flocking to the "Boulangerie," among them Ross Lee Finney, a young composer from Minnesota, who had worked his way to Europe by playing in a shipboard jazz orchestra. Copland's visit to Gargenville that summer is still vivid to Finney: "His presence made such an impact on me! Nadia was to play the organ at

Letter from Roy Harris, 1933 (date in Copland's hand).

Chartres Cathedral and we all traveled together with her by car. Aaron spoke so eloquently about being an *American* composer and understanding your roots that he made me consider my Midwest background just as valuable as what I was experiencing in France. It was a crucial period for me, and Aaron's influence lasted a very long time."[2]

Copland must have been voicing his relief at being out of the stultifying atmosphere in Germany, but he soon discovered that Gargenville offered its own problems. Citkowitz and Harris, both close to Copland, were not compatible and their constant bickering for Nadia's attentions made Copland feel responsible, since it was he who had sent them to her in the first place. After Copland's return to the States, Israel and Roy confided their troubles and complaints to him, each viewing relationships from his own side of the triangle: Israel's fifteen and seventeen-page letters tightly packed with bitter complaints against Roy's insensitive nature and his wife's impossible behavior; Roy's sprawling messages venting his homesickness for California and his impatience with French rules and restrictions ("Aaron, can't we go together to live in California? Short of that, send me garden seeds for next year from New York. . . . I would like to introduce some good melons, sweet corn and potatoes to Juziers farmers from America. . . ."). And Nadia's spidery European script on her ubiquitous black-bordered paper reporting her pupils' progress, asking Aaron's advice and counsel, and causing Aaron to respond (19 December 1927): "Is he [Israel] behaving himself? I often have had visions of him causing you untold trouble and annoyance. Reassure me, please!" Nadia's response: "Now with Israel—he has *improved immensely*—and we must find the money for him—to make it easier—I will not take on the $3.00 for the 2nd lesson a week. I am too glad to bring this little help to a born musician and such a nice boy—" About Roy, she wrote, "great beauties in Roy's symphony—hope you will be pleased—when order will come with, what a musician he can be. . . ."

Aaron wrote regularly to Israel, "knowing how much he needs my moral support," thus making Roy jealous. Both depended on Copland for contacts at home, especially with Koussevitzky, and for programming, teaching, and lecturing about their music. In addition, Citkowitz was helpless about financial matters and depended on Aaron for support. "Last year," wrote Citkowitz in December 1927, "I was so bent on going to Paris that I totally overlooked the means . . . the thought of a job doesn't make me hysterical as it did. . . ." But Israel did not find a job. Alma Wertheim gave $160 toward his support, while Aaron and Nadia continued to look for another patroness, even though Copland's own situation was little short of precarious. Copland sailed from Cherbourg 10 September 1927 (on the R.M.S. *Berengaria,* second class). When he arrived in New York, the Guggenheim Fellowships had run out, and he had to face the serious problem of how to make a living.

When Paul Rosenfeld offered to turn the music courses he had been delivering at the New School for Social Research over to Copland, the timing could not have been better. For the next ten years, the New School would provide a modest and dependable source of income. Best of all, Copland could work in the field of music and still have time for composing. The $50 fee paid for each two-hour session one evening a week was a lot of money then; later, when the courses became popular, the New School paid a percentage of the tuitions. The courses were valuable in another way: they provided an opportunity for Copland to observe and evaluate modern music, to consider antecedents and developments, and to view his own music in the context of history, all at a time when he was taking stock of his situation and considering his directions. Every Friday evening, Copland went down to lecture at 465 West 23rd Street (in 1931 the New School moved to 66 West 12th). The lectures proved to be more time-consuming than the young musician had imagined—modern music was the principal subject, most scores were unpublished and unrecorded, and Copland had to play the musical examples himself on the piano.[3] Neither experience nor musical education were required from the sixty-eight people who registered for "The Appreciation of Modern Music" in the fall of 1927. They included a few music teachers and students, businessmen, secretaries, librarians, a playwright (Elmer Rice, then young and unknown), and several others who wrote "no occupation at present" on their applications. The first course ended on 28 December with a concert arranged by Copland of works by Krenek, Stravinsky, Hindemith, Cowell, Ravel, Webern, and Copland.[4]

Lecturing held a challenge similar to that of composing—how to communicate the pleasure and excitement of modern music without being patronizing or jeopardizing quality. The New School classes provided one kind of listener; later (at Harvard, for example) Copland would face different audiences. He wrote to Nadia (16 October 1927): "My lectures are going brilliantly. I have already played Oedipus, Création du monde, Hindemith op. 37, etc. If I weren't a composer it would be very amusing. But as it is, it is even difficult for me to give up several months of the year . . . and it is practically impossible to do any concentrated work on composition unless I devote my entire energies to it. . . ." Israel Citkowitz wrote from Paris: "Your lectures are turning out marvellously and in other words you have again proven that it is impossible for Aaron Copland to make a wrong step—almost as impossible for you to make a wrong one as for me to make a right one. . . ." Copland responded by preparing "Lecture IX, The Youngest Generation in America," that included Citkowitz, Antheil, Sessions, Ornstein, and Harris. An undated memo in Marc Blitzstein's papers describes his friend's teaching: "Copland's lecturing, like his written criticism, is notable for a flat undecorated honesty. He is no felicitous phraser, he has little grace of speech, few quips; and sometimes one stops listening. Almost always something important is missed."[5]

In 1938 when Copland taught general music appreciation rather than modern music, his popular course became the basis for his first book. According to the composer, a gentleman came up to him after a lecture one evening and said, "Mr. Copland, I don't know if you know it or not, but you are talking a book. Next year we'll send a girl down here from McGraw-Hill and she'll take down verbatim what you say." At the end of the following year's series, Copland was presented with the basis of *What to Listen For in Music*. The book has been translated into eleven languages, among them Dutch, Egyptian, German, Italian, Persian, Portuguese, Spanish, and Swedish. A revised version was published in 1957.

At the close of 1927, Copland's frustration at not composing was mounting, and he wrote to Boulanger in a tone that was a rare departure from his usual "lucky guy" attitude: the score for "As It Fell Upon a Day" sent to Universal in Vienna had been ignored; the violin pieces sent to Strecker made no impression; and the letter Mademoiselle had suggested he send to Mengelberg remained unanswered. But to balance the bad news, he had a commission from Professor Amédée L. Hettich of the Paris Conservatoire for a "vocalise-étude,"[6] and *Music for the Theatre* was being transformed into a German ballet, *Tragödie im Suden, ein Ballet in Fünf Sätze*. (Copland had met Hans Heinsheimer, from Universal's opera department, in Frankfurt during the ISCM Festival; he suggested the ballet version and proceeded to write the scenario himself.) Copland wrote to Boulanger: "The ballet story is appallingly melodramatic, but the action has been well put to the music, and I have no doubt that the good German opera public will be delighted. The Universal assures me that a production is certain, even possible this season yet. For once, it is pleasant to sit back and watch a formidable organization like the Universal do the unpleasant business of finding performances. . . ."[7] The letter ended with: "I've written no new works, hélas! When I think that 1927 is coming to a close and that I have produced no work signed 1927, I assure you I have a sinking feeling of the heart. It is as if the entire year were wasted. This won't happen again if I can help it." When Copland realized that commitments for 1928 were already filling his calendar, he announced to the New School that he would not teach until the following fall.

Copland kept diaries at various times in his life, primarily when traveling. The only entries of an introspective, personal nature were made between 1927 and 1928. These reflect the more serious side of his personality at that time. Rereading them in 1982, Copland hooted with laughter at their naiveté, but remarked that they still make sense some fifty-four years later:

DEC. 1927: I have two principles of living which seem apparently, and possibly are actually, contradictory. First: everything is good which makes me act otherwise from my normal self. Second: never do anything which betrays my true nature.

The first tells me to get drunk, the second tells me that if I get drunk I betray my true nature.

The ideal would be for my true nature to tell me to leave my normal self. But if it doesn't, should I force it? Thus, the problem.

(Make a list of examples of the first rule and of the second, thus: the first says to live adventurously, the second to live carefully.

The first says experience everything, since all experience is good; the second says experience only that which is admirable and good.)

Tonight it seems to me that I should force myself a little, like one forces a child to take music lessons for the sake of finding any possible latent talent; that is, get drunk twice anyhow if only to prove to myself conclusively that it is not in my true nature to get drunk. (This has other applications!)

My ever-present fear is that by thinking that I know myself, i.e., my *normal* self completely, I may circumscribe whatever latent possibilities I may have.

MAR. 1928: I am anxious above all things to perfect myself. I am bourgeois to the core! This seemingly gratuitous 'perfectionnement' (since I wish it for no reasons of worldly glory or heavenly bliss) comes from an inborn sense of economy, getting the best possible out of my own being. H. is amused when I pass a store and say, "Too bad, they couldn't make it pay." I am anxious to become a more profound person because it supremely satisfies my sense of economy (order) that one being should render the utmost possible profit (good).

Gide says, "Those who differ from me most attract me most." I might have written that. . . . My imagination takes fire when I am given a glimpse of the workings of a being different from myself. Our differences throw into a stronger light my true self.

According to Gerald Sykes, "Gide was close to Aaron's thinking then. He was reading a great deal and was considerably more introverted than he became later. That's why the music of this period had a distinct feeling of introversion. Aaron lived sparsely, almost monastically, and was as unostentatious and undemanding as anyone I've ever met—not like men who have been spoiled by their wives and are used to living much more sumptuously than Aaron ever thought of doing. Composing and reading were most important to him."[8]

Early in the new year Copland began to compose again. He wrote two short pieces for string quartet: *Lento Molto* was paired with an earlier piece for string quartet, *Rondino*, composed in Paris in 1923. *Lento Molto* was not planned as a companion piece to the *Rondino*. Its four short pages of homophonic texture and sustained tranquillity contrast with the earlier work.[9] Since neither piece was long enough to stand on its own, Copland decided to pair them for performance in the spring of 1928. Together they

Manuscript page of the first violin part of a string quartet movement,
recently rediscovered by and dedicated to Vivian Perlis.

have remained as *Two Pieces for String Quartet.* A rescored version for
string orchestra was made during the summer of 1928, and Koussevitzky
presented them at the end of the year in Boston, where critics and audiences received *Two Pieces for String Orchestra* as a minor novelty. The
two pieces, presumably Copland's only works for quartet, have continued
to be programmed in both versions.

But Copland wrote another movement for string quartet, probably during the early part of 1928. The undated parts, carefully copied in the composer's hand, were discovered among the composer's manuscripts at the Library of Congress. The score has not come to light. Mentions of a string quartet movement in correspondence to Boulanger and others refer either to this long-forgotten piece or to the *Lento Molto*. Copland to Boulanger (June 1928): "When I look back at the winter it seems to me that the only real thing accomplished was the fact that I have finished my slow movement for string quartet. I have just made a copy for you because I am most anxious to know what you think of it. Please show it to Roy and to Israel. (I dedicated it to Roy because it was his enthusiasm for the opening phrase which gave me the incentive to finish it.)" *Lento Molto* is indeed dedicated to Harris. Boulanger responded (23 September 1928): "This piece for string quartet is a masterpiece—so moving, so deep, so simple. . . ." About a month later, Harris wrote to Copland, complaining, "Have not received your string quartet dedicated to a 'budding talent.' " The "new" quartet movement is of approximately six minutes duration, in three parts, with an *assez vite* between slow sections. The piece undoubtedly will be performed and published, adding a third work by Copland to the string quartet literature.[10]

Soon after Copland met Roger Sessions in 1926, they began to discuss the need for a concert series to implement the League of Composers presentations. These two most promising young American composers of the twenties were good friends and colleagues for several years. But the original picture of them has been so varnished over by layers of time and events that they are no longer viewed in relation to each other as they once were. Copland and Sessions were to move in such different directions that even they themselves do not recall a time, long ago, when they stood in the same place. But from Sessions' early letters to Copland, the friendship between the two young composers is evident. Sessions' first letter from Paris was written out of enthusiasm for Copland's *Symphony for Organ and Orchestra* and with concern about some of the younger composer's ideas and activities:

This afternoon I heard Nadia play your symphony, and while I am not in the habit of writing this particular kind of letter I can't refrain from giving you a piece of my mind on the subject. First of all the symphony is magnificent, and I was more impressed than I can tell you. While one does not, as you know perfectly well, get everything from a work on one hearing, I did carry away a big impression—a really big one. It was a revelation and a surprise to me—a revelation in an absolute sense, and a surprise, because the other works of yours which

I know did not lead me to share to the full Nadia's opinion of you—an opinion of which I am sure you must be aware and which I need not enlarge upon.

Sessions continued giving Copland a "piece of my mind" for *Music for the Theatre* and for wasting time on propaganda for other young Americans, including himself. Sessions lightly chastised Copland for thinking of himself as a New York figure rather than an international one. Copland responded, and on behalf of *Modern Music* invited Sessions to write an article. Sessions agreed, "on one condition—that you never ask for another!"[11] He thanked Copland for speaking to Koussevitzky and Henry A. Moe of the Guggenheim Foundation in his behalf. This letter and many others that followed were long, affectionate, worrisome, apologetic, and occasionally contradictory. For example (from 25 February 1929), "Would he [Copland] forgive the previous letters? Were they still on speaking terms? . . . Barbara tells me always that, to people who don't know me well, I misrepresent myself, and that what I intend as purely ironic and picturesque emphasis is taken seriously. . . . I would be the last to advise you *seriously* not to take an interest in other people's music for I can see that it is so much a part of you—we are quite different in that way. . . ." Sessions admired Copland's article on jazz in *Modern Music* and expressed a desire to hear the *Piano Concerto*. He was very annoyed with "a female relative" in Boston who had sent reviews, implying that Sessions would be pleased to read unfavorable criticism about a rival.

Barbara and Roger Sessions expected to be in the States from 15 March to 30 April 1927 and hoped to see as much of Copland as possible. It was in that spring and summer that the composers first discussed starting a concert series. Roger, from Florence on 3 September 1927:

> I think your ideas for the young composers' idea are excellent and subscribe to them heartily. . . . I shall hope to be of some use in practice, if not in theory. . . . My ideas at first blush would be to have both kinds of concerts—one or two each season, perhaps, of the most ambitious kind, and several of the smaller kind. . . . I agree that "liberal despotism" is the only possible form of government—with the final accent on the despotism rather than on the liberal; and in my capacity as co-despot I gladly pledge cooperation!

Other matters relating to the concerts were mentioned, such as an age limit of thirty-five for composers to be included. "I have some ideas which I think we had better discuss *viva voce* than try to put within the limits of human sized mail. . . ." Both composers agreed in the meantime to look for financial support. Through Minna Lederman, Copland met Mary Sen-

144

ior Churchill, the wife of an architect, Henry Churchill. She was well-to-do in her own right and about Copland's age, interested in the arts and willing to support an adventurous idea. By mail, Copland and Sessions explored titles for the series. As late as 15 March 1928, only five weeks before the first concert, Sessions wrote jokingly, "the 'Enemies of Music'—suggested by a sort of converse of the old Puritan proverb that Hell is paved with good intentions. . . . Please do not gather from this that I approach the problem in a flippant spirit!" They discussed and discarded "Laboratory Concerts," and finally agreed on "The Copland–Sessions Concerts of Contemporary Music." The timing was ironic, for no sooner was the name chosen than Sessions received the Rome Prize and an American Academy in Rome Fellowship. Not only would he be outside New York, he would be out of the country for most of the concerts; therefore, his position would necessarily be as adviser rather than active co-director. In later years, Copland was convinced that Sessions, always conservative and cautious about the use of his name, was sorry he had agreed to its use for the concert series. It is not entirely true, however, that Sessions "did little more than lend my name," as he has claimed.[12] His letters reveal a fuller involvement and influence than that, although they also reflect an increasing sense of concern over his absentee status, and a devotion and admiration for Copland.

Sessions was teaching at Smith College in Northampton, Massachusetts, in the spring of 1928 before returning to Europe. That March he wrote to Copland:

> . . . you must know how much good it does me to see something of you, and to be in touch with you. It has been the chief compensation and a rather "formidable" one, for a dull and disappointing winter in which many lingering illusions over my native country have disappeared. . . . If ever I had any doubts about your future—and I never did have any serious ones— . . . nothing seems surer to me now; and it is more than a comfort to me to feel that way, when my own future seems to me constantly to be hanging in the balance and or worse. *Yours* is something that I take absolutely for granted, and I have not—for all my doubting nature—had the suspicion of a feeling that I was deceiving myself. Furthermore, you are the only person over here with whom I feel quite myself. . . .[13]

As the time for the first Copland–Sessions concert drew near, even Barbara Sessions helped out by writing the prospectus that appeared in the program. She sent it to Copland from Northampton in draft form for changes and corrections. Letters flew back and forth. Sessions wrote (26

March): "You have my O.K. on everything practical . . . the title seems very good. . . ." Sessions wrote on 30 March: "I trust your judgment entirely. I'm only sorry [Quincy] Porter is the best I can contribute in the way of composers. . . . As to my playing percussion in V.T.'s [Thomson] work I leave that also to you. Your mild surprise took me a little aback, and I don't know that I want to, so to speak, put such a definite seal of approval on this music without knowing it better. . . ." Sessions went after Theodore Chanler for a piece and Copland wrote to George Antheil. Finally, from Sessions to Copland on 5 April: "Your letter sounds as if you had found this thing more work than you had bargained for—I sincerely hope not. I don't object to M.C. [Churchill] and M.L. [Lederman] helping out, but I do think it is a crime if it seriously upsets you—I only know how one undertakes sometimes to do a thing that grows bigger than one would think. . . ."

The first season featured works by eleven American composers with concerts on 22 April and 6 May 1928 at the Edyth Totten Theatre at 247 West 48th Street (later renamed the President Theatre). Neither Copland nor Sessions was represented with music at the first concert. Copland's only performing duty was the percussion part (in place of Sessions) in Thomson's *Five Phrases from the "Song of Solomon."* Sessions had not been able to complete the piano sonata promised for the opening. Copland, with programs already printed and distributed, reprinted them, substituting Carlos Chávez' *Sonata for Piano* (played by Chávez). Thus, reports on the program for the first Copland–Sessions concert have varied through the years, depending on which of the two printed programs was used as the source of information. Sessions was home in Northampton at the time, working desperately to put the *Sonata* into playable condition for the second concert of the series. He wrote to Copland: "Don't *worry* about the *Sonata*. It isn't finished but I *swear* to you it will be ready in time—you can count on it absolutely. Also, I like it. . . ."

Barbara Sessions wrote to Copland from Northampton after the first concert: "We hated not being there. . . . It certainly looks as if things got a splendid send-off and I should think you and Mrs. Churchill would be more than gratified—we thought of you all to be sure, and we shall have to make up for our disappointment by having a marvelous time when we do come. . . ." Sessions' plan was to be in New York from 5 May to 10 May. From Barbara: "Roger wants me to ask you what you intend to do if and when asked to join the League . . . what would we do, Aaron, without your worldly wisdom?—to say nothing of all the other reasons we shall have for

1928

Dear Aaron, —

Thanks for your letter — You don't know how much moral food it did me — I am quite excited, & thinking of nothing but my sonata — it is by far my best work, & has been also a marvelous experience. In very many ways it leaves the symphony far behind. Though it is not as large a work.

Your letter breathes a most exhilarating atmosphere & I am crazy to get to N.Y. — Cheer up, I want as much as you to get the sonata done, & am working from twelve to fifteen hours a day on it. B—

arranges my life perfectly, including recreation — you would be amused — & John Duke has fragments, which he plays marvelously — When I reach N.Y. I will be a nervous wreck, but I will have something to show for it. Incidentally this work is teaching me some method, though I'm far from being the "food machine" that Stravinsky claims he is!

Thanks for the particularly wise letter — & forgive this incoherent one.

R—

...etter from Roger Sessions.

PROGRAM OF THE FIRST
COPLAND-SESSIONS CONCERT
APRIL TWENTY-SECOND AT 8.30 IN THE EVENING

ASSISTING ARTISTS
Radiana Pazmor, Mezzo-Contralto
Ruth Warfield, Violinist   Percy Such, Cellist
Hans Lange, Violinist   Lamar Stringfield, Flautist
Harry Cumpson, Pianist   Guy D'Isere, Clarinetist
John Duke, Pianist   David Swaan, Bassoonist

PROGRAM

SONATA FOR VIOLIN AND PIANO
Allegro energico   THEODORE CHANLER
Lento moderato
Scherzando   Ruth Warfield · Harry Cumpson

THREE PIECES FOR FLUTE, CLARINET
AND BASSOON   WALTER PISTON
Allegro scherzando
Lento
Allegro   Lamar Stringfield · Guy D'Isere · David Swaan

SONATA FOR PIANO   ROGER SESSIONS
Andante · Allegro · Andante · Vivo   John Duke
(played without pause)

FIVE PHRASES FROM THE "SONG
OF SOLOMON"   VIRGIL THOMPSON
For Voice and Percussion   Radiana Pazmor

THREE SONATINAS   CARLOS CHAVEZ
a) Cello and Piano
b) Piano Solo
c) Violin and Piano
Hans Lange · Percy Such · Harry Cumpson

MASON AND HAMLIN PIANO

PROGRAM OF THE FIRST
COPLAND-SESSIONS CONCERT
APRIL TWENTY-SECOND AT 8.30 IN THE EVENING

ASSISTING ARTISTS
Radiana Pazmor, Mezzo-Contralto
Ruth Warfield, Violinist   Percy Such, Cellist
Hans Lange, Violinist   Lamar Stringfield, Flautist
Harry Cumpson, Pianist   Leon Wiesen, Clarinetist
Carlos Chavez, Pianist   David Swaan, Bassoonist

PROGRAM

SONATA FOR VIOLIN AND PIANO
Allegro energico   THEODORE CHANLER
Lento moderato
Scherzando   Ruth Warfield · Harry Cumpson

THREE PIECES FOR FLUTE, CLARINET
AND BASSOON   WALTER PISTON
Allegro scherzando
Lento
Allegro   Lamar Stringfield · Leon Wiesen · David Swaan

SONATA FOR PIANO   CARLOS CHAVEZ
Moderato · Poco mosso · Lentamente · Conciso
(played without pause)   Played by the composer

FIVE PHRASES FROM THE "SONG
OF SOLOMON"   VIRGIL THOMSON
For Voice and Percussion   Radiana Pazmor

THREE SONATINAS   CARLOS CHAVEZ
a) Cello and Piano
b) Piano Solo
c) Violin and Piano
Hans Lange · Percy Such · Harry Cumpson

MASON AND HAMLIN PIANO

Left: Program from the first Copland-Sessions Concert, 22 April 1928, including Sessions' *Piano Sonata. Right:* Replacement program, showing the substitution of Chávez' *Piano Sonata.*

missing you far too much, that alone makes me tremble to think of putting an ocean between us. . . ." After the first concert, Mary Churchill sent clippings to Northampton, and Sessions responded: "At least we received a good deal of attention. Downes has risen 100 percent or more in my estimation—he alone seems to have realized that the event could be of any importance whatever, and his very timidity is a good sign . . . it means, at least, that he is afraid to commit himself too soon. . . . Henderson rather surprised me—he seemed next best, in spite of being an old war horse. . . ."

Both directors were present at the second concert on 6 May. Copland's *Two Pieces for String Quartet* was performed, and two movements of Sessions' still incomplete *Piano Sonata* were played by John Duke. Duke, who was teaching at Smith, recalls that Sessions brought the music to him almost page by page to learn. "But as time went on, and it wasn't finished, Roger was in a terrible state about it and finally decided to just have me play the first two movements with an improvised ending to the second movement. I'll never forget the struggle he had. He used to stay up drinking black coffee, and by the time we went to New York, Roger was about all in. We had to change trains in Springfield, and he had to lie down on the station seat there. But we made it to New York and I actually played the *Sonata* at the concert...."[14] Copland performed in a *Violin and Piano Sonata* by Robert Delaney, a composer favored by Boulanger, and in the Quincy Porter *Quintet*. Richard Buhlig, a well-known pianist who was closely associated with West Coast composers, presented works by Ruth Crawford, Adolph Weiss, and Dane Rudhyar. In writing about the first season, critics pointed out that American composers had not yet found an American sound. Edward Burlingame Hill for *Modern Music* and Paul Rosenfeld both voiced disappointment that despite the "affirm America" movement, the musical works all sounded much like Stravinsky or Schoenberg. Three more seasons of Copland–Sessions Concerts would follow, making a total of ten concerts, eight in New York, and one each in Paris and London. Copland took the presentation of them very seriously, as he did his lecturing, although for many years he has enjoyed telling about the lady who came up to him after a Copland–Sessions concert to say, "Mr. Copland, I just *love* your sessions!"

Roger Sessions[15]

I was enthusiastic about the Copland–Sessions Concerts, but there was nothing I could do because I went to Europe for eight years—three in Florence, three in Rome, and two in Germany. Aaron and I began to move in different directions musically. He wanted to create an American music. I didn't believe in that and don't believe it can be done like that—you create music and if it's genuine and spontaneous music written by an American, why then it is American music. These things have to grow naturally. For me, nationalism is the wrong approach.[16] Anyway, I don't think it did much good. For any composer I admired in the past, nationalism was not an issue. After all, Bach and Mozart were influenced by Italian music— they didn't think of nationalism.

If it is written in places that I studied with Nadia Boulanger, it's not true. I knew and saw her often; furthermore, when I first met her I thought

I would like to study with her, but I was very young and inexperienced and did not know the rest of Europe then. I came to disapprove of Nadia. She was really a businesswoman, not a disinterested musician at all. Nadia was overworking for her students. People don't realize it, but there were musicians who had nothing to do with Nadia Boulanger. And she had some strange ideas about the U.S. She thought it was a young, inexperienced country that did not know its way around and should have a guardian, and that France should be its guide. I soon discovered there were other countries in the world.

In Rome I met Otto Klemperer who said I must come to Germany. He introduced me to all the musicians. In the second year, Hitler came to power, and the Germans became very anti-Semitic, but Klemperer didn't see it. My wife and I saw it very clearly; furthermore, I knew I met Nazis. Each night I had dinner with British newspaper correspondents, and we knew what was going on, but the Nazis didn't dare bother us for the moment. Later I heard I was being watched. I could and did say whatever I chose and am rather proud of that. I went to Florence, my favorite European city, for the first spring festival. It was clear that Hitler and Mussolini were two quite different things—all the Germans I knew went to Florence to hear the festival. I was asked to pick up Alban Berg at the train when he arrived from Austria, and he was asking me what was going on in Germany!

I don't understand how anyone can say there was jealousy between Aaron and myself. How can you be jealous if someone is doing something different than you? If Aaron and I had a dispute, I don't recall it now, so it could not have been very important. I have always liked Aaron very much even though we haven't seen each other often in recent years.

American composers may not have sounded independent in 1928 at the Copland–Sessions Concerts, but for the first time they were taking responsibility for presenting their own music. The concerts gave young composers a confidence that would lead to other performances, as well as to the founding of the American Composers Alliance and the American Music Center and to the establishment of American-based publication and recording companies. With their first season successfully accomplished, the co-directors left town—Sessions for Europe and Copland for his first taste of the American West.

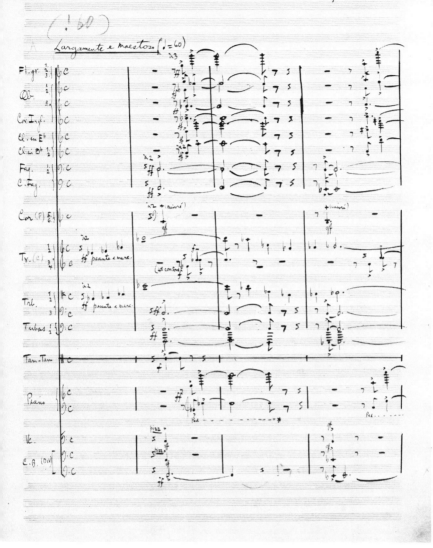

Music for Musicians

1928-1930

I visited Santa Fe, New Mexico, for the first time in the summer of 1928. When in 1977 and 1982 I was invited to participate in the Santa Fe Chamber Music Festival, I could not help but compare the bustling Santa Fe of today with the sleepy old Spanish town I first saw in 1928. I had heard about Santa Fe from artist and writer friends who told me I could find an inexpensive room with a piano there. Santa Fe proved to be the quiet place I needed before going on to Los Angeles to play my *Piano Concerto* at the Hollywood Bowl. I had in mind to compose two works—a trio and an orchestral piece—and I thought I could make headway on both, since the thematic material was already worked out in my head. I even had fragments of the orchestral piece written down and had played them for Roger before leaving New York. During the past season, my activities and responsibilities had been so demanding that I had not been able to find uninterrupted blocks of time needed for composing. I *had* to give lectures to make a living, I was committed to the Copland–Sessions Concerts and to presenting performances of modern music at the New School,[1] and countless other demands made inroads on my time, such as finding support for Israel Citkowitz in Paris. Santa Fe would provide the privacy I so desperately needed. It seemed strange to be away from Paris at this time of year, and I wrote to Nadia (June 1928): "I suppose it is time for me to see America a little, and then of course playing at the Bowl is an excellent introduction to the Pacific Coast. Still, I do miss the rue Ballu very much and I feel very much out of what is going on. Perhaps, during the summer you will be able to find a little time to write me. . . ."

The quiet time alone in Santa Fe would serve another purpose. I had an important decision to make, indeed a crucial one at this time in my career: whether to take advantage of the tempting offers that were coming my way from abroad, or to stay in New York, furthering the causes of American music while continuing my own work. Carlos Chávez[2] wanted me to come to Mexico to play the *Piano Concerto* with the Orquesta Sinfónica de

ORQUESTA SINFONICA MEXICANA

Director, CARLOS CHAVEZ

TEMPORADA 1928-1929

ULTIMO CONCIERTO
EN EL

TEATRO ESPERANZA IRIS
=== EL ===

DOMINGO 3
DE FEBRERO DE 1929, A LAS 11 HORAS

PROGRAMA:

J. L. MARISCAL	SINFONIA
SAINT - SAENS	CONCIERTO EN SI B. PARA VIOLIN Y PIANO
	SOLISTA, SILVESTRE REVUELTAS
AARON COPLAND	MUSIC FOR THE THEATRE
HONEGGER	PACIFIC 231

PRECIOS:

Luneta	$ 2.00
Anfiteatro	„ 2.00
Segundos numerados	„ 1.25
General de Segundos	„ 1.00
Galería numerada	„ 0.75
Galería general	„ 0.50

BOLETOS DE VENTA EN J. F. VELAZQUEZ Y HERMANO, BALDERAS 74;
EDITORIAL CULTURA, ARGENTINA, 5, AGENCIA MISRACHI, AV. JUAREZ, 10.

Wednesday

Dear Aaron

Next Sunday is the first concert. Your work is rehearsing all right. My players are excellent. I am assuring you now a fine performance. For Music for the Theatre I use 8 1st, 8 2nd, 6 Violas, 6 cellos, 4 Basses. I am sure it is well to be like this. I did not want to use full strings that you know are generous in our orchestra. I hope for a great success, you and for me — With love — Carl

Above: Program from Mexico [for] Copland's *Music for the Theatre* [with] the note from Carlos Chávez w[ritten] on the reverse of the program. *Left*: Photograph of conductor [Albert] Coates, actress Norma Shearer, [and] Copland, Hollywood, 1928.

Courtesy Astor, Lenox, Tilden Foundations, New York Public Library, Music Division.

México in Mexico City, and Roger was urging me to try for the Rome Prize. He pointed out that I could win it and thus have all my time for composing, while at home I had to teach and be dependent on uncertain prizes and commissions. My answer was, "What would happen to our concerts?" But Roger did not consider this reason enough not to try for the Rome Prize. Even Israel put in a word for my returning to Europe, writing: "Only some absurd scruples about concerts and duties may keep you in the U.S.A." Nevertheless, sometime during that quiet summer in Santa Fe, my mind was made up. I would stay in New York. I would continue to teach at the New School and to accept lecture engagements. I would direct the Copland–Sessions Concerts. And I would write a major orchestral work for a competition sponsored by RCA Victor that was offering a $25,000 prize to the winner.[3] I wrote to Chávez with apologies and assurances of a long visit to Mexico later and suggested he substitute *Music for the Theatre* for the *Piano Concerto* in his February concert. I wrote to Roger about the Victor competition and my plan to submit a work.

I rested, worked on the *Vocalise*[4] for Professor Hettich in Paris, and practiced for my appearance at the Hollywood Bowl on 20 July. To my amazement, when I stepped off the train in Los Angeles, I was met by manager, president, chairman, photographers, reporters—and two men moving a piano! Someone had cooked up a Hollywood publicity stunt for me to play jazz to the crowds and photographers at the railroad station. I had a heck of a time convincing them that I didn't play jazz, nor was I any good at improvising. I doubt they believed me! I was put up at the Hollywood Plaza Hotel, but had little chance to enjoy the posh surroundings. Not enough rehearsal time had been scheduled for the *Concerto* performance. I wrote to Chávez, "The *Concerto* caused almost a 'skandal'! But it was very amusing to play before the crowd of 17,000 people." After the quiet of Santa Fe, the attention of the press, the radio interviews, and the presence of movie stars was exciting. I was particularly impressed with meeting Charlie Chaplin. After Los Angeles, I spent a week with Henry Cowell in San Francisco. He arranged a reception with members of the New Music Society. They asked to publish "As It Fell Upon a Day" in the *New Music Quarterly* (July 1929), and I invited Henry to send a piece for the next Copland–Sessions Concerts.

After returning East, the remainder of the summer was spent at the MacDowell Colony. Clurman and Gerald Sykes were already there (Sykes had stayed at my place in New York while I was in Santa Fe). I reported to them on the "winning of the West" and got down to concentrated work

on the trio and orchestral piece. Long letters from Roger, who was in Juziers for the summer, were added to those from Israel, Roy, and Nadia. At
first, Roger sent reports on that lopsided triangle, but as the summer pro-
gressed, it seemed that he too became part of the shape of life in Juziers.
One fifteen-page letter from Roger (25 July) ended with a P.S.: "Barbara
reminds me that I could have gotten about $30 from Minna L. for an arti-
cle the size of this letter! . . ." Roger was concerned about Nadia's health.
"She drives to Fontainebleau and back each week, and while she is there
she leads a life which can't help but be a terrific strain—teaching from 7
A.M. till late in the evening without any let-up, even for lunch—she eats a
banana or two at noon apparently. . . . She drives very fast and has a way of
sometimes missing a collision by the skin of her teeth. . . ." Later that
summer, Roger wrote again (19 August): "Nadia is still strange and seems
to have something on her mind that she is working herself to death to forget."

Mademoiselle's friends and students seemed to have no idea of what
was troubling her. I have read criticism of Boulanger for keeping her personal life private. But this was the French way—it would not have been
appropriate for Nadia to confide in her students.[5] Israel described Mademoiselle that summer (11 August 1928): "I'm quite at ease with her now
and our relations are much warmer and closer. She has such a wealth of
feelings and sympathy and emotion and understanding. I'm continually
amazed and am stricken at such a rare fusion of musicianship, intellect,
feeling, intuition, etc. . . ." Whatever was disturbing Nadia, she confided
this much to me at the end of the summer (23 September 1928):

> Have still one head, two hands and even place for affection—unbelievable, is it
> not? But so— And I feel quite miserable—hating unfaithfulness over all and
> with it, lack of courage. But . . . it has to be confessed that after such a year,
> courage is very low, but very! This preludium played—I declare my shame
> killed, and everything already better—Now necessary to proceed with order: . . .
> Terrible not to be able to speak—but you feel, dear Aaron with what an ad-
> miration, an affection these awkward words are going to you. . . .

I stayed at the MacDowell Colony as long as possible, working against
time to finish the trio, knowing that my return to West 78th Street meant
putting it aside again. I returned just in time to deliver the first of my lectures at the New School. This fall, my series was called "Masterworks of
Modern Music," each lecture illustrating a subject or a style of music with
a major work.[6] Looking back at my lecture notes fills me with renewed

wonder and respect for the New School for the opportunity it gave me to explore such topics. These lectures would have been enough to occupy me, but I had several additional commitments: I joined the League of Composers in the fall of 1928, though I was not on the board until 1932, and I was helping to organize the Cos Cob Press, an early effort to assist young American composers to publish music that would not be taken on by established publishers. It was funded by Alma Wertheim. Cos Cob gave composers 50 percent of music sales, rather than the usual 10 percent. Alma and Edwin F. Kalmus, the vice-president, depended on my advice and contacts. While it lasted Cos Cob gave a much-needed boost to American music. In 1938 Cos Cob merged with Arrow Music Press, and in 1956 both catalogues were taken over by Boosey & Hawkes. My own music benefited from Cos Cob, in view of the fact that several of my early works were published by it: the *Dance Symphony, First Symphony, Music for the Theatre, Concerto for Piano and Orchestra, Piano Variations,* and *Vitebsk.*

Thanks to Mary Churchill's help, a small office at 1601 Steinway Hall was rented for the Copland–Sessions Concerts. Henry Cowell and Colin McPhee came to New York for the first concert, 30 December, which included Henry's *Seven Paragraphs for String Trio.* McPhee played Nikolai Lopatnikoff's *Sonatina for Piano,* earlier approved by Roger and Nadia in Paris. John Duke performed Bernard Wagenaar's *Sonata for Piano,* and Marc Blitzstein was represented by *Four Songs for Baritone and Piano,* with texts by Whitman. Roger and I both thought George Antheil deserved further hearing, so we were pleased when he sent his *Second String Quartet.* Roger was in Rome, and his promised set of short piano études did not arrive in time for the concert.

The reaction of the press was distressing; I would not have been troubled by bad reviews—I had seen enough of those—but for the critics to call the music *conservative* was a blow to our purpose of presenting stimulating modern music. Olin Downes dismissed the evening as unmemorable: "Music of such poor, weak, and childish character as to afford no justification for public performance. . . ."[7] Antheil's quartet received a particularly poor press and was viewed as an apology for his earlier and scandalous *Ballet mécanique.* Although Roger and I agreed that we should keep the concerts going, we were both becoming more and more concerned about his absentee status. Roger wrote (17 January 1929), ". . . I have already given the thing—the problem as you state it—a good deal of thought, and have reached certain conclusions—the chief one being that it

Letter from Alma Wertheim, 1930.

Financial statement for the first two
years of the Copland-Sessions
Concerts, compiled by Copland.

would be a great mistake to give them up. My 'moral support' as you so kindly put it has I fear not been a too tangible quantity; I hope to improve it . . . and besides, I have reason to believe that press announcements and similar matters may have looked up since you wrote." Roger was right. The second concert on 24 February stirred up considerably more interest. Included was a rather dissonant *Sonata for Violin and Piano* by the European Alexander Lipsky, three songs by Vladimir Dukelsky (who would become better known as the film music composer Vernon Duke), and Roy Harris' *Piano Sonata*, played by Harry Cumpson. But it was the final work on the program that woke up the audience—Virgil Thomson's *Capital Capitals*.[8] Composed for male quartet with piano accompaniment and an outrageous text by Gertrude Stein, the work struck the audience as hilariously funny. Virgil directed the proceedings from the piano and accepted "bravos" at the end. He described the occasion vividly in his own autobiography.[9] I conveyed my relief to Roger that the critics at least showed some interest in the music, but the situation engendered by his absence was growing increasingly difficult. Roger wrote (22 March 1929):

> The point is simply that I have no means of knowing the situation in any real sense when I am absolutely ignorant of some of the music that is being played. I have as much confidence in you as I would have in anyone; and yet—in spite of the fact that I myself am wholly responsible for this situation—I am beginning to realize the very great inconveniences as well as the risks involved in my being a completely irresponsible partner. I have to all intents and purposes signed a blank page, and sponsored, as a musician and a composer, something for which I have no responsibility at all; and I have no sure means of knowing, as things are now, whether I would be willing to take that responsibility for the works that are played at the concerts.

Roger was also disturbed by the publicity, which included pictures and biographies of us two directors. "I had understood that we were to keep in the background," he wrote, and suggested we meet for a "good leisurely talk in May or June" to go over our policies and plans. When I suggested we plan a Copland–Sessions concert in Paris, Roger answered, "Don't you think it is a little premature; that our concerts have not really established themselves sufficiently in America. . . ." Not wanting to abandon the idea, I responded that I would proceed without using our name.

Nadia agreed that a concert of American music in Paris was a good idea. When Mary Churchill offered to pay expenses, I canceled a third Copland–Sessions concert that was tentatively planned for 7 April in New York. About the title for the Paris concert, I simply wrote Nadia (19 April

1929) that we had changed our minds and decided to call it "Concert d'oeuvres des jeunes compositeurs américains." I still hoped to include Roger and asked Nadia to urge him to agree that his *Three Choral Preludes* be on the program. I wrote to Nadia (19 April 1929):

> I hope you will be willing to play them. I know how busy you are but is it too much to ask you also to play the piano part in Roy's "Sextette"[10] and in my Trio (the Trio is *not* difficult). One more word. Be sure that in the last analysis I leave everything in your hands. Whatever you do I'm certain in advance will be right. Unfortunately I can't be in Paris as soon as I had hoped. Because my orchestral piece is not nearly finished I have put off my sailing until May 29 which should bring me to Paris about June 4.

Mary Churchill was in Paris, and I knew she would help Nadia with arrangements. While Mary was in France, I had the use of her country house in Briarcliff Manor, just outside New York. I made a hasty retreat out of the city and went to work.

Looking back at the past season, I realized that the main event for me had been the premiere of *Vitebsk*. The League of Composers had asked for a new work, offering a performance by no less a pianist than Walter Gieseking and two members of the Pro Arte Quartet, violinist Alphonse Onnou and cellist Robert Maas. The score had been finished at the Mac-Dowell Colony in September, but I was still copying parts two weeks before the concert. Gerald Sykes, who lived nearby and worked downtown, would come by at eight in the morning, pick up the parts I made during the night, and deliver them downtown to where the performers were rehearsing.

Based on a Jewish folk song, the trio has often been cited as my only "Jewish" work. But when I was younger, I had set traditional Hebrew melodies for cello and piano,[11] and in the thirties I made arrangements of some Jewish folk songs that were published.[12] In 1926 and 1932 respectively, Roger Sessions and Virgil Thomson wrote about the Jewish elements in my music.[13] It seems to me that my use of Jewish themes was similar to my use of jazz—Jewish influences were present in my music, even when I did not refer to them overtly. I have often been asked why I wrote "cowboy" music rather than "Jewish" music. I never thought about these things at the time, but it must have been partly because I grew up in the Eastern European tradition and there was no novelty to it. Every American boy is fascinated with cowboys and Indians, and I was no exception. Also, my mother had grown up in the American West. Many artists (writers in particular) have claimed that they work best out of their

Above: Manuscript page from the
sketch score of *Vitebsk.*
Right: Published arrangement of a
"Hora" by Copland.

own experiences. But for me it was not necessary to have an experience in order to compose about it. I preferred to imagine being on a horse without actually getting on one! In any case, I never gave much thought to including or excluding *any* kind of influence from my work. It was always a musical stimulus that got me started, as when I heard the folk theme that the Polish-Jewish author S. Ansky used in his play *The Dybbuk.*[14] It appealed to me just as it had to him. Vitebsk, a small Russian village, was the playwright's home; it was there he had heard and transcribed the tune. It seemed an appropriate title for my trio based on the same tune. Years later when I traveled in the Soviet Union, the Russians were amazed that any composer would name a piece of music after the city of Vitebsk, a large industrial complex resembling Pittsburgh or Cleveland!

The overall nature of *Vitebsk* is basically a dramatic character study. It is a tripartite, slow–fast–slow form. The introductory opening, a series of major and minor triads struck simultaneously on the piano, is followed by resultant quarter-tone intervals that enhance the Hebraic atmosphere of the piece and set the scene for the appearance of the Jewish melody played by the cello, the instrument that continues to maintain a leading role throughout the section. (The cello's deep tone seemed appropriate for the *molto espressivo* I hoped to achieve.) The fast section is a Chagall-like grotesquerie that reaches a wild climax and interrupts itself in mid-course, causing a dramatic pause. The main theme returns in unison two octaves apart played by violin and cello, punctuated by clangorous chords on the piano. A short coda leads to a quiet ending.

The full title of the trio is *Vitebsk (Study on a Jewish Theme)*, and it was my intention to reflect the harshness and drama of Jewish life in White Russia. So it did not surprise me when the work was described as "hard," "dry," and "dissonant." Performers and audiences have told me that they find *Vitebsk* a strangely moving work. Musically, I knew I had found something that I intended to explore further as soon as I finished the orchestral piece, which would be titled *Symphonic Ode. Vitebsk* has been performed frequently (often with me at the piano), and always more successfully than at the premiere, 16 February 1929, at Town Hall where my trio was played after a *Sonata* by Karol Rathaus and before a work by Mario Castelnuovo-Tedesco. The League's audiences knew what to expect—they came to these concerts to hear contemporary music. But, according to Lehman Engel, who was present at the premiere:[15]

> It resembled nothing less than a Mack Sennett comedy. The cellist was heavy-set (to put it politely), and as he came on stage carrying his large instrument, he

knocked over the violinist's stand. While bending over to retrieve the music, he dropped his cello, and it knocked over the violist's stand. There was music all over the floor. Finally, when they were seated and ready to begin, a cello string broke with a loud noise! It was hilarious. For some reason, the nature of the piece and its strange name continued to strike the audience as funny! Laughter was mixed with applause at the end.

This was hardly the reception I had anticipated. I decided to give *Vitebsk* another hearing at the upcoming Paris concert.

A month before my sailing date, I had to face the fact that I would not be able to finish the *Symphonic Ode* in time for the RCA Victor competition. This was to be my first big orchestral piece since the jazz-inspired *Concerto*. I was attempting something different, and the work was not proceeding as quickly as I had anticipated. Does anyone but the composer, I wonder, realize the sheer physical labor involved in writing down all those notes and musical symbols in a way that will eventually translate into sound by a large symphony orchestra in a concert hall? This phase of composing has little to do with creativity or inspiration, and each composer has his own method of getting the job done. For me it went this way: over a period of time, I made sketches, jotted down fragments, and when the time was right, arranged these fragments into their inevitable order. You must shape the material so that it is logical—just those notes and no others are needed to complete the thought. You eliminate, you revamp. In short, you seek out the inevitable conclusion of what you started by showing it *has* to go one way and no other. That's what I mean by inevitability. I would make piano sketches and polish and refine them with the appropriate instrumental sounds in my mind along the way. (I would occasionally make jottings for the instrumentation on the piano score.)

A long symphonic work such as the *Ode* naturally presented more problems than a short piece. The *Ode* in its original version was to be scored for a Mahler-like oversized orchestra with eight horns, five trumpets, three trombones, and two tubas. I was not able to finish the orchestral score before leaving for Europe. It would have been a shame not to submit anything to the competition, so I searched my scores for a substitute. Since most of the ballet *Grohg* was unpublished, I found considerable usable material other than *Cortège macabre* and *Dance of the Adolescent* that had been taken from it earlier. By working nights and days for weeks, I extracted three dances from the ballet score, gave it the title *Dance Symphony,* and delivered the score to the competition officials just in time for their end-of-May deadline.

Exhausted, I left Mary Churchill's house. This experience had made me more than ever determined to find more time for composing. The way was suddenly opened by an offer from my well-to-do cousin Percy Uris to support me for a full year with no strings attached! These were lean and hungry years, and although I found it somewhat degrading to accept money this way, I knew that I could not live as a full-time composer by commissions alone. Percy asked me to think it over—but I did not have to consider my answer for long. The judges for the Victor competition decided that none of the works submitted warranted the full $25,000 prize, so they divided it into four awards: $5,000 each to Louis Gruenberg, Ernest Bloch, and myself, with a $10,000 prize to Robert Russell Bennett, who had submitted two compositions. I was more than satisfied to have won the $5,000, which would keep me going for a year, and I asked Percy if his offer could begin a year later, in 1930. Considering his generosity, I am somewhat embarrassed to see now what I wrote then (16 May 1929): "My only objection is that you have no personal conviction about the value of the stuff I turn out, but must take it on hearsay. When a person has a real appreciation of the product I turn out, it is easier for me to accept the wherewithal for turning out that product. . . ." Percy graciously agreed to my proposal. I left Mary Churchill's house knowing that my financial future was secure, and with the anticipation of a rest on shipboard and a reunion with friends in Paris, I felt like a caged animal set free!

In May 1929 Mary wrote that she had met with Nadia in Paris and was terribly impressed with her and all the trouble she was taking for the June concert: "Boulanger reports to me of 'great complications.' I am sure there have been terrific ones, far beyond my knowledge. I feel hopeful that your presence will dissipate them. Nothing has been said about defraying preliminary expenses. But since I am departing and to forestall any possible needs, I have just deposited $800 in your name at the G.T. Co. . . ." I arrived to find that Nadia had organized everything beautifully. The Salle Chopin was reserved (about 500 seats), and Roy was rehearsing performers for his work. I waited as long as possible for music to arrive from Roger, but finally the program had to be decided without him. Nadia, who had decided not to perform, went all out to make the occasion a gala event by inviting the French musical and social elite and the many Americans studying and visiting Paris that spring. Mary Churchill returned to Paris in time to attend the concert with Minna, Israel, Roy, and Marc Blitzstein. The music was all new to Paris except for Virgil's songs. The reviews were mixed: Virgil got high marks from several critics, including the *Interna-*

tional Herald Tribune, while Roland Petit in *La Revue musicale* praised my pieces. Far more important than individual reactions was the recognition by French critics and an international audience that America had composers ready to be heard in Paris, the artistic capital of the world.

It seemed a good idea to be close to Nadia while working on the *Ode*, so for the summer of 1929, Israel and I took rooms in Juziers chez Mme Blondel. My work was finally going along well. When Roger wrote from Switzerland inviting me to visit and sending train schedules, I had to refuse. On 12 July he suggested we take a trip together ("bring old clothes"), and I responded by suggesting we meet in Paris in September, before my return to the States, to discuss plans for the third Copland–Sessions Concerts. Roger replied, jokingly, "Apparently you will stay in that little mudhole instead of coming to be near us!"

Koussevitzky had invited me (and several other composers) to present a new symphonic work for the fiftieth anniversary of the Boston Symphony Orchestra in 1931. When I remarked that I intended an expanded instrumentation for this work, he assured me I could have as many brass and percussion players as I wanted—after all, Koussevitzky pointed out, this was to be a special occasion, and he emphasized, "They vill expect, they vill expect!" The Boston Symphony anniversary celebration would be a perfect occasion for the premiere of the *Symphonic Ode*. I had been striving for something grand and dramatic in this work. Composed over a two-year span that was a transitional period for me, the *Ode* is a transitional work—a summing up as well as a looking ahead. Perhaps this was my way of announcing, at about the time of my thirtieth birthday, that I was grown up. The *Ode* resembles me at the time, full of ideas and ideals, introspective and serious, but still showing touches of youthful jazz days, reflections of a Jewish heritage, remnants of Paris (Boulanger's *la grande ligne*), influences of Mahler (the orchestration) and Stravinsky (motor rhythms). Looking ahead, one can hear in the *Ode* the beginnings of a purer, non-programmatic style, an attempt toward an economy of material and transparency of texture that would be taken much further in the next few years in the *Piano Variations*, the *Short Symphony*, and *Statements for Orchestra*. In the *Ode*, a twenty-minute one-movement composition, I was attempting to write a piece of music with an unbroken logic so thoroughly unified that the very last note bears a relation to the first. I used a two-measure blues motif (from my *Nocturne* for violin and piano of 1926) as the musical basis of all five sections. This budding interest in formal structure would become more absorbing in my subsequent works, along with a continuing fascination for polyrhythmic experimentation.

The title *Symphonic Ode* is not meant to imply connection with a literary idea. It is not an ode *to* anything in particular, but rather a spirit that is to be found in the music itself. When questioned about what this spirit was supposed to be, my response (as quoted in several contemporary newspaper interviews and program notes) was as follows: "What that particular spirit is, is not for me to say. In another connection, André Gide has well expressed my meaning: 'Before explaining my book to others, I wait for them to explain it to me. To wish to explain it first would be to restrain its meaning prematurely, because even if we know what we wish to say we cannot know if we have said *only* that. And what interests me especially is what I have put into my book without my own knowledge.' "[16] The exploration of the unconscious in Gide's writings was one of the influences moving me toward a style in which my music was to stand as pure and absolute, limited in no way by a programmatic or extra-musical connotation.

I wrote an explanation of the complicated meters in the *Ode* on the title page of the sketch-score:

Version for the conductor:	7/8	4/8	9/8	10/8	12/8
to be beat:	3	4	4	4	4

I had even included a short piano piece in 10/16 rhythm.[17] These complicated rhythms and frequently changing tempi caused Koussevitzky and the orchestra players great difficulty. Since most of the rhythms could be beat in 4/4, they could not understand why I had not *written* them in 4/4! After the first rehearsal, Koussevitzky informed me that the men could not play the *Ode* as written. I laughed at the notion that these were difficult rhythms and told Koussevitzky that there was nothing to it. He replied: "Come up to Boston and take over the rehearsal yourself. For me, the orchestra has been able to play only three bars of the piece in a full hour of rehearsal." I was reluctant to make changes in the score two weeks before the scheduled premiere, so I went to Boston, and Koussevitzky turned a rehearsal over to me. I described the incident in a letter to Israel (29 May 1930):

> I finally heard the 'Ode'! I conducted it myself one morning at a rehearsal in Boston while Koussevitzky listened from the auditorium. I only really heard the slow parts, the fast parts were ruined by being played too slow. The end sounds gloriously. It was a revealing experience. The upshot was that I have for all time

a obra vigorosa del mpositor Copland

Por *JOSE BARROS SIERRA*

opland pertenece a la nue-
ción de músicos america-
preocupación máxima con-
libertarse de las influen-
ionales con el fin de crear
a que sea genuinamente
. Con una firme educa-
al, hecha parcialmente en
arón Copland, músico de
nto con un grupo de jó-
positores, entre quienes
tran Roger Sessions, Roy
rgil Thomson, Henry Co-
uños otros, está logrando
o imponer su música en
americanos y europeos,
en un principio con hos-
los tradicionalistas, son
te aceptados estos nue-
sitores por un considera-
iel público y por las prin-
antaciones sinfónicas de
Unidos. Buena prueba de
es el hecho de que la
sinfónica de Boston, diri-
Conseulzizky haya sido la
a la "Oda Sinfónica" que
avez nos dió a conocer en
concierto de la Orquesta
le México. Todos estos sí-
positores se hallan unidos
piración idéntica, no obs-

tante las grandes diferencias tem-
peramentales que existen entre ellos,
y ahora parecen haber entablado
estrechas relaciones con los nuevos
músicos de México. Este intercam-
bio no puede menos de resultar be-
néfico para ambos grupos, y también
para esta nueva música que empie-
za a surgir del Continente y que
cuenta ya con muy distinguidos ex-
ponentes.

Para completar esta obra de
cooperación continental, quisiéramos
también conocer a los nuevos compositores de Sud América, entre los
cuales existen ya nombres tan jus-
tamente conocidos como los del uru-
guayo Fabini y el brasileño Villa-
lobos.

Aaron Copland no era desconocido
de nuestro público antes de ejecu-
tarse su "Oda Sinfónica". En diver-
sas ocasiones y particularmente en
una reciente audición del Conservatorio, se habían ejecutado obras su-
yas. Y hasta el compositor mismo
interpretó en el Teatro Orientación
sus Variaciones para piano. Pero
esta última obra suya, es segura-
mente, junto con las Variaciones, la
más acabado, lo más personal y le

(Sigue en la Página 8a, Columna Primera)

Da. Carmen R. C. de Amor
Da. Adela S. de Cárdenas
Da. Margarita S.
. Carolina Amor
. Ma. Luisa Lópe
ía
. Josefa Pimentel
Carlos Prieto
. G. Conway
Eduardo Mestre G.
rto V. Pesqueira
César R. Margáin ---
Alejandro Quijano, Presidente

UNA OBRA VIGOROSA DEL COMPOSITOR...

(Viene de la cuarta plana)

más perfecto que Copland ha pro-
ducido hasta ahora. Magnífica es

esta "Oda Sinfónica", que acusa una
firme orientación en el joven compositor. En un principio Copland,
como otros muchos compositores,

aprovechó el jazz como elemento di-
recto en sus obras. El deseo de no
repetirse y una concepción más am-
plia del arte musical, han hecho que
Aaron Copland haya prescindido de
ese procedimiento, con lo cual su
música ha ganado mucho en impor-
tancia y posibilidades. Difícil como
es esta obra en donde la más gran-
diosa solemnidad alterna con la li-
gereza intrascendente, nuestra Orquesta supo darle una excelente in-
terpretación, a la que contribuyó
principalmente, el Director, Carlos
Chávez, cuya fuerte personalidad ha
adquirido en los dos últimos concier-
tos, un extraordinario relieve.

Salvador Ordóñez Ochoa, nuestro
excelente pianista, nos ofreció una
versión admirable del Concierto de
Tcherepnine. Este artista volvió a
triunfar decisivamente, y esperamos
que la entusiasta acogida que le tri-
butó el público habrá de estimular-
lo a presentarse con más frecuen-
cia en audiciones públicas. La obra
de Tcherepnine, es de las que ofre-
cen grandes posibilidades de luci-
miento a un artista de experiencia,
como lo es Ordóñez, quien contó,
además, con una eficaz colaboración
de Carlos Chávez y de la Orquesta.

También escuchamos "La siesta de
un fauno" de Claudio Debussy, en
una versión excelente, y "Escalas"
del francés Jacques Ibert, que aun-
que menos cuidadosamente inter-
pretado que las anteriores obras no
dejó de gustar por su colorido bri-
llante y sugestivo.

José BARROS SIERRA

F.

new Aaron Copland belongs to the
generation of American musicians
whose principal preoccupation
is to free themselves from
traditional influences with
the idea of creating a genuinely
American music. With a full
musical education, made
partially in Europe, A. C.,
musician of 31 years, together
with a group of composers,
among whom are Roger
Sessions, Roy Harris, Virgil
Thomson, Henry Cowell and others
have little by little gotten
their music performed in
American and European music
centers ...... the proof is

that this Ode was first performed by
the Boston Symphony under Roussevitzky
A. C. was not known to our
lic before the performance of the Ode, but
work, with his Variations is the most finished
and perfect that he has written to date
is Ode is magnificent and shows a firm
ection in the composer etc.

One of several newspaper reviews of the *Symphonic Ode* sent by Copland
to his parents from Mexico City.

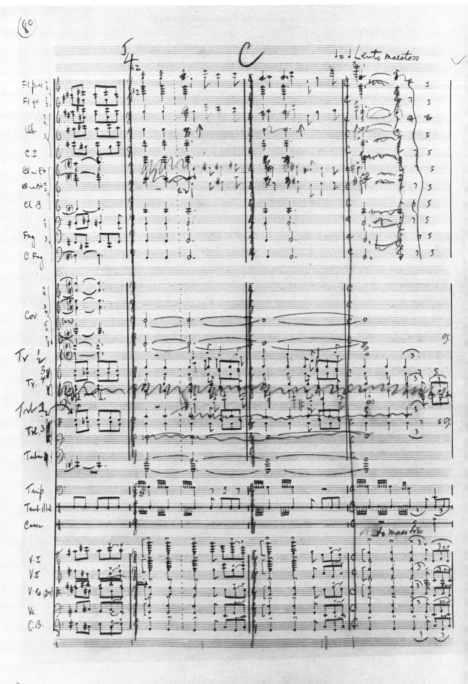

Manuscript page from the revised *Symphonic Ode*.

given up trying to make music look on paper what it actually sounds like. Applied to the Ode it means that I must completely rewrite the barring of the fast parts throughout. I'm working on it now and have discovered how much easier certain sections might have been written. For example, one part which originally had 13 changes of time—3/4, 7/8, 5/8 etc.—is now entirely 4/4. I never believed it could be done till I tried. So that not a note of the piece will be changed but it will look entirely different on paper. When I think of the loss of time and money (the parts must be completely recopied and recorrected) I could weep. On top of this, I played it at the piano for Hertzka, head of Universal Ed, who happened to be here at Alma's one night, and when he heard it was scored for a Mahlerian orchestra he advised her against publishing it. (Not that she'll take his advice.) "Why you're crazy man," says he, "there are not ten orchestras in all Europe that can supply 18 brass instruments." This darling 'Ode' seems to be having a hard time in a cruel world.

After the rehearsal in Boston, I returned to New York and wrote to Koussevitzky (27 March 1930): "Cher ami, May I suggest that the premiere of the *Symphonic Ode* be postponed to the next season in order that I can revise the notation further." Probably relieved, Koussevitzky agreed, and the journalists had a field day writing about the Copland score that was so modern it could not be played even by the Boston Symphony Orchestra. I was questioned about it constantly. But actually, the changes were minor revisions in notation merely to simplify the parts for the musicians and the conductor. After the *Ode* was finally heard in Boston on 19 February 1932, Koussevitzky conducted it in New York (3 March). Paul Rosenfeld and H. T. Parker of the Boston *Transcript* reviewed it favorably, describing it as "grand," but Lawrence Gilman of *The New York Times*, previously an admirer, was disappointed in a work he characterized as "impotent and unrewarding." Audiences were disturbed by what they considered dissonance. Nonetheless, I have always regarded the *Symphonic Ode* as an important work. I tried hard for something there, and I feel that I succeeded in what I attempted. As was my custom, at the end of the conductor's score (eighty-six ink manuscript pages with Koussevitzky's blue pencil markings) I inscribed the places and dates of completion: "Königstein, Germany–New York 1927/Santa Fe–Peterboro 1928/Briarcliff Manor–Juziers–NY 1929." The *Symphonic Ode* had not been easy to compose, and it was difficult to perform, particularly at a time when orchestral performers were not trained to play rhythms that have since become standard. Kirkpatrick admired the piece and made a two-piano arrangement that we played together several times.[18] John recalls one such occasion:

Roy Harris invited Aaron and me to play the Ode in my two-piano version. It was about 1935 in Princeton at the Westminster Choir School. I had done an original and a revised version. I was fond of the original which was shorter. Somehow, we got our signals crossed, and I started out on the shorter version, while Aaron took the longer one. Of course, we discovered it right away. Aaron, fortunately, could improvise in the style of Copland, but it was a traumatic experience![19]

After Marc Blitzstein heard us, he commented: "It is strangely richer in the 2 piano transcription than in its original form. . . ." Carlos Chávez conducted the *Ode* on 18 November 1932 during my first visit to Mexico City. I wrote to Koussevitzky about the Mexican orchestra (13 November 1932): "What they lack in technique is made up with love in their Latin-American way. . . . I only realize now on rehearing the *Ode* to what an extent it is inextricably bound up in my mind with you and the Orchestra and that unforgettable week when it was first brought to life. . . ." After the Mexican performance, the *Ode* was not heard again until 1946, when the Juilliard Orchestra took it up under Thor Johnson's direction.

Koussevitzky and I were both disappointed that the *Ode* was so rarely performed. At the time of the Juilliard concert, I contemplated a revision. The opportunity to undertake one came along in 1955, when the Boston Symphony Orchestra and the Koussevitzky Music Foundation offered a commission to honor the seventy-fifth anniversary of the orchestra's founding. Since Koussevitzky had always held the *Symphonic Ode* in high regard, it seemed appropriate to prepare a new version of the work he had introduced twenty-five years earlier. The overall shape and character remained unaltered, but, for practical reasons, the size of the orchestra was reduced and further notation changes were made of the difficult rhythms. (They are still not child's play. At a pre-eightieth birthday celebration in June 1980, when the New York Philharmonic invited me to conduct the *Ode*, some of the players behaved as though they were on vacation, and it came as a surprise to them that Copland's old *Ode* still made them sit up and work!) Changes in the revision were as follows: certain pages that seemed excessively bony were filled out with fuller textures; the opening and closing sections originally written quite high for brass and strings were lowered; completely new measures were substituted only at the start of the 7/4 section leading to the ending; three pages that had been cut from the end of the slow section at the time of the premiere were restored. The revised *Symphonic Ode* is dedicated to the memory of Serge and Natalie Koussevitzky. It was first performed under the baton of Charles Munch in

Boston, 3 February 1956. I cannot say that the revised version led to many more performances than the original, and it was not until 1973 that a recording was made by the London Symphony Orchestra, myself conducting.

At the end of the summer of 1929, when I was leaving France, one opinion was most important to me. I arrived at my stateroom on the *Aquitania* and found a letter from Nadia:

> How happy I would be if I could express what your Ode brought me as feeling of greatness, of power, of deepness—but you know my struggles with words &—I am quite miserable! This time more than ever, I have understood who you are, what you come to say, & how you are ready to give it a definite form. The clarity is still more astonishing when one thinks how complex is the language—& the work is in my head as if I had heard it many times & carefully studied it. I am so happy. You know what admiration I always have had for you—what confidence—But such a work is however a surprise—& such a moving one. Shall never forget the progression leading to the end, so magnificent—& so many details which now sing in my memory forever I suppose. Why would you ever speak to people—if they love your music, how well they know and love you— Will not try to explain—you know better than myself what I mean—(could you not when orchestrated, send the sketch—I should like so much to speak of the work).

Although it was the height of the Depression when I returned to New York from France that fall, the recent economic disaster did not have an immediate effect on my own situation. I was accustomed to living on very little and owned nothing of value except my piano and scores. Not wanting to pay rent on an apartment while away from the city, I had put these in storage and had given up my apartment. My Uris cousins owned real estate, and since there were many apartments empty in New York during the Depression, they offered me one in the Montclair Hotel on Lexington Avenue at 49th Street. Once settled, I resumed my lectures at the New School. Roger wrote from Italy with recommendations and scores for inclusion in the third season of our Copland–Sessions Concerts, scheduled for February, March, and April 1930. Roger's determination to take more responsibility for programming stimulated him to search for new talent among young Europeans and the Americans living in Europe. The Copland–Sessions Concerts are often, and correctly, described as an early attempt to support American composers; however, as I review the programs for the third season, I am struck by the wide range of nationalities represented.

The first concert, on 9 February 1930 at Steinway Concert Hall, featured songs by an eighteen-year-old Italian, Nino Rota, then studying at the Curtis Institute. (Roger was responsible for sending these, which he found "fresh, genuine and musical.") Also included were the young Englishman Jeffrey Mark, Robert Russell Bennett, Vladimir Dukelsky, Robert Delaney, and Henry Brant. Brant was only seventeen years old, recently arrived from Canada, highly recommended by Henry Cowell, and introduced to me by my former piano teacher, Clarence Adler. The second concert, on 16 March, featured "older" composers: Theodore Chanler (*Sonata for Violin and Piano*), Charles Griffes (*Piano Sonata*, played by Jesús María Sanromá), Leo Ornstein (*Three Moods, Six Poems, Two Dances*, performed by Ornstein), Chávez (*Sonata* played by Sanromá), and my *Vitebsk* (Clarence Adler as pianist). Roger wrote (11 April): ". . . I am delighted that the concerts are going so well, and am sure the last one will be excellent with Fitelberg & Israel & Roy, it ought to—I don't know Roy's Quartet, but I hear excellent things about it . . . & wish I could hear it . . . I am delighted that Bedford is proving itself good for you. . . ." Roger had been responsible for finding Jerzy Fitelberg's *Second Piano Sonata* and songs by Jean Binet, which were sung by Ethel Codd Luening. Kodály's Hungarian pupils Pál Kadosa and Istvan Szelanyi gave additional international flavor, as did a work by the Hungarian Imre Weisshaus. The critics praised Roy's *String Quartet*, but in general, the press gave little attention to the series. However, we had good audiences and a faithful list of subscribers who paid a dollar at each concert for any seat in the house.

The "Bedford" referred to by Roger was the village of Bedford in New York, where I had rented a small house on Hook Road. I left New York City on 1 January 1930 with my lectures finished and the *Ode* orchestration complete. I was most anxious to work on a piano piece that had been in my mind for some time. Gerald Sykes was writing a book and was also in need of a quiet place, so he came to Bedford with me. Only the Copland–Sessions Concerts and the most necessary trips took us from Bedford Village that winter and spring. The Depression was beginning to limit out-of-town lecture recitals. The only one that season was at the Arts Club of Chicago (6 April) on "The Younger Generation of American Composers"—Sessions, Harris, Antheil, Weiss, Thomson, and Copland. That winter in Bedford I became closer to Gerald. I was always close to Clurman, but he was having a love affair during this time and developing a whole new set of friends who believed in him fervently. I wrote to Israel (29 May 1930): "Harold's on his way to being one of the really important critics in America," and continued, "I am totally absorbed with the new piano piece and pleased with my progress. . . . For the moment it is called 'theme and variations.' It's a new form for me and lends itself beautifully to my particular kind of development from a single germ. But it needs time to fully flower and won't be done probably until the end of the summer. . . ."

Gerald Sykes[20]

Aaron was driving the first time we went to Bedford. There was a terrible snowstorm, and we came face to face with the Kenseco Dam—a very disturbing experience! But we were put straight and went on to Bedford Village. Aaron has often said that he does not like to compose with anyone around, but perhaps this was different because I am a writer, not a musician. I worked upstairs in the house that we rented together, and I knew from past experience in his loft that listening to him compose did not upset me. Aaron was terribly systematic in his preparation for this piano piece. He brought "tons" of music with him and began by playing works from as far back as the fifteenth century, then on to piano pieces by Mozart, Haydn, and others. As time went on, Aaron moved into piano works by Brahms and Schumann. He developed an affection for Liszt, and I recall his admiration for Liszt's enormous technical skill. Meanwhile, he was making notes while familiarizing himself very systematically with a great deal of piano literature. It was an education for me! We discussed the Variations *almost note by note—I think that was the main reason Aaron dedicated it to me. And maybe he also wanted to thank me for my patience. But it wasn't patience at all. Something special was happening. I was seeing Aaron in an inspired moment, and yet he was tranquil and even-tempered, even though he was pressured by time and responsibilities. I lived with the* Piano Variations *for months. It was a wonderful experience—Aaron at his best.*

From the start, my first major piano piece, the *Piano Variations,* had a "rightness." The piece flowed naturally and never seemed to get "stuck" as the *Ode* had, although I worked on it for about two years, off and on. After a concentrated period of composing, I would often find it beneficial to put a piece aside for a while. My critical faculty flowed stronger when I was composing than at other times, and such breaks served to refresh me and to renew my sense of objectivity. Composers vary on this—some like to work all in one fell swoop. My method is slower and perhaps safer, since it leaves less chance of falling too much in love with what one is doing. If a composer's critical instincts are in good shape, the slower approach seems to have more possibility for lasting results.

The *Piano Variations*, eleven minutes in length, consists of twenty variations and a coda. It was not composed in the consecutive order of its finished state. I am told that this is at odds with what I have written about the piece—that each variation is meant to develop organically from the previous one and all contribute to a carefully constructed whole. While this is so, it is also true that I worked on the variations individually, not knowing exactly where or how they would eventually fit together. I cannot explain this contradiction. One fine day when the time was right, the order of the variations fell into place. That time was not to come until after we left Bedford Village for Yaddo, the beautiful estate in Saratoga Springs, New York, that had been endowed as an artists' colony, where Gerald, Clurman, and I had been invited to spend the summer of 1930. It was there I derived, from the sixty-two pages of sketches I had carried with me to Yaddo, the seventeen-page score of the *Piano Variations*.

bei Strub
uhlandstr 3
Berlin - Charlottenburg
Nov 10

Dear Miss Stein, —

The proposed concert I mentioned to you
at Pillignin has worked out. The British Music Society
has agreed to sponsor a concert of American chamber
music on Dec 16 at Aeolian Hall. Your Capital Capitals
will be sung by the Tudor Singers with Virgil coming
from Paris to play his own accompaniment. I think that
assures a good performance. Other items on the program
are Sessions' Piano Sonata, my Piano Variations, Carlos
Chavez Sonatina, Citkowitz's Songs to texts of Joyce, and
very probably Freddy's Sonata for Oboe and Clarinet. I expect
Freddy will come to London to hear his piece ~~who~~ — it will be
his debut as composer, you know.

It occurred to me that there might be people in London
who ~~would~~ would not hear of the concert through the ordinary
channels, but who would be glad to hear the Capitals
if they knew they were being given. If you know of any
such, I'd be glad to have their names and addresses and
will see to it that notices are sent them. Any other suggestions you might have for the furthering of the concert would
be welcome.

I'm sorry to say that I wont be able to pass through
Paris on the way to London. I suppose its too much to hope to
see you in London.

Kind regards for Miss Toclas

Sincerely
Aaron Copland

Yaddo and Mexico

1930-1932

Y addo[1] became so much a part of my life that I tend to forget how strange the name sounds to those not familiar with it. In fact, the story behind Yaddo is a strange and tragic tale resembling an opera in which all the main characters mysteriously expire before the final curtain. In 1881 a wealthy and handsome young couple, Katrina and Spencer Trask, purchased a five-hundred-acre property for a summer home in Saratoga Springs, a town with the reputation of a very elegant resort. The Trasks restored the original house and grounds. This couple—so idealistic, liberal, and generous in their dedication to the arts—was stalked by tragedy. Their first son died in infancy, and the house at Yaddo burned to the ground. Soon afterward a young daughter, overhearing her parents describe their lives as "shadowed," which she could not pronounce, called the place "Yaddo," and the name stuck. The Trasks built a Gothic-style mansion on the site of the old house and several smaller buildings and beautiful gardens. But tragedy struck again when the daughter and a younger son died. The parents never recovered from this terrible blow: Katrina Trask fell ill and spent the rest of her life as an invalid; Spencer Trask suffered financial reverses in 1909 and was the only person killed in a freak train accident. About ten years before his death, Spencer and Katrina Trask made plans to endow Yaddo as a retreat for creative artists. Its doors were opened to guests in 1926.

When Clurman met me at the Saratoga railroad station in July 1930, he looked very inhibited, having already received a note from Elizabeth Ames, executive director of Yaddo, requesting that he not monopolize my time! Actually, few rules were imposed on anyone, and we had the privacy necessary for ideal working conditions. When Mrs. Ames had a suggestion or criticism, her custom was to leave a blue note in the appropriate mailbox. Those of us who were at Yaddo during the early years have been heard to quote a South American composer who visited Yaddo: "Watch out, or you get blue in the box!" I described my turret studio to Israel: "It is the perfect setting for an outdoor performance of the Tower Scene in 'Pelléas.' I am working extraordinarily well because of it. For the rest, one lives like a wifeless bourgeois—eats well, sleeps in a soft bed, and relaxes in cushioned chairs."

Teddy Chanler arrived and I played parts of the *Ode* for him, but I was still keeping the *Variations* to myself. When I wrote to John Kirkpatrick about the piece, calling it "Thematic Variations," he responded, advising me to find a better title. I wrote back, "I should like to call them like Bach did the 'Goldberg Variations'—but thus far haven't been able to think up a good one." Jottings on pencil sketches indicate that I was considering several titles: "Melodic Variations, Twenty Melodic Variations, Thematic Variations, Fantasie on an Original Theme, Variations for Piano, Variations on a Theme, Chaconne, Declamations on a Serious Theme, Theme and Variations." I worked steadily on the piece with only one trip away on 9 August to perform my *Piano Concerto* at Lewisohn Stadium in New York, Albert Coates conducting. (Israel Citkowitz had returned from France, and he met me for a reunion and to attend the concert.) Returning to Yaddo, I roamed the magnificent grounds and began to dream of a festival that might be established there. What had started with the Copland–Sessions Concerts in an attempt to promote the younger generation of composers, I hoped might continue at Yaddo. I always thought of myself as part of a group effort; now it seemed I was to be the ringleader. When I approached Mrs. Ames with the idea for a festival of contemporary American music, she was not unenthusiastic and promised to bring the matter to Yaddo's board of directors.

I did not return to New York until the beginning of November 1930, just in time to begin my lectures. Roger had been visiting his family in Massachusetts all summer and was anxious to discuss our programs for the next Copland–Sessions Concerts. After we met, he sent a letter from shipboard as he left for Europe (29 November 1930): "Our visit was quite perfect in every respect. Among the most important things for me was that I felt that the Copland–Sessions friendship prospered—I am specially happy about that...." Two hundred people had enrolled for my New School lectures, and I was teaching Herman Chaloff privately. Figuring my basic expenses at $35 a week, I spent $12 for a room (this fall at the Hotel Lafayette); $15 for food; and $8 for secretarial work—I had to take an extra job that paid $5 for three hours of judging music applicants for the New School. I was also practicing the *Piano Variations* for its premiere on a League of Composers program scheduled for 4 January 1931. The only concert pianist I felt could play the *Variations* at that time was Walter Gieseking, who had participated in the premiere of *Vitebsk*. But he was "not available"; I thought perhaps he had had enough of my modern music. Later, Gieseking wrote from Berlin (22 June 1931):

> During the last week I found time to try out your Variations. This composition is very interesting and most original, but I do not know an audience which would accept such crude dissonances without protesting, except perhaps the League of Composers people in N.Y. and some of the group of the ISCM. I am sorry that I must say that I do not see any possibility of playing your Variations. . . . I am sure you will understand that a work of such severity of style is not possible among the normal type of concert-goers.

But I was pleased to be playing the piece myself. The *Variations* filled a special niche as the first of my works where I felt very sure of myself; I knew that if someone else had written a piece using the same materials, it would have evolved quite differently. Moreover, I knew how difficult it would be to explain my intentions to another pianist. On the other hand I was aware that my piano playing did not measure up to concert artist quality. When Virgil Thomson criticized my "hardness of tone," he had justification—my natural attack tends to be hard without that roundness of tone that a concert pianist develops. No doubt I played the *Piano Variations* like the composer I am, although Arthur Berger, my composer-critic friend, admired my playing: "Copland got every ounce of sonority from each tone and it was a good thing too, because there weren't that many tones in the piece!"[2]

After the New York premiere critics were negative, including the *Times* and the *Herald Tribune*, where Jerome D. Bohm wrote, "Mr. Copland, always a composer of radical tendencies, has in these variations sardonically thumbed his nose at all of those esthetic attributes which have hitherto been considered essential to the creation of music. . . ." It was not until I played the *Variations* at Yaddo in 1932 that the piece really made an impression. Paul Rosenfeld described the occasion: "No previous performance had revealed its greatness as fully as this at Yaddo, and the power of its contracted, slowly progressive volumes with their flinty, metallic sonorities. . . . One felt its author the composer of the coming decades. . . ."[3] The *Variations* drew a lot of attention because it was new and strange. Arthur Berger wrote: "The *Variations* made an impression in the early thirties that was profound and exciting,"[4] and Marc Blitzstein described the piece as "Lithic."

Among the unusual aspects of the *Piano Variations* are irregular rhythmic patterns within the fundamentally straightforward 4/4 design. The work has been called dissonant, moody, nervous, bare, stark, lonely, concise, precise, and austere. But I was utterly convinced about it, and I was not going to be upset by early unfavorable reactions. In fact I assumed there would be temporary difficulty in having this composition accepted. My family naturally thought it was impractical to write works not easily grasped by an audience. Obviously, it *does* cut down on the number of potential listeners and even potential performers. But after all, you don't write music thinking, "Is this practical?" If you write something for instruments not readily available, or that is so long people don't want to spend that much time on any one piece—those are practical considerations that might justifiably cross your mind. But I don't think one composes to be practical. That's *too* sensible. You have to be more adventuresome than that. But you do have to be truly convinced about the value of what you are doing, otherwise there are many reasons for not doing it—minimal financial gain, no favorable criticism in the papers the next morning. You really must be brave, but the bravery is derived from inner conviction. I was absolutely sure that I had put down what I wanted to put down and that it was meaningful to me. It was wise to assume that it was going to take some time before other people would come around to understanding and appreciating it. That has, after all, been the history of much new effort in music.

What kind of music is the *Piano Variations?* It has been said more than once that "Copland doesn't like to talk about his music." I suppose this is as good a time as any to respond to that charge. I admit that I am uneasy with strict technical analysis, just as I have always been disinclined toward rigid methods of composition. I prefer to leave theoretical analysis to those who are experts in theory and analysis. Even then, I feel uncomfortable with strict analysis when it takes the place of discussing relevant matters such as the harmonic structure, rhythmic life, and dynamics of the music. I have occasionally had the experience of not immediately recognizing my own work when it is dissected in this manner! In addition, analysis may be misleading about a composer's intentions, for it can lead to the division of a lifetime of composing into arbitrary style periods. Furthermore, and in a more general sense, my reluctance to discuss musical works stems in part from the realization that our language is woefully inadequate to the task of describing musical experiences.

Having said all this, I will nevertheless take up the challenge and at-

Manuscript page from the *Piano Variations*, 1930.

tempt some comments of a musical nature about the *Piano Variations*, one of the few pieces in which I *did* make use to some extent, but in my own way, of the method invented by Arnold Schoenberg that came to be known as "twelve tone" and from which developed "serialism." The *Variations* incorporates a four-note motive on which the entire piece is based. Almost every note and chord in the piece relates back to these four notes. The *Variations* cannot be said to have been written according to all the rules of Schoenberg's method—for example, I repeat tones in their original form—but I have no doubt that the construction of the piece shows his influence. We were all at that time influenced by both Stravinsky and Schoenberg to some degree. I never rejected Schoenberg's ideas, even though I was closer to the French way of doing things. I believe that any method which proves itself so forceful an influence on the music of our times must be of considerable interest. In fact, I lectured about serialism at the New School as early as 1928. For me as a composer, the twelve-tone method was a way of thinking about music from a different perspective, somewhat like looking at a picture from a different angle so that you see things you might not have noticed otherwise. It was an aid in freshening the way I wrote at a time when I felt the need of change, and so I view it as an enrichment. It forced me into a different, more fragmented kind of melodic writing that in turn resulted in chords I had rarely used before. Thus my harmonic writing was affected in the *Piano Variations*, and in the works that followed—the *Short Symphony* and *Statements for Orchestra*. These pieces are more dissonant than my earlier works, yet I did not give up tonality. If a composer is secure in his judgment, his sense of what is musically valid does not change when he adopts a "new" method. The same judgment is applied to whatever the musical action, no matter what the method may be. Otherwise, one runs a strong risk of merely playing games. As for the traditional theme and variations form, this also I adapted to my own use. The twenty brief variations divide into two sections of ten without episodes or breaks between them, resulting in a sound that flows freely without discernible divisions.

The *Piano Variations* is more serious in intent and feeling than my earlier playful jazz pieces, and it is sharper, more orderly and logical than the declamatory and epic proportions of the *Ode*. Not only was the public perplexed at the direction I took with the *Variations*; some of my friends and colleagues were puzzled, too, and they questioned me about it. To one friend, the poet Lola Ridge, who greatly admired the *Ode*, I wrote (21 April 1931):

Let me see if I can make more clear what I mean in relation to the Ode and the Variations. To affirm the world is meaningless, unless one also affirms the tragic reality which is at the core of existence. To live on—to develop means, as I see it, to enter always more and more deeply into the very essence of tragic reality. The Ode is an affirmation, of course, with tragic implications. The Variations also affirm, but the reality they affirm is more particularized, it is the reality of our own age and time, while the reality of the Ode is more usual and understandable because it leans more on older and related affirmations with which we are to a degree, already familiar. I don't wish to underestimate the Ode in favor of the Variations but I feel sure that there is a certain essence of contemporary reality which is expressed in the Variations which I was too young to grasp at the writing of the Ode. You will find a certain relation between the Ode and an occasional movement in the grandiose style by Gustav Mahler but it would be much more difficult to relate the Variations to any of the older composers. . . .

Schoenberg was not the sole influence on my work at this time. Frugality and economy were the order of the day; social and economic conditions could not help but affect the music world. Considering these factors, I was fortunate to have the *Variations* published by Cos Cob in 1932.[5] When Martha Graham asked for permission to choreograph the work, I was utterly astonished that anyone would consider this kind of music suitable for dance. The result was *Dithyrambic*. It was my introduction to Martha's unusual and innovative ideas. Her appearances in *Dithyrambic* that season were much talked about and praised, although her choreography was considered as complex and abstruse as my music. If it took some time for audiences and critics to appreciate the *Piano Variations*, concert artists seemed to recognize its worth. As early as 1933, Victor Babin performed the *Variations* at the Eleventh ISCM Festival, and John Kirkpatrick included it in an all-American program at Town Hall in 1936. Through the years, I have had the satisfaction of many performances by wonderful pianists, among them Leonard Bernstein, John Browning, Paul Jacobs, Grant Johannesen, William Kapell, Noel Lee, William Masselos, Robert Miller, Ursula Oppens, Leo Smit, Hilde Somer, and Beveridge Webster.

The idea of transcribing the *Piano Variations* for orchestra was a recurrent one in my mind for some time. A commission from the Louisville Symphony Orchestra gave the incentive to carry out the project. The work was completed on 31 December 1957, and the *Orchestral Variations* was premiered by the Louisville Orchestra with Robert Whitney conducting on 5 March 1958. I wrote the program notes, as I preferred to do when invited. The following is derived from my notes of 1958.

My purpose was not to recreate orchestral sounds reminiscent of the quality of the piano, but rather to re-think the sonorous possibilities of the composition itself in terms of orchestral color. I could not have done this when the *Variations* was new, but with the perspective of twenty-seven years, it was not difficult to orchestrate the piece using the original as a piano sketch with orchestral possibilities. The overall plan remains the same, but the bar lines have been shifted in some instances to facilitate or-chestral performance.

The brass, in subdued tones, open the work and the theme is presented in a restrained vein. The quiet feeling persists until Variation VII when the mood becomes bolder. In variation VIII and IX, singing string tones predominate, and in XI, the oboe is heard in duet with a solo flute. From Variation XII on, the climax builds steadily with an increasing use of brass. Variation XVIII is a Scherzo, with flute and clarinet taking the lead. A section for drums closes the last Variation and leads to a brilliant-sounding Coda.

The Louisville *Courier Journal* carried a review the day after the pre-miere of the *Orchestral Variations* under the heading: "New-Old Copland Work Cheered, Also Jeered." Critic William Mootz assessed the audi-ence's reaction as "mostly bewildered." By year's end, Bernstein was con-ducting the work with the New York Philharmonic at Carnegie Hall. After the performance of 5 December 1958 Howard Taubman of *The New York Times* wrote: "The music has not changed; our capacity to respond has." Taubman admired the *Orchestral Variations*; personally, I am fond of both versions, although neither are performed enough to suit me. Occa-sionally I hit the jackpot—and the *Piano Variations* and *Orchestral Varia-tions* are included on the same program.

The Depression was affecting the general quality of life in New York. From the carefree twenties, we had plunged into a grim and difficult pe-riod. The artist is always the first to suffer, particularly in America, where he does not have the respect enjoyed by creative artists abroad. In the early spring of 1931, I wrote music for a Theatre Guild production, *Miracle at Verdun*, by Hans Chlumberg. Sensing hard times ahead, I planned a long trip to Europe to begin after the final New York Copland–Sessions series. Roger and I had agreed that the time had come to present something un-usual. We decided on a film program with music to be played by thirty members of the New York Philharmonic–Symphony Orchestra conducted by Hugh Ross. It took place 15 March 1931 at the Broadhurst Theatre and was considered "arty" and very daring. Included were three films by

A PROGRAM OF

Music and Films

HUGH ROSS, CONDUCTOR

●

American and European Films
with music written especially for them by
American and European Composers

●

Three films by **Ralph Steiner**
"H₂ O"
"Surf and Seaweed"
"Mechanical Principles"

One film by **Cavalcanti**
"La P'tite Lilie"

Film music by **Marc Blitzstein**
Colin McPhee
Darius Milhaud

Music for small orchestra by

Roger Sessions
"The Black Maskers"

Aaron Copland
"Music for the Theatre"

TICKETS $1., $2., $3.
may be obtained from
Copland-Sessions Concerts
Room 1505, Steinway Building,
113 West 57th Street, or at
Broadhurst Theatre.

A small orch╎
of thirty m╎
Philharmonic-Sy╎

Sunday╎

March 15th,

Broadhur╎

235 West╎

Above: "Music and Films," the program for the Fourth Season of the Copland-Sessions Concerts, 15 March 1932.
Right: Photographer Ralph Steiner with Copland, 1932.

Photograph by Victor Kraft.

the young avant-garde photographer Ralph Steiner, one with music by Blitzstein and two with scores by McPhee; films by Cavalcanti and news clips with scores by Milhaud; my *Music for the Theatre*; and Sessions' *Black Maskers*. Roger had sent his music suggesting to me that we use parts of the score: "parts I, V and VIII are best for this performance. . . . I give you carte blanche." A funny thing happened during Steiner's film, *Mechanical Principles*. The film broke, and we had to switch the order of the program on the spot. It must have been handled smoothly, because the papers the following day assumed that *Mechanical Principles* was *meant*

THE PHILADELPHIA ORCHESTRA
FOUNDED 1900

ALEXANDER VAN RENSSELAER
PRESIDENT
WILLIAM JAY TURNER
VICE PRESIDENT
WILLIAM PHILIP BARBA
SECRETARY

LEOPOLD STOKOWSKI   OSSIP GABRILOWITSCH
CONDUCTORS

PACKARD BUILDING, PHILADELPHIA

ARTHUR JUDSON
MANAGER
LOUIS A. MATTSON
ASSISTANT MANAGER

CONFIDENTIAL

October 29th, 1930.

Dear Mr. Copeland -

      I am greatly looking forward to having the material of your new Symphony and to beginning work at it in rehearsal with the Orchestra.

      I should like to write to you about a matter in confidence, which is this -

      I am trying to develop an electrical orchestra, and I am wondering whether it would interest you to compose something for electrical instruments. In any case whether the matter interests you or not please do not speak about it, as I wish to keep this matter confidential until I am ready to act.

      Yours sincerely,

LEOPOLD STOKOWSKI

Mr. Aaron Copeland,

Letter from Leopold Stokowski.

to be given in two parts with the Copland and the Sessions music sandwiched between.

Leopold Stokowski had been promising to schedule the premiere of my *Dance Symphony* since 1930, and he finally did so on 15 April 1931, with the Philadelphia Orchestra at the Academy of Music. It was interesting to hear a work I had composed so long ago—the *Dance Symphony*, derived from my early ballet *Grohg*, was given the famous "Stokie" treatment, programmed between his flamboyant orchestral arrangements of Bach and Wagner. The title of the concert reflected the hard times affecting musicians—"Emergency Concert for the Benefit of the Unemployed Musicians of Philadelphia by the Philadelphia Orchestra." From the Benjamin Franklin Hotel after the concert, I expressed critical views of Stokowski's conducting in a lengthy letter to Koussevitzky:

> At any moment you are liable to be shocked by his superficiality of feeling or some detail which is completely out of style with the rest. . . . (the public of course doesn't understand this because everything he does sounds so effective. . . .) He [Stokowski] seems well pleased with the *Dance Symphony* and says he will repeat it at his regular concerts next season. . . . I liked it very much in parts but not as a whole. . . .[6]

Soon after the Philadelphia premiere, I left for Europe, taking with me some sketches for my *Short Symphony*. In Paris I joined up with a new young friend who had been studying composition with me, Paul Frederick Bowles, who was gifted in both music and literature. One of his admirers was Gertrude Stein, who called him "Freddy." We planned to visit her before going on to Berlin for May and June. It was because of Paul that I got to spend a weekend visiting Miss Stein and Miss Toklas in their country home near Grenoble. This visit was described in *The Autobiography of Alice B. Toklas*:

> A young man who first made Gertrude Stein's acquaintance by writing engaging letters from America is Paul Frederick Bowles. Gertrude Stein says of him that he is delightful and sensible in summer but neither delightful nor sensible in winter. Aaron Copeland [sic] came to see us with Bowles in the summer and Gertrude Stein liked him immensely. Bowles told Gertrude Stein and it pleased her that Copeland said threateningly to him when as usual in the winter he was neither delightful nor sensible, if you do not work now when you are twenty when you are thirty, nobody will love you.[7]

Miss Stein (I have *always* called her *Miss* Stein) drove us around in her

Ford on Saturday afternoon on a tour of the countryside. When we casually mentioned that we planned to go to the Riviera for the summer or perhaps Tangier, she said, "Ohhh, of course go to Tangier. It is a marvelous place. You must forget the Riviera in summer. That's so *awful*, so full of Americans." She quite literally talked us into changing our plans, and instead of the Riviera, we headed for Tangier. Tangier was the most exotic place I had ever visited. From there, I wrote to Miss Stein (25 August 1931):

> Tangier is responsible for my not writing sooner. It wasn't easy getting settled. It took a week to find a house and furnish it. We have an African piano which looks like a piano but which sounds like hell! It would sound all right if we could only get a piano tuner who can tune. But they tell me he's not easily found in Morocco. We tried one man who put it more out of tune than it was before he touched it. These are problems you are happily free of, but they make my stay somewhat precarious. Still, if I should have to leave tomorrow, I'd be glad you sent us, because it *is* lovely to see, and so I have to thank you on that score too. . . .

I had brought only one volume of music to Tangier with me—Mozart's Quartets and Quintets—and some music writing paper. But I found the atmosphere not conducive to composing, although I tried to work a little every day. In the evening Paul and I would sit outside a café to watch the local scene. One day, we were invited to lunch at the home of an Arab family. I recall that the women disappeared at the sound of a stranger approaching. Only the male members of the family were allowed to be present, and we all ate with our hands out of a common bowl. Paul stayed behind in Tangier when I left. He is still there, fifty years later!

Paul Bowles[8]

In the winter of 1929–30 Henry Cowell gave me a letter of introduction to Aaron, who was living at the Hotel Lexington on the corner of 49th Street. I showed him my music and he agreed to teach me harmony. For counterpoint he thought I should try to go to Paris and study with Boulanger. I was obliged, however, to return to the University of Virginia at the beginning of February. At Easter time Aaron came to Charlottesville, where I proudly introduced him to members of the faculty. In August of that year, thanks to Aaron's intercession, I was invited to Yaddo, where he had a

Copland with Paul Bowles, 1932.

studio in the woods (he was working on the Variations*). During that au-
tumn and winter in New York I had a harmony lesson with him nearly
every day. He was due to go to Berlin in the spring, and it was decided that
I would accompany him. In March I sailed for Paris. About a fortnight
later Aaron arrived. I took him to Gertrude Stein's and she invited him to
visit Bilignin later in the year. We stayed only a short time in Paris, being
eager to get to Berlin and settle down. Aaron already knew where he was
going to live. . . . Edouard Roditi had given me letters for Stephen
Spender and Christopher Isherwood, among others. Aaron was less interested than I in exploring the town and leading a social life, but he did
consent to having lunch each day with Isherwood, Jean Ross, and Spender
at the Café des Westens. We saw* Fidelio *at the Kroll-Opera and* Das
Rheingold *at the Staats-Oper, and we went to a festival at Bad Pyrmont,
where Bartók played. In the summer we returned to Paris, and Aaron went
on to Oxford where the ISCM Festival was being held. We met again at
Gertrude Stein's in Bilignin. It was Stein who suggested that we try Tangier instead of Villefranche, where friends of Aaron were summering. So,*

when we had finished our visit at Bilignin, we set out for Morocco. I don't think Aaron really enjoyed being there, but he made the best of it, and even went to Fez. He returned to Berlin about 1 October.

I saw Aaron in the summer of 1932 when I arrived back in the States. He was engrossed in leading the Young Composers' Group. I remember an unpropitious first meeting with them, after which Aaron shook his head ruefully (grinning nevertheless) remarking on the reluctance of the other young composers to accept me. I returned to Morocco. The next time I was in New York was in the spring of 1935, and Aaron was living at the Hotel Empire. . . . It was that summer that Aaron, Virgil, George Antheil and I went up to Hartford as hired performers at a party given by the Austins (Chick Austin was the curator of the Wadsworth Atheneum there). The same group, with Marc Blitzstein replacing Antheil, performed at another party in New York, at the house of Mrs. Murray Crane. All this was Virgil's idea; he believed very strongly that music should be paid for. (We all believed it, but he did the campaigning.) In the years that followed, I would see Aaron at parties in Edwin Denby's loft, or at the house of Kirk and Constance Askew. We saw each other often until I came here to live permanently in Morocco.

It seemed that I produced concerts of modern American music wherever I found myself during those years. (It is surprising that I did not attempt one in Tangier!) During the late spring months in Berlin, I stayed in the apartment of a violinist, Max Strub. Within a short time I realized that German audiences knew nothing of American orchestral music beyond a few jazz-inspired pieces, so I arranged a concert of four orchestral works by Americans for the following 9 December, to be sponsored by the ISCM and conducted by Ernest Ansermet. Only one piece was a jazz-inspired work—Louis Gruenberg's *Jazz Suite*. The others were Carl Ruggles' *Portals*, Sessions' *First Symphony*, and my *First Symphony*, which would be the premiere of the new version without organ. Ruggles, a generation older than the rest of us, had worked out an original system of composition. I admired *Portals* and later, in 1965, when I had begun to conduct frequently, I programmed it again in London. I had met Ruggles in New York in the late twenties at the Stieglitz gallery, and when I wrote to ask permission to include *Portals* in the Berlin program, Ruggles responded (9 September 1931): "If you are at the rehearsals, everything will be fine I'm sure. . . ."

Also in December, the final Copland–Sessions concert took place at the Aeolian Hall in London. It featured American chamber music. It is difficult enough to arrange concerts of contemporary American music under the best of conditions, but when the principal participants are scattered around the globe such an undertaking borders on the impossible. During the planning stages, Bowles was in Tangier and then Paris, Citkowitz in New York, Thomson in Paris, I in Berlin, and the concert in London! Various performers were in other locations. This was Paul Bowles' debut as composer, and he was understandably anxious: "I didn't receive your letter until ten days or more after you had written it. . . . I shall start making the parts, but God knows how right they will be. I wish there were some way of your seeing them before I send them to London. Oh dear, oh dear! I insist on getting them done in time for the rehearsals. In fact I should blow up and die immediately if it could not come off on account of lack of time. . . ." I answered Paul to bolster his courage, and then wrote to Israel, who had promised me new songs for the concert (18 July 1931):

> Your letter was not calculated to bring joy to the heart of an arranger of festivals! Your old songs would look like rank partisanship. . . . I would even be willing to risk that, but I really think you owe it to your "public," to America, to Nadia, to Roger, to me to arrange your life in such a way that it all leads to the production of at least *one* new oeuvre a year. . . . And remember that all the ideals and ideas we have can best be advanced by tangible examples. There aren't so many of us that we can afford to have you loll by the wayside. . . .

But Israel did not complete his "Blake" songs and sent only one new work to be added to the four "Joyce" songs of the previous year. I wrote to Virgil about *Capital Capitals* (29 October 1931): "Will you come to London to coach the singers . . . and play the piano part at the concert? Say yes— or I'm lost. I'll be there myself and am to play the Chávez *Sonatina* and my *Piano Variations*. . . ." Virgil agreed, and I wrote to Gertrude Stein on 10 November hoping (in vain) that she might attend the concert.

Lest it appear that these concerts of modern music were all glowing successes, let me assure you that this one was not. I no longer recall the details of what went awry, but in a letter written to Virgil later (29 January 1932), I thanked him for being so nice "considering the concert was going about as bad as possible." By the turn of the new year I was in New York, staying in Harold and Stella's apartment at 52 West 58th Street while they were away. Edmund Wilson lived in the building. Clurman was deeply involved with the Group Theatre, which he had started in 1930, and the

Stieglitz crowd was still going strong. Several of them lived in the neighborhood, so I saw them often, and by now, Paul Strand, Orson Welles, Mary and Ralph Steiner, William Lescaze, and Carl Van Vechten were also my friends. (After Mary and Ralph divorced in 1933, Mary married Lescaze.) Everyone greeted my arrival home as though I had been away for years, particularly the young composers in town. They often came to my studio in the evening, so when Elie Siegmeister asked if I would be the informal leader of a group of composers to meet every few weeks, it seemed a natural development. The only attempt at organization was to find a name—the Young Composers' Group.

The "regulars" were Arthur Berger, Henry Brant, Israel Citkowitz, Lehman Engel, Vivian Fine, Irwin Heilner, Bernard Herrmann, Jerome Moross, and Elie Siegmeister. They decided on an age limit of twenty-five (except for me, of course). Other than that, there were no rules. We met informally every few weeks during 1932. Visitors came, or were invited when they were in town—Bowles, Chávez, Blitzstein, Antheil, Kirkpatrick, and Thomson. Conversation was very lively, ranging through all aspects of modern music. When things got "hot," I would play the role of peacemaker. Once, I wrote on a postcard announcing the time and place of a meeting—"No polemics!" When Bowles and Virgil were visitors, the regulars were less than friendly toward the expatriates. The Young Composers were interested in the situation of the American composer. Vivan Fine recalls: "There was not a lot of brotherly and sisterly love. We played and severely criticized each other's music."[9] According to Lehman Engel, some of the criticism was unwarranted: "Benny [Herrmann] always said, 'It stinks!'—no matter what was played. Aaron was the watchdog and took a back seat. He never tried to steer things. I never saw him angry, although heaven knows everyone else was hot-headed at those meetings. We used to tease Aaron—not about his music, but about money. We were students, so naturally we had nothing, but in our eyes, Aaron was a success, yet he always looked for a place to live that was free."[10] Henry Brant wrote a piece called *5 and 10 Cent Store Music*, and the gang all agreed it was his best so far.

Henry Brant[11]

Of the composers at the Young Composers' Group meetings, the most voluble in expressing his views was Bernard Herrmann. The one who

brought in the most new music and played it was myself. I had no rivals—
I could write faster than anyone else. And Arthur Berger was the critic
among us. On one occasion, he, or somebody else perhaps, brought in a
clipping from the New York Sun where the critic was W. J. Henderson.
He wrote an article wondering if young people, when they met to talk
about music these days, ever pronounced the word "beauty." We decided
to satisfy Mr. Henderson and all pronounce "beauty"—and we did so,
with expression! There was always a fair amount of excited talk. The entire
group was present at the First Yaddo Festival. While there we had meet-
ings in the evening something like the ones at Aaron's apartment. We im-
provised in the avant-garde styles of the time and did burlesques of some
of the new pieces just played. Marc Blitzstein had written a quartet in
three slow movements—we did a burlesque of that, four hands, conducted
by Bernard Herrmann. From time to time someone would bring in a piece
perhaps unknown to all of us—something by Eisler, Ives, or Webern that
we'd never seen before. We'd say, "Vivian, play it!" (Vivian was the best
sight reader in the group.) Then we would discuss what it was, when the
composer wrote it, who else was doing something like it. We really wanted
to collect information about new things in music. The idea of writing in
the neoclassic Stravinskian manner was something that occurred only to
me at that time. I was the first one in the group to do it. Some of the boys
criticized it as a pointless conservatism. The views of the group were much
more open than later was the case among young composers, and there was
much greater curiosity to find out the range of what was going on. Aaron's
attitude throughout was one of encouragement.

I can recall one episode in which Bernard Herrmann, who had the worst
handwriting of anyone there, brought in a new piece that was just a scrawl.
But he explained it, not hesitating to point out its significant qualities. He
spoke in a flippant way about spilling coffee on some of it and so forth, and
Aaron said, "Now look, Benny, you've taken the trouble to do it. It's not
right for you to be flippant about what you do, because it clearly means a
lot to you to do it. And you musn't give others the impression that it
shouldn't mean much to them." (These are not Aaron's exact words, but
it's the sense of what he said, and in a very friendly way to which offense
couldn't possibly be taken.) Aaron introduced music to us also. On one
occasion it was Milhaud's The Misfortunes of Orpheus. *Vivian played it,*
we tried to sing the parts, and Aaron spoke about the harmony, which he
said is Milhaud's only, because of its—he used the word—"drugged"
quality, which no other composer quite has. Occasionally Aaron would

bring in such a piece, usually something he himself happened to be study-
ing. Even though we didn't continue the group for long, it was valued, be-
cause this was our only opportunity to get some sort of idea of what was
happening.

Brant wrote to me after Arthur Berger published an article about the
Young Composers' Group in *Trend*,[12] a magazine that ran from 1932 to
1935 (18 July 1932): "You should get Berger to talk to you about 'vitality
and sterility' which have very special implications for him. Moross and
Vivian are vital, *I* am sterile. . . ." The group was so often at odds with
each other individually that I feared for its survival when I left for Mexico
later in 1932. Brant wrote again (22 November 1932): "Let me give you
inside and authoritative assurance that the group will hold together, if not
because of common sympathies at least on account of common objects for
ridicule." Siegmeister and Heilner organized a concert of music by members of the group, to which I was invited as honored guest. But I was in
Mexico. Siegmeister wrote (22 December 1932):

> To break the suspense I might as well tell you that the date of our program is
> Jan. 15—so you'd better cut your Mexican stay short if you want to be in on the
> fun. The best thing about our bunch is nobody likes anybody else's music—
> wouldn't touch it with a ten foot pole. Exceptions are me and Irwin—I like
> *both* his and my stuff and he says he thinks we're both terrible. We've decided
> the best thing for the success of the concert is to have the group meet as rarely
> as possible. It always ends up in a fight or in somebody singing songs they heard
> in a Harlem speakeasy (not published by Schirmer, or Cos Cob). Two weeks
> ago the gang got together and Benny showed quite remarkable talents as a "dis-
> euse"—giving Ruth Draper character sketches of the modern composers, from
> Sibelius through Roger Sessions down to Vivian Fine and Jerry Moross. Then
> we had a lot of fun going thru those songs in the Ives 114 which he marks,
> "Though there is no danger of it, I hope these songs will not be sung—at least
> not in public."

The concert was the climax of the Young Composers' Group. After my
return from Mexico, we did not meet again.

Koussevitzky finally conducted the *Symphonic Ode* in the spring of 1932.
I wrote to Virgil in Paris (14 March 1932): "I was hoping you could hear
my *Ode* which Koussie is doing in New York next week. When he did it in
Boston last week the *Transcript* printed your article (but they cut out the

tickling duchesses and seducing housemaids line!)."[13] Virgil and I had known each other since our student years in Paris, but now we were more closely in touch because we had a mutual friend in Paul Bowles, who went to Paris at my urging to have counterpoint lessons with Nadia. Virgil, who had become disenchanted with our former teacher, was urging Bowles to study with Paul Dukas. I received a nine-page letter from Virgil stating his case against Nadia, and ending: "Nadia is not the same as when we were there. . . . I've told you my story and you can give him [Bowles] any advice you want and he will follow it because he believes in you and I shant say any more about it. I've sent Nadia pupils for years and very little good has come of them, none for European purposes. This is the first time I've done otherwise. I think it's time to change. . . ." I responded:

You certainly state the case *against* N.B. well enough and I'm not so blind as to be unaware that there is such a thing. In relation to Paul . . . there is no matter where or how a pupil learns his stuff just so that he learns it. Therefore it makes no difference whether he studies with N.B. or Dukas. But I know absolutely nothing about Dukas as teacher and I do know N.B. can teach counterpoint so I naturally send my friends to N.B. Secondly, it is useless to be a pupil if you are unwilling to enter into a pupil-teacher relationship (Roy was too old to do this and so were you in 1926). I'm all for the teacher influencing the pupil—it doesn't matter what pet ideas the teacher happens to have or what means are employed to drive them home—the pupil should swallow them whole for a time and if he has any guts he'll throw them overboard soon enough. If not, it proves he's just a pupil and it doesn't matter whom he studies with. I know N.B.'s pet ideas and I know the maternal means she employs but I know nothing of Dukas' pet ideas etc. So it boils down to sending pupils to a known quantity. As soon as I feel the disadvantages outweigh the advantages to be gained from being N.B.'s pupil I'll stop sending pupils, but that time hasn't come yet.

Virgil and I continued to disagree about Paul. I worried about his lack of discipline, and Virgil wrote (28 August 1932): "You are shocked because he won't follow the conventional education of a young man of talent. He is frightfully impressed by what you tell him and gets awfully worried because he can't do it." I, in turn, thought that Paul liked to have someone worry about him. I wrote to Virgil (5 December 1933): "And so I play the role of worrier. You encourage him and I'll worry him and together we'll do very well by him." (As it turned out, within a short time Paul was very sick with typhoid and did indeed worry us all.)

This would not be the only time Virgil and I disagreed. We are not much alike in temperament and personality, but we have never had a falling out, even though it has been assumed in the music world that there was terrific competition between us. I doubt either of us would deny this completely, but we could always carry on our friendship and collegial activities—I think because we were honest with each other. We said and wrote what we thought, no holds barred. For instance, in 1931 after Virgil sent me a copy of his *Violin Sonata*, I wrote (5 April): "I think it has lovely things in it, particularly the second movement, but I also think that you are often much too easy with yourself as for instance the too-Handel-like beginning of that 2nd movement and the theme with arpeggio accompaniment of the 4th movement. . . . What I like about the piece are those moments of seemingly effortless musicality which are utterly simple and deeply charming. . . ." It was also in 1931 that Minna suggested I invite Virgil to write the article on me for *Modern Music's* "American Composers" series. I made the request (29 January 1931): "From my standpoint, don't for an instant feel the slightest obligation to do the article on my account. . . . And if you should decide to do it nothing but your honestest judgment would please me. . . ." When the piece had appeared, I wrote again (27 January 1932): "Thanks for the article. All my friends thought it very swell. It made me understand *your* music much better. And it will help me make mine better I hope. . . ." After *What to Listen For in Music* was published in 1938, Virgil wrote to me in not the most complimentary manner. I countered (2 May 1939): "The whole book is a kind of outline of facts. It never occurred to me that anyone would look for an original contribution to musical theory in it. . . . The damn thing was never meant for you to read in the first place—" On the other hand, I have always considered Virgil a superb writer and critic. Reviewing his book *The State of Music*, I stated categorically: ". . . the most original book on music that America has produced."[14] Virgil went to live in Paris but kept in touch. I thought he should be in America and said so. I wrote (15 February 1940): "Come home and help instead of sending all that good advice from Paris." Virgil and I have been colleagues through many years. At a dinner at the Plaza Hotel in honor of Virgil's seventy-fifth birthday in November 1971, as part of the entertainment I parodied my *Lincoln Portrait:* "Born in Missouri, raised in Kansas City, and lived in Paris, France, this is what Virgil said: 'I have never known an artist of any kind, who didn't do better work when he got properly paid for it.' And this is what he said: 'Always beware of ex-composers; their one aim in life is to discourage the writing of music!' " I continued, "When standing erect, he is five feet four inches tall, and this is what he said: 'A concert is a meal. It is a feast, a ham sandwich, a chocolate sundae, nourishment to be absorbed with pleasure and digested by unconscious processes.' " And I concluded, "Virgil Thomson, best all-around music critic in the U.S. is everlasting in the memory of those he criticized." Joking aside, Virgil and I have often worked together to give American composers a surer footing in the world of music. Later in our lives, recognition and honors came to both of us, among them membership in the National Institute and Academy of Arts and Letters. In 1956 Virgil agreed to make the presentation to me of their Gold Medal in Music, and I was given the pleasure of presenting him with that prestigious award in 1966.

Virgil Thomson [15]

Minna had tried to get me to write for her when I was going back to France to live there in 1925, and I didn't want to do it. I was giving up all that kind of thing. I'd been writing regularly for Vanity Fair *magazine, and I had been playing the organ professionally, teaching at Harvard, and all that. I said, "Enough of this! My mind has got all of everybody else's music in it." So I went off to be in Paris, where you don't hear music unless you really want to—at least it doesn't come to you over the air or around the neighbors—and I was walking out on this business of writing. Well, Minna didn't like that idea, so about five years later she asked Aaron to get me to write an article about him. That was my first break back into writing. Minna was shocked when she first saw the piece—she took a strong gulp and then said, "But this is* very *good!" I used the word "Jewish," you see, and the League of Composers—one hundred percent Jewish—was not accustomed to the word. But I was not bringing up the Jewish question, but the identity. It's as if you couldn't mention to me that my family were Southern Baptists! I used it legitimately, I'm sure, to explain certain psychological traits in Aaron. I thought he was a prophet calling out to Israel. The music has little counterpoint—it's one man speaking with a lone voice. Anyway, Minna had an enormously good editorial sense. She knew a good piece from a not good piece, an interesting piece from a not interesting one. She could even take kids and train them. Minna has a huge place—if anybody wanted to give it to her—in the literacy of the American musical composing group. And in the twenty-two years of her magazine, everybody wrote there. Well, I did this piece on Aaron and it was successful, and I got on with Minna, chiefly by corre-*

AARON COPLAND 1538 L. WASHINGTON STREET PEEKSKILL, N.Y. 10566

Jan 23 1971

Dear Virgil:
Just re-read the pretty letter you sent for my 70th birthday album, with its excerpt from your forthcoming book. Has ever a composer had a more generous friend? I doubt it.
Thank you — and affectionate greetings
Aaron

P.S. I'm looking forward to reading the book!

VIRGIL THOMSON 222 WEST 23rd STREET NEW YORK 11, N.Y.

d. A: 27 January '71
Your letter ought to be framed and no doubt will be by my heirs.
You and I have worked together for about fifty years now and never tried to kid each other.
Thanks for existing!
Ever warmly
Virgil

Above: Letter from Copland to Thomson, 23 January 1971.
Left: From Thomson to Copla[n] January 1971.

spondence, of course. After that I would write things for Modern Music from time to time. I got $25 for each piece.

Aaron introduced me to his Young Composers' Group when I came back for visits. He had the great gift of being a good colleague, and we became good, loyal colleagues. Some of his friends have tried to provoke quarrels, and maybe mine have, too—I don't know. But we weren't having any. Aaron and I were sold on the same general idea, that composers are not rival cheats at some show game on the street. We're all members of the same Fifth Avenue Merchants' Association, and our future and our present depend on being good colleagues.

For the first twenty years of Aaron's career as a composer he carried his American colleagues along with him, because he was successful before anybody else. When he gave concerts, we would be in on it. That included the Copland–Sessions Concerts for which Copland was the charm boy and Sessions was the heavy. Aaron was a strict orchestral and chamber music man and not really as complex a modernist as Sessions, but a good card-carrying modernist nevertheless. He needed support early on and found it from Alma Wertheim and others. He figured out, I think, that he would not make unnecessary enemies. But he never hesitated to make enemies where it could not be done otherwise. Since we were young together, I was aware of some things that could annoy or worry Aaron, but he always went about those matters in a straightforward way by trying to find a solution. And, if you can't find a solution—you live with it. As time went on, Aaron became the patron of American musical youth just like Darius Milhaud in Paris—all the young went through Darius somehow or other. And like that, Aaron looked at everybody, encouraged them if necessary, discouraged them if necessary. He was valuable as a talent filter for Koussevitzky, and he took it all quite seriously.

I made his musical portrait and when you do that, things turn up. Once you start looking at someone closely, you find things you hadn't expected at all. Aaron turned out to be a long, steady, indefatigable pastoral. And some of the best music he's written is pastoral. I don't see the sidewalks of New York in Aaron as some others do. Aaron, the son of immigrants, adopted the countryside, and as I wrote in that first piece, he's the Jewish preacher telling people right and wrong. That's an historical and inherited trait from his family and religious background. Also from Aaron's family is his good sense about business. Whenever it came to the question of a commission by the same person, when Aaron and I would compare notes about how much we were getting or how much to ask, it inevitably turned out that Aaron asked more and got it! But he did it all so gently. I asked him once what he did if he found a publisher charging something he's not supposed to, and he simply answered, "Well, I would just write a letter." Ralph Hawkes from Boosey & Hawkes liked Aaron and saw a good business there and so got him a contract with the London house. It was Aaron who, when I first came back to America in 1940, introduced me to Ralph and recommended that he take me on also. Hawkes tried it. I took him one little choral piece, and he sent me a long, handwritten contract—one of those British contracts—everything pretty in it. Since I couldn't make it out myself, I took it to a young lawyer who wrote Boosey & Hawkes a letter. Ralph didn't answer it. He just sent my music right back, and it never went further. But Aaron had tried; he always did his best to help his fellow composers.

Aaron was involved in the theater personally through Clurman and by musical example through me. I wrote opera, ballet, and film music before he did these things, and I did them in a straightforward manner. There came a time when Aaron needed a simpler approach. He has said and written that I'm one of the few composers who influenced him. The foreign models were Shostakovich and Kurt Weill, and the American model, Virgil Thomson. In the thirties the whole of New York musical and intellectual life was moving into a theory of trade unionism, even occasionally reading Karl Marx. Theater was definitely where things were heading during and after the Depression. And the social content of theater and films was moving away from complexity—any theater audience wants music that is accessible. Didactic modernism gets nowhere with them. It just doesn't communicate in the theater, whether union theater or Broadway capitalist theater or film for great chunks of the population.

Aaron's quite a good conductor—not a star but very competent. Since he stopped writing music, a fact which he deeply regrets but can't do anything about, it's something for him to do. He can travel around the world making money and getting his own music distributed and there's absolutely nothing wrong with it. I've done a bit of it myself. I've never had as many dates as he has, and I don't suppose I'm as dependable a conductor. He's very straightforward about it.

Aaron was the president of young American music, and then middle-aged American music, because he had tact, good business sense about colleagues, and loyalty. He conquered Mexico through Chávez, and he inherited England with Benjie's [Benjamin Britten] permission—and Benjie had veto power there. Aaron made good friends all over the world. He was *always president of American music of any age or any place he happened to be.*

As soon as the dates for the First Festival of Contemporary Music at Yaddo were set for 30 April and 1 May, 1932, I wrote to Virgil and Paul Bowles in Paris and to Roy Harris in California for pieces. Roy answered, "I will write you a work for string quartet and flute—one movement about 12 minutes . . . will be written 'pronto.' . . . Love to you old boy—more power to you, an ancient and tenacious friend. . . ." Bowles sent five songs on his own texts and Virgil a setting of Max Jacob's *Stabat Mater* with string quartet accompaniment (after the festival, I recommended the *Stabat* to Cos Cob for publication). From the Young Composers' Group, I invited Henry Brant and Vivian Fine to submit works and another young composer-pianist, Oscar Levant, whom I had met at an evening at the Gershwins in New York that past winter. He had played part of an unfinished jazzy piano *Sonatina* for the guests, and I encouraged him to complete it for a premiere at Yaddo.[16] I drew also on the League of Composers and former Boulanger students. In all, eighteen composers were included on three concerts, divided between Saturday morning and evening, and Sunday afternoon.[17] A Conference for Critics and Composers was scheduled for Sunday morning. Of all the pieces performed, highest praise went to Roger's *Sonata for Piano* (by now in its complete state), seven songs by Charles Ives, and my *Piano Variations.* George Antheil had been scheduled to perform four piano pieces on Saturday evening. When he canceled at the last moment, I substituted the *Piano Variations.* Perhaps this was a blessing in disguise, for while I was playing, I sensed the music reaching this Yaddo audience in a way that it had not done in New York a year earlier. Both Arthur Berger and Paul Rosenfeld corroborated this in reviews of the festival. Re-reading them, I am reminded that after several requests, I played the *Variations* again on Sunday.

The Ives songs, performed by baritone Hubert Linscott with myself at the piano, were received with great interest—this was the first time a group of professional musicians were paying serious attention to Ives. It was a turning point in the recognition of his music. Arthur Berger was prophetic when he wrote in his review for the *Daily Mirror:* "History is being made in our midst."[18] The Young Composers' Group had "discovered" Ives in the early thirties. Benny Herrmann, Irwin Heilner, and Jerry Moross were particularly enthusiastic, and Ives became an influence on their music. It's

Top: Elizabeth Ames, Copland, and other guests on the porch at Yaddo, 1933.
Bottom: Group photograph at Yaddo, 1932.
Opposite top: Group photograph at Yaddo, 1932. Copland (center) behind Vivian Fine, to the right of Lehman Engel; Roy Harris is left of Engel; and Paul Bowles is third from the right side.
Opposite bottom: Program for the First Festival of Contemporary Music at Yaddo, 1932.

First Festival
of
Contemporary American Music

Yaddo

Saratoga Springs
New York

April thirtieth and May first
nineteen hundred thirty-two

ASSISTING ARTISTS

ADA MAC LEISH, Soprano   HUBERT LINSCOTT, Baritone
JESUS MARIA SANROMA, Pianist   JOHN KIRKPATRICK, Pianist
GEORGES LAURENT, Flutist

HANS LANGE QUARTET

H. LANGE, First Violin   Z. KURTHY, Viola
A. SCHULLER, Second Violin   P. SUCH, Cello

LEAGUE OF COMPOSERS QUARTET

N. BEREZOWSKY, First Violin   M. STILLMAN, Viola
M. MUSCANTO, Second Violin   D. FREED, Cello

COMPOSER-PIANISTS

GEORGE ANTHEIL   AARON COPLAND
VIVIAN FINE   OSCAR LEVANT

THIRD CONCERT

SUNDAY AFTERNOON   **MAY FIRST**
At two-fifteen

SONATA FOR FLUTE AND PIANO   *Walter Piston*
  1. Allegro moderato e grazioso   2. Adagio
  3. Allegro vivace
MR. LAURENT and MR. SANROMA

* SEVEN SONGS   *Charles Ives*
  1. The Indians (Charles Sprague)
  2. Walking (Ives)
  3. Serenity (Whittier)
  4. Maple Leaves (Thomas B. Aldrich)
  5. The See'r (Ives)
  6. Evening (Milton)
  7. Charlie Rutlage (Cowboy Ballads)
MR. LINSCOTT and MR. COPLAND

* SUITE FOR FLUTE AND PIANO   *Henry Brant*
  1. Madrigal   2. Minuet   3. Saraband   4. Toccata
MR. LAURENT and MR. SANROMA

INTERMISSION

PIANO VARIATIONS (1930)   *Aaron Copland*
THE COMPOSER

SUITE FOR FLUTE SOLO   *Wallingford Riegger*
  1. Moderato   2. Vivace   3. Molto con sentimento
  4. Allegro ironico
MR. LAURENT

† SECOND STRING QUARTET   *Silvestre Revueltas*
Allegro giocoso—Lento—Molto vivace—Allegro molto sostenuto
HANS LANGE QUARTET

true that I was not much interested in Ives until Benny pushed me into looking at 114 *Songs*, a volume that Ives had published privately in 1922.[19] When I *did* investigate, I was amazed. There we were in the twenties searching for a composer from the older generation with an "American sound," and here was Charles Ives composing this incredible music—totally unknown to us! I wrote for permission to include a selection of his songs at Yaddo (7 March 1932), and he sent me a rather curious copy of the 114 *Songs* (several pages had been cut out or removed, and I never found out why).[20] I chose seven with an eye toward representing the incredibly wide variety of style and moods in the song collection.[21] Following the First Yaddo Festival, I arranged for these seven songs to be published by Cos Cob Press—the first commercial publication of songs by Charles Ives.

When planning the Second Yaddo Festival I included another Ives song, "Where the Eagle Cannot See," and wrote to John Kirkpatrick (11 September 1933): "Will you have the Ives sonata movement ('Alcotts' from 'Concord') with you (and in the fingers) in case somebody gets sick and we need a substitute?" Our Young Composers' Group had heard John play this at a meeting, and all were interested and impressed. A postcard sent to Ives requesting publicity photographs remained unanswered; years later, I saw it in the Ives Collection at Yale—scribbled over with characteristic Ives fury against publicity. In 1933 when preparing an article on the 114 *Songs* for *Modern Music*,[22] I wrote again to the composer with a list of questions. This time Ives responded cordially and in great detail.[23] After Yaddo I tried in vain to interest Koussevitzky in performing an Ives orchestral piece. In the forties the Arrow Music Press, with which I was involved, published some Ives music, and I recall that the composer returned every royalty check for us to use toward publishing other composers' works. As Ives' music gradually emerged, it had an increasingly influential effect on younger composers and eventually on the position of the American composer in the international musical scene.

Paul Rosenfeld, who had been an Ives supporter even before Yaddo, admired the performance of the seven songs at Yaddo, but the rest of the program did not please him. He objected to Yaddo as being a reflection of my own personal taste rather than a representation of the very best American music available. But in practical terms it was absolutely necessary for me to deal primarily with composers who were my friends and colleagues. After all, the music was mostly unpublished and unrecorded, and neither scores nor parts were available. Rosenfeld would publish his criticism in

Letter from Charles Ives to Copland (date in Copland's hand).

Discoveries of a Music Critic,[24] but soon after the festival he wrote them directly to me (15 June 1932):

> . . . you must know that I was not very happy about it all until the latter half of the second program . . . I have come to the conclusion that the best that can be done for all American composers, the weak and the strong, is for the makers of programs to put the strongest foot forward at all times. . . . I prefer Ruggles to Berezowsky and Moross to Brant or Fine. . . . As for Gruenberg: why prefer him

to Jerome Kern or Gershwin: they too have works which are short and characteristic in technique and content: I really like Ole Man Ribber.... Ornstein's songs seem on a par with Bennett's and one of Rudhyar's moments are worth several of Berezowsky's. As for Cowell and Weiss, I am surprised that you see no reasons for their inclusion in programs which featured Thomson and Blitzstein. Cowell at least makes interesting sounds....

Alfred H. Meyer reviewed the Yaddo Festival for *Modern Music*. He appraised the music, complimented the performers, and commented, "American music need no longer step aside for Europe...."[25] Rosenfeld, Berger, Meyer, and Irving Kolodin were the only critics who came to the festival. As chairman of the Sunday conference, "Critics and Composers," it was up to me to express the anger and frustration felt by the composers. I said that the time had arrived for critics to adopt new attitudes, and I accused the critics of neglect and lack of curiosity. I urged my colleagues to join together for their own mutual benefit. "Frankly," I concluded, "under such circumstances I consider daily newspaper criticism a menace, and we would be better off without it!" The following morning, an Associated Press dispatch informed readers of *The New York Times*: "The long-standing feud between composers and critics flared into the open at a conference in Yaddo, the Spencer Trask mansion." I described the blow-up to Virgil, who was in Paris (10 May 1932): "The critics were conspicuous by their absence. I lit into them at a conference. An AP reporter got the story, and thereby stirred a hornets' nest. There is now a case going on of Copland vs the Critics. Since they always treated me with kid gloves they consider it rank ingratitude—biting the hand that fed my reputation...." I wrote a response to the *Times*:

> ... It would be naive to imagine that a conference between critics and composers was arranged at the First Festival of Contemporary Music at Yaddo for the childish purpose of giving composers an opportunity to tell the critics where "to get off at," as the saying goes. On the contrary, our purpose was the thoroughly serious one of considering the relation between the American composer and the music critics of the daily press and to discover what might be done to make that relationship more vital and more important than it now is. ... Far from being a "menace" to the composer, he is an absolute necessity....

But the *Times* music critic, Olin Downes, had the last word. "Who," he asked rhetorically, "has created music remotely cognizant of the things that palpitate in such modern American novels as *Arrowsmith* or dramas with such a terrible intensity as *Mourning Becomes Electra*?" Roger Sessions wrote from Italy wondering why I would even bother myself with critics in this way. But I decided to go further by expanding my remarks into an article for *Modern Music* in which I asked that the critics attend concerts of the League and the Pan American Association of Composers, and furthermore, that they study scores of new works. "If they knew all this music, and knew it well, they would realize that there is something alive and growing on our own soil which deserves to be championed; for like any new growth, American music needs nurturing. . . ." And I pleaded for just one critic "who will concern himself in the creation of an American music to the same degree as Edward Evans in English music, of Henri Prunières in French music. Is that too much to ask?"[26]

It seemed likely that Yaddo would take the place of the Copland–Sessions Concerts, so Roger and I decided to give up our joint effort. Henry Brant coined a phrase at about this time that has become familiar, but that I am not particularly fond of. Henry wrote (2 May 1932): "You are destined to become the 'Dean of American Composers.' The names of your disciples are so far not well established, but such as already exist are even now known as 'Coplandites.' . . . Do you think the late season was so bad for American music? 1. Composers group actually started. 2. Yaddo festival and its notice. 3. Ives began to be noticed."

For the Second Festival of Contemporary American Music at Yaddo in 1933, a Central Music Committee was formed: Richard Donovan, Robert Russell Bennett, Wallingford Riegger, Randall Thompson, and myself as chairman. To further broaden our scope, representatives were chosen in various cities in the East (Piston in Boston, Bernard Rogers in Rochester, Blitzstein in Philadelphia, Carl Engel in Washington); West (Harris in Los Angeles, Cowell in San Francisco); and in Europe (Thomson in Paris), and Mexico (Chávez in Mexico City). We hoped to expand this plan further. There were again three concerts—two on Saturday, 30 September; one on Sunday afternoon, 1 October. The Sunday conference with Roger Sessions as chairman featured a discussion between "Interpretive Artists and Composers." A lively session evolved around the social uses of music. Several composers from the original festival were on the program in 1933, while others were being represented for the first time. Nothing of my own was performed.[27] Partly in response to Rosenfeld's criticism, Cowell and Ruggles were now included. George Antheil had canceled in 1932; I wrote again to him in Paris, and finally had a response (7 September 1933) after his return to America: "I should like to play at Yaddo, (1) The Death of Machines Sonata (2) Preludes from '100 piano preludes to Femme Cent Tete of Max Ernst's' and (3) Sonatina 1932. This ought to be enough if not too much. All three works are related to the 'Death of the Machines' Sonata. . . . I have dedicated the Sonatina to you, Aaron, in admiration of your work, and in appreciation of your friendship."

Randall Thompson reviewed the festival for *Modern Music:* "Gone the nonconformity, gone the hearty satisfaction of smashing everything in sight; gone the passionate conviction, gone the spirit of the Mohawk trail. . . ."[28] Well, the festival reflected the times—and the times were calling for a swing away from the experimentalism of the twenties. The Second Yaddo Festival demonstrated the growing need for a simpler, more accessible musical language.

After 1933 I was not to present contemporary American music festivals at Yaddo after all. Following the Second Festival, I proposed that Yaddo be sponsored by the U.S. Section of the ISCM, and I wrote my reasons and suggestions in a lengthy report to Elizabeth Ames, who took the proposal to the Yaddo board of directors. I received a letter from Mrs. Ames (5 May 1934): "It is now very clear to me that it will be impossible for Yaddo to make any decision this spring about when or how the third festival shall be held. . . ." The festivals did not resume until 1936, and then it was to present programs combining "old" and "new" music. I was no longer associated with them. In 1940 Yaddo returned to my original idea of all-contemporary American music, but the war then caused a hiatus of six years. The festivals resumed in 1946, 1949, and 1952. The final celebration honored Yaddo's twenty-five years of service to creative artists. When the concert opened with my *Piano Variations* played by John Kirkpatrick, I was in the audience in the Yaddo music room of the mansion where I had played the piece twenty years earlier.

In the spring of 1932 I stayed on at Yaddo to work on the *Short Symphony* and *Statements for Orchestra,* two of my most serious compositions that followed in the style of the *Piano Variations.* I wrote to Kirkpatrick (22 June 1932): "My new work is being upset by the fact that I've started still a newer and am working on the two simultaneously. The newest piece will have 4 or 5 short movements. I have one of these already. . . . Of the other, I have two of the three movements practically done." This, the *Short Symphony,* was written at intervals between 1931 and 1933 in a variety of places from Morocco to Mexico. It is a bare fifteen minutes in length, but as was the case with the *Variations,* those minutes are concentrated in meaning. If I expended a great deal of time and effort on the

Short Symphony, it was because I was determined to write as perfected a piece as I possibly could. I had briefly considered naming the piece (at Chávez' suggestion) "The Bounding Line" until another friend (I no longer recall who) wisely advised against it, pointing out that "bounding" seemed more like "boundary" than the "bounce" I had in mind. The *Short Symphony* is actually my *Second Symphony* and is occasionally referred to that way. It is in three movements—fast, slow, fast—to be played without pause. The first movement's main impetus is rhythmic, with a scherzo-like quality. All melodic figures result from a nine-note sequence—a kind of row—from the opening two bars. The second movement, tranquil in feeling, contrasts with the first movement and with the finale, which is again rhythmically intricate, bright in color and free in form. The orchestration includes a heckelphone (baritone oboe), but there are no trombones, and the nature of the music calls for an enlarged chamber orchestra, rather than the full sound of the symphonic ensemble.

The *Short Symphony* has a curious performance history. Both Stokowski and Koussevitzky announced performances, but gave it up because of the rhythmic difficulties. Koussevitzky considered the piece for a year and a half. When I asked him, "Is it too difficult?" he responded, "Non, ce n'est pas trop difficile, c'est impossible!" Exactly one week later, Chávez gave the world premiere in Mexico City (23 November 1934) with the Orquesta Sinfónica de México. Carlos sent the program and wrote (1 December 1934):

> . . . We had ten rehearsals . . . the orchestra men were at first skeptical but by the third rehearsal or so they had a real genuine and growing interest. . . . It is impossible to tell you in a few words how much I enjoy the Little Symphony: I already begin to write an essay on it. . . . The way each and every note comes out from the other as the *only* natural and logic possible one, is simply unprecedented in the whole history of music. . . . There has been very much talk about music in which everything is essential, nothing superfluous, but, as far as I know, exists, yes, *the talk* about such music, but not the music itself. The Little Symphony is the first realization I know of that, and yet, the human content, the ironic expression, is purely emotional. . . .

And I responded (31 December 1934): "How I wish I could have heard it. And what a strange feeling it gives me to think that you have heard a piece of mine which I have not yet heard. . . ." The *Short Symphony* is dedicated to Chávez. From the start, he called it the "Little Symphony," and through the years, he never referred to it as anything else.

Partly due to the fact that the piece did not get a performance in the

Manuscript page from the two-piano sketch score of the *Short Symphony*.

Manuscript page from the orchestral ink score of the *Short Symphony*.

States, I prepared the *Sextet*, an arrangement for clarinet, string quartet, and piano in 1937 while summering in Mexico. The *Sextet* was first performed in New York at Town Hall in 1939 by a Juilliard graduate ensemble. It was announced for the 1941 ISCM Festival and a CBS radio broadcast in connection with it but was abandoned due to the difficulty of the piece and the number of rehearsals required.

The *Short Symphony* itself finally had its U.S. premiere when Leopold Stokowski conducted the NBC Symphony in a broadcast from the famous 8-H studio in the RCA Building. Even then Stokowski told me, "It is still a difficult work to perform, and even more so to interpret." But it *can* be done—in 1955 I conducted the Sudwestfunk Orchestra, and I wrote to Virgil (24 September), "I'm having a scrumptious time this week . . . they play 5/8–7/8 in their sleep—and with *ten* rehearsals in five days the *Short Symphony* sounds like 'Eine Kleine Nachtmusik'!" Leonard Bernstein conducted the first American public performance of the *Short Symphony* in 1957 with the Philharmonic–Symphony Society of New York on a program that included Roy Harris' *Third Symphony.*

I think of the *Short Symphony* as one of "my neglected children" and am perhaps more fond of these works *because* they receive so much less attention. But at least on special occasions they have occasional hearings. For a seventieth birthday celebration, I conducted the *Short Symphony* in an all-Copland program with the New York Philharmonic, and at about the same time, it was finally played for the first time by the BSO under Seiji Ozawa. In my eightieth year I was invited to conduct the *Short Symphony* at Carnegie Hall. Between rehearsals, a violinist came up to me and said, "In my opinion *you*, Mr. Copland, taught American orchestras to play in 5/4!" I'm sure this is an exaggeration, but even today, with orchestra players capable of complicated rhythms and harmonies, the *Short Symphony* and the *Sextet* are not easy for performers. On a European tour early in 1981, I was scheduled to conduct the *Symphony* in Brussels, and it was canceled for lack of extra rehearsal time; and when the Chamber Music Society of Lincoln Center played the *Sextet* on 31 October and 2 November 1980, *The New York Times* reviewer, Joseph Horowitz, wrote (2 November 1980): "It is fiendishly difficult to negotiate cleanly . . . however frustrating Mr. Copland's tangle of syncopations, cross-rhythms and shifting meters may seem to the performer, there are no gratuitous difficulties in the *Sextet*. . . ." One would think that most of the terrors of both versions would have worn off by now for players as well as listeners. One learns to have patience.[29]

I had been promising Chávez a visit to Mexico for several years. The time had come—especially since I was promised an all-Copland program in a series conducted by Chávez at the Conservatorio Nacional de México. I wrote to Chávez (8 August 1932): "You'll be glad to hear that I am studying Spanish and reading a great deal about Mexico, so that I think I can already find my way around the City without a guide! I am spending a quiet summer in New York, working on the same new orchestral piece which I hope to finish in Mexico. And looking forward 'passionement' to my Mexican trip." In my next letter (18 August 1932), I explained my plans. I would drive my car as far as Laredo and take the train to Mexico City, leaving New York 24 August. I wrote: "I am bringing with me a young violinist who is a pupil, companion, secretary and friend. His name is Victor Kraftsov. I'm sure you will like him." (When Victor dropped the last three letters from his name, I no longer recall—it seems to me I *always* knew him as Victor Kraft!) I had a telegram from Chávez that the all-Copland program—the first ever given anywhere—would take place 2 September. I was determined not to miss such an occasion, so we left New York precipitously and drove to Laredo in eight days, arriving in Mexico City on the morning of the concert.

I wrote "Dear Ma and Pa" letters from Mexico during my five-month visit there just as I had from France eleven years earlier, and the letters covered the same subjects—money, food, and weather: "You can get a regular meal in the swellest American restaurant for 2 pesos (60¢)." I called Cuernavaca "a Mexican Atlantic City," and sent programs and reviews regularly with my translations, asking Ma and Pa to share them with the family. I wrote home about the attractive small apartment Chávez had found us in Mexico City and described the excitement surrounding the all-Copland concert and the informal and enthusiastic spirit that prevailed. The program, presented by the Conservatorio Nacional de México, at the Teatro de Orientacion, included the following works: *Two Pieces for String Quartet*; *Piano Variations* (Jésus Durón Ruiz, pianist); "The House on the Hill" and "An Immorality" for chorus directed by Chávez; and *Music for the Theatre* performed by the conservatory orchestra under Chávez, who spoke about my music from the stage during the intermission. Several of these works were repeated a few weeks later.

Life was quieter for me in Mexico than in New York. The telephone did not ring so often, and I was able to fulfill a commission from the League for a piece to be performed in April. While in Mexico, I composed two *Elegies for Violin and Viola*. (When I decided to use this material in

Copland and Victor Kraft, Mexico, 1932.

Statements, I withdrew the *Elegies* from my list of works.)[30] I spent a great deal of time with Chávez. We had much in common. His dedication to improving conditions for Mexican music was similar to my own efforts in American music. But in Mexico the general educational facilities and music in particular were far behind what we had in the States. Chávez and I admired each other's music, and I was amazed to see where he had come from and how he had taught himself almost everything he knew without formal instruction. Chávez knew what he wanted and was very forceful in getting results; he had the orchestras, although lacking in the kind of technical expertise we had in America, playing more contemporary music than I had ever heard performed anywhere in a short period of time. I wrote to Virgil (5 December):

> Chávez has complete control of the musical situation here. I wish you knew him personally—he's about as nice a guy as you could hope to meet. They've been playing a lot of stuff here so that I begin to feel as famous as Gershwin. Mexico has turned out even grander than I expected—and I expected pretty grand things. The best is the people—there's nothing remotely like them in Europe. They are really the "people"—nothing in them is striving to be bourgeois. In their overalls and bare feet they are not only poetic but positively "émouvant."

III
Viernes 2 de Septiembre
a las 20.30 horas

2 Piezas para Cuarteto de Cuerda   COPLAND
Cuarteto del Conservatorio
Violín 1o.	Higinio Ruvalcaba
Violín 2o.	Filiberto Nava
Viola	Jesús Mendoza
Violoncello	Luis G. Galindo

Variaciones   COPLAND
Piano Solo JESUS DURON RUIZ
2 Piezas para Coro y Piano   COPLAND
Upon the hills
An inmorality
Coro del Conservatorio
Dirección CARLOS CHAVEZ

INTERMEDIO

Music for the Theatre   COPLAND
Prologue
Dance
Interlude
Burlesque
Epilogue
Orquesta del Conservatorio
Dirección CARLOS CHAVEZ

Top: Program of the first all-Copland concert,
Mexico City, conducted by Carlos Chávez.
Above: Copland visiting a family in
Tlalpam, Mexico.
Left: Copland, Mexico, 1932.

I was beginning to sense something in the Mexican character that was especially sympathetic. When Chávez took me to an unusual night spot called El Salón México, the atmosphere of this dance hall impressed me, and I came away with the germ of a musical idea. I wrote about Mexico to several friends. Gerald Sykes responded that he particularly liked my description of the "silence of the Mexican crowds." But in the concert hall they really let one know how they felt about the music. I could sense approval on 18 November when Chávez conducted the *Symphonic Ode* with the Orquesta Sinfónica in the Teatro Hidalgo. But I recall another occasion when I performed my *Piano Concerto* and some of the listeners took a dislike to it and began to hiss with characteristic Latin vigor. Others in the audience began to shush the hissers with equal vehemence, and between the hissing and the shushing, such a tumult was raised that I looked apprehensively at Chávez for a sign as to whether to stop the performance or go on to the bitter end. "We go on!" muttered Chávez grimly. So we did, and I wondered all the while whether it was the correct thing to take a bow to hisses. At the finish, however, there was sufficient applause to drown the hisses and the bow was definitely indicated.

Our last two months in Mexico were spent in the rural small town of Tlalpam. Before leaving Mexico, Victor wanted to experience swimming in the Pacific, so we had a few days' vacation in Acapulco. We then took the train to Laredo to pick up our car. As we crossed the border, I had a sharp pang at leaving Mexico, and I wrote to Chávez from our first stop, San Antonio (2 January 1933): "It took me three years in France to get as close a feeling to the country as I was able to get in these few months in Mexico." Victor and I took turns driving back to New York. We made one-night stops in Houston, Montgomery, Atlanta, Savannah, Charleston, Raleigh, Richmond, and Washington. From Savannah, ten days before arriving home, I wrote to Mary Lescaze (13 January):

Mexico was a rich time. Outwardly nothing happened and inwardly all was calm. Yet I'm left with the impression of having had an enriching experience. It comes, no doubt, from the nature of the country and the people. Europe now seems conventional to me by comparison. Mexico offers something fresh and pure and wholesome—a quality which is deeply unconventionalized. The source of it is the Indian blood which is so prevalent. I sensed the influence of the Indian background everywhere—even in the landscape. And I must be something of an Indian myself or how else explain the sympathetic chord it awakens in me. Of course I'm going back someday.

Interlude III

Some periods in history are long and stable, with changes so gradual as to be imperceptible; others are short and volatile, with political and economic forces causing sudden shifts that quickly affect the climate. In describing the abrupt change from the twenties to the thirties, George Orwell wrote, "Suddenly we got out of the twilight of the gods into a sort of Boy Scout atmosphere of bare knees and community singing."[1] And Aaron Copland's friend Mary Lescaze recalled, "One morning in 1930 I opened my closet to find everything out of style. I stored away the high-heeled dancing slippers and went out to buy 'sensible' shoes."[2] The glamour of French culture, the exclusivity of the avant garde, the champagne, formal clothes, and lighthearted parties were replaced by earnest groups discussing serious matters in a charged atmosphere of liberalism and social consciousness: Trotskyism, Marxism, and Stalinism were discussed endlessly by the Young Peoples Socialist League and the Young Communist League, and aspects of American culture were written about in *The New Republic* and *The American Mercury*. The role of the arts in society was a favorite topic for debate at the Group Theatre, the Young Composers' Group, and the conferences at Yaddo. If a time in history can be located and defined by catch words and phrases, "the masses," "the proletariat," "workers' causes," and "comrade" would henceforth identify the thirties.

In the arts, modernism was "old hat" and realism was "in." "Social Realism became not *a* style of the period but *the* style of the period," wrote Tom Wolfe about the art world. "Even the most dedicated Modernists were intimidated.... For more than ten years from about 1930 to 1941, the artists themselves, in Europe and America, suspended the Modern movement.... Left politics did that for them...."[3] Paradoxically, political radicalism produced conservative results in the arts. Social Realism at its worst was propaganda; at best, an art that could be understood and enjoyed by the masses—one that was far from the experimentation and innovation that characterized the twenties. The thirties are considered dull and plodding when compared to the flamboyant years preceding them. But for many, these were the "fervent years" of commitment to social and national causes—years when artists had the rare experience of feeling wanted and needed.

Copland was not by nature a political person; he joined neither Socialist nor Communist Party, but for a time in the early thirties he was what might be called a fellow traveler. When questioned about his leftist activities, his answer is simply, "It seemed the thing to do at the time." In fact, so many artists were caught up in the strong wave of sympathy for socialism that it *was* the thing to do. The Party slogan, "Communism is twentieth-century Americanism," took full advantage of the "affirm America" movement. In any case, Copland, cautious as he was about politics, was never a loner and would not have found it natural to go underground with those modernists holding to the doctrine of "art for art's sake." Irving Howe, as a young political activist in the thirties, wrote: "Things had gone profoundly wrong. No later discounting of the radicalism of the thirties can wipe away this simple truth. Things had gone wrong not only in America but still more in Europe." Socialism offered a hope of restoring order and improving conditions. Howe also made the point that many politically active artists were from Jewish immigrant families: "Socialism was not merely politics or an idea. It was an encompassing culture, a style of perceiving and judging through which to structure their lives . . . culture could be a high calling. What excited them was the idea of breaking away, of willing a new life. They meant to declare themselves citizens of the world—and if that succeeded, might then become the writers of this country."[4] These ideas were not new to Copland and Clurman. Hadn't they been expressing "cultural politics" for American music and drama since their student years in Paris?

Several influences nudged Copland toward the Left: Mexico and the "people"; the Depression (by now affecting Copland's own family); the Marxist concept of "art for society's sake" espoused by Hanns Eisler and Marc Blitzstein; the lack of an audience for Copland's most recent compositions; and the political idealism of Clurman and the Group Theatre. Considering the repercussions for those who were involved in left-wing activities, it is hardly surprising that Clurman did not deal with his own or the Group's politics in his later published writings. But his letters to Copland at the time were filled with political discussions. After one particularly stimulating visit to the John Reed Club, Clurman wrote (24 May 1932):

It is clear to me that people like us are the real revolutionaries in America today and that we are revolutionary in our function as artists and leaders. If we continue to perfect our experience in the deepest sense which means relating ourselves as completely as is natural to our temperaments and interest to people around us with the same interests we shall be doing more for the revolutionary change of society . . . than all the theoretical communists in America. . . . The Artist's job today is to fight like hell to be an artist which means to find his kindred, to fight for them too and to relate it to as many still living people as possible . . . and perhaps the Aaron Coplands—because they are as aware of their *world* as well as their art—are in the final analysis the greater artists as well as the greater revolutionaries. . . .

Copland was close to the Group Theatre[5] from the time of its formation in the winter of 1930–31 when Clurman, Lee Strasberg, and Cheryl Crawford invited young theater people to meet with them on Friday evenings after showtime for discussions and lectures by the directors and others—among them, Waldo Frank on the relationship of the theater to the American social system and Copland on the uses of modern music in the theater. When the Group ran out of meeting places, Copland offered his Copland–Sessions office at Steinway Hall. Among those who attended regularly were Stella Adler, Morris Carnovsky, John Garfield, Robert Lewis, Sandy Meisner, Clifford Odets, and Franchot Tone. About the Group's beginnings, Clurman wrote:

. . . one had to divine an approach that might be common to all the members. . . . It was this that added a dimension to the talks and to the whole atmosphere around the Group, that was to become its distinguishing mark, its strength, its impediment, and its wound. . . . For this reason photographers like Paul Strand and Ralph Steiner, a musician like Aaron Copland, an architect like William Lescaze, and many others not directly connected with the theatre found these meetings, and the subsequent development of the group that emerged from them, both stimulating and relevant to their own fields of interest. . . .[6]

Twenty-eight who attended the first winter meetings became the Group Theatre. The following summer the directors found a place in the country, at Brookfield Center, Connecticut, where they all lived and worked together in an atmosphere of high dedication—dissecting, debating, and rehearsing two plays for production in New York. Visitors were welcome to join in the discussions; they included Maxwell Anderson, Copland, Waldo Frank, Gerald Sykes, Paul Strand, and Ralph Steiner. Director Bobby

Lewis, then a young actor with the Group, recalls that they were all great talkers, himself included—and Clurman most of all:

> Clurman *never* tired of talking about the theater! Once Franchot [Tone] despaired of getting a particular play ready in time for performance. I said, "Don't worry. Harold will never stop *talking* long enough for a production to take place!" But Harold had to define what our theater was. He believed that theater was an *idea*, not a building or a complex. The Group Theatre's idea was to reflect the life of their times. We practiced a common technique derived from the Stanislavsky system of the Moscow Art Theatre—not a star system, but an ensemble theater. In ten years, twenty-five plays were produced. The Group was an influence all over the world—even felt to this day through their own actions, and subsequently from the Actors Studio which came out of it.[7]

Clurman had always confided his troubles to Copland. Now he had almost more than he could handle: artistic, personal, and financial. Never realistic about money, Clurman loaned what he had to Group members, who were constantly broke, and then turned to Copland for help. From Boston (12 February 1932):

> I want to borrow some money. $150 from *you*. We got only ½ salary last week. We shall get only ⅓ salary this. Can we get out of Boston?—We won't receive any more salary at all till we open the Anderson play—in three weeks. . . . If for any of a hundred reasons—"good" or "bad"—you can't lend me this money, don't feel badly about it at all. I shall accept—without a reason and without a doubt. Since all things you do are *right* to me (Always 100%) I don't feel embarrassed at asking you either—tho I don't like it. And I don't feel sad because money is really a minor trouble to me now. . . . I'm getting all clear within me and strong and am preparing myself for a bunch of real "socks." . . .

Clurman and his co-directors managed to hold the Group together through many "socks." They survived the first two seasons and the second summer at Dover Furnace, New York, but during the third season, the Group was close to bankruptcy. They were saved at the last moment when an arrangement was made to exchange four nights a week of entertainment at Green Mansions, an adult camp in the Adirondacks, for a place to live and work. Copland had helped the Group earlier by introducing them to potential donors (Mary Churchill was one), and he continued to write to benefactors on their behalf; in return, he was named Group Associate. In the summer of 1933, when Copland himself was feeling the pinch of the Depression, a few young actors invited him to stay for free in a house on Friends Lake in Chestertown near Green Mansions.

During that summer Clifford Odets and Copland began a lasting friendship. Odets was passionate about music and would frequently turn to it during turbulent periods in his life; he was often at the piano at Green Mansions. According to Bobby Lewis, who was a cellist in his early years, "Sandy Meisner was really a fine pianist, but Cliff was an amateur who thought he was a musician."[8] Odets joined the Communist Party, but Copland preferred to stay closer to Clurman's less keenly focused political idealism. Clurman and the actress Stella Adler, recently married, traveled to Russia together in the spring of 1934 to see the Moscow Art Theatre in action and to meet Stanislavsky. From Clurman to Copland (15 June 1934): "I'd like to go back to the U.S.S.R. next spring! Let's go together!" Clurman was invited to return in 1935, but Copland could not afford to travel there at his own expense. After his return, Clurman wrote impressions of Russia and of the Group (31 July 1934): "They still want automobiles, good parts, cocktails while they are building a revolutionary theatre. They still are Americans who do not understand the element of sacrifice in the making of an integrated world. Russia gave me that picture clearly. . . ."

Clurman urged Odets and Copland to collaborate on a play, *The Silent Partner*, described by Odets as "presenting the problems of a symphony, in contrast to . . . less ambitious chamber works. . . ."[9] But the play was dropped after several trials and revisions, before music was written for it. Copland did not work on a play with the Group Theatre until 1938 when he composed incidental music for an experimental drama, *The Quiet City*, by Irwin Shaw. This also was dropped after two dress rehearsals. Clurman wrote, "All that remained of our hard work was a lovely score by Aaron Copland, which is not infrequently heard nowadays at orchestral concerts."[10] And Bobby Lewis commented, "This was a good example of Aaron's frugality—he just scooped up all those pages of music and *used* them later!"[11] Copland maintained friendships with several Group Theatre members for many years—Elia Kazan, Lewis, Odets. He always attended performances in New York, and later, every production Clurman had anything to do with. "I don't remember *ever* being at a theater without Harold."[12] (In 1980 Copland went to the Harold Clurman Theater for a memorial tribute to his lifelong friend, and as Clurman's associates and friends took the stage to reminisce about him, Copland mused, "Where is Harold? He would enjoy this more than anybody!")

In 1933 even Copland's normally ebullient spirits were low. "This damn Depression!" he wrote to composer Silvestre Revueltas in Mexico.

Accepting the invitation to join the League of Composers board in 1932, Copland hoped to implement their programs with music by younger composers, but as he wrote to Chávez (16 December 1933): "It is hard to put new life into the old girl!" Alma Wertheim (now Wiener) turned the Cos Cob Press over to Copland to run for two years on a reduced budget, which allowed for publication of only a few works a year. The fall of the American dollar abroad and the impending threat of Nazism chased composers to the United States, the Europeans running away and the Americans dashing back. No longer was there anyone to study with in Europe. Copland wrote to Chávez: "Everyone is now in New York—Varèse, Antheil, Roy Harris, Sessions, Cowell etc.—but the feeling of camaraderie is not strong. The younger group of composers who I brought together have even less of an 'esprit de corps.' Last year they were very busy getting famous—this year they are students again, several of them studying with Sessions. . . ." And about conditions at home: "Here in the U.S. we composers have no possibility of directing the musical affairs of the nation—on the contrary, since my return, I have the impression that more and more we are working in a vacuum. There seems to me less than ever a real rapport between the public and the composers and of course that is a very important way of creating an audience, and being in contact with an audience. When one has done that, one can compose with real joy." This increasing discontent with the attitudes toward contemporary music in America opened Copland further to left-wing causes.

The Pierre Degeyter Club (named after the composer of the "Internationale") was a branch of the Workers Music League (the WML, later renamed the American Music League or AML). They were controlled by the Communist-backed International Music Bureau. The Degeyter Club's headquarters were at 5 East 19th Street in New York, and there were branches in Philadelphia and Boston. Under its auspices were choruses, an orchestra, and a Composers Collective. The Degeyter Club invited Copland to play a recital on 16 March 1934. He asked John Kirkpatrick and a few others to join him. (One work was Kirkpatrick's two-piano arrangement of Copland's Piano Concerto.) Charles Seeger under the pseudonym of Carl Sands reviewed the concert in the Daily Worker.[13] Copland, in his introductory remarks, had warned the predominantly working-class audience against viewing his compositions from a revolutionary angle. Sands wrote:

> . . . the composer spoke with charming naiveté, claiming that he had not, at the time of their composition, any ideas of that sort in his head. This reviewer held

tightly to his seat, waiting for the avalanche to fall, but not one single member of the large audience took him up on the point, which clearly challenges the very basis upon which the club is organized. . . . The issue was all the clearer because the composer's progress from ivory tower to within hailing distance of the proletariat was plainly and graphically told in his music. . . .

What might really have been "naive" was the presentation of such music for an audience, many of whom were hearing their first concert music of any kind. Part way through the difficult *Piano Variations*, several people stomped out. Sands concluded his review: "How about some show there, comrades, of revolutionary discipline, not to speak of courtesy and musical taste?" Undaunted, a few months later on 11 May 1934, Copland presented a symposium with his colleagues Roy Harris, Elie Siegmeister, and Charles Seeger on "The Problems of the Composer in Modern Society."

The Composers Collective[14] was initiated by Jacob Schaefer, Leon Charles, and Henry Cowell after the three had conducted a seminar in the writing of songs for the masses. Although the Collective was under the auspices of the Degeyter Club, the members wanted more independence and a wider membership than the Party-controlled Degeyter Club would allow; they soon made a point of calling themselves the "Composers Collective of New York." There was never a complete break from the parent organization, but friction and disagreements increased during the years of the Collective's existence, from 1931 to 1936.[15] The Degeyter Club was on East 19th Street and the headquarters of the Collective at 47 East 12th; however, the composers usually met Saturday afternoons at 5430 Sixth Avenue in a shabby loft where there was an old upright piano. In a newsletter published by the American Music League, Marc Blitzstein, secretary of the Collective, listed the group's aims:

> . . . the writing of (1) Mass Songs, dealing with immediate social issues . . . to be sung at meetings, on parades, and on picket lines; (2) Choral music for professional as well as non-professional choruses, dealing in a broader way with the social scene. . . . (3) Solo songs, on social themes to be sung at meetings and concentrate the attention on the subjective, private emotions to the exclusion of the realistic social questions. (4) Instrumental music, to carry on the best musical traditions of the past, now threatened by the collapse of bourgeois culture. . . .[16]

Who belonged to the Composers Collective? In an interview, Charles Seeger answered, "That is what I never say!"[17] A membership list of the Collective is not readily obtainable for several reasons: members have been reluctant to name names; attendance varied from one time to another (for example, Cowell was in at the start and soon out, while Henry Leland Clarke came into the Collective in the late fall of 1934); and several participants took pseudonyms, adding to the confusion. Clarke points out, "It was dangerous to belong to the Collective, and even more dangerous later on to have been connected with it."[18] Clarke took the pseudonym Jonathan Fairbanks, and Elie Siegmeister recalls, "I took the name L. E. Swift, but sometimes I'd forget which name I was using. One time I was listed on a program as Swift conducting the Daily Workers Chorus in an arrangement by Siegmeister!"[19] Marc Blitzstein's minutes from meetings in the spring and summer of 1935 list the Executive Committee of the Collective as Sands, Chair; Swift, Treasurer; Blitzstein, Secretary; and George Maynard.[20] Blitzstein made a distinction between regular members and sympathetic composers; among the latter, "Aaron Copland, who came into a meeting (11 April 1935) for five minutes. . . ." Hanns Eisler was the member most strongly affiliated with the Communist Party. He attended meetings of the Collective when he was in New York. According to Clarke, "[Lahn] Adohmyan was the spearhead of the group and a strong follower of Eisler, but he went off to Spain in the Lincoln Brigade." Jacob Schaefer, older than most of the composers in the Collective, headed a Jewish chorus, the Freiheit Gesang Farein, and a mandolin orchestra. Schaefer was critical of the regulars for writing music too difficult for his workers to sing and play. Earl Robinson said, "We spent an awful lot of time talking about whether pure music, that is, instrumental music, could be useful for our purposes. I said no, and Seeger agreed with me. None of us used folk music at all until he and I started pushing it in 1934 and '35. . . ."[21] And Clarke considers that the Collective may have been the start of socially significant folk song in America.

The Workers Song Book No. 1 (1934) and Songs of the People were prepared by the Collective and published by the Workers Music League. Composers included were Carl Sands (Seeger), L. E. Swift (Siegmeister), Jacob Schaefer, Lahn Adohmyan, Janet Barnes (Jeannette Barnett), Jonathan Fairbanks (Clarke), Copland, Earl Robinson, Hanns Eisler, Stefan Volpe (Wolpe), Karl Vollmer, S. C. Richards (Riegger), A. Davidenko, and George Maynard. Workers Song Book No. 1 was reviewed by Copland in the New Masses. He called it ". . . the first adequate collection of revolutionary songs for American workers." In assessing the songs, Copland noted, "On the whole, Carl Sands seems to me to have written the best songs. . . . These may not be great songs, but they display a directness of attack and a sure technical grasp which is refreshing. . . ."[22]

Charles Seeger (Sands)[23]

Henry Cowell took me around to this composers' group and I lectured on the dictatorship of the linguistic—making fun, of course, of the dictatorship of the proletariat. I said, "Now, it's all right for you people who are interested in things like that, but what dictates the proletariat? It's language. And they are absolutely in the thrall of language. They may think they can get free of the bosses, and perhaps they will, but the bosses are enthralled with language too. Everybody is. And then if you straighten that out, this theory of yours—Marxism—doesn't make sense." Well, they were very nice about it and they said, "Of course, we don't agree with what you said, but what you said is very interesting." In other words, they wanted to get me in! So I joined.

The Composers Collective met every week, wintertime, composing songs for the labor movement. It was Communist-controlled. We had a competition for a May Day song in '34. The words were submitted to a committee first and were published in the old New Masses, *and then a committee was appointed to receive the settings of it. And I was chairman of the meeting which went over the final songs, words and music, so that I spoke last. And of course Aaron Copland won the prize. He wrote a beautiful song. It really was a splendid thing. It was magnificent. We all agreed. We criticized everybody's contribution, and they criticized themselves— true Communist style (as far as I know there was only one real Communist member there, Marc Blitzstein). Henry was out by this time. In California, I think. Also, he wasn't too interested. . . . It came to me, and I criticized my piece. "You know, I'll agree that mine is just about the worst of the whole lot, but I'll put it to you this way," I said to Copland. "Everybody here knows that your song is best. But do you think it will ever be sung on the picket line? And anyway, who would carry a piano into the streets May First or any time?" Well, Aaron was very nice and he said, "No, I don't suppose it ever will be sung in a picket line." He'd made some freak modulations, and some big skips of sevenths in it, had some dissonances, key changes all over the place. "Well," I said, "take mine, for instance. I haven't tried to make a piece of music I admire. I tried to write a piece of music that I think might be sung on the picket line. Do you think there is anybody in New York who couldn't join in with this the second time they hear it?"*

Copland's song, "Into the Streets May First!" was set to a poem by Alfred Hayes provided by the Collective. After the contest, the song was published in the *New Masses*[24] and later in the *Workers Songbook No. 2* (1935). An article by Ashley Pettis preceded the music in the magazine: "The *New Masses* feel that the time is ripe for the development of music by the various composers of America for the constantly increasing number of singing workers; a music which is characteristic of them, truly representative of their awakening consciousness and growing power; of their determination and hopes. With this in mind, Alfred Hayes' poem, 'Into the Streets May First!' was sent out to the Composers Collective of the Pierre Degeyter Club, New York, as well as to a group comprising some of the most accomplished musicians of America."[25] Pettis listed the contributors: "Lahn Adohmyan, Aaron Copland, Isadore Freed, Wallingford Riegger, Carl Sands, Mitya Stillman, L. E. Swift, and one composer who conceals his identity under the nom de plume 'XYZ.' " Pettis discussed each song and gave reasons for the committee's unanimous choice of Copland's. Earl Robinson recalls, "We *agreed*, but we all commiserated over Aaron's song." Pettis wrote as if to prepare his readers: "Its spirit is identical with that of the poem. The unfamiliar, 'experimental' nature of the harmonies which occur occasionally, does not tend to make the unsophisticated singer question. . . . Some of the intervals may be somewhat difficult upon a first hearing or singing, but we believe the ear will very readily accustom itself to their sound." Pettis announced that the song would be performed by the Workers Music League at their Second Annual American Workers Music Olympiad (29 April 1934). "The entire ensemble of 800 voices, comprising the revolutionary workers' choruses of New York will participate. . . ."

In 1935 Earl Robinson won a competition sponsored by the left-wing Downtown Music School. The prize was free lessons donated by composer Aaron Copland. "Aaron was a wonderful teacher," claimed Robinson. "He never would say *how* to compose, but when I brought in a jazz-style fugue, he'd play Milhaud's *Création du monde* to demonstrate the use of jazz in concert music. In the summers I went to the Party Camp, Unity Camp. While there in 1936 I composed two songs—'Joe Hill' and 'Old Abe Lincoln,' and I showed them to Aaron. He seemed impressed with the alternation of song and speech in 'Abe,' and with the phrase, 'and these are the words he said.' (Aaron may also have heard my 'Ballad for Americans' in '38 or '39, which includes the same section from Gettysburg Address used by Aaron in *Lincoln Portrait*, and the spoken words, 'Abraham Lin-

"Into the Streets May First" as published in *The New Masses*, 1 May 1934.

coln said that on November 19, 1863.') When Aaron was composing *Lincoln Portrait*, he said to me, 'Earl, I'm stealing some of your thunder.' "[26]

Copland contributed occasional articles and performances to left-wing organizations in the spring of 1935. These articles could hardly be called agitprop. In one, the first issue of *Music Vanguard*, featuring Hanns Eisler on the German workers' music movement, Copland almost seemed to be taking an anti-Party line. He wrote, "The young composer who allies himself with the proletarian movement must do so not with the feeling that he has found an easy solution, but with a full realization of what such a step means, if his work is to be of permanent value to the workers and their cause. . . . But as for myself, I admit to a certain uneasiness of feeling til that 'first symphony,' quintet or proletarian oratorio is forthcoming."[27] A "Gedenkschrift" for Hanns Eisler compiled 17 April 1935 by Seeger included a "Sketch for a Worker's Song" by Copland. Also, in *The American Mercury*, in an issue featuring Emma Goldman on communism in Russia, Copland wrote a straightforward report on a resurgence of activity in American music, with this warning: "It is not even now appreciated that

Above: Sketch page from 1933 with segments of *El Salón México* and *Statements*.
Left: Copland, 1933.
Photograph by Ralph Steiner.

a serious and important type of composer functions among us; nor, as a man, is he properly understood. . . . It cannot be doubted that he occupies little or no place even today in the mind of the public at large."[28] Copland was caught in the dilemma of wanting to reach the "people," but not wanting to use his own music for propaganda. He was not the only composer to face this problem—members of the Collective debated it often, and Henry Cowell and Wallingford Riegger were even less interested than Copland in adapting or changing their music-writing skills and talents to suit Party songs and marches.

The summer of 1934 held an unexpected political experience. When Copland's cousin, Leo Harris, offered him a rent-free cottage on a lake in Minnesota, he accepted, thinking that a period of isolation from the musical, political, and social pressures of New York would be beneficial. Copland and Victor Kraft drove to Lavinia, Minnesota, to the cottage on Lake Bemidji. From there Copland wrote to Roger Sessions that it offered all the advantages of an art colony with none of the disadvantages. He settled down to work on *Statements for Orchestra*, moving ahead steadily to orchestrate five of the projected seven movements. When Victor and Aaron drove into town, they saw Swedes, Germans, radical farmers, tourists, Indians, and lumberjacks coming in and out of Bemidji. One day Victor was amazed to see a little wizened woman selling the *Daily Worker* on a street corner. Then they attended a picnic supper hosted by "red" farmers. Copland wrote to Israel Citkowitz (summer 1934):

> If they were a strange sight to me, I was no less of one to them. It was the first time that many of them had seen an "intellectual"! . . . I wish you could have seen them—the true Third Estate, the very material that makes revolution. What struck me particularly was the fact that there is no "type-communist" among them, such as we see on 14th St. They look like any other of the farmers around here, all of them individuals, clearly etched in my mind. And desperately poor. None can afford more than a 10¢ pamphlet. (With that in mind I appealed to the Group for funds and they sent me a collection of $30 which I presented to the unit here for their literature fund.)

When the farmers asked Copland to talk to the crowd, he at first demurred, but later accepted, making his one and only political speech to farmers in Bemidji, Minnesota.

Copland's political contributions included an occasional benefit performance. On 17 May 1936 at the first Festival of the American Music League, were represented seventeen organizations, among them German, Italian, and Lithuanian choruses, the Fur Workers' Chorus singing in

Yiddish, the Freiheit Mandolin Orchestra, along with many individuals. Copland was featured as "one of America's outstanding composers, performing his 'Children's Pieces for Piano.' "[29]

That Copland's music was influenced by the social and political climate cannot be discounted. Convinced that the American people could be reached by good new music, over and over again he asked audiences to open their minds, to "take off the ear muffs," to be less conservative, to give music a chance. He took great pains to teach and to write "what to listen for in music." It was only fair, he considered, that in return the composer meet his audience part way. The challenge was to find a way without sacrificing musical values. Copland wrote, "To compose music of 'socialist realism' has stumped even so naturally gifted a man as Shostakovitch."[30] Never again would Copland attempt to reach a more popular audience with a "workers' song" or for political reasons. When the Popular Front came along in 1935 bringing a wider recognition and appreciation of American folk music, the way was opened for Copland to adopt a simpler, more direct musical style using quotation or simulation of folk tunes in productions outside the concert hall—ballet, theater, radio, and film. Copland was again about to set out in a new direction; as before, the change would not be abrupt or exclusive. For over a year, he worked concurrently on *Statements for Orchestra* and *El Salón México*, the former in his "old" austere style; the latter, the first of the "new" popular works. While he was so occupied at Lake Bemidji, a request came from Ruth Page in Chicago for music for a ballet. Copland wrote to Chávez (15 October 1935): "I almost had *two* new orchestral works finished when I had to interrupt them to do a ballet to be performed at the Chicago Opera in November. . . ."

Music for the People

1934-1937

Ruth Page was ballet director of the Chicago Grand Opera Company and a well-known dancer and choreographer. When she produced ballets for her own company, the Ruth Page Ballets, she often commissioned music by contemporary composers. Ruth had heard my jazzy *Music for the Theatre*, so she invited me to compose music for a ballet about murder in a nightclub. It was late August 1934; the ballet was scheduled for November. Victor and I drove from Lake Bemidji to Duluth and took a train to Chicago. I discussed the proposal with Ruth and with Nicholas Remisoff, who was to design the staging and costumes. The ballet, *Hear Ye! Hear Ye!*, was to take place in a courtroom, and the plot consisted of three witnesses giving highly divergent accounts of the same nightclub murder; *Hear Ye! Hear Ye!* was a *Rashomon* type of story.[1] Ruth, who was married to a lawyer, wrote the scenario. The idea sounded dramatic, different, and lively. It would be my first experience writing music for a ballet and knowing in advance that it would actually be staged. After a week of discussions, I signed on the dotted line and dashed back to Bemidji to get to work on the ballet, putting *Statements* and *El Salón México* aside for the time being.

Ruth had given me the scenario and "some suggestions to the composer." The cast of characters was as follows: the judge, prosecuting and defense attorneys, six masked jurymen, a crowd of marionettes, twelve chorus girls, a nightclub hostess (Mae West type), her maid, a honeymoon couple, a Negro waiter, a cabaret dancer (Ruth Page), a male dancer, a jealous chorus girl, and a maniac. I was expected to write an overture, several jazz-influenced dances, and various special effects. After five weeks, I returned to Chicago with a working score of forty minutes of music[2]— most of it new, some of it drawn from my earlier ballet *Grohg*. Ruth put me up at her house on Lake Michigan so that we could work closely together. I finished the orchestral score and turned it over to the conductor, Rudolph Ganz, a few weeks before the premiere on 30 November. The day after the opening, the Chicago *Herald* reported: "It was an exciting night at the Opera last night when for the first time a whole evening was devoted to ballet. . . . It was a full house. . . . There was, of course, a great deal of discussion about *Hear Ye! Hear Ye!* the new ballet, which had its premiere. . . ." The program consisted of *La Guiablesse* (music by William Grant Still), danced by Katherine Dunham and an all-black dance group; the premiere of *Hear Ye!*; the premiere of *Gold Standard* (music by Jacques Ibert); and *Iberian Monotone* (to Ravel's *Bolero*), danced by Ruth Page.

Remisoff had designed flashy costumes and vivid effects for *Hear Ye!*[3] During the overture, a movie projector flashed lurid headlines onto a large overhead screen: "RED-HOT JAZZ!" "MURDER!" "GUILTY!" The music incorporated segments of "The Star Spangled Banner," distorted to convey the corruption of legal systems and courts of law. For a bride and groom scene, I prepared a parody of Mendelssohn's "Wedding March." It seemed an effective way to emphasize the cynicism behind the innocence of newlyweds amid white doves and flowers. And for the doves, I composed a flowing flute passage in descending thirds. The ballet ended with the judge going berserk and the opposing lawyers gaily leaving the stage arm-in-arm to the dissonant "Star Spangled Banner." The gala evening was topped off with an elegant supper party thrown by Harold McCormick at the Electric Club, known for its spectacular view of the city. *Hear Ye!* was repeated in Chicago a few weeks later, and Ruth retained it in the repertoire for several seasons. I conducted it myself in New York on 1 and 2 March 1936.

In Chicago the reviews had centered on Ruth Page and the dancers; later, Cecil Michener Smith wrote: "Certainly the music is thoroughly representative of the American scene, and makes no obsequious bows toward any foreign authority."[4] In New York criticisms varied. Jerome D. Bohm in the *Herald Tribune*: "The idea is fraught with possibilities for excitement which are never quite realized; but for those who had never attended one of Minsky's burlesques, there was a suggestively attired and writhing bevy of chorus girls and Miss Page's own costume was perhaps a trifle more immodest than necessity demanded. . . ." And W. J. Henderson in the *Sun*: "The music by Mr. Copland demonstrated again that composer's instinct for the theater. He has made a score which perfectly fits the story and the action. It has a modernist sting in harmony and pungent rhythm, and its incursions into the realm of jazz are made with the certainty of a musician who knows his way about the town." Soon after the

Chicago premiere, I wrote to Chávez (31 December 1934): "It was an experience for me to hear my music with stage action. Now I should like to write an opera, or at any rate, more music for the stage."

I arranged a suite from the ballet that was performed at an all-Copland concert sponsored by the WPA Composers Forum–Laboratory in 1937, but I decided to give it up, drawing from the suite only one section that became Blues No. 2 in my *Four Piano Blues*. I prefer that the original ballet score remain unpublished. The music was really incidental to the dance, and I have discovered that some music is more incidental than others! Nevertheless, Ruth Page's ballet was important as my first collaborative experience of this kind, and it left me open to other offers for ballets that would be central to my musical life in the next decade. In more practical terms, it was satisfying for me, a slow writer, to produce a successful score in so short a time.

While in Chicago I received an interesting letter from Walter Piston (15 November 1934): "What would be your reaction toward the possibility of teaching my composition class at Harvard during the second half-year?" The idea of teaching at Harvard was an impressive one to a fellow who had never gone to college. I wrote to Paul Bowles (8 January 1935): "I think it is very brave of them to have me, don't you?" Little did I realize what enduring benefits would come from teaching at Harvard. Years later I met Douglas Moore for lunch at the Harvard Club in New York. I looked around wistfully, commenting, "I wish I could belong to a place like this!" My friend asked why I didn't join, and I said, "Don't be silly—I never even went to college." "Don't *you* be silly," responded Douglas. "*You* taught at Harvard!" Next thing I knew I was signed in as a member of the Harvard Club, and I have used it as my home-away-from-home since I moved to the country.

In February of 1935 I got off the train in Boston and was put up temporarily at Harvard's Eliot House in Cambridge. I wrote to Victor Kraft (3 February 1935): "About 300 boys live here, eat here, etc. Rather exclusive and expensive, and of course *very* plain. I have nine boys in my class and one girl from Radcliffe." My teaching duties were not demanding—only three hours a week on Tuesdays and Thursdays. I enjoyed the students and was delighted to see Koussevitzky and attend rehearsals of the orchestra. After settling into rooms at 15 Sumner Road, I was able to teach a few private students. One, a Mrs. Rappaport, said, "Please make my lessons a little modernistic." While in Cambridge I saw quite a lot of Arthur Berger and got to know a few Harvard music professors—Hugo Leichtentritt and

Edward Burlingame Hill, whom I had met earlier at Fontainebleau. And I attended lectures by Alfred North Whitehead on the subject of "Time." When I returned to New York, I had no permanent home, so between leaving Harvard and going to the MacDowell Colony I stayed at Alma Wertheim's apartment on 57th Street and Second Avenue. There I completed the orchestration of *Statements for Orchestra*, dedicating the piece to Mary Churchill. It was used to satisfy a commission from the League of Composers for a new orchestral work to be played by the Minneapolis Symphony under the baton of a young conductor named Eugene Ormandy.

The title, *Statements for Orchestra*, was chosen to indicate terse, short movements of well-defined character lasting only about three minutes. Instead of the original plan for seven short movements, *Statements* was finished with six. Each was given an additional title as an aid to the public in understanding what I had in mind when writing the movements: "Militant" is based on a single theme announced in unison by three flutes, two oboes, bassoon, and strings; "Cryptic" is orchestrated for brass and flute alone, with an occasional use of bass clarinet and bassoon; "Dogmatic" is an allegro in tripartite form, the mid-section quoting from my *Piano Variations;* "Subjective" is the final resting place of *Elegies for Violin and Viola* and is scored for strings without double basses; "Jingo," utilizing the full orchestra, is a rondo form on a chromatic melody with occasional bows to a well-known tune, "The Sidewalks of New York"; and the final section, "Prophetic," is rhapsodic in form and centers on a chorale-like melody sung by the solo trumpet. Occasionally, only four of the six statements are programmed, as on a concert in honor of my seventy-fifth birthday at Alice Tully Hall when Dennis Russell Davies chose to conduct I, IV, V, and VI; at other times, only the first four are played. This strikes me as somewhat ironic, considering that only the last two movements were played for the premiere of *Statements* in Minneapolis—first on an NBC network broadcast on 9 January 1936 and then at a symphony concert on 21 February 1936. My music was again considered "too difficult," although *Statements for Orchestra* is not nearly so demanding for performers as the *Short Symphony. Statements* was not heard in its entirety until 1942, when Dimitri Mitropoulos conducted it with the New York Philharmonic.

Of the reviews, I am most fond of Virgil's, printed in the *Herald Tribune* following the concert of 7 January 1942: "Aaron Copland's six shortish pieces grouped together under the name of 'Statements' are succinct and stylish music. They are clearly written and very, very personal. . . . The whole group is a manly bouquet, fresh and sweet and sincere and frank and straightforward. . . . They were admirably played, too, the dryness of Mitropoulos' interpretation suiting to a T that of the Copland musical style." Subsequently, I conducted the work for a recording with the London Symphony Orchestra. To my disappointment, *Statements* remains one of my lesser-known scores.

In the summer of 1935 I was assigned the very same studio at the MacDowell Colony that I had in 1925, and I was struck with the fact that it had been ten years since my first visit. I worked on *El Salón México* and wrote a chorus for the Henry Street Music School where I was teaching part time. They had asked for a work that could be sung by the Girls' Glee Club. The result was "What Do We Plant?", a short and simple setting of a text by Henry Abbey for soprano and alto voices with piano accompaniment. I have always liked the idea of young people singing and playing my music. After all, they grow up and become our audiences. That summer I also composed two piano pieces for a collection Lazare Saminsky and Isadore Freed were editing for Carl Fischer.[5] "Sunday Afternoon Music" and "The Young Pioneers" are again short (two and three pages respectively) and easy to play, while still introducing young ears to the contemporary idiom. The title "The Young Pioneers" has a double meaning, for I had in mind instilling in young piano students the courage to attempt music that is somewhat "modern." After the collection of these piano pieces for young performers was played in 1936, Lehman Engel wrote, "Here is real and welcome *Gebrauchsmusik* for America. . . ."[6] My interest in composing for young people escalated to the point where I was considering a suggestion made by Grace Spofford, head of the Henry Street Settlement, that I write an opera for high school students. I wrote to Chávez from the MacDowell Colony (28 August 1935):

> It becomes increasingly difficult to have the sense that there is any public for our music—the public that can afford to pay for concerts is quite simply not interested. . . . In a period of such economic and general social tension music itself seems unimportant—at least to those middle class people who up to now have been our audiences. Is it the same in Mexico? Also, this has personal repercussions. It is no longer easy to be published (the Cos Cob has discontinued publishing for a year already and I don't know when they will resume)—I must make some money in order to live which uses up much valuable time and energy. I mention all these things not to give you the idea that I am discouraged in any essential way, but merely to show you that I have good reasons to feel sympathetic with your own struggles. It is just in such times as these that friends like we are should encourage and sustain each other. . . .

Also from the Colony in the summer of 1935, I wrote to Victor Kraft, then working in Chicago: "There are no famous 'names' at MacDowell this summer. It is a good place to work—there's simply nothing else to do!" In midsummer two young composer friends arrived: Nicolas ("Nicky") Slonimsky and David Diamond.

David Diamond[7]

I had heard the Prelude *from his* First Symphony *played in a chamber music concert at the Eastman School—I was still studying there in '33 and '34. I was so moved by the* Prelude *that I wrote him I loved it and where could one see the score? He answered, "The score is published by Cos Cob." Sure enough I found it in the Sibley Library. But what was nice was that he sent me the original score of it. (I gave it as a gift to the Sibley Music Library.) I was delighted when Aaron wrote saying we could meet. It was the spring of '35. I was living at the YMHA and studying at the Dalcroze Institute with Roger Sessions, and Aaron was living in an apartment with a tiny bedroom and a very narrow living room with a piano. He said, "Oh, I remember you very well, because you sent a batch of music to me all done up in colored paper." He played the* Short Symphony *for me, and I was very impressed. He wanted to hear what I'd done, so I played the* Eight Piano Pieces *for Children which I'd just finished working on with Sessions, and he liked them. He said, "I'd like to have you come to some of the League of Composers Concerts." When I first came to New York, Lazare Saminsky, being on the League board as well as Aaron, was trying to get me started. I looked up Saminsky's book,* Music of Our Day, *and I thought what he said about Aaron outrageous.[8] There was no love lost between Aaron and Lazare Saminsky. He'd always let out, "Now I hope you aren't seeing too much of our dear Mr. Copland." I'd say, "Why, Mr. Saminsky?" And he'd say, "I just don't think you should come under the influence of Copland. I think you should follow Sessions." I said, "Well, I am—Sessions is my teacher." (You see, I depended financially on Saminsky's help. He would give me a few dollars to add to the $5 a week my family sent me.)*

It was through Aaron I met people in the Group Theatre—the whole original group. And Clifford Odets, a great friend of Aaron's. It's still my feeling that had Clifford come through with that opera libretto that they talked about doing—what an opera with Aaron's dramatic sense it could have been![9] *Cliff went off to Hollywood, and Aaron lived in his apartment at 1 University Place. Cliff turned the apartment over because Aaron didn't have much money in those days. I met Israel Citkowitz at Aaron's place; Israel and Aaron were very close. Stella [Adler] would come over too. I would rush across from the West Side over to University Place and visit Aaron and walk him over to the New School. From then on, he sort of kept his eye on me.*

Naturally, Aaron adored Nadia and had great respect for Koussevitzky. But he also knew Koussevitzky's limitations. I always found that Aaron's great talent and why, probably, his career went as it did, was his innate, natural sense of diplomacy. Aaron felt I should study with Boulanger, so in '37 I went to Fontainebleau. Nadia got me a scholarship. She had been here in America, Aaron introduced me, and I played some things for her. Nadia spoke in such a way about Aaron that you felt the love and the admiration all the time. Once, I'll never forget, she said, "You're a very fortunate young man to have a friend like Aaron," and I knew exactly what she meant.

When Aaron came over to Paris I had a rented studio in a music store on the rue de Rennes. I showed him the Flute Quintet, which I dedicated to him. He'd often say to me, "You write too much, David Diamond," and, "David Diamond, be more selective!" One day Aaron said, "Lincoln Kirstein wants me to do a ballet." I said, "What do you mean, a ballet? Why doesn't he do the one you did for Ruth Page?" (I had never heard Hear Ye! Hear Ye!) He said, "Oh no, no. This has gotta be new, it's gotta be about cowboys, and as a matter of fact, I've gotta go right now to the post office and pick up another book of cowboy tunes from Lincoln." So off we went.

Back at the studio Aaron rented next to mine, he played through some of the tunes for Billy the Kid. I thought to myself, "This is amazing!" Except for El Salón México, I didn't think of Aaron as using folk material yet. He had played the Short Symphony for me, and Statements for Orchestra, which I fell in love with—especially the "Prophetic" one. (On a photo Aaron sent me, he wrote: "To David, the lover of Prophetic Statements.") I used to go around humming that, and I suggested he put the word "nobilemente" in the score. Aaron asked me, "Do you think I'll ever hear a complete performance of Statements?" I would be bewildered. Here he's being played by the Boston Symphony, but he can't hear a complete performance of Statements! Finally, I went to Mitropoulos and said, "Dimitri, please! There is this great piece of Copland's. Won't you play

it?" He said, "Get me the score." I bring him Statements, *and he schedules it for 7 January* 1942. *So Aaron finally heard* Statements for Orchestra. *But in Paris in '37 I couldn't figure out how he was going to use folk
tunes with this spare, severe style of his. I thought, "Oh, gee, this is not
Aaron!" Look, at my age then, everything had to be* THE *masterpiece. I
had seen the* Ode *in manuscript, and I was fascinated. I thought, "This is
what I think of Aaron." So naturally I was very curious.*

*I remember that when Arthur Berger, Donald Fuller, and I went to a
rehearsal of* Billy, *we were impressed and surprised at Aaron's stick technique. He certainly had what one calls know-how. I used to wonder, "Is
Lenny giving Aaron tips?" Everybody in that orchestra that Lincoln Kirstein got together was talking about how clear Aaron's beat was; even
Gene Loring, who did the choreography and danced the part of Billy, said,
"It's just so wonderful having Aaron there in that pit." I felt Aaron was a
born conductor the moment I saw him, and I'm sure it's been borne out
by the fact that he's the only successful composer-conductor since Stravinsky that I know of.*

When Ravel died in December of '37, I sat down and in two days wrote
Elegy for Ravel *for brass, harps, and percussion. Aaron was very taken with
it, and said: "I wonder if Koussie would be interested in this? It might be a
little over-severe for him, but anyway, I'd like you to meet Koussevitzky."
So at one of the concerts when the Boston Symphony came, he brought
me backstage and introduced me. I can still remember the going over I got
by Madame! While Koussevitzky was talking, I could feel her standing at
the other side of the room—like a hawk—she had a rather marvelous nose
like Lillian Hellman's. Well, Aaron reported to me that Koussie liked the
way I looked. (Actually, he was interested in the shirt I was wearing. I liked
dark shirts like Alfred Knopf wore.) So Koussevitzky took the* Elegy. *He
said, "I vill let you know." [Richard] Burgin read through it with the orchestra. "Too cerebral," Koussie said, pronouncing it "ce-ray-bral." I told
Aaron about it, and he just said, "Well, these things take time."*

I began working on my First Symphony *at Yaddo. Aaron was not on too
good terms with Mrs. Ames. She said that Aaron was concentrating too
much on one specific kind of music, and that his coterie was only the
League of Composers gang. She wanted to be broader, to take in some of
the New England composers. And, as a matter of fact, Richard Donovan
and Quincy Porter ran Yaddo after Aaron was not in the picture any more.
In the forties, Elizabeth [Ames] told me that she liked Aaron very much
and thought he was a magnificent composer, but she didn't like this con-*

David Diamond, his sister Sabrina, and Copland at the MacDowell Colony, 1935.

stant special group. She should talk, of all people, 'cause she was always favoring a group of her own as guests. Later on, she threw me out!

In New York in the forties, I played fiddle in the Hit Parade *orchestra to make a living. I would come up to Aaron's loft when he was working on the* Violin Sonata. *I showed him things about harmonics in the last movement, and I said, "Aaron, it would be a little awkward to jump from a low note all the way up in the tenth position. Why don't you make it an artificial harmonic?" We played the* Violin Sonata *together in a "loft performance" before it was premiered at a League concert. Aaron had these musical evenings where we'd all come. He would say, "David, take care of the stuff to eat," so I'd go to the shops on Tenth Avenue and bring things. I would always cook up a storm, because I was a good cook.*

Lenny and Aaron were my two authorities. With Aaron it would be, "David, why do you let things go so easily?" He didn't know what to make of all this music that was pouring out of me. He used to say, "I don't know how you do it! You're a mess emotionally. And stop making scenes all the time in public." One time, Lenny was conducting the Boston Symphony in New York (12 February 1947). I had been at a party, and I was a little late in leaving, and I'd had two manhattans, no more. I rushed up the steps of Carnegie Hall, and the doors were closed. So I knocked gently on the glass. Todd Perry, [George E.] Judd's assistant, came to the door. I took a swipe at Perry. Performance over, not a note heard, I went back-stage, charged in, and made a dreadful scene with Judd [manager of the BSO from 1934 to 1954], finally heaping all the abuse on Margaret Grant [executive secretary to Koussevitzky] and Betty Bean [then working at Boosey & Hawkes]. Result? Aaron grabs me by the shoulder and says, "Come on!" Never before have I seen Aaron angry. Never! He maneu-vered me out, put me into a cab, and said, "You're drunk and I want you to go home." I said, "Aaron, I'm not going home." He said, "You're going right home." I take the cab down only as far as Sixth Avenue, get out, and go right back to the Russian Tea Room. In come Lenny, Jennie Tourel, Aaron, Harold Clurman, and Stella. Aaron said: "I thought I told you to go home!" They go into the back. I see I'm being ignored, and they're punishing me. So I go out very, very upset and go home.[10]

The following day I wrote to Lenny, Judd, and a long, long letter to Aaron, to which he replied a masterpiece, beginning: "Dear David, you truth teller. Now I'm going to tell a few truths about you that you ought to know. . . ." And he enumerates. "And now, I want you to seriously think about help. You must see someone." And it was true. I was upset because I could not find work, and I couldn't understand—I'm being noticed, good things are said about my talent, and a job I can't get! I didn't think I was difficult; I just said what I thought, and in those days you didn't do that. Aaron and Lenny asked people to give contributions to a fund for my analysis. It gave me much more insight about why I was a psychosomatic mess. It was wonderful the way Aaron and Lenny got it together for me, and that letter is the finest letter I've ever received. I think there was a real devotion that remains to this day. After all, how many of the old friends are left of that period?

In the forties when I saw what Aaron was doing for film music, I thought, "At last, something's happening!" I heard that extraordinary chord for the scene in Of Mice and Men where he takes the hand and he crushes it! This is what film music's all about. I would battle people like Sessions who made remarks to me about Aaron's selling himself out. Roger didn't even like El Salón México, you see. He liked the Aaron of the Piano Variations. But to me, the situation is like Stravinsky. Aaron is Aaron in whatever style. I must say, I like the Aaron of the jazzy things less. They strike me as being less vital to Aaron's big talent. But certainly not the Americana.

I played fiddle in Wonderful Town *for several weeks in the fifties and stayed in Marc's [Blitzstein] apartment. Now, while I'm in that, to the pit comes one day a woman who hands over a document. I thought it was a message, so I take it, and it's a subpoena to appear before the House Un-American Activities Committee. Naturally, I panic, so I called Aaron. "What do I do?" "David," he said, "take it easy. Just do what the legal advisers tell you." I said, "I'm not going to inform on anybody." Aaron said, "Well, naturally, I hope not." I said, "What, however, if I'm asked a question directly about you, about Lenny?" He said, "You say what you feel you have to say." That's all. This was Aaron's wonderful way of advising me—you do what you have to do, say what you feel you have to say. But I could see he was upset. He was upset because I was emotional. Really, I was in a state. Here comes a man, and in five minutes I'm absolutely tranquilized by his particular kind of quiet.*

From '35 on, Aaron and I have always kept in touch, even during those fifteen years from '51 through '65 when I lived in Italy. Aaron would come abroad, and we'd meet. When I was staying at Aaron's in Peekskill before I went to Greece this past summer, we were sitting out on the terrace, and Aaron said, "David, it looks very bad for Harold." There was a kind of thing that happened in his face that I could feel. But now this is Aaron going into his eightieth year. In past years, when Colin McPhee died or Varèse, even Chávez, which is not too long ago—Aaron said very little. I could never really know how deep the pain was. There's never a scene with Aaron. He knows exactly what dignity means in the sense of how far you go emotionally.

I think Aaron senses very strongly the acclamation now. There's something about filling a huge place like Carnegie Hall with the kind of warmth felt at his eightieth birthday concert. They weren't all friends there, either—they were people who have loved his music for decades. Aaron was always leading and helping, but never with a sense of "I'm a big wheeler-dealer." There's a kind of childlike quality about Aaron, so that even people who are jealous (and I knew several through the years who were very jealous) show their warmth for Aaron, because they feel and admit he deserves every bit of it. Because he has done so much for others. It's a marvelous thing to see this happening to Aaron—it's all coming full circle. Because the early years seem so close to me, all the more do I feel this is extraordinary, his reaching eighty and achieving all that. Maybe for Aaron it all seems far away, those years that to me seem like yesterday.

In the fall of 1935 my cousin Percy Uris loaned me a small apartment at the Hotel Lafayette on 9th Street and University Place. After a few months I moved into another Uris building at 1 University Place where Odets was living. I was occupied with producing a special concert series of five evenings, each one devoted entirely to the music of an American composer. Included were Harris, Thomson, Sessions, Piston, and myself—what Virgil called "America's up-and-at-'em commando unit."[11] At Mary Lescaze's suggestion, I had written to a patroness, Mrs. Leonard Elmhirst, pointing out that rarely had there been "one-man concerts" of American music, though it was commonplace for painters to hold one-man shows. I explained that the New School was offering their auditorium without a fee, and admission was to be $1 with receipts to be equally divided between the school and the composer of the evening. I asked Mrs. Elmhirst to contribute $1,000 for performers' fees. Once granted, I set to work on programs and arrangements. Since I had been away all summer and the first concert was scheduled for 11 October, my own evening would have to come first. I sent an urgent request to John Kirkpatrick (15 September 1935): "Can you help me out? Mrs. Luening is to do the Song Group on the 11th, but all 3 songs are in storage! Could you bring with you: Old Poem, Pastorale, and Vocalise?"

I counted on John for much more than the scores—in fact, he was the featured performer of the evening, playing my *Piano Variations*, and with me, his two-piano arrangements of the *Symphonic Ode* and *El Salón México*, which was not yet finished in its orchestration. (I had sent John the first part in September, while still working on the orchestration.) One reviewer commented that it was easy to understand why concertgoers would go to *Porgy and Bess* and stay away from a concert like mine "by the hundreds of thousands, which is why Mr. Copland's music is not performed more frequently than it is." Evidently my reputation as a wild-eyed modernist was still secure! On the final concert of 6 December I had planned to play Walter Piston's two-piano arrangement of his *Piano Concerto* with Kirkpatrick. But I wrote to John (7 November 1935): "After due consideration I've decided that the Piston oeuvre is beyond my powers—pianistically speaking. Unless you have any violent objections I plan to invite Miss Gertrude Bonime, who recently played and played well at Virgil's WPA concert to take my place. This hurts me more than it does you." As I looked around at the all-too-familiar small group at these concerts, I knew that I wanted to see a larger and more varied audience for contemporary music.

I was already "experimenting" with a different style of writing in two compositions, *El Salón México* in its finishing stages, and a high school opera. I had no thought of rejecting one kind of music for another—only the feeling that it was time to try something new. *El Salón México* had been "in the works" since my first trip to Mexico in 1932 when I came away from that colorful dance hall in Mexico City with Chávez. I had read about the hall for the first time in a guidebook about tourist entertainment: "Harlem type night-club for the peepul, grand Cuban orchestra, Salón México. Three halls: one for people dressed in your way, one for people dressed in overalls but shod, and one for the barefoot." A sign on a wall of the dance hall read: "Please don't throw lighted cigarette butts on the floor so the ladies don't burn their feet." A guard, stationed at the bottom of the steps leading to the three halls, would nonchalantly frisk you as you started up the stairs to be sure you had checked all your "artillery" at the door and to collect the 1 peso charged for admittance to any of the three halls. When the dance hall closed at 5:00 A.M., it hardly seemed worthwhile to some of the overalled patrons to travel all the way home, so they curled themselves up on chairs around the walls for a quick two-hour snooze before going to a seven o'clock job in the morning.

I realized that it would be foolish for me to attempt to translate some of the more profound sides of Mexico into musical sounds—the ancient civilizations or the revolutionary Mexico of our own time—for that, one really had to know a country well. But my thoughts kept returning to that dance hall. It wasn't so much the music or the dances that attracted me as the spirit of the place. In some inexplicable way, while milling about in those crowded halls, I had felt a live contact with the Mexican "people"—that electric sense one gets sometimes in far-off places, of suddenly knowing the essence of a people—their humanity, their shyness, their dignity and unique charm. I remember quite well that it was at such a moment I conceived the idea of composing a piece about Mexico and naming it *El Salón México*. But to have an idea for a piece of music is far from having the piece itself! I began (as I often did) by collecting musical themes or tunes out of which a composition might eventually emerge. It seemed natural to use popular Mexican melodies for thematic material; after all, Chabrier and Debussy didn't hesitate to help themselves to the melodic riches of Spain. There was no reason I should not use the tunes of the hispanic land on our southern doorstep. My purpose was not merely to quote literally, but to heighten without in any way falsifying the natural simplicity of Mexican tunes.

Frances Toor, a resident American in Mexico City, had published an unpretentious little collection, *Cancionero Mexicano*.[12] I used tunes from that and from an erudite book by Rubén M. Campos, *El Folklore y la Música Mexicana*.[13] "El Mosco" is the most direct quotation of a complete melody. I also used "El Palo Verde," "La Jesusita," and "La Malacate." If quotation of folk tunes is a sure way for a composer to translate the flavor of a foreign people into musical terms, it also presents a formal problem when used in a symphonic composition. Most composers have found that there is little that can be done with such material except repeat it. In *El Salón México* I decided to use a modified potpourri in which the Mexican themes or fragments and extensions thereof are sometimes inextricably mixed. For example, before the final climax I present the folk tunes simultaneously in their original keys and rhythms. The result is a kind of polytonality that achieves the frenetic whirl I had in mind before the end, when all is resolved with a plain unadorned triad.

I wrote to Chávez about *El Salón México* with some embarrassment (15 October 1932): "I am terribly afraid of what *you* will say of the 'Salón México'—perhaps it is not Mexican at all, and I would feel so foolish. But in America del Norte it may sound Mexican!" And again (28 August 1935): "What it would sound like in Mexico I can't imagine, but everyone here for whom I have played it seems to think it is very gay and amusing." Oddly enough, this composition celebrating Mexico was completed in Bemidji, Minnesota. My Mexican impressions must have been very strong ones! Other projects intervened, so the orchestration was not fully completed until 1936, two years after Bemidji, when I was again in Mexico with Victor. (*El Salón México* is dedicated to Victor Kraft.) To my great relief, when I played it for Chávez in New York, he asked to conduct it after the orchestration was finished. The world premiere of *El Salón México* was in Mexico City on 27 August 1937, Chávez conducting the Orquesta Sinfónica de México at the Palacio de Bellas Artes. Despite Chávez' enthusiasm, I still felt nervous about what the Mexicans might think of a "gringo" meddling with their native melodies. At the first of the final rehearsals that I attended, an unexpected incident took place that completely reassured me. As I entered the hall the orchestral players, who were in the thick of a Beethoven symphony, suddenly stopped what they were doing and began to applaud vigorously. What they were expressing, I soon realized, was not so much their appreciation of one composer's work, as their pleasure and pride in the fact that a foreign composer had found their own familiar tunes worthy of treatment.

I was moved by that gesture, and the reviews that appeared in the newspapers after the premiere were no less kind. They seemed to agree that *El Salón México* might well be taken for Mexican music—"as Mexican as the music of Revueltas," which was like saying at that time, "as American as the music of Gershwin." The only typical Mexican percussion instrument I asked for in the score was the gourd. There have been times when no one seemed to know where to find a gourd. One such instance was in London in July 1938 at the sixteenth ISCM Festival with Sir Adrian Boult conducting. Also, I requested that the traditional orchestral E-flat clarinet play with the flavor of a native Mexican instrument. At the first American performance of *El Salón México* on 14 October that same year, the BSO clarinetist Rosario Mazzeo under Koussevitzky's direction handled this wonderfully, as he did on the recording for Victor Records in 1939. *El Salón* was not easy to perform; it presented rhythmic intricacies for the conductor and the players.

The 1938 ISCM concert in London turned out to be an important occasion for me. It was there I first met Benjamin Britten, and it was Ben who introduced and recommended me to Ralph Hawkes of the British publishing firm, Boosey & Hawkes. Mr. Hawkes offered to publish one work, I asked him to take three; we settled on two. Later, I signed permanently with Boosey & Hawkes. I have been very satisfied with this arrangement, though at times I wonder at someone like myself, so involved with American music, having a British music publisher! In New York Hans Heinsheimer was working for Boosey, Hawkes, Belwin, Inc. (as it was then named in America). Business was very slow, according to Heinsheimer,[14] so when Ralph Hawkes sent fifty copies of *El Salón México*, Heinsheimer was delighted. He called my piece an "American Bolero" and proceeded to fill orders for scores and rental parts that soon came in from all over. One year after publication in 1938, Boosey put together a list of orchestras that had played *El Salón México*: fourteen American orchestras ranging from the BSO to the Women's Symphony in Chicago; two radio orchestras; and five foreign ensembles. Never in my wildest dreams did I expect this kind of acceptance for the piece![15]

Boosey & Hawkes, wanting to make the most from this unexpected windfall, suggested a piano arrangement. Heinsheimer asked me for someone who could do it quickly and cheaply. I suggested a young musician who had just come to town. According to Heinsheimer: "The young man was also badly in need of money and would therefore do the job for a really miserable fee. This, of course, clinched the deal. We asked Copland to go ahead and order it and after a few days a young Adonis delivered the arrangement, played it brilliantly and convincingly on what was alleged to be a piano . . . and left, happily, with his little check. His name is still to be found on the piano version of *El Salón México*. The young man was Leonard Bernstein."[16] Lenny also made a two-piano arrangement.[17] My first meeting with Lenny Bernstein was on my thirty-seventh birthday, when he was a student at Harvard. We both happened to be at a dance recital by Anna Sokolow in New York. I invited him along with a few friends to the loft afterward for an impromptu party. When Lenny heard *El Salón México* at its first performance by the BSO in 1938, he sensed what I was after and wrote (20 October 1938): "I wish these people could see that a composer is just as serious when he writes a work, even if the piece is not defeatist (that Worker word again) and Weltschmerzy and misanthropic and long. . . ."

El Salón México caught on quickly, and it started the ball rolling toward the popular success and wide audience I had only just begun to think about. Toscanini conducted *El Salón* in a broadcast with the NBC Symphony Orchestra on 14 March 1942.[18] (I was amazed when Walter Toscanini found a piano arrangement of it among his father's papers; he sent me a photocopy in 1961.) Lenny conducted *El Salón* for the New York Philharmonic Young People's Concerts; I particularly recall one such performance on my sixtieth birthday. The score has also been used by several choreographers—among them, Doris Humphrey, José Limón, and most recently Eliot Feld for *La Vida*. *El Salón* was adapted by Johnny Green for a film released in the United States by MGM as *Fiesta* starring Esther Williams and Ricardo Montalban, and in Italy as *La Matadora*. The published piano version of his adaptation is called *Fantasia Mexicana*. *El Salón* was also arranged for concert band by Mark Hindeley in 1972. It was one of my first recorded pieces—in 1939, with the BSO under Koussevitzky for RCA Victor. Lenny included "Saloon" (as we called it) in his conducting debut with the BSO on 8 February 1944.

After hearing the piece played for one of my seventieth birthday celebration concerts, I was still explaining to an interviewer what Lenny seemed to know in 1938. "As I see it, music that is born complex is not inherently better or worse than music that is born simple." But my turn to a simpler style in *El Salón* and other pieces that followed puzzled some of my colleagues. Roger Sessions did not approve of my move to a "popular" style, nor did Arthur Berger. After *El Salón*, I occasionally had the strange sensation of being divided in half—the austere, intellectual modernist on one

Eliot E51
Camb
Oct 1938

Dear Aaron,

It's going to be hard to keep this from being a fan letter. The concert was gorgeous — even the Dvořák. I still don't sleep much from the pounding of

in my head. In any event, it's a secure feeling to know we have a master in America. I mean that too (don't pooh-pooh). I sat aghast at the solid sureness of that construction of yours. Timed to perfection. Not an extra beat. Just long enough for its material. Orchestral handling plus. Invention superb. And yet, with all that technique, it was a perfect rollercoaster ride. And it's not the exhaustible kind of cleverness (like français, or his ilk).

I want seriously to have the chance to study with you soon. My heart's in it. Never have I come across anyone capable of such immediate absorption of musical material, possessing at the same time a fine critical sense with the ability to put that criticism into words — successfully. This is not rot. The little demonstration you gave with those early things of mine proved it to me conclusively.

I saw the Group Theatre bunch today and they all asked for and about you. Odets, true to form, thinks the Salón México "light," also Mozart except the G minor Symphony. That angers me terrifically. I wish these people could see that a composer is just as serious when he writes a work, even if the piece is not defeatist (that Wonder word again) and Weltschmerz and misanthropic and long. Light piece, indeed. I tremble when I think of producing something like the Salón.

Casting is a wretched business. It's slow but sure. And so tiring. (What word from the Marc?) But I think we'll have a fine show.

Let me hear soon. As Dame Fortune said to you backstage last Saturday night, "On to bigger & nobler things."

Always,
Lenny

PS — I hope you're really haunted by

Maybe not convincing, but maybe haunting.

letter from Leonard Bernstein, 1938
(date in Copland's hand).

Top: The first page of a piano arrangement of *El Salón México* by Arturo Toscanini.
Bottom: Program for a Japanese-American Music Festival in Tokyo, 22 June 1948, featuring Copland and Roy Harris, and including *El Salón México*.

side; the accessible, popular composer on the other. I have addressed this issue several times in print, and in a letter to Arthur Berger I wrote at some length (16 April 1943):

> . . . for the sake of drawing sharp distinctions you rather overdo the dichotomy between my "severe" and "simple" styles. The inference is that only the severe style is really serious. I don't believe that. What I was trying for in the simpler works was only partly a larger audience; they also gave me a chance to try for a home-spun musical idiom similar to what I was trying for in a more hectic fashion in the earlier jazz works. In other words, it was not only musical functionalism that was in question, but also musical language. . . . I like to think that I have touched off for myself and others a kind of musical naturalness that we have badly needed. . . .

Lehman Engel, as a young conductor of the children's choruses at the Henry Street Settlement Music School, agreed with Grace Spofford, head of the school, that I should compose an opera for children under their auspices. (Lehman had conducted Kurt Weill's *Der Jasager* there before Miss Spofford's tenure.) I agreed and chose my friend, the dance critic and poet Edwin Denby, to write the libretto. I had known Edwin since the twenties in Germany where he had lived and worked as a dancer and writer of opera librettos and dance scenarios. Since his return from Germany, we had seen each other often in New York. My plan was to compose the opera during the summer of 1936 in the quiet town of Tlaxcala, Mexico. Edwin gave me a draft libretto to take along and promised to come to Tlaxcala late in the summer to work with me. I wrote to Koussevitzky from Tlaxcala, "I hope to finish my high school opera here," and to David Diamond (4 July 1936):

> V. and I have gotten lost in the wilds of Mexico. Tlaxcala is a provincial town, very typical and very old. It was all here long before Cortez arrived—and it looks it. We live on top of a hill opposite a 17th century church . . . in a 5 room house, Mexican style, (that is, without any windows!) that costs $14 a month. (It appears we were robbed. It should have been $7!) and we have a cook— Maria. It's all incredibly quiet and picturesque and hopelessly Mexican. No one in the whole town of Tlaxcala talks any English. . . . For the first week I did nothing but hunt for a piano. There was nothing in this town that could boast the name. Then I travelled to Puebla—an hour trip over incredible roads . . . I was getting desperate—for the performance of my Concerto is only 3 weeks off. Today I think I found something that will do—the Padre of the church across the way came to the rescue with a sort of a piano that was discovered in the vestry. Such is life in Mexico.

When I returned to New York in the fall of 1936, *The Second Hurricane* was well under way. I took a quiet room at the Empire Hotel for $8.50 a week and rented a studio in a loft building close by where I would disturb no one with my late night banging. Finally, my belongings came out of storage! The hotel flourishes today where it stood in 1936, but the old building at 115 West 63rd, where my studio was, is the present site of Lincoln Center. You had to go up four steep flights of rickety stairs to get there, passing the other tenants on the way up: the Borinquen Democratic Association, the Comité-Femeninos-Unidos, Flavors by F. W. Kaye & Co. That chocolate scent was so strong, I can smell it now by just thinking about it. I began to have informal gatherings in the loft, serving only beer and pretzels, unless David or Victor shopped and cooked. The first such gathering was in January. About ten composers and a few painters came; Paul Bowles played his new ballet music, and I played some of the opera. I worried that there were not enough seats, but people sat on the cot and on cushions on the floor. The loft went over in a big way. It was a novelty before the time when composers and artists sought out lofts to live and work in. The only way one could get into the place at night was to yell very loud from the street. I would have to run all the way down to open the door. After Victor returned from Paris and Spain as a press photographer, he lived in the loft and set up a darkroom there. We had a few robberies aimed at Victor's photographic equipment. But I chose that hideaway because it was one of the few places in the city where one could make music at any hour of the day or night without jeopardizing the lease. The loft cost $25 a month with no heat (we improvised).

I resumed lectures at the New School (a "music alertness course for intelligent listening") and worked on *The Second Hurricane* whenever I could between other projects. Minna had put me in charge of a column in *Modern Music*, "Scores and Records." It was one of five regular columns; the others were on theater, film, dance, and radio. I considered this a very good deal, since it meant receiving recordings and scores free. It was also a good way to keep in touch with the latest developments. My first article (November–December 1936) began: "Our title, we hope, is prophetic. The time may not be far off when recording companies will issue scores with their records, and publishing firms records with their scores. . . ." Unfortunately, I was overly optimistic, for this prophecy has never been realized. In May–June 1937 I announced the resumption of publication by the Cos Cob Press. One of the scores of interest was Ives' *Washington's Birthday*, the first movement of the *Holidays Symphony* published by

Top: Copland's loft.
Bottom: Copland and Clurman in the loft, 1937.

COPLAND / 1 9 0 0 – 1 9 4 2

Cowell's New Music Orchestra Series. I wrote about this work, composed in 1913, "What unique things Ives was doing during that period! And what a shocking lack of interest to this very day on the part of our major symphonic organizations in this true pioneer musician." In the January–February 1938 issue I covered "Swing" recordings: ". . . the master of them all is still Duke Ellington. . . . Ellington is a composer, by which I mean, he comes nearer to knowing how to make a piece hang together than the others." In March–April 1938 I included newly published pieces by Conlon Nancarrow, the *Toccata* for violin and piano and *Prelude and Blues* for piano: "These short works show a remarkable surety in an unknown composer, plus a degree of invention and imagination that immediately gives him a place among our talented younger men." The May–June column of "Scores and Records" described two young prizewinners, William Schuman and David Diamond: "Schuman is, so far as I am concerned, the musical find of the year. There is nothing puny or miniature about this young man's talent. If he fails he will fail on a grand scale . . . it seems to me that Schuman is a composer who is going places." I wrote "Scores and Records" for *Modern Music* until the spring of 1939, when I turned it over to Colin McPhee.

Another project of the 1936–37 season was a commission from the Columbia Broadcasting System for an orchestral work to be composed specifically for radio. CBS awarded six such commissions, to Louis Gruenberg, Howard Hanson, Roy Harris, Walter Piston, William Grant Still, and myself. Radio was an exciting new medium—the very idea of reaching so many people with a single performance! I believed that radio was an important new field for the American composer to explore, and I welcomed the chance to compose music that would lend itself to the unique opportunities of radio performance. *Radio Serenade* (as my piece was first called) is in one movement of about twelve minutes' duration in a style designed to bridge the gap between modern composition and the need for a wider public. It was written expressly for a large audience of inexperienced listeners, rather than for the more limited number of sophisticated devotees of the concert hall. Deems Taylor, CBS's Consultant on Music, wrote to give me instructions (28 September 1936): "The instrumentation shall be that of the average radio concert orchestra—that is 37 players. Bear in mind that the string section, playing before the microphone sounds much fuller than it would in a concert hall." CBS even invited the composers to visit the studios for a demonstration of "various effects possible with instru-

254

ments on the microphone." I decided to use several special effects in the orchestration: a muted trumpet ("felt hat over bell"), other trumpet mutes, a flutist standing at the microphone, bassoons and saxophones for jazz effects, and a vibraphone. To increase audience interest, CBS announced a contest for the best title. (I was to use *Music for Radio* until the winner was announced.)

From January on, work on my high school opera became so all-engrossing that I had to put the radio piece aside, but my plan was to orchestrate it immediately after the April opera premiere. In the spring however, I left New York with the score still unfinished. From Mexico I wrote to the authorities for a two-week extension and they agreed. Somehow I got the score and parts to CBS for a broadcast on 25 July 1937 on the program called "Everybody's Music," Howard Barlow conducting. The announcer informed the audience that a prize would be given for the most suitable title. "The prize," he jokingly added, "has no great allure in terms of cash value, although it might someday be a collector's item. Ha ha." The winner was to receive the original score, personally autographed by the composer. Over a thousand suggestions came from the United States and Canada. Davidson Taylor, head of the music section of CBS, sent the titles on to me in Mexico. I responded by telegram: HAVE READ ALL TITLE SUGGESTIONS STOP ASTONISHED AND DELIGHTED BY NUMBER AND VARIETY STOP NO ONE TITLE COMPLETELY SATISFACTORY STOP ACCEPT GLADLY AS IMAGINATIVE SUBTITLE SAGA OF THE PRAIRIE STOP CLOSE RUNNERS UP PRAIRIE TRAVEL STOP JOURNEY OF THE EARLY PIONEERS STOP AMERICAN PIONEER. I had used a cowboy tune in the second of the four sections, so the western titles seemed most appropriate. (The piece, of course, had been composed entirely on West 63rd Street in New York City.) A sampling from the titles submitted suggests that a piece of music can evoke a wide variety of associations in the minds of an audience: The Inca's Prayer to the Sun, Machine Age, Spiritual Ecstasy, Sunday at Coney Island, Marconi's World Message, Transatlantic Liner Ascending Ambrose Channel, Subway Traveler, Boy Scout Jamboree, Journey of the British Patrol Across Arabia, Adventures in the Life of a Robot, Futile Search for Order Out of Chaos.

In 1968 when there was no longer live music on radio, *Music for Radio, Saga of the Prairie* was renamed *Prairie Journal.* But somehow the piece has never been called anything but *Music for Radio.* After the winner of the contest was announced in 1937, the lady who had submitted *Saga of*

Manuscript page from *The Second Hurricane*.

the Prairie was sent my original score as promised. Miss Ruth Leonhardt of Grosse Pointe, Michigan, where are you now?[19]

The premiere of *The Second Hurricane* was scheduled for 21 April 1937, with Lehman Engel conducting. When Sandy Meisner could not serve as director, I took Denby's advice about a young actor-director, Orson Welles, whom Denby called "the most talented person in town." We went to see him, and after I played parts of the score, Orson accepted. The newspapers seemed to enjoy the idea that a dyed-in-the-wool modernist was writing an opera for schoolchildren, so they gave a great deal of attention to every step along the way, particularly the casting. Those kids must have gotten a kick out of seeing their names in the *Times* and *Tribune!* Clearly, we would not present this school opera quietly and skip town if all did not go well. If it was going to be a flop, it would be a big one. The idea of an opera for high school performers appealed to the press, I suppose, for the same reasons it appealed to me. There's a certain excitement in hearing your music sung and played by an enthusiastic group of youngsters that no highly trained organization of grown-up professionals can produce.

Furthermore, it was pleasant to envisage musical contact with an entirely new audience—the youth of America. In a way, *The Second Hurricane* was inspired by them. I had in mind the remarkable growth of school music organizations throughout the country, particularly those in the Middle West, the Far West, and the Southwest. I heard tales of creditable performances with charming fresh voices and good orchestral technique, but with little repertoire to choose from other than arrangements of Gilbert and Sullivan operettas and tenth-rate imitations of Broadway musicals. The Henry Street Settlement supplied the impetus by offering the Grand Street Playhouse and their Music School as proving ground for a production of a work especially designed for high school students. My motives were not all unselfish—the usual run of symphony audiences submitted to new music when it was played *at* them, but never showed signs of really wanting it. The atmosphere had become deadening. It was anything but conducive to the creation of new works. Yet the composer must compose! A school opera seemed a good momentary solution for one composer, at any rate.

Lehman Engel and I decided on a grown-up chorus from the Henry Street Settlement for the parents' chorus and a student one from Seward High School for the pupils' chorus. Daily rehearsals became part of their curriculum. Lehman got together a professional orchestra to supplement a few teachers from the Henry Street School. The leading parts were cast from the Professional Children's School. When Orson and I went to choose the cast, we were amazed and delighted at the talent and naturalness of the kids. The only difficult casting was the part of Fat—there were no fat boys with bass voices except one, and he had a distinctly Brooklyn accent. Since the opera takes place in the Midwest, the boy had to be replaced. I felt terribly cruel! The part of Jeff, meant for a boy soprano, was not quite right because our Jeff was a little too old, and his voice had changed. But the others seemed perfect. Our only professional adult actor filled the part of the aviator. His name was Joseph Cotten, and he received $10 a performance.

Mary Lescaze began to organize drives for fund raising. She invited prospective donors to her attractive modern town house. At the first of these gatherings, Edwin Denby read a synopsis of the libretto, and I played some of the music. Lehman, who was more outgoing, asked for contributions. Mrs. Leopold Stokowski and Dorothy Norman gave $100 each to match Mary's starter; $875 was collected that day. Since expenses for three performances were figured at $2,250, Mary invited another group—Carl Van Vechten, Constance and Kirk Askew, Lincoln Kirstein, Chávez, and others. Rudy Burckhardt, Denby's Swiss filmmaker friend, showed two films. In one, 145 West 21 (Denby's address), I "acted" the part of a roofer. Denby and the lyricist John Latouche were also in it. It was an amateur production with recorded piano music by Paul Bowles, but it gave everyone a laugh, and more funds were collected. By the beginning of March we had about $1,500 toward the total; the rest was to be made up in ticket sales. I wrote these details to Victor and concluded: "I can think of nothing else but the opera performance. I will always remember this spring as the hurricane season."

Denby and I had agreed from the start that all stage business was to be simple and natural, and that we would keep before us at all times the premise that this opera was for American youngsters to relate to in their everyday lives and language. Settings, costumes, and orchestration had to be elastic—stretching to accommodate the circumstances and simple enough for young people to put together themselves. It could be performed with two pianos for accompaniment or with an ensemble of thirty, as we had for the premiere. There was to be no curtain and no operatic posturing. Denby explored the problems of creating and choosing a viable opera libretto in an article for Modern Music.[20] In writing The Second Hurricane, he adapted his ideas to the framework of a school libretto.

Copland and John LaTouche as they appeared in Rudy Burckhardt's short film, "145 West 21."
The title refers to Edwin Denby's address.

Edwin Denby [21]

When Aaron asked me to write the text for an opera, the first thing I won-dered about was the costuming—what kind of costumes could students possibly know how to wear on stage? Once we realized that it was best not to have any costumes at all, the story came easily. I read in the daily news-papers accounts of floods and airplane rescues in the Midwest. I added hurricanes for excitement, not realizing that hurricanes do not go inland. The plot was simple as it should be, and was finished in a few days. But when Aaron needed four extra lines of song, it took me ten days to write them! The plot went this way: an aviator comes to the principal of a high school for volunteers to help in flood relief. The principal chooses six pupils, four boys (Butch, Fat, Gip, Lowrie) and two girls (Gwen and Queenie), and off they go in the airplane. It falters and is forced down in a deserted spot near a great river. They unload, and the plane leaves for help. The young people begin to quarrel when they are left to fend for themselves. A small Negro boy, Jefferson Brown [Jeff], appears. He is afraid and lonely. The students fight over the food, while a chorus of parents on stage comment and a chorus of pupils reply. The six students decide to leave in different directions in search of the nearest town. It is then that the hurricane hits hard. They gratefully find each other again and are rescued by a search plane. The moral of the story is stated in the Epilogue:

> *The newspapers made a story out of it like a lot of others.*
> *That's not what we think of, now it's all over.*
> *We got an idea of what life would be like with everybody pulling together,*
> *If each wasn't trying to get ahead of all the rest—*
> *What it's like when you feel you belong together,*
> *With a sort of love making you feel easy.*
> *We'll remember that feeling even if we six drift apart—*
> *A happy easy feeling, like freedom, real freedom.*

We subtitled Second Hurricane a *"play opera"* because of the talking parts. The writing of these came naturally to me, from my experience with German opera. Once the libretto was finished, I stepped out of the picture. I regretted not being around to help Aaron and for the excitement of the premiere, but Rudy Burckhardt and I had an opportunity to go to Haiti, and so we left at the end of February. A few years later I happened to be in Akron, Ohio, when the local high school was putting on a production of The Second Hurricane. I could go incognito. It was a real school production with football players in it and lots of enthusiasm and individual touches. Later on in New York, I saw another version by an almost all-black cast at the Museum of Modern Art. They did some very funny parodies of the text. It was totally different from the Ohio production.

Aaron was eager to do another opera, a grown-up one, and we both promised to think about subjects. I looked into various biographies and historical figures, but nothing seemed right until I was traveling in the Southwest and heard an old-timer, "Arizona Bill," tell a legend of the Southwest. I no longer remember the story, but I was so taken with the subject that I made a libretto based on it. But I had some difficulty getting permission from the storyteller, and then Aaron was not convinced that it was what he wanted. It was put aside, and we never did do another opera together.

The musical challenge with *The Second Hurricane* was to see how simple I could be without losing my musical identity. I wished to be simple to the point of ordinariness. I chose mild and consonant harmonies and easy rhythms. This worked well for the colloquial passages of the libretto where the music approaches operetta, but in the more dramatic moments, it was difficult to make the distinction between grand opera and high school opera. The opera is ninety minutes in duration, in two acts, with seven soloists, three spoken parts, a mixed chorus, and an orchestra using saxophone and a musical saw (or theremin). The music is divided into ten "numbers," with the spoken scenes taking away the necessity for recitative. There is only one motif that is repeated. It appears at the very beginning and again at the end of the opera and typifies the spirit of adventure. For our own work, Denby and I identified each main character with a central motivation or emotion—Fat was "loneliness," Queenie "adolescent love," etc. Jazz elements seemed appropriate for youthful bounce and optimism, and even for jitteriness in a few of the scary scenes.

Denby and I corresponded about the characters from the time I was first writing the music in Tlaxcala. About Queenie, he wrote:

> Queenie ought to have a song that would be musically very sweet and coo-ing. I don't think you need understand the words, but get the feeling of floating in contentment that isn't rationally crystallized, like singing vocalise. It is the tenderest and most intimate personal spot in the piece, the moment that expresses the individual when he or she is sure of his environment. . . . The grace that flows out of a person when he feels sure of contact with everything. It's not an effort and it's not an affirmation. . . . Fat's song is the opposite, being complete loneliness: only I think it should be not ugly just the same, but also attractive. . . .

Denby's depth of understanding and involvement with these fictitious characters helped me enormously. For "Queenie's Song" I wrote a high, long, and sustained melodic line over slowly moving harmonies. (This "aria" has occasionally been used as a solo song; Ethel Luening performed it in a Town Hall recital on 22 March 1937 before the opera premiere.) *Hurricane* was the first work in which I incorporated a North American folk tune—the revolutionary song, "The Capture of Burgoyne." The score of *The Second Hurricane* has been likened to the school of *Gebrauchsmusik* current in Germany some years earlier, but I felt I had attempted something more ambitious than music "written for use."

Rehearsal schedules and arrangements were complicated. In addition to a cast and orchestra totaling close to 150, Denby had included a ballet

Denby, Copland, and Bernstein studying the score of *The Second Hurricane*.

pantomime describing what the children imagine rescue work to be like. Orson did not care for this ballet sequence, and it was finally removed from the production. Orson's ideas for staging were original—the two choruses were on stage, and the orchestra was placed on a platform at the rear with the conductor facing the audience. Denby wrote from Haiti: "I wouldn't worry over Orson's part, and I hope his unpunctuality at rehearsals is not bad. He works very hard. You'll see, the best thing to do is to show him you trust him and leave him alone." I took Denby's advice. Orson got busy with staging Marc's *The Cradle Will Rock*, and once the concept for *Hurricane* was set, he left much of the actual work to Hiram Sherman. Virgil was helpful, and Lehman called him "the midwife" of the production. Lehman told me he was amazed at how "cool and relaxed" I was during all this. I asked him why he thought so, and he replied, "Well, you rarely come to rehearsals." The fact was, I had no time for rehears-

The original cast of *The Second Hurricane.*

als—I was frantically finishing the orchestration! But one evening I stepped in to hear the first rehearsal at Henry Street of the Chorus of Parents and the Chorus of Pupils singing together with the orchestra. I wrote to Chávez, "It sounded like Beethoven's Ninth Symphony!" Everyone was so obviously having a good time that it smoothed my frazzled nerves. "If only the audience enjoys themselves half as much," I thought, "all will be well." Edwin wrote: "I don't know how we can resist coming back! Perhaps you'd better save two seats. . . . Don't worry—if one kid is good, the whole thing will work."

The audience for the premiere were adults from what was called the "carriage trade." Due to the organizational efforts of Mary Lescaze, New York's high society found its way down to the Playhouse at 466 Grand Street in a driving rainstorm to see *The Second Hurricane.* Two performances followed, and a CBS radio broadcast (9 May 1937) in which a narrator took the place of the choruses. Following the premiere, Francis D. Perkins wrote in the *Herald Tribune:* "It should prove a very appropriate vehicle for schools throughout the country wishing to present musico-dramatic performances with homegrown talents and without going to great expense for settings and properties. Thus it can be welcomed as a valuable contribution." Some critics called the opera "dull," and others recognized that an opera for high school performers had to be in a musical style suitable for its use. The libretto came in for some adverse criticism, particularly from Europeans and Americans used to hearing only European opera; they found it hard to swallow a plot that we had purposely made simple and natural. But Virgil appreciated what we were after:

> The music is vigorous and noble. The libretto is fresh and is permeated with a great sweetness. Linguistically it is the finest English libretto in some years. . . . Unfortunately the show peters out before the end, the plot falling to pieces at the very moment when our anxiety is greatest about the fate of the characters. . . . Please, Messrs Copland and Denby, do that last part over at greater length and tell us the "real adventure" that you promised us in the beginning. . . . It is nonetheless, of course, a remarkable work. . . .[22]

I had promised to send reviews to Edwin. Some critics called the libretto "innocuous" and "naive," so I wrote reminding him that it takes about fifty years for a musical work to be appreciated. I believed then that Edwin Denby had as good an idea of what a libretto should and should not be as anyone in the country. Edwin responded: "I have to laugh when I think of how when we're eighty the Metropolitan will give it with Martinelli as Gip and Flagstadt as Queenie, and everybody will be completely serious about it. . . . I think you ought to write another opera for grown ups."

In 1938 excerpts of *Hurricane* were presented, sponsored by *New Masses* with comments by Orson Welles and performances by the Lehman Engel Singers and myself. Productions out of town were not as frequent as we had hoped, but there were a few—in Alaska, California, Ohio, and Tennessee. Paul Hindemith put on parts of *Hurricane* at the Berkshire Music Center's second season of 1941. Leonard Bernstein directed the opera in 1942 at the Peabody Playhouse in Boston. The opera's theme of cooperation was particularly appropriate during the war years, so the Treasury Department sponsored a radio broadcast for the sale of U.S. War Savings Bonds, with the late Alfred Wallenstein conducting a cast from the High School of Music and Art. And in the mid-forties, The Composers Laboratory–Forum in San Francisco produced *The Second Hurricane.*

Lenny's television production in 1960 with students from Music and Art drew fresh attention to *Hurricane*. I was in Russia, but Denby described it to me:

> Lennie's 2nd Hurricane was an adorable show.... the children looked heavenly, sang musically ... being New Yorkers they also acted like so many little Lennies, no harm at all.... Musically it was immeasurably better than any performance ever, and the beautiful freshness of the music is ravishing. Lennie played it for drama, as you would expect, a trifle extra fast and extra slow if one knows the piece, but he gave it a fascinating over-all pace.... The spoken text was cut (He wrote and talked the introductory and connecting narration—and sang all the words—inaudibly).... I don't mind the spoken scenes being cut....

This version was recorded with Lenny conducting and narrating. In 1961 Charles Schwartz invited me to do the narration in a concert version at the Composers' Showcase at the Museum of Modern Art, again with students from Music and Art, Seymour Lipkin conducting. More recently Sarah Caldwell's Opera New England presented the opera at various high schools, drawing on local talent.

C. C. Birchard asked to publish the score soon after the premiere in 1937. This may read like a simple statement, but simple it was not. Various performance requests had to be postponed in 1938 during the publication procedures. Would the cuts from the original be reinstated? Would changes be made in the text—for example, could the word "durn" be allowed in print? What about the ballet? These questions and hundreds of others were discussed and decided by mail between Denby in Haiti, Mr. Birchard in Boston, and myself in New York, followed by tedious proofreading of libretto, piano-vocal score, choral and orchestral parts. By late 1938 *The Second Hurricane* was available in published form. The final chorus, "That's the Idea of Freedom," was also released separately by the American Book Company to whom I sold the rights for $50. I was happy to get it, having made only $100 from the opera.

The $500 commission from CBS for the radio piece would not be forthcoming until the goods were delivered, and I would not be ready to do this until summer. A course planned for the New School on "Contemporary Piano Literature" had been abandoned because only two people had signed up for it. (I took this as yet another sign that the public was in no mood for modern music.) I did get $100 from the New School as compensation for all the preparation, and a few fees tided me over—for a lecture on Stravinsky given in Cleveland in February, and for the performance of my *Dance Symphony* by the New York Philharmonic under Artur Rodzinski in a concert sponsored by the League on 11 April. Rodzinski had postponed the performance once already, and when word came that the orchestra did not want to play the piece, I told Claire Reis that I would quit the League in protest if they canceled again. Claire, in her best fighting mood, stormed over to see Rodzinski and told him the League would collapse without me. It was all very unpleasant and spoiled any fun a performance might have been. On top of it, the piece was not played well. It surprised me to hear the reviewers call it "well crafted," since even to me it sounded confused in spots. I was particularly chagrined because Nadia had arrived a few days earlier and was at the performance.

A look at my bank balance persuaded me to cancel a booking on the *Normandie* for the end of April. My idea had been to meet Victor in Paris and travel to Russia with him during the summer. A Russian delegate had promised to get me invited and to find out if I had rubles being held there from the publication of "Into the Streets May First!", but I never heard from him after he left the United States. Also, I wanted to be on hand for the radio broadcast of *The Second Hurricane* announced for 9 May, and for the wedding of my friend Peggy (Rosamond) Rosenbaum in Philadelphia.

Rosamond (Peggy) Bernier[23]

When I first met Aaron, I was at Sarah Lawrence. Some of my friends there were going to Mexico for the holidays, and my father, who was connected with the Philadelphia Orchestra and knew Carlos Chávez, wrote to him to tell him I was coming. So when I arrived in the summer of 1936, Chávez picked me up and invited me to a rehearsal of his Sinfónica de México. The rehearsal took place in a disaffected church because a "light and power" strike made the regular hall unusable. I went, and was very amused at the scene of this orchestra filled with Indian faces—and what were they rehearsing but Aaron's Piano Concerto! And Aaron was playing the piano. I sat at rehearsal watching him in absolute delight. He was so pleased with the music and with the orchestra. He was just so happy, bouncing up and down on the piano stool to the jazzy rhythms, and beaming. This orchestra of Chávez's had a very flexible rhythmic sense, but a peculiar nasal quality of sound. I was enchanted to see the composer so clearly enjoying his own music.

I went to the performance, and afterward we all went out to a nightclub for supper. Immediately I thought Aaron was the most wonderful man I ever met, and I fell in love with him on the spot and never changed. Aaron was radiant—he laughed and laughed—and we talked. He told me he lived in Tlaxcala, several hours from Mexico City, and he mentioned that he couldn't find any marmalade there and he missed that. So what did I do but enroll some boyfriend to drive me to Tlaxcala with a great load of marmalade. I arrived, and Aaron thought I was out of my mind! There he was with Victor Kraft in a small house with a rickety upright piano, and he was working on The Second Hurricane. He sat down and played some of it, and I've never forgotten him singing "I'm sad and all alone and awfully far away. I wish I was back home, but I just have to stay. . . ." It was so improbable somehow—Aaron in this small Mexican village writing an opera! He told me that the local priest had come down to pay a courtesy call, and said, "Since you are a 'musico,' please play something." Aaron was embarrassed to say he was not that kind of "musico," but he managed to play a popular Mexican tune for his visitor.

When I went back to Sarah Lawrence, Aaron came out several times to see me; I was in New York City regularly for harp lessons with Carlos Salzedo. Aaron would take me places with him. He took me to my first grown-up party at the Askews (the Askews had a famous salon, Tchelitchew and Dalí were regulars), and it seemed to me like the height of glamour. Aaron was amused by this, but he was never taken in by that world. He was comfortable in it, but he had just as much fun at the Automat. I used to go to Aaron's ramshackle loft. It was so dusty that once I saved my pocket money to get it cleaned—he thought that was crazy! And I would go with him like the composer's wife to concerts and pick up programs to be sure he would have them for his archives. I met Edwin Denby through Aaron, and Paul and Jane Bowles, Harold Clurman, Clifford Odets, and all the Group Theatre people. And of course the composers.

Aaron was sort of a combination father figure and mentor, and I don't know what he made of me then. I think he was probably amused by my devotion, and since it was totally undemanding, it didn't cause any problems of any kind. I always felt that life was better when Aaron was around. When he came into a room, it was literally like a light coming on. I think that everybody else felt that too. Somehow, one was safer with Aaron there—he had a marvelous equilibrium which comforted one. I never intruded in any way on Aaron's personal life, and I knew that anything of that sort would make him uncomfortable. And I never inflicted my own *personal life on him. Our relationship was absolutely cloudless. When I was married to Lew Riley, Aaron was already a loved friend, and he came from New York for the wedding, which was in the garden of my father's house in Philadelphia. He knew that I liked "Gip's Song" from The Second Hurricane very much, so he showed up at the wedding with "Gip's Song" scored, as he said, for "Peggy's harp and Lew's guitar." So we had a Copland work specially written out for us.*

In 1941 or '42, Aaron invited me for a weekend at Tanglewood. So off I went to his tiny rented house in Stockbridge. The first morning I showed up in my dressing gown for breakfast, and Aaron looked at me and said wistfully, "Is that what girls wear?" I think he was quite pleased to have a feminine presence there. He seemed terribly proud to have me around, and he showed me off, introducing me to everyone. That's when I met Lenny for the first time. I recall him playing the piano and being Lenny in Aaron's house, and Aaron saying, "There's no doubt about that one!" Lenny had a tremendous feeling for Aaron. He simply adored him. It was the link between Lenny and myself. We have a devoted friendship also, but we always talk about Aaron. That never changes. Lenny and Aaron were both at my wedding to John Russell in 1975.

I was very fond of Victor Kraft in the early years. He was terribly handsome, but so unsure of himself. In 1941 I was very ill and in hospital here in New York; Victor took care of me when I came out. And Aaron came to visit me in hospital on my birthday with a gift of Gide's essay on Montaigne, signed by Gide, that belonged to him. (Gide meant a lot to that generation of Americans.) Victor was intuitive, affectionate, always taking up lost causes. He was like a character out of a Russian novel. Victor and Aaron were totally different. Victor was very musical. He would be outraged when things weren't right at concerts of Aaron's music and would get terribly angry with Aaron for adapting pieces from his own music instead of writing something new.

When Lew Riley and I lived in Mexico and then South America, we went on seeing Aaron. We would go to a favorite bar in Mexico City—La Cucaracha, and although Aaron almost never drank, he would occasionally have a daiquiri. He was unworldly in some ways; I recall how puzzled he was that Lew had to have his cocktail and that on our travels through remote places, the search for ice for the cocktail drink took on such intensity. We were in South America when Aaron was sent on his first "goodwill tour" in 1941, so we met in Bogotá in August. Aaron did quite nicely in Spanish (*his favorite word was "tropical"*). He never changed, however different his surroundings might be, and we could see how his simplicity and his true intelligence reached everyone. We were together in Havana in December and heard the news about Pearl Harbor on the radio and later walked on the beach and talked about it. I remember seeing Aaron off occasionally on planes or trains and noticing that he took scores of all kinds to read the way other people take magazines and books.

In Paris, just after the war, I went to visit Nadia Boulanger at Aaron's suggestion. It was bitterly cold in her rue Ballu apartment. Absolutely freezing. She was extremely kind to me because of Aaron. Before I left for home, she came by to see me at the Crillon. I wasn't there, so she left a goodbye gift. Do you know what she left?—a piece of soap and a box of Kleenex—the most precious things in Paris then. At that time, when I was with Vogue magazine, Nadia did an article for me about the young French composers she was championing. Years later, in the early seventies, when Aaron came to conduct in Paris, he and I went together to one of her famous receptions. In the total darkness of the hall downstairs, Aaron reached out automatically and found the light switch—he had been coming there for decades. To Aaron's amusement, the refreshments on offer were as spartan as in his student days. Mademoiselle Boulanger simply didn't bother about such things. But her delight in seeing Aaron was evident. (Aaron himself never paid much attention to food, nor to the decor of his surroundings.)

In 1946, also for Vogue, I asked Minna Lederman for a piece on composers, about John Cage, Aaron, and others. I had Irving Penn photograph Aaron. Whenever I was in New York and there was something special going on in the music world, Aaron would ask me to be his "date." Once I was visiting him in the country—it was 1967—and I was wearing a light dress. Suddenly, it turned cold and Aaron lent me a big heavy dark green sweater. I kept it and wore it for walks during a weekend at a famous French château that season. When I sent a photo of me in it to Aaron, he said, "I never dreamed anything of mine would go around looking so elegant in a place like that." I still have the sweater in my house in Connecticut and I love it. No matter how much times goes by, we keep in touch. I am always moved by the expression of delight on Aaron's face when he catches sight of me, and by his happy, unmistakably Aaron shout of "Peggy!"

All things considered, especially financial, June 1937 seemed like a good time to accept Clurman's invitation to visit Hollywood to try for a film contract. I had followed George Antheil's column in *Modern Music*, "On the Hollywood Front," with great interest. "Something is going on in Hollywood," Antheil wrote. "Composers may remain aloof to it, but only at the peril of being left behind, esthetically perhaps as well as financially."[24] Clurman, who was working for Walter Wanger, was trying to act unofficially as my agent. He talked to Alfred Newman of United Artists, Nat Finston of MGM, and Boros Morros at Paramount on my behalf. Harold wrote (5 May 1937): "Morros says he knows that you have a good reputation, etc. but will you be 'adaptable,' will you adjust yourself, will you realize the *practical* problems! . . . So I say, Copland is as practical as Louis B. Mayer, as adaptable as an English diplomat, a regular mumzer! (agents' stuff!) Alright says B.M. 'How much?'—$5,000 for a score, and no more than 8 weeks at that price, I tell him. . . ."

They asked to see some of my scores at MGM, and Clurman went around telling everyone to listen to the broadcast of *Hurricane*. Harold reported (18 May): "I asked Morros immediately if he had heard the broadcast. He had and liked it very much. He is sold on you. . . . He feels that you ought to be put on an important picture that needs an impressive score." There was talk of a new art form among composers, called "picture music." Schoenberg and Stravinsky had been invited by Morros to do scores for Paramount and Honegger was to compose music for *Joan of Arc* at RKO. Harold urged me to make my presence known in Hollywood soon. Antheil still made me wary: he warned that it was difficult to get a commission for a film score without prior film credits; that Hollywood was a "closed corporation"; and, "No one should attempt to come out unless he can write 'piano scores' at the rate of fifteen to thirty pages a day. Speed is still one of the main requisites of the picture business."[25] But I gathered my courage and decided to go to Hollywood for the month of June. On the train trip out, I was accompanied by Stella Adler's nine-year-old daughter Ellen, whom Harold asked me to bring along. From the *Santa Fe Chief*, I wrote to Victor back in New York: "It's like traveling with a pet poodle everyone admires."

When I saw Harold's small house on South Maple Drive, which looked to me like a cross between Brooklyn's Flatbush Avenue and the newer sections of Mexico City, I took a room at the Hollywood Franklin Hotel and rented a small piano. George Antheil and Kurt Weill came by to take me to dinner and Luther Adler invited me to the Brown Derby restaurant, where I was introduced to James Cagney and to Harpo Marx, who was unrecognizable without the wig. It seemed that everyone was either just going to or just returning from the Brown Derby! Harold took me around to several sets at United Artists and to Paramount to meet His Majesty, Boros Morros, who immediately started to call me "Aaron." I saw Cliff Odets and his wife, Luise Rainer, and the Group people. I wrote to Victor, "They are fed up with Hollywood and yearning for the heat and grime of N.Y." Oscar Levant took me to visit George and Ira Gershwin. I was impressed with the swimming pool and tennis court in their "backyard." It was hard for me to realize that you could get all that for writing songs and lyrics! I wrote other impressions to Victor (June 1937):

Hollywood is not nearly as composer-conscious as Antheil's articles would make one think. The whole idea of their wanting "different" music comes solely from Morros' playing around with the idea of Stravinsky, Schoenberg, et al. The conditions of work are very unsatisfactory. Antheil says the cutter can ruin 5 weeks of work by dubbing music indiscriminately. The only thing for sure is there's money here. . . . Antheil and his wife have an art gallery and have invited me to do a concert in a series. I will be wiring you for music from the loft. Saw Gershwin and spoke with him. He had heard the opera broadcast and asked for a copy. Also said he'd sign my application for membership in ASCAP. . . .

The Group turned out for my concert en masse. Levant played the two-piano arrangement of the *Piano Concerto* with me brilliantly, Jerry Moross took the second piano part in *El Salón México*, and I performed the *Piano Variations.* I left Hollywood for Mexico at the beginning of July without a film contract. Antheil was right about needing a film credit in order to snag a contract in Hollywood. But how was one to go about that?

In Tlaxcala, the Padre from the church across the way had opened the house for us. I preferred this out-of-the-way place to the suburban living in Hollywood. After *Music for Radio* was finished and sent off to CBS, I went into Mexico City from 13 to 24 July. Elizabeth Sprague Coolidge had invited me to the First Festival of Pan American Chamber Music, where compositions from the Americas (including my *Music for the Theatre*, which I conducted) were presented in six concerts under Chávez' direction. Back in Tlaxcala, I arranged the *Short Symphony* as the *Sextet.* After the world premiere of *El Salón México* on 27 August in Mexico City, Victor headed to Haiti to visit Rudy Burckhardt, and I took a slow train to Vera Cruz, and then a boat to Havana for a few days, before going on to New York. Every restaurant, café, and nightclub in Havana had two orchestras—a rhumba band and a "danzón" sextet. They played alternately, and the music never stopped. The sonority of the danzón was intriguing—predominantly flute that sounded like a clear bright whistle, combined with violin, piano, double bass, muted trumpet, and traps. The music itself is very simple, but it had me fascinated as a lesson in what could be done with a few notes if the rhythms are amusing and the sonority interesting. I thought at the time that I would someday try a piece based on the Cuban danzón.

Music for Use

1937-1939

Arriving back in New York, I found that three hundred people had signed up for my course, "What to Listen For in Music," and I could look forward to the lectures becoming a book at the close of the series. A few private students still came to me from the Henry Street School. I took my old room back at the Empire Hotel. Victor was away, and Paul Bowles was staying in my loft temporarily. While I was gone, the entire building had been painted bright yellow with red doors and black borders. I went to several rehearsals of Clifford Odets' *Golden Boy,* since this was the only way to see Clurman, and to the opening night and party afterward at Bobby Lewis'. Finally, the Group Theatre had a success!

Roy Harris and Roger Sessions were both in New York that fall, and we were all involved with a composers' committee to support a bill in Congress for a National Fine Arts Department. It seems to me that I spent a great deal of time at meetings—the Fine Arts Bill Executive Committee, the League, Lehman Engel's publishing project that would become Arrow Music Press, and a Composers' Protection Society. Although the Federal Arts Bill was not passed through Congress, our efforts crystallized the aims of composers toward helping themselves, particularly as concerned the collecting of performance fees. The right to a performance fee was established by law, but composers had been cautious about exercising that right for fear it would act as a deterrent to performances. But the time had come for composers of serious music to insist on benefits similar to those made possible by ASCAP for composers of popular music. Thus the American Composers Alliance (ACA) came into being.

Forty-eight composers attended an organizational meeting on 19 December 1937 at the Beethoven Association. I was appointed chairman of the temporary executive committee mandated to draw up aims and objectives. On the committee were Marion Bauer, Roy Harris, Goddard Lieberson, Douglas Moore, Quincy Porter, Wallingford Riegger, Roger Sessions, Elie Siegmeister, Virgil Thomson, and Bernard Wagenaar. Siegmeister presented a list of ideas for discussion; we evolved a program of fifteen points that was presented to a second meeting of the general membership in February 1938. Officers were elected: Copland, president; Lieberson, vice-president; Harrison Kerr, secretary; Henry Gerstlé, treasurer. I would serve as president of the ACA for the next seven years, until 1945. There was a sense of excitement and optimism at those first meetings. Our program of aims was sent to newspapers and critics, and we held a drive for membership, resulting in an enrollment of 184 composers. The list included some odd bedfellows—Walter Damrosch and Arnold Schoenberg, Ferde Grofé and Elliott Carter. We announced ourselves in *Modern Music:*

> The Composers Organize. A Proclamation. The American composer of serious music is about to proclaim a new principle for his work as a creative artist. He intends to campaign for the right to make a living by composing. . . . The elementary principle that every composer is worth his wage has never been established . . . the American Composers Alliance announces two objectives: first to regularize and collect all fees pertaining to performance of their copyrighted music, in other words, to protect the economic rights of the composer; second, to stimulate interest in the performance of American music, thereby increasing the economic returns.[1]

The ACA was to be considered "the official voice of the American composer." We published a bulletin, a simple brochure that grew as the organization itself gained strength. Our first *ACA Bulletin* of April 1938 listed aims and stated needs: "The composer plays a very minor role in the musical counsels of the nation. WE WISH TO CHANGE THAT! The composer comes last instead of first in the musical scheme of things. WE WISH TO CHANGE THAT!" In 1939 we added a rotating advisory board, and in 1940 chapters were formed in Los Angeles and Chicago. Harrison Kerr was heroic in managing ACA affairs. In the early forties we ran into problems stemming from the necessity to choose between affiliation with ASCAP or BMI. (Until 1938 ASCAP had been the principal collector of performance fees. BMI was founded when radio broadcasting grew, with the function of licensing radio rights and with the idea of breaking the ASCAP monopoly.) As members of ASCAP, Virgil and I of course preferred that ACA connect with them; others, Roger Sessions included, sided with BMI. ASCAP was reluctant to settle an agreement to control the collection of fees for ACA. After three years of discussions between the ACA and ASCAP (not always friendly), a decision was made when BMI offered a contract of $10,000 for ACA radio rights in 1944. We needed the money. Those who held dual membership in ASCAP and ACA were forced to choose one or the other. I resigned as president of ACA, and Otto Luening was elected in 1945. Otto had been learning the "business of music," and as he wrote in his autobiography, "We now became composer-businessmen."[2]

Since ASCAP and BMI continued to battle through most of the fifties, Otto's increasing awareness of American music in the business world was invaluable to ACA. David Rubin and Roger Goeb followed Harrison Kerr as executive secretaries. Roger set up a library of scores in 1951 at the BMI offices and the Laurel Leaf Award for distinguished service to contemporary American music was established (I was honored to receive it in 1968). By 1953 ACA had a regular radio program on WNYC. When Oliver Daniel became ACA's coordinating manager, he improved the *Bulletin*, initiated concert series at museums in New York City, and established outposts of support for new music all over this country and abroad. He was a founding father of Composers Recordings, Inc. (CRI) in 1954.[3] Oliver made it possible for ACA to change and grow with the times instead of being left behind them. The building of CRI's catalogue and the high quality of its recordings have been influential in promoting American contemporary music. In 1978 the American Composers Orchestra (ACO), the first orchestra devoted entirely to American music, was formed. It is currently headed by Francis Thorne; Nicolas Roussakis presides over ACA. What was begun in 1937 continues today, in stimulating performances, commissioning new works, and creating the necessary publicity for the American composer.

By 1938 and 1939 American music was thriving and growing, but the infant, represented by several groups, the ACA among them, was in need of parental authority. Among those publishing and recording American music were New Music Editions and New Music Quarterly Recordings (led by Luening after Cowell), and the Arrow Music Press, founded in 1938 by Blitzstein, Engel, Thomson, and myself. American music was being published, but no one knew how to distribute it. Luening had discussed the lack of a central library and distribution facility with Quincy Porter and Henry Moe of the Guggenheim Foundation. Together with Thomas Whitney Surette, they founded the Council for the Advancement and Diffusion of American Music. At their suggestion, in March 1939 a group met at my studio to incorporate the American Music Center

(AMC). I represented Arrow Music Press and ACA; Howard Hanson, the Eastman School Publications and Recordings; Marion Bauer, the Society for the Publication of American Music; and Porter, Yaddo and the New England Conservatory Recordings. The American Music Center office opened in November 1939 at 37 West 42nd Street in New York City. The idea was for the center to be a nonprofit dealer for distributing published music by American composers at list price. Announcements were sent to newspapers in various cities. Luening served as chairman of AMC boards for twenty years, and Harrison Kerr was again indefatigable as secretary; later Ray Green was just as tireless.

We had a lot of trouble with the publishers at first. They would not believe that we were nonprofit and refused to send us music, either on consignment or on a dealer's discount. Schirmer was particularly resistant, and their influence spread to the other publishers. Eventually, we came to terms. A rental library of orchestral manuscripts was established and composers were invited to place scores in it. The Center, although dependent on funding sources, has grown and prospered. It houses and runs a large and active library of scores, records, and videotapes of all kinds of music, and it is a much-needed clearinghouse for information about every aspect of composition and performance in the United States. After being actively involved with the AMC for many years, I was awarded their "Letter of Distinction" in 1970, and then again in 1975. Along with many of our country's composers, I am still a proud member of the American Music Center.

I have already told the story of how my lectures, "What to Listen For in Music," became a book. It is true that after the first year's lectures, a gentleman approached me, saying "Mr. Copland, you are speaking a book," but it was up to me to coordinate these materials and prepare them for publication. Also, I had agreed to formulate a study outline to use in conjunction with the book.[4] So in the spring of 1938 I accepted Roy Harris' offer to use his place in Princeton while he was away. When the manuscript was finished, I left for Europe.

It had been seven years since my last trip abroad. I went first to London for the ISCM Festival, where *El Salón México* was performed, and then to Paris. I carried with me two collections of "cowboy" tunes given me before I left New York by Lincoln Kirstein, leading American dance impresario and director of Ballet Caravan. When Lincoln Kirstein asked for a ballet, it was a foregone conclusion that it would be an American subject. Lincoln was attempting to move ballet away from the established Russian traditions and I could not have been more sympathetic with his aims. Still, I was wary of tackling a cowboy theme. Lincoln arranged discussions with Eugene Loring, choreographer for the ballet, and showed me sketches of Jared French's costumes.[5] When I suggested that, as a composer born in Brooklyn, I knew nothing about the Wild West, Lincoln informed me that Loring's scenario for *Billy the Kid* was based on the real life story of William Bonney, a notorious cowboy who had been born in New York![6] Lincoln was persuasive, and it did not take long to convince me that if I could work with Mexican tunes in *El Salón México*, I might try home-grown ones for a ballet. Thus during the summer of 1938 I found myself writing a cowboy ballet in Paris.

It is a delicate operation to put fresh and unconventional harmonies to well-known melodies without spoiling their naturalness; moreover, for an orchestral score, one must expand, contract, rearrange, and superimpose the bare tunes themselves, giving them something of one's own touch. That is what I tried to do, always keeping in mind my resolve to write plainly—not only because I had become convinced that simplicity was the way out of isolation for the contemporary composer, but because I have never liked music to get in the way of the thing it is supposedly aiding. If it is a question of expressing the deepest ideas of one's own soul, then you write a symphony. But if you are involved in a stage presentation, the eye is the thing, and music must play a more modest role. There was another reason for being simple in *Billy the Kid*. Our hero, Billy, may have been a complex character from a psychological standpoint but as a stage figure in a ballet, he is a simple figure—a boy bandit who brags that he has killed twenty-one men, "not counting Indians." To use or not to use cowboy songs as the basis for my ballet score was a decision left up to me. So said Lincoln as he slipped two tune books under my arm. I have never been particularly impressed with the musical beauties of the cowboy song as such. The words are usually delightful, and the manner of singing needs no praise from me. But neither the words nor the delivery are of much use in a purely orchestral ballet score, so I was left with the tunes themselves, which, I repeat, are often less than exciting. Nevertheless, I took the songs abroad with me.

While in London I received a letter from Elliott Carter (23 June 1938), who was at that time music director for Ballet Caravan, informing me of the instrumentation (an orchestra of about fifty) and enclosing the scenario, several pages of "Notes on Billy the Kid's Character," and suggestions to the composer. Lincoln sent a third collection of tunes to me in Paris. There in a studio on the rue de Rennes next door to David Diamond, I began to compose *Billy the Kid*. Perhaps there is something different about a cowboy song in Paris. Whatever the reasons, it was not long before I found myself hopelessly involved with "Great Grand-Dad," "Git Along Little Dogies," "The Old Chisholm Trail," "Goodbye, Old Paint," and "The Dying Cowboy." David looked on in wonder as I played "Trouble for the Range Cook." I assured him that I would not use "Home on the Range"—I decided to draw the line someplace!

Billy the Kid concerns itself with significant moments in the life of this infamous character of the American Southwest, known to the Mexicans as "El Chivato," or simply, "The Keed." The ballet begins and ends on the open prairie. The first scene is a street in a frontier town. Cowboys saunter into town, some on horseback, others on foot with lassoes; some Mexican women do a *Jarabe*, which is interrupted by a fight between two drunks. Attracted by the gathering crowd, Billy, a boy of twelve, is seen for the first time, with his mother. The brawl turns ugly, guns are drawn, and in some unaccountable way, Billy's mother is killed. Without an instant's hesitation, in cold fury, Billy draws a knife from a cowhand's sheath and stabs his mother's slayers. His short but famous career has begun. In swift succession we see episodes in Billy's later life—at night, under the stars, in a quiet card game with his outlaw friends; hunted by a posse led by his former friend Pat Garrett; in a gun battle. A celebration takes place when he is captured. Billy makes one of his legendary escapes from prison. Tired and worn out in the desert, Billy rests with his girl. Finally the posse catches up with him.

Eugene Loring[7]

Lincoln gave me The Life and Times of William Bonney *and said, "Read it and try to get a ballet out of it." I had never been west of the Mississippi, but I did an outline, and after Copland got involved, we filled in the action. We decided to use silence whenever Billy kills someone, and the sound of a gun only when Billy himself is killed. We discussed using props, but decided against guns. Each time Billy fires, he does a double pirouette before shooting as though an explosion of fury is going through his body. Billy's victims are always called "Alias" in various characterizations. Since no one knew of a real girlfriend for Billy, we idealized that re-*

lationship and treated the Sweetheart as an imaginary character. But the critics, John Martin among them, criticized our use of the Sweetheart's toe shoes among the cowboy boots. We got fond of Billy, although we knew we would finally have to kill him. Aaron composed a march for use at the beginning and end of the ballet to symbolize law and order.

Billy was my most successful work; it was a hit from the start and was danced all over South America with great success—in Nicaragua it was called Billy el Niño. *In our western states, there were still a few old-timers who remembered Billy. One came backstage in San Francisco to tell us that it was all fine, except that Billy really shot left-handed!* Billy the Kid *was the first full-fledged American ballet in style and form as well as content; it was the prototype for the later "western" ballets of De Mille, Robbins, and others that would become American dance classics.*

The premiere of *Billy* was scheduled for October 1938. I went to the MacDowell Colony for the month of September. It was my fourth visit. The first day in the mountain air was always wonderful, and it seemed like unbelievable luxury to have a closet in which to hang my clothes, a shower, and clean sheets in a clean room with no dust anywhere! I was put into Chapman Studio, which I had occupied in 1928, away from the sight and sound of everyone. I enjoyed the ten-minute walk to and from Colony Hall. I reached the very end of the ballet, but then got stuck on the last two minutes. (Perhaps because I knew I would have to begin the drudgery of orchestration as soon as I finished the actual composing.) I stayed in my studio all day, occasionally lighting a fire, eating a basket lunch that arrived on the doorstep daily (except for Sundays when we had midday dinner at the Hall—always chicken and ice cream—exactly the same as in 1925). As a respite from orchestration, which made me feel like an automaton, I worked on a piece for baritone solo and chorus, "Lark," based on a poem by Genevieve Taggard, for the Dessoff Choir commissioned by (and dedicated to) Alma (Wertheim) Wiener who sang in the chorus.[8] (Why the Dessoff Choir did not premiere "Lark" I no longer recall. It did not have a performance until 13 April 1943, when the Collegiate Chorale under Robert Shaw sang the premiere at the Museum of Modern Art in New York.)

A letter was forwarded to me at the Colony from William Schuman, a young composer whom I had met the previous winter. He wrote informing me of the radio broadcast of his *Second Symphony.* I listened and was impressed—with him and with CBS for choosing that kind of American music to present on "Everybody's Music." I wrote to Victor (September 1938): ". . . what I like about it is that it seems to be music that comes from a real urge, which gives it an immediacy of feeling that gets everyone who hears it. If he can build on that, we've got something there." I also received a letter from Lincoln with an encouraging response to the piano score of *Billy*: "I can tell you without an exaggeration that it is the best music we have ever had. . . ."

As September wore on at the Colony, the rains came, the river overflowed its banks and flooded the town. There were no papers, no mail, no lights. I left my studio one day and could not return again because streams were flowing across the road. I spent the night on a mattress on the floor in Colony Hall. The next day I tried to reach my studio. The scene was incredible. What one day had been a lovely pine woods now looked like the most desolate war-torn swamp. The road that had taken ten minutes for me to walk took two men with axes two and a half hours to hack their way through. After the hurricane subsided, they found my studio intact and all my stuff safe (including the score for *The Second Hurricane*); only I had to move my music to a new studio to go on working.

The orchestration for *Billy* was finally finished, but I had to make a difficult decision. I wanted to hear Koussevitzky and the BSO rehearse *El Salón México* for the performance of 14 October, but could not afford a hotel. My checking account showed a balance of $6.93! Just then, Koussevitzky wrote, inviting me to stay in his "sanitorium" at 88 Druce Street. I was pleased to be back in Boston—the orchestra was wonderful with my piece, and I enjoyed an evening at Harvard with Lenny Bernstein and his friends, and another at Walter Piston's with Ernst Krenek and Quincy Porter.

Lincoln Kirstein sent a check that made it possible for me to travel to Chicago for the opening of *Billy the Kid*, which was presented by the Ballet Caravan on 6 October 1938, with Eugene Loring in the title role and Marie Jeanne in the part of Billy's Mexican Sweetheart. Michael Kidd was a cowboy in the cast,[9] and I met a young dancer, Jerome Robbins, who also had a minor part. The music was performed on two pianos by Juilliard students Arthur Gold and Walter Hendl, and by them on tour before the New York premiere, which took place at the Martin Beck Theatre, sponsored by the American Lyric Theatre on 24 May 1939, Fritz Kitzinger conducting. Preceding *Billy* on the program was *Pocahontas*, with music by Elliott Carter. (After Elliott later arranged his *Pocahontas Suite* from

The cast of *Billy the Kid* with Erick Hawkins, Eugene Loring,
and Lew Christensen, center.

the ballet, I sent the score to Koussevitzky with a note (25 September
1939): "He [Carter] has never been played as yet by any major orchestra,
and this is his first important orchestral work. I need not tell you about the
quality of the piece as you can see that for yourself." Unfortunately, Koussevitzky was not convinced.)

The reviews of the ballet *Billy the Kid* were consistently excellent; to my
surprise, even *Time* magazine (5 June 1939) ran a picture and article in
their music section. "His music for the 'character-ballet' *Billy the Kid*,
much of it based on cowboy songs, was close-knit, percussive, incisive,
wasting not a grace note in its evocation of the dapper, New York–born
killer who flourished in the Southwest in the '70s and '80s. The choreography of Eugene Loring and the dancing of the Ballet Caravan were no less
exciting." I cannot remember another work of mine that was so unani-
mously well received. *Billy the Kid* was revived by Ballet Caravan in the
1941 season, Gene Loring still in the title role with Alicia Alonso as the
Sweetheart; in 1943 by Ballet Theatre with Michael Kidd; and in 1948 at
the Metropolitan Opera House with John Kriza and Alicia Alonso. Ballet
Theatre took *Billy* on tour to Europe in 1950, but in 1960 the Russians
refused it on the grounds that the story glorifies a lawbreaker. In May 1962
Billy was presented at the White House at the request of President and
Mrs. John F. Kennedy in honor of the visiting president of the Ivory Coast

Republic. As recently as 1976, Clive Barnes wrote in *The New York Times*, "With its score still fresh as a wind on the prairies, the ballet maintains its interest and charms to this day."[10]

Lincoln Kirstein[11]

The cowboy tunes—yes—I gave them to Aaron and the original idea for the Processional at the beginning of Billy *somehow came from Martha [Graham]. I don't recall much about* Billy *because I don't want to. I didn't like what the ballet became after I agreed to let Ballet Theatre do it. I do care about Aaron though—a saint—the sweetest man I ever knew. He always understood if something didn't work out. Like* Time Table *to his* Music for the Theatre.[12] *Aaron was different about music for the dance than other composers—he took it more seriously and recognized the challenge of translating into sound what one sees on stage.*

In the summer of 1939 I arranged *Billy the Kid* as an orchestral suite, utilizing about two-thirds of the original ballet score. The Suite is in six connected movements, which match the action of the ballet.[13] An introductory prelude, "The Open Prairie," presents a pastoral theme harmonized in open fifths that gives the impression of space and isolation. The second section, "Street in a Frontier Town," is lively and full of action; for western flavor I used quotations from "Great Grand-Dad," "The Old Chisholm Trail," and "Git Along Little Dogies" (but not in traditional harmonies and rhythms), a Mexican dance featuring a theme in 5/8, and "Goodbye, Old Paint" introduced by an unusual 7/8 rhythm. The third section, "Card Game at Night," has a sinister sound achieved by strings built on triads and segments of "Bury Me Not on the Lone Prairie." "Gun Battle," the fourth movement, makes generous use of percussion. The fifth, "Celebration After Billy's Capture," depicts the townspeople rejoicing in the saloon, where an out-of-tune player piano sets the scene. "Billy's Demise," the final section of the Suite, makes use of material from the introduction, but with different coloration to convey the idea of a new dawn breaking over the prairie.

The Suite is programmatic, but I used musical ideas to tell the story and rhythmic interest to lift the music above a mere collection of folk tunes. For instance, the percussive gunfight is conveyed by rhythmic action instead of simulated gunfire, and the frontier town street scene is a kaleidoscope of tunes, sparked with dissonance and polyrhythms, interrupted by sudden silences. Dance and jazz devices are present, such as the off-beat rhythm of "Great Grand-Dad."

Billy the Kid is one of my most frequently performed works. Lenny recorded it with the RCA Victor Symphony, and other recordings have been made. In addition to the complete ballet score and the Suite, "Prairie Night," "Celebration," and "Waltz" are published individually for full and reduced orchestras. ("Waltz" was not included in the Suite.) Philip J. Lang made a band arrangement of "Waltz," and both "Waltz" and "Celebration" have been arranged for violin and piano (edited by Louis Kaufman) and cello and piano (edited by Gregor Piatigorsky). Also published is a piano solo from *Billy* arranged by Lukas Foss, and a collection of excerpts taken by myself from an early two-piano version of the complete ballet. The music has been used in several films.

When I began to get royalty checks of $40 in 1940 after each performance of *Billy the Kid*, I thought it was *amazing*. After all, I had been paid a commission by Kirstein to compose it. It seemed like getting money for doing absolutely nothing! It was after *Billy*, when I was almost forty years old, that my mother finally said the money spent on piano lessons for me was not wasted.

An Outdoor Overture owes its existence to the persuasive powers of Alexander Richter, head of the music department of the High School of Music and Art. He had witnessed a performance of *The Second Hurricane* and made up his mind that I was the man to write a work for his school orchestra. I liked the idea of the High School of Music and Art—that gifted students could prepare their careers in the arts at such a school without sacrificing a general education. Richter won me over when he explained that my work would be the opening gun in a campaign the school planned to undertake with the slogan: "American Music for American Youth." I found this so irresistible that I interrupted my orchestration for *Billy the Kid* in the fall of 1938 to write the piece. Mr. Richter suggested a single movement between five and ten minutes in length and optimistic in tone, that would appeal to the adolescent youth of this country. Richter added (13 June 1938): "I am reminded that boards of education throughout this country do not take to ultra-modern composition. It seems to be against the 'institutions of our forefathers,' and what-not. I do not know how you will respond to this hideous reminder, but again I trust your good taste in the matter."

When I played the piano sketch for him, Richter remarked that it seemed to have an open-air quality. Together we hit on the title *An Outdoor Overture*. It is scored for the usual symphony orchestra, but without tuba. "Don't forget the percussion section!" said Mr. Richter. The percussion section was therefore not forgotten.

The premiere performances of *An Outdoor Overture* were conducted by Alexander Richter on 16 and 17 December 1938 with his school orchestra. The piece is dedicated to the High School of Music and Art. The first performance by a "regular" symphony orchestra was given by the Federal Symphony conducted by Alexander Smallens in an all-American concert sponsored by the WPA Composers Forum–Laboratory concerts for the New York World's Fair at Carnegie Hall on 7 May 1939. It included pieces by the Guggenheim award winners in composition, William Schuman and Roy Harris. The World's Fair's symbols of the trylon and perisphere appeared on all the advance leaflets and programs. After the performance, Elliott Carter, writing in *Modern Music*, chastised music critics for not paying attention to it: " 'An Outdoor Overture' . . . contains some of his finest and most personal music. Its opening is as lofty and beautiful as any passage that has been written by a contemporary composer. It is Copland in his 'prophetic' vein which runs through all his works . . . never before . . . has he expressed it so simply and directly."[14] Lenny Bernstein included *An Outdoor Overture* in the debut concert of his New York City Symphony at City Center on 8 October 1945, explaining in a newspaper interview: "A lot of people thought it was kid stuff and refused to play it. I'm very proud of my orchestra—they're young and they're terrific!" In 1954 Cecil Smith wrote in a program note for the London Philharmonic Orchestra: "Youth and freedom and tireless energy are the subject matter of the Overture. This is music without poetising, without introversion. Perhaps it is already a period piece: it is music without a care in the world. Could any composer anywhere have written it after 1938?"

Early in 1939 I provided two scores for plays that never got to Broadway. One was the Mercury Theatre's *Five Kings*; the other, the Group Theatre's *Quiet City*. Orson Welles produced, directed, and starred in *Five Kings*, an adaptation and compilation of three Shakespearean plays—*Henry IV*, Parts I and II, and *Henry V*. Burgess Meredith was also featured in the production. Orson gave me a script, and I wrote music where cues were indicated. The orchestra consisted of eight instruments plus organ. I composed "battle" music, fanfares, and even adapted a few

French and English traditional tunes.[15] *Five Kings* opened at the Colonial Theatre in Boston at the end of February and closed in Philadelphia in March. An unsigned review in the *Enquirer* stated (21 March 1939): "Shakespeare would hardly have recognized himself in this edition and acting." I explained to Virgil in Paris (1 May 1939): "My career in the theatre has been a flop—through no fault of my own I hasten to add. Orson's stock is very low at the moment. Last year's hero arouses very little sympathy."

Undaunted by the failure of *Five Kings*, I accepted Clurman's offer to compose music for Irwin Shaw's *Quiet City*, considered too experimental for outside backers—the Group Theatre had to produce it with their own funds. The play was billed as a "realistic fantasy," a contradiction in terms that only meant the stylistic differences made for difficulties in production. The script was about a young trumpet player who imagined the night thoughts of many different people in a great city and played trumpet to express his emotions and to arouse the consciences of the other characters and of the audience. After reading the play, I composed music that I hoped would evoke the inner distress of the central character. Clurman and Elia Kazan, the director, agreed that *Quiet City* needed a free and imaginative treatment. They and the cast, which included Frances Farmer, struggled valiantly to make the play convincing, but after two try-out performances in April, *Quiet City* was dropped. I arranged orchestral studies from *Five Kings* and *Quiet City*, but dropped the former from my catalogue.

The original version of *Quiet City* called for trumpet, saxophone, clarinet, and piano.[16] In arranging the suite for trumpet and string orchestra, I added an English horn for contrast and to give the trumpeter breathing spaces. I cannot take credit for what a few reviewers called my affinity to Whitman's "mystic trumpeter" or Ives' persistent soloist in *The Unanswered Question*. My trumpet player was simply an attempt to mirror the troubled main character, David Mellnikoff, of Irwin Shaw's play. In fact, one of my markings for the trumpeter is to play "nervously." But *Quiet City* seems to have become a musical entity, superseding the original reasons for its composition. The work has been called "atmospheric" and "reflective," and David Mellnikoff has long since been forgotten!

The orchestration was completed in late September 1940 in Lenox, Massachusetts; the score is dedicated to Ralph Hawkes of my publishers Boosey & Hawkes. The first performance was by the Saidenberg Little Symphony, on 28 January 1941 at Town Hall, conducted by Daniel Saidenberg. The following summer Koussevitzky conducted *Quiet City* at Tanglewood, and again when he was guest conductor for the first time with the New York Philharmonic (19 February 1942). The Suite is performed frequently and for some reason is particularly admired by the British. Since it is mostly quiet, it fills a niche in concert programs. When I conducted the suite with the London Symphony Orchestra soon after my eightieth birthday, it turned out to be anything but a quiet occasion. The elderly heating system in Royal Albert Hall on that cold December evening rattled and thumped so persistently that it was necessary to stop the orchestra and leave the stage. But we played the piece through after intermission, when the noise disappeared as suddenly as it had started.

The World's Fair brought forth an unusual commission—composing music for a puppet show, *From Sorcery to Science*, to be shown at the Hall of Pharmacy. The cast of characters included a Chinese medicine man, an old witch with a head seven feet long and an eye that lit up and popped, a hawk-faced medieval alchemist, an African witch doctor, two modern scientists, a modern druggist, and a modern beautiful girl. The action took place on a large revolving stage. The puppets for this ten-minute show were not your ordinary puppets but twelve-foot-high creations designed and made by the artist and puppeteer Remo Bufano, who had earlier designed the impressive puppets for the operas sponsored by the League of Composers at the Metropolitan—De Falla's *El Retablo de Maese Pedro* and Stravinsky's *Oedipus Rex*. The plot of *From Sorcery to Science*, such as it was, was narrated by a voice familiar from radio. I can hear it now, "This is Lowell Thomas coming to you from the Hall of Pharmacy at the New York World's Fair . . ." The music was to provide atmosphere, background, and continuity. I used two pianos and a wide variety of percussion for the various effects needed—temple blocks, tambourine, cymbals, chimes, tam-tam, gourd, ratchet, maracas. When the show's run was over, I retrieved the music with the idea of someday developing the musical material further, but the score was lost before I could do so. Only recently, a sketch score has turned up at the Music Division of the Lincoln Center Library.[17]

The New Yorker of 3 June 1939 subheaded its music column "Mr. Copland Here, There, and at the Fair." In under two months' time, *Billy the Kid*, *An Outdoor Overture*, *From Sorcery to Science*, and music for *The City* were introduced. *The City*, a documentary film, was produced specifically for showing at the World's Fair. It was directed and filmed by

Manuscript page, *From Sorcery to Science*, a puppet show produced
for the 1939 New York World's Fair.

Ralph Steiner and Willard Van Dyke, and it was Ralph who brought me into the project. In 1939 the film documentary was a new and exciting concept. Several films on science, medicine, and social problems were shown at the Little Theatre of the Science and Education Building at the Fair. The original idea for *The City* was conceived by Pare Lorentz[18] (already known for *The Plow That Broke the Plains* and *The River*, both with music by Virgil Thomson). A poetic commentary, written by Lewis Mumford and narrated by Morris Carnovsky, leads the viewer from the scene of a peaceful New England village— "The town was us and we were part of it"—through the blight of industrialism—"Smoke makes prosperity, no matter if you choke on it"—and finally to the new "Green City where children play under trees and the people who laid out this place didn't forget that air and sun was what we need for growing." The American Institute of Planners, a prestigious group of scholars, architects, and city planners, were consultants for *The City*; they were convinced that American cities could and should be decentralized to mirror the spirit of the small town. Steiner and Van Dyke traveled through thirty states filming Americans at work and play. They edited 4,000 feet from the 100,000 feet they shot, for a forty-four-minute film that cost $50,000 to produce. The Carnegie Corporation of New York made a grant toward assisting the production.

Composing music for film is not in itself "easier" than writing concert music except that the form, length, and general tone are set in advance, so the composer does not have to make those initial decisions. After Steiner showed me a rough cut of *The City*, I composed music to fit the five sections.[19] The nature of the visual material called for strongly contrasting musical sections to dramatically underline the differences between country and city life. The film avoided two major pitfalls of documentaries, preachiness and symbolism, and the result was a human intimacy that appealed to all kinds of audiences. I realized when composing music for *The City*, my first film credit, that the composer is in a special position to appreciate what music does for a film because he sees it first without any music. Movie audiences may not consciously realize they are listening to music when they view a film, but it works on their emotions nonetheless. And if the soundtrack breaks down for a moment, the realization of what the music adds becomes acute. While composing for *The City*, I learned the most basic rule: A film is not a concert; the music is meant to help the picture.

The City was premiered on 26 May 1939, and thereafter was open to the public daily for the duration of the World's Fair. The score was praised along with the film in such widely read magazines as *Time*, *Life*, and *The New York Times Magazine*, as well as in film and music journals. I was fortunate that *The City* was such a good film; in fact, I am told that it has become a classic in the art of the documentary. *The City* started me as a film composer, a direction I would pursue on and off during the next decade. It gave me the credit I needed to approach Hollywood again, and it helped make 1939 the year my name became better known to the American public.

Two offers from CBS that summer influenced my decision to stay close to New York City: one, to introduce and comment on radio broadcasts from Lewisohn Stadium; the other, to compose a short work for the "School of the Air" series. The radio broadcasts were canceled, but the commission brought forth *John Henry*. At a rented cottage in Woodstock, New York, I began to work on *John Henry* by going through the collection of folk tunes put together by Alan Lomax, who was responsible for the radio series and the commission, which carried with it the stipulation that the piece make use of an American folk song. John Henry, as we all know, was a nineteenth-century hero, a black man so strong that hundreds of legends and songs grew up describing his heroic feats. The one I chose is based on the well-known railroad ballad. In it, John Henry pits his strong arms against the speed of a steam pile-driver and wins the contest, but dies in the effort. Knowing my audience was to be a young one, and that young people like their music exciting and not too long, I kept *John Henry* down to less than four minutes and called it "a descriptive fantasy."[20] A clarinet introduces the theme, and to add to the excitement and help achieve the sound of a train and John Henry's hammer, the scoring calls for triangle, anvil, sandpaper blocks, train whistle, and piano, in addition to a chamber orchestra. The material lent itself easily to unorthodox rhythms and harmonies, which I hoped to introduce to young performers and listeners. *John Henry* was broadcast in March 1940, conducted by Howard Barlow and the Columbia Broadcasting Symphony. The original version suited its purpose well enough, but after radio ceased broadcasting live music, I revised the work in 1952 so that it could be performed by high school orchestras as a concert piece.

Most vivid to me about the summer of 1939, which was spent in Woodstock, is Benjamin Britten. Ben and the singer Peter Pears had left England when conditions worsened in Europe—first for Canada and then New York. We had met in England at the ISCM Festival of 1938, and I

ST. JOVITE STATION
PROVINCE OF QUEBEC
CANADA

June 8ᵉ 939

Dear Aaron,

When are you? Don't you dare say you're already left for the South without telling me! Our plans now are these as follows: Leave here for Toronto 7ᵃ — Grand Rapids 12ᵉ, Toronto 18ᵉ (three Variations ∼ Radio) Ottawa (possibly) 20ᵉ, New York 25ᵉ — or a few days later for a week - perhaps — While we find somewhere to go for the two summer months — i.e. unless you've got any bright suggestions. We'll put off decisions until hearing from you — so please write — to 10 Shuter St. Toronto.

How was Billy the Kid? I hear the Caravans been a great success — was that because of you?

Affectionately,

Ben

Above: Letter from Benjamin Britten to Copland, June 1939.
Left: Copland with Britten, c. 1950.

had spent a weekend at their place, the Old Mill at Snape in Suffolk.[21] (The mill and village were as quaint and charming as the address sounded; Britten's studio was in a converted tower of the mill.) We hit it off well together from the start. I had with me the proofs of *The Second Hurricane*. It didn't take much persuasion to get me to play it from start to finish, singing all the parts of principals and chorus in the usual composer fashion. In return, Ben played me the first version of his *Piano Concerto*.[22] Less than a year after this visit, Britten and Pears were on their way to Canada. I wrote, "Dear Benjie, How perfectly extraordinary to think of you here on this side of the water! I can't get used to the idea—but I will."

When I settled on Woodstock for the summer, Ben and Peter decided to take a place close by. Ben and I found we had a great deal in common. We had the distinct feeling of a relationship as composers of the same generation, as well as friends. We played tennis (he always won) and had time for talk and relaxation. Ben was young and very gifted—a delightful person who knew what he wanted to say and said it without fuss or trouble. He was not a hale fellow, but rather quiet, even shy, and quite British. And his music is very direct and British while at the same time very personal. His was a natural and spontaneous gift—Ben was what is called a born musician. His talent was unforced, his training impeccable. He had been a prodigy, so by the time I knew him, he was an accomplished musician.

During that summer in Woodstock we played many things through for each other; Ben was a fine pianist and a great accompanist. Always able to compose what fit his temperament, he wrote music in a modern style, yet without danger of upsetting an audience. I thought of him as the voice of England in the contemporary musical scene, and he, in turn, considered me the American spokesman. We had many of the same sympathies, musical and other kinds, and we knew we faced similar problems. Toward the end of August, Ben and Peter left Woodstock. They worried constantly about whether to return to England. I wrote to Ben: "You owe it to England to stay here. After all, anyone can shoot a gun—but how many can write music like you?" Ben had financial problems, so when I went to Hollywood in 1940 and got an agent (Abe Meyer of MCA), I arranged for a film contract for Britten. "If they get you no work in 4 months," I wrote, "the contract is null and void. I think it's safe to sign it. Anyhow, I signed one just like it."

During the three years Ben stayed in America, we saw each other frequently; he and Peter were living on Long Island and we would meet at my loft or attend concerts together. They drove to Tanglewood to see me on the Fourth of July weekend of 1940, and after Ben and Peter returned to England, we kept in touch with each other. In 1945 *Peter Grimes* made Ben famous, and of course Peter Pears sang the title role. It is a great challenge to write opera that really works on stage—very few people are able to do that. Ben's vocal music is very fresh, singable, and effective. He composed many things with Peter's great talent as a singer in mind. After Ben and Peter founded the Aldeburgh Festival, I visited and conducted there and became active in finding support for Aldeburgh in America. It's a great tragedy that Benjie died in 1976 with so much music still in him. I remember him with great fondness, and when I think of him, my thoughts most often go back to the summer of 1939 in Woodstock.

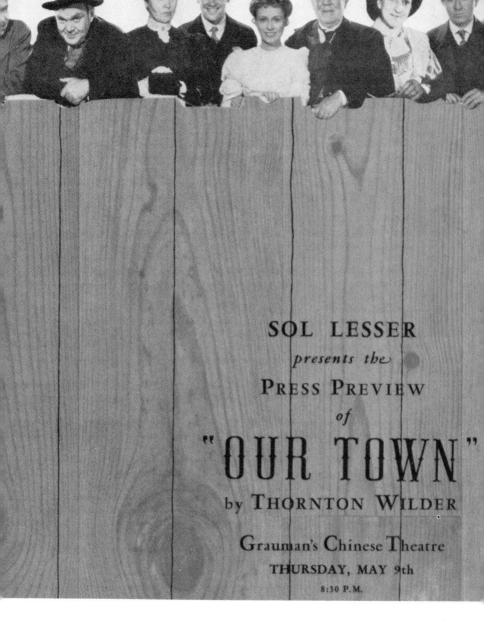

SOL LESSER
presents the
PRESS PREVIEW
of
"OUR TOWN"
by THORNTON WILDER

Grauman's Chinese Theatre
THURSDAY, MAY 9th
8:30 P.M.

Hollywood

1939-1940

I had been working on a piano piece (the *Sonata*) in Woodstock with no thought of Hollywood. But it seems that *The City* was playing in a movie theater out there and was seen by the producers, who earlier on had not been convinced by my symphonies, opera, and chamber music. Now I finally had a film credit, and I was in! A telegram arrived from Hal Roach, producer, and Lewis Milestone, director, asking me to write the musical score for *Of Mice and Men*, a film version of John Steinbeck's prize-winning play. I flew to the West Coast in October of 1939—my first long plane trip. Why they had waited until the film was completely shot to find their composer, I have no idea. I viewed *Of Mice and Men* twice, but once was enough to know how fortunate I was to have this film offered for my first major movie score. Milestone had translated the fine Steinbeck play into a film that was true to the original, rich in detail, and perhaps even more intense than the play. He captured the poignancy of the simple California ranch hands and enhanced the conception with perfect casting: Lon Chaney, Jr., as the hulking simple-minded Lennie; Burgess Meredith as George, who cares for his childlike buddy with touching dependence; and Betty Field in the only female role. They were directed with rare insight into the characterizations. Here was an American theme, by a great American writer, demanding appropriate music. Obviously, Lewis Milestone, a cousin of Nathan Milstein, was not the ordinary Hollywood director. He was willing to let me do as I saw fit and gave me none of the usual "advice." (He actually added four seconds to the film for the sake of the musical score when I told him it was needed for a particular scene.) Milestone sensed that there were scenes where music should take over to express the emotions of the characters, and others involved with the production wanted a composer who would not follow the formulae for movie music. Not even the music director got in my way.

Once settled, I wrote to Koussevitzky from the apartment rented for me by the studio in the Chateau Elysée on Franklin Avenue (18 October

1939): "Hollywood is an extraordinary place. You must come out here sometime. It's like nothing else in the world. Thank heavens." My arrival did not go unnoticed. *Stage and Screen* of 30 October announced that my appearance on the Hal Roach set was causing something of a stir. "No one has mentioned modern music yet, in conferences. In fact, Copland himself, isn't sure of his approach." Actually, I could not begin to work on any approach until I solved the difficult problem of finding recorded music to use temporarily for the "sneak" previews to which audiences were invited and requested to fill out questionnaires, giving opinions and criticisms of the movie. The producers would go to these previews to see how the movie was being received and to consider changes. During the previews I set to work on the score at a frantic pace. Fortunately I enjoyed working late at night. I liked the studio lot best when it was deserted and seemed to resemble a medieval village or a western ghost town. I had been given a cue sheet marking the parts of the picture for which I was to compose the music, and I had met with Milestone and Roach. They knew my objections to the lush sort of Hollywood music that often had little relationship to the action, emotions, or ideas in a movie. Full-blown symphonic music throughout a film might be fine for a nineteenth-century theme like that of *Wuthering Heights*, but it was not appropriate to the California wheat ranch in *Of Mice and Men*. I discovered that piano music was not suitable either for outdoor scenes, so I tried more natural-sounding instrumentation—solo flute, flutes together, and a guitar for a campfire scene. I insisted on doing the orchestration myself. (Often Hollywood composers turned this job over to arrangers who orchestrated every film they worked on the same way.)

I had a great deal to learn about the technical aspects of filmmaking. Just keeping the music out of the way of the spoken dialogue was not easy—from a composer's point of view, there is always too much talk in movies! I decided to work with a movieola (making it possible for me to run the film back and forth by myself)—the movieola was set up next to an upright piano, and I could turn the knob while sitting at the instrument. The movieola was not the favored way of working on a film in Hollywood then; most composers simply wrote the score to the timings after seeing the film once through. But I was genuinely moved by *Of Mice and Men* and by the inspired performances, and I found that the scenes induced the music if I turned to them while composing.

I made certain decisions: I would not use the leitmotif idea à la Wagner whereby each central character is identified with a theme; I would not quote folk tunes; and I would not underline every piece of the action (I disliked this kind of "mickey-mousing" that composer Max Steiner was so fond of). In certain segments, the music had to reflect the action, at least in a general way. For the big fight scene between Curly and Lennie, I wrote dissonant music by Hollywood standards. I found little difficulty with other dramatic sections where the music could take over: the opening sequence showing George and Lennie running after a train and jumping into a boxcar; the scene where Lennie crushes Curly's hand to the accompaniment of one grinding chord that lasts about twenty seconds; the segment where the old dog is killed; and the ending with about eight minutes worth of continuous music and little dialogue. All these came easily. But the background music was difficult for me. It seemed a strange assignment to write music that is actually meant to be uninteresting. Yet this kind of "neutral" sound is often needed to "warm" the screen or to connect one piece of action to another.

While working on *Of Mice and Men,* I thought of George Antheil's warning about speed-writing. All of a sudden, everyone seemed to be in a frightful hurry—they all sat down to wait for the composer while valuable time passed. I was given about six weeks, but often movie scores were done in much less time. If the shooting of a script would take longer than planned, time would be lopped off the composer's end. I expressed the opinion at the studio that a composer ought to work directly with the picture while it was being filmed. At least when my score was finished there was no cutting. I was told that this was unusual for Hollywood. I had expected problems about the modern-sounding spots, but there were no complaints, even though at the previews with my completed score, the ladies had shown some dissatisfaction with the "raw" and "masculine" aspects of the picture, which my music served to emphasize.

Once the score was finished, I was anxious to hear what the music actually sounded like when put with the film. The players were very experienced, and recording day was wonderful. It seemed pretty fancy to me that we could record more than one sound track and mix them, as in the opening sequence, which begins with outside action and switches to inside a boxcar, showing a hobo playing the Jew's harp. We superimposed the realistic sound of the Jew's harp onto the nonrealistic background of the orchestral music. The orchestra was required to play everything at about the same dynamic level, since the sound adjustments were not made until the time of dubbing with the film. Every composer dreads the dubbing room. The awful thing that happens there, from the composer's standpoint, is that the music starts to disappear. The score that was so clear and satisfying when recorded gets further away the minute anyone on the screen opens his mouth! It is a moment for great self-control. In a position to ruin everything was not a musician, but a sound engineer. I made some mild objections, but I was asked, "Haven't you heard of the union?" Moreover, the particular sound man assigned to *Of Mice and Men* was overly sensitive to criticism, and so it was difficult to give any. Whenever I *would* say something, it was too late—the spot was already dubbed! Another problem that affected the composer and could give him grave discomfort was that there was not a way yet invented to predetermine sound levels in the theaters. Adjustments would be left up to each theater manager. It seemed to me utterly ridiculous to take so much pain about proper levels for the music and dialogue and then leave it all up to chance in the theaters.

My overall experience with *Of Mice and Men* was a good one. I was satisfied that the score enhanced the movie, making it more intense and more meaningful. To some in Hollywood my music was strange, lean, and dissonant; to others it spoke with a new incisiveness and clarity. I was an outsider to Hollywood, but I did not condescend to compose film music; I worked hard at it. Perhaps this is why I was accepted. And I genuinely liked some things about the film industry, particularly that music was made to be used on a daily basis, and that composers were actually needed there. Also, the accent was entirely on the *living* composer. But I was puzzled at why film composers were so isolated from the rest of the music world! In 1939 there were four major figures—Erich Korngold, Max Steiner, Alfred Newman, and Herbert Stoddard—and these men were not known outside of Hollywood.

The premiere of *Of Mice and Men* on the West Coast on 22 December 1939 was an all-out glamorous Hollywood opening night. I stayed in California just long enough to attend. Another picture was offered to me right away, but I turned it down because it was not a very good one. My agent was absolutely shocked! Several people were surprised to see me back in New York. There seemed to be an idea that once one went to Hollywood, he was lost forever to the rest of the music world! But I could enjoy going back and forth to California occasionally without moving there. It was such a nice change from New York—the weather was beautiful, and the pay was good. Furthermore, film music was a very live subject as a new art form and open for serious discussion. Back in New York, I lectured about it at the Museum of Modern Art and wrote a few articles about my first Hollywood experience.[1]

Top: Manuscript, sketch of the "Dog Scene" from *Of Mice and Men.*
Bottom: Congratulatory telegram from Thornton Wilder to Copland. (Mabel Daniels was a composer living in Peterborough.)

If some were surprised at my prompt return from Hollywood, others were relieved. The affairs of the League and of ACA had piled up while I was away. I continued to give lectures in and out of town, although I was no longer teaching regularly at the New School. Discussions were under way toward a new book. Finally I was experiencing some modest financial success, and I was able to buy a typewriter and have repairs made on my car. But it was not a happy time. With the threat of impending war, the atmosphere was one of nervousness and insecurity—everyone was worrying about friends and relatives abroad and those at home who might have to go into the service. I wrote to Ben Britten, "I find it hard as hell to go on putting down notes on paper as if nothing were happening." Composers as well as writers and artists were drawn to patriotic and nostalgic themes, and the American public, fearing violence to come, was comforted by works like Thornton Wilder's *Our Town*, which looked back at an America of simple, homespun values that seemed to have been lost. When Sol Lesser, the Hollywood producer, asked me to compose the musical score for the screen version of the play about life in the small town of Grover's Corners, New Hampshire, U.S.A., I welcomed the opportunity. For one thing, I admired Wilder's play; for another, I was irritated that film music had become so pat, so conventionalized, when the medium was still so young. *Our Town* was the perfect vehicle for putting to the test opinions I had voiced in the press—that film music should follow the organic structure of a story, and that the music must be appropriate to the nature of that story. *Our Town* could not have been further from *Of Mice and Men* in subject, setting, characters, and feeling. Here was my chance to show that a composer, within a short period of time, could write different-sounding scores, each appropriate to the film it accompanied. Finally, the fact that Wilder had written most of *Our Town* at the MacDowell Colony, and that Grover's Corners was patterned after Peterborough, New Hampshire, was too much for me to resist. I flew to Hollywood on a sleeper plane. It took all night and I felt like a hero.

Thornton Wilder worked closely with Sol Lesser on the film scenario. As a play, *Our Town* had certain technical features that were "filmic": flashbacks, a narrator, and fast scene changes. But the subject matter and the treatment were not ones that would normally be expected in a Hollywood movie. The play is essentially plotless in the usual sense of the term (it was frequently called quasi-documentary), it is innocent of romantic intrigue, and deals entirely with unassuming, everyday people in simple settings, with virtually no scenery. For the film version, Wilder and Lesser were counting on the music to translate the transcendental aspects of the story. As with *Of Mice and Men*, most of *Our Town* was filmed before my arrival in Hollywood. In New York after reading the play, I wrote some musical themes and later marveled that they seemed so right when put with the picture. Lesser asked if I would use popular tunes in the score. But I felt that the songs of the period of *Our Town*, numbers like "Down on the Farm" and "Give My Regards to Broadway," were inappropriate to the spirit of the film; moreover, considering the eternal, universal qualities of the story, direct quotes would have pinned the period down too specifically. But I used harmonies suggestive of church hymns associated with small New England towns of the early twentieth century.

In practical terms I worked in much the same way as I had on *Of Mice and Men*, first viewing the film several times with Sam Wood, the director, and then using a moviola placed next to a piano while composing the music. Again I was moved by the beauty of the film. The poignancy of the play was intact, and there was a haunting quality that made it all very touching. *Our Town* dared to be simple and at times very funny; it challenged me to meet its high standards. The performances were exceptional—Martha Scott as Emily and Frank Craven as the narrator recreated their roles from the stage production; other leading roles were taken by William Holden, Fay Bainter, Beulah Bondi, and Guy Kibbee. This was not an ordinary motion picture. The camera itself seemed to become animate, and the characters spoke directly to it. Once the narrator actually placed his hand before the camera lens to stop a sequence and introduce the next.

My job was to create the atmosphere of a typical New Hampshire town and to reflect the shifts from the real to the fantasy world. Because of the nostalgic nature of the story, most of the music had to be in slow tempo. I was mystified as to how to get some variety into it and wrote to Victor, "I'd give my shirt for one decent 'allegro.' " Percussion instruments and all but a few brass were omitted. I relied on strings, woodwinds, and the combination of flutes and clarinets for lyric effects. Since *Our Town* was devoid of violence, dissonance and jazz rhythms were avoided. In the open countryside scenes, I tried for clean and clear sounds and in general used straightforward harmonies and rhythms that would project the serenity and sense of security of the play. The most difficult problems came when scoring the graveyard scene where Emily joins the ranks of the dead. It was not meant to be morbid or depressing, so any hint of funereal music would have been out of place. In keeping with the metaphysical mood, I used choral sequences with unusual harmonies, hoping that their unconformity would suggest something of the preternatural quality of the scene.

Sol Lesser gave me an office with a view at United Artists' lot, but I worked with my back to the window, since the view was of huge gas tanks, hardly conducive to recalling the rural charms of New England. In four weeks I wrote a score of over forty-three minutes—two weeks less than it took to compose *Of Mice and Men*. Being mostly slow, the music did not take as long to write. Any composer will tell you that it does not take as long to write one half-note as it does to write four eighths.

Our Town had its Hollywood preview at Grauman's Chinese Theater on 9 May 1940. Lawrence Morton wrote, "Hollywood is to be congratulated, Roach and Lesser highly praised for acquiring Copland's services . . . he has a passion for the expression of the American spirit in music. It is not only new in Hollywood but to all of musical America."[2] The world premiere took place in Boston on 24 May, named "Our Town Day" by the mayor. The New York opening was held at Radio City Music Hall on 13 June, where the film shared the bill with the Music Hall Grand Organ, the March of Time, the Music Hall Symphony, and the Rockettes. Critics were unanimous in praise and in agreement that the picture was even more deeply moving than the play. Bosley Crowther of *The New York Times* wrote (14 June 1940): "We hesitate to employ superlatives, but of *Our Town* the least we can say is that it captures on film the simple beauties and truths of humble folks as very few pictures ever do; it is rich and ennobling in its plain philosophy—and it gives one a passionate desire to enjoy the fullness of life even in these good old days of today."

I lost no time in arranging about ten minutes of music from the film score for a suite that was broadcast a few days before the film opening in New York by the CBS Orchestra under Howard Barlow's direction. (I was the regular commentator for the program.) After the film premiere, I took some time to prepare a more careful version of an *Our Town* suite that was introduced at a Boston Pops concert on 7 May 1944 by Leonard Bernstein, to whom the piece is dedicated. I conducted the London Symphony Orchestra for a recording, and I arranged excerpts for piano that are published and have been performed by several pianists, among them Andor Foldes and Leo Smit.[3]

Interlude IV

It was a long way from Hollywood to Tanglewood, but to Copland in the summer of 1940, Lenox, Massachusetts, looked like Grover's Corners, U.S.A. Copland felt far more comfortable in the Berkshires than in California. By this time he was more often described as "the Dean of American Composers" than "that wild young modernist," and since he had always looked more like a teacher or a businessman than a brooding genius, he did not have to change his style of dress, cut his hair, or shave off a beard. Nevertheless, Copland's casual and breezy manner has always invited informality. To this day it is not unusual to hear a friendly, "Hi Aaron," called from across a street in New York City by a total stranger. It would have been difficult to imagine such freedom with Paul Hindemith, the other composer invited by Koussevitzky to teach during the first season of the Berkshire Music Center.

Koussevitzky had often talked to Copland of his plan: " . . . a Center where the greatest living composers would teach the art of composition, the greatest virtuosi the art of performance, and the greatest conductors the mystery of conducting orchestras and choruses . . . such an elite would result in a creation of new and great values in art . . . and in the education and training of a new generation of American artists."[1] Koussevitzky had been nurturing this dream since his youth in Russia. When the Boston Symphony replaced the New York Philharmonic after the first two seasons of the Berkshire Music Festival, Koussevitzky lost no time in convincing his trustees that a Music Center was necessary and important. Only three concerts were held during the summer of 1936 in an open field under a tent in Stockbridge. In 1937 the 210-acre Tanglewood estate was donated to the trustees of the orchestra by the Tappan family, and again the festival was made up of three concerts. When a typical Berkshire rainstorm almost drowned out a performance of the *Ride of the Valkyries*, a funding drive was begun on the spot. By 1938, the "Shed" designed by Eliel Saarinen was built, and the concerts increased to six. Copland's *Music for the The-*

atre was one of the works performed that season. On a beautiful site over-looking the lake, the Shed has continued to be the principal facility for the Berkshire Music Festival, or "Tanglewood," as the largest and most fa-mous of American summer music festivals is generally called.[2] In 1939 and 1940 the festivals included nine concerts each season. At the opening ceremony of the Berkshire Music Center (BMC) on 8 July 1940, a chorus sang Randall Thompson's newly composed "Alleluia," which has become a tradition at each summer's opening. Koussevitzky, affectionately called "The Doctor" by everyone, gave a speech in which he reminded the peace-ful gathering that at that very moment similarly beautiful landscapes in Europe were being destroyed by war. "If ever there was a time to speak of music, it is now in the New World."

There was at least one member of that audience who needed no re-minders about the European war situation. Paul Hindemith wrote to his wife, Gertrud, still unable to leave Europe, that the Berkshires brought to mind North Switzerland. Hindemith, in America since the previous Feb-ruary, had endured a difficult winter of teaching in Buffalo, where neither the weather nor the students were satisfactory; moreover, he was con-cerned about Gertrud's safety. Hindemith's music, performed frequently worldwide during those years, had been banned in Nazi Germany since 1934. In 1937–38 the composer traveled to America primarily to attend a concert in Washington of his works sponsored by Elizabeth Sprague Coo-lidge. When he returned to Germany, he found conditions had worsened, so he and his wife moved to Switzerland, and then he came on to America. Tanglewood was a godsend after Buffalo, especially since Hindemith had no idea until midsummer where he would go next.[3] The two composition teachers at Tanglewood had little in common; Hindemith did not take the American composer seriously, and Copland, while admiring Hindemith's musical talent and craftsmanship, considered the German a "deep-dyed academician." Perhaps Koussevitzky had chosen two such different per-sonalities with an eye toward exposing students to a broad range of musical styles and methods. More likely he was pleased to have both the most fa-mous German composer and the best-known American at his new school. Furthermore the Maestro knew that he could depend on Aaron to keep the peace.

Koussevitzky planned the Music Center with two divisions: an Institute of Advanced Study, to include the composers and their students, Dr. Her-bert Graf's "opera dramatics" program, and Koussevitzky's conducting students; and the Academy, or Department of Music and Culture, for more general students to sing in the chorus and perform in the orchestra.[4] The first season, Olin Downes gave a lecture series on "Music and Integrity," and Abram Chasins discoursed on "Ornamentation." Archibald T. Davison of Harvard, Randall Thompson, the director at Curtis, and Howard Abell of the Milton Academy all lectured. Hindemith wrote to Gertrud in Switzerland (14 July 1940): "I am living in two very nice and quiet rented rooms in the home of Mr. Driscoll, pastor of the Congregational Church in Lenox . . . Tanglewood is a blend of Donaueschingen, Ankara, and the Berlin Hochschule, and everything going on here seems to be good. I am naturally a very 'famous' teacher here and the students have already spread rumors about all of the surprising things I am doing with them. . . ."[5]

Thirteen composition students had been accepted by Koussevitzky, who with Copland's help had reviewed scores and applications during the previous spring. Requests to study with one or the other composer were honored; otherwise students were arbitrarily assigned. On arrival, Hindemith was given his list of students: John Colman, Norman Dello Joio, Lukas Foss, John Klein, Harold Shapero, Robert Strassburg, and Charles Naginski. Colman had studied briefly with Hindemith in Berlin. He had received some encouragement, but also advice that he seek a conservatory education. Colman applied from his second year at Juilliard to study with Hindemith at Tanglewood, but Hindemith refused to have him in his class. In an interview Colman said, "My feelings were hurt badly by Hindemith's behavior. But Copland said, 'I'll teach you,' and although I did not particularly want to study with Copland, wasn't that nice of him!"[6]

Hindemith met with his six students daily; in addition he taught two evening classes a week to the Academy. Hindemith wrote to Herbert Fromm, a former student from Buffalo, with whom he had become friendly (15 July 1940):

> The students (at least, the so-called composers) are awful. There was some conflict at first since they all came with large scores and wanted recognition, and they showed no love for me. They did not like at all to have to start small and hated the idea of having to sing what they had written. But when I made them work for hours at the blackboard on strict counterpoint exercises and they saw that none of them was able to solve even the simplest ones, they became pliable, relented and are now quite good and mannerly. . . .

In the years to follow, Hindemith would teach many American composition students with varying results and influence.[7] But two qualities were obvious from the start—Hindemith was an absolutely extraordinary musician with a powerful and difficult personality.

Harold Shapero[8]

I wanted to study with Hindemith because he wrote fast and I wanted to get the secret of how to do that. I was always getting stuck. But it didn't rub off on me. The first shocking thing was that I was not going to be allowed to hear any of my compositions that summer. He would not look at our compositions or allow them to be played. Instead, we had exercises in two-voice counterpoint. Hindemith was more interested in what we could do on the spot right then and there that summer. Also, we were assigned an instrument to be learned, one quite the opposite of what we ordinarily played. I was a pianist, so I took the trumpet. Hindemith demanded a lot of work. I would come back to my room—Tanglewood was not very organized that first year—I had five jumping musician roommates in one room at the Cranwell School, including Lenny Bernstein, Arthur Winograd cellist, Raphael Hillyer violist, and a clarinetist. I was trying to compose in this mess. (And I drove them crazy with my trumpet.) I complained to Hindemith and he said, "You can go to the woods." I had the stupidity or nastiness to say, "Well, the bugs get all over your music paper." Hindemith considered this disrespectful. He went to Copland and complained about this fresh student. So immediately we had a confrontation. Years later Copland remembered the way Hindemith came running to him, saying, "That young man Shapero is impossible," and then two seconds later me coming in, screaming, "That Hindemith, he's a monster." That's how it started, but it finished up a lot better.

The main thing about Hindemith as a teacher in those days was his energy. He met us five days a week for five hours every morning with a little time off for a swim. That degree of involvement was staggering when you consider he had already been writing his own music each morning before he started with us. To me, he resembled an electric motor, a little dynamo. Short, compact, with very strong muscles. And he sort of churned and left a wake. He swam that way too. He was a powerhouse personality. As a teacher he did some interesting things with us. But he would really put us down. All of us. He would think nothing of telling us we were terrible, we had no technique, and so forth. We may not have had much, true, but we

Buffalo N.Y., Hotel Lenox
March 4.th 40

Dear Mr. Copland, I just received a letter from Boston, concerning the Berkshire-work. It seems to be necessary to have some discussion about this subject, and since I learned that you are willing to come to New York for this purpose, I would be very glad, if you could arrange your coming for next Sunday (10.). I shall arrive in the morning and would wait for you at 12 noon in the hall of the Hotel Roosevelt, where I am staying. I hope you will not refuse to have lunch with me. If I don't receive a reply, I suppose that you agree with my proposition.

Yours very sincerely

Paul Hindemith

Above: Letter from Paul Hindemith, 1940.
Right: Copland, Hindemith, Margaret Grant, and friend at Tanglewood, summer 1940.

weren't absolute zeros! At first he was martinetlike but he did sort of mellow, or else we got used to him. His procedure was to sit at the piano with each member of the class who brought a piece in. He'd put the piece up with a page of blank music paper to the right. He had a pencil which was one of those push-button types. When he wanted to go fast, he didn't even have to bother to turn the pencil. He could just squeeze it—bang, bang, bang—as though he was a human musical typewriter. He'd look at your piece, scan it with his eye quickly and have you play it if you insisted, but he didn't need that. He'd immediately make judgments: "This is pretty . . . this isn't a bad way to go, this is a wrong modulation." And then he'd rewrite your piece for you while you were waiting—just like having your pants pressed! Pure Hindemith just by changing an interval here and rhythms there. It was always better of course. You realized you were being dominated, yet the process of watching him write at that speed with technical strength and coherence was awesome. "Well, you know," he said, when I told him I was impressed, "it's taken me a long time to come to the point where there's no time lost between my head, elbow, and arm." In other words, his mind and pencil.

From having started off wrong, he took a shine to me and to Lukas Foss, and invited us to visit him for private instruction after the Tanglewood semester. So I came breathless into the house in Lenox, and there was a big sheet of orchestral paper on his desk that had a motive on it with a big fermata. I said, "That's an interesting motive." "Yes, it looks pretty good," replied Hindemith. Then we went with the paper to the park in Lenox with a bunch of manuscript paper and he said, "Okay, fill the page with melodies. I'll be back." I didn't know what to do. So I filled the page full of Hindemith-like melodies to please him. He came back in a couple of hours, looked quickly, and said, "That's not it. Keep writing. Write melodies, okay?" We went on this way for two or three days, all morning and all afternoon on the park bench. I didn't have the vaguest idea of what he was after! In desperation, in the middle of these things I was trying to write Hindemith-style, I finally put down a melody from a little woodwind trio I had written as a freshman at Harvard. That day when he came by, he came right to that tune and said, "That's it. You finally found it, build on it." All I could think was, "Thank goodness, it's over. I don't have to sit here any more!" He was very pleasant, and by that time, we all thought he was lovable! In the meantime, while I was on that park bench, he had written the entire first movement of his E-flat Symphony.

Copland met with his students individually—not in class as Hindemith did—and he held orchestration classes a few times a week. His students were Josef Alexander, Harold Brown, Donald Fuller, Charles Jones, Robert Palmer, John Verrall, and John Colman (after Hindemith refused him). Copland delivered four lectures to the Academy that summer: Berlioz; Musical Form; American Music; and Debussy, Schoenberg, and Stravinsky. Compared with Hindemith, Copland was supportive, but Robert Palmer makes this point: "It is important to remember that Aaron was as sharp a critic as I've ever come across. He could put his finger on trouble spots, but without tearing a work down. He didn't always like what was brought to him, but if he liked a work, you could be *sure* that he did. What was remarkable about Aaron as a teacher was this combination of giving the necessary criticism without ruining a young composer's confidence."[9] Copland thought that students could learn a great deal from hearing their pieces played and that it was wasteful not to take advantage of the performers who were right at hand. (After regular classes ended, Copland got together with composers and performers who had stayed on at Tanglewood, and they read through works not played earlier. "But don't tell Hindemith!" warned Copland.) Hindemith wrote to Gertrud: "Copland wants to have his students' works performed and always speaks of them as finished composers, while I consider mine to be raw beginners in need of appropriate training. Koussevitzky is completely on my side and happily agrees with my decision to forbid anything by my students to be performed." This is a rather surprising statement, since it has been thought that Koussevitzky did not agree with Hindemith's teaching methods.[10] But nothing in Hindemith's correspondence indicates problems between the two. In fact, late in August Hindemith wrote to Gertrud: "He has offered me no less than the Directorship of the entire school, but I am not particularly attracted by that. . . ."

Koussevitzky's conducting students were Leonard Bernstein, Lukas Foss, Richard Bales, and Thor Johnson. Each received a scholarship of $50. Copland saw as much of Bernstein as the frantic pace of the six-week term allowed. Harold Shapero soon became Copland's close friend, and Lukas Foss, who had searched out Copland at the Empire Hotel in 1937 when Foss was only fifteen, also knew Copland well by the summer of 1940. Foss would run to Aaron whenever Hindemith threw him out of class after saying, "Write in any style you want, but write in my style while you study with me. At least you'll have my world, then eventually maybe you'll have your own." And Foss finally thought that Hindemith was right

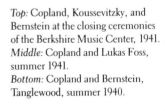

Top: Copland, Koussevitzky, and Bernstein at the closing ceremonies of the Berkshire Music Center, 1941.
Middle: Copland and Lukas Foss, summer 1941.
Bottom: Copland and Bernstein, Tanglewood, summer 1940.

and went on to study with him at Yale. In an interview, Foss talked about Hindemith and Copland: "They got along because Copland never *doesn't* get along. But I think Aaron had a hard time. Because Hindemith would say things like 'Why should my pupils study orchestration with you? If anybody knows orchestration, it's me!' *That* kind of thing, which no American would say. And Aaron would answer mildly, 'Well, it just happens to be something I like to teach.' "[11]

In midsummer one of Hindemith's composition students, Charles Naginski, drowned. Because of Hindemith's reputation as a taskmaster, the tragic incident caused speculation about whether Naginski had taken his own life. Hindemith wrote to Gertrud (6 August):

> I have one less student—he was drowned night before last. He would go in the lake every morning with the class but he could not swim and so just paddled around a little. In spite of that, he went alone last Sunday afternoon to a nearby lake to bathe. When he did not return the police dragged the lake and found him dead. He was 31 years old and somewhat neurotic. Perhaps I could have straightened him out in time (he wanted to come to Yale to study); he was not overly talented but could have been quite good. The school was rather upset over the incident.[12]

Harold Shapero recalls composition class the next morning as silent and deadly. "After about two hours went by, the tension got extreme. And Hindemith suddenly burst out and said, 'They say I killed him.' Nobody could reply to that. Hindemith wasn't unsympathetic. He tried to figure out what he'd done and if it could have been his fault. He did talk about it. And then we let it lie, and that was the end of it."

Although Naginski's death cast a shadow on the BMC's first season, the Festival Concerts during the final three weeks were a diversion. Each performance attracted from between eight to ten thousand people. Eleanor Roosevelt was one of the famous guests at a Tanglewood concert that summer, and even Toscanini made an unannounced visit. The major American work conducted by Koussevitzky was Roy Harris' *Third Symphony*. Hindemith's symphony *Mathis der Maler* was given a great deal of attention. Hindemith found Tanglewood so attractive that he stayed in Lenox for a few weeks after the season to work on his symphony before going to New Haven to begin a new life as Professor of Music at Yale.

Copland also remained to work on the *Quiet City* suite and to compose an organ piece commissioned by H. W. Gray, the English publishers. (Gray had invited several American composers to write short organ works for a series: Frederick Jacobi, Douglas Moore, Piston, Sessions, Leo

Sowerby, and Bernard Wagenaar.) Copland composed a four-page piece first called *Improvisation*, in three sections, the outer ones quiet with polytonal harmonies, enclosing a contrasting midsection. The title was changed to *Episode*. It was played first by William Strickland in March 1941, soon after publication.[13] Hindemith and Copland were both sufficiently impressed with the BMC's first season to agree to return the next season. Copland shared Koussevitzky's elation and enthusiasm at having so many superb musicians and students together in one place. The Center was Koussevitzky's pride and joy until his death in 1951, and for Copland, a very special place to return to year after year for twenty-one memorable summers over a span of twenty-five years.

At the close of the summer of 1940, Harold Clurman, always philosophical on special occasions, wrote to his friend:

> The thirties had a certain drive—the Depression and the realistic mood . . . ten years of the Group. . . . What has happened? All around me I notice a new thing. People are not talking so many generalities. They are not driving forward with a vague hope or a collective optimism: they are asking themselves—Who am I? What am I? Where do I belong? . . . in a word, taking stock. . . . The period of the 1940s will be one of reaction. Don't you think all this will show itself in music too somehow? What is happening to your own work? Or don't you have too conscious a sense of it? I know you have always been able to work without theory or too much consciousness. Still . . .

The fact is that Copland composed little after his return to New York in the fall of 1940. The atmosphere, so filled with uncertainty and turmoil, was not conducive to writing music. Victor, who had been working as a photographer's assistant during the summer months, was waiting to be called into the service; Blitzstein was already in uniform; and Copland worried about Nadia—would she make it safely out of Europe in time? Béla Bartók had banned his music from broadcast in Nazi countries, causing furor in his native Hungary, and Copland joined with others in forming an American Music League to support his brave gesture. But otherwise Copland had no outlet for his patriotic feelings. Socialist activities had slowed down after the WPA's Federal Music Project came into being, paying artists for performing civic duties. The war years would be difficult ones for composers. Few in the service could work in the field of music; those at home had to choose between creating patriotic works or composing in isolation. Roger Sessions, who disliked overt nationalism in art, addressed the issue again in an article called "American Music and the

Crisis" in which he stated, "The composer is faced by the impossibility of finding his public within himself."[14]

Copland wrote to the Department of State offering his services. While waiting for an answer, he immersed himself in organizational activities—the League, the Arrow Music Press, the ACA, the American Music Center. His fortieth birthday was celebrated quietly with his family. Copland, usually casual and philosophical about birthdays, was less so about this one. David Diamond wrote to him (19 November 1940): "I am sorry my birthday greetings upset you. Really, Aaron, I only meant it in all sincerity. . . . Just the same I hope you have forty more and I never forget one."

The time seemed right for considering a suggestion from Whittlesey House for a second book, so Copland began to organize and collect materials. In *What to Listen For in Music*, his target had been the general listening audience; but for his next book, he wanted to tackle the problems of contemporary music. The result was *Our New Music*, published in the fall of 1941, a year after Copland began to assemble articles written previously for *Modern Music* and other journals.

Our New Music was not meant to be a dictionary of modern music or a prediction of who the most promising young composers of the future would be; rather, it was intended as a guide to mainstream developments in contemporary music. Copland began by tracing the roots of modernism in the nineteenth century, giving emphasis to Moussorgsky as a pivotal figure. Two main sections followed: one on European composers, the other on Americans. Of Schoenberg and the twelve-tone system, Copland wrote: "Already it begins to sound surprisingly dated. . . . It creates a certain monotony of effect that severely limits its variety of expression. . . . But for a long time to come it is likely to be of interest principally to specialists and connoisseurs rather than to the generality of music lovers. . . ." (Later, Copland would admit that the twelve-tone movement "took a position no one could have foreseen—that is one of vital importance after World War II.") Included in the European section were early and later Stravinsky, Bartók, Ravel and Roussel, Satie and *Les Six*, and Milhaud. In the American chapter, Copland examined six contemporaries: Ives, Harris, Sessions, Piston, Thomson, and Blitzstein. Chávez was given a full chapter, and Copland himself was represented by the reprinting of an autobiographical sketch, "Composer from Brooklyn," which had first appeared in 1938 in the *Magazine of Art*. Concluding chapters reviewed the role of the media—radio, film, and phonograph music. About the change to a new decade, Copland wrote: "The decade 1930–1940 marked the end of the experimental phase of contemporary music. For almost forty years, music had passed through a series of revolutionary crises, as a result of which all the stultifying rules of harmony, rhythmic phrase, and melodic construction had been broken down. By 1930, composers everywhere began to sense the necessity for consolidating the gains made for their art. . . ." Copland believed that the pendulum had swung into a period in which "the more revolutionary twenties were normalized, one of new simplicity that has left certain of our musical elite with a sense of being let down."

Olin Downes' review in *The New York Times* (19 October 1941) praised *Our New Music* for "brilliant and admirable pages," but criticized Copland for claiming that modern music was ready for the mainstream of musical listening. Copland responded: "My book is not a plea for any kind of musical modernism. It is quite simply a statement of my picture of what modern music is and how it got that way." Downes followed Copland's letter with a second article (30 November), setting off a heated debate. Theodore Chanler's review of *Our New Music* in *Modern Music* was titled, "The New Romanticism,"[15] and Virgil Thomson reviewed *Our New Music* for the *Tribune* as a "Fireside Chat from the President of American Music." Thomson praised the book: "What gives it its unique quality among books about modern music, is its gentlemanly, its humane tone. . . . There are bitter books and pugnacious books and log-rolling books and joke books about that subject. Practically nowhere else is there a book on modern music at once so enlightened and so sweetly frank as Mr. Copland's." Thomson explained that Copland was not all sweetness— "He grants to each of his friends and enemies no more or no less than what is fair. His friends and his enemies both may well be grateful for his having placed them in the line-up at all and for not having hogged the center place himself."

Certain remarks in "Composer from Brooklyn" were viewed as a retreat from Copland's long-standing support of modern music. For example: "During these years I began to feel an increasing dissatisfaction with the relations of the music-loving public and the living composer. The old 'special' public of the modern music concerts had fallen away, and the conventional concert public continued apathetic or indifferent to anything but the established classics. It seemed to me that we composers were in danger of working in a vacuum. . . . My most recent works, in their separate ways, embody this tendency toward an imposed simplicity." Copland did not intend his remarks as a rebuttal of former works, but they were frequently taken as such; moreover, publication in book form gave them emphasis.

When preparing a later revised version of *Our New Music*, Copland was relieved to have an opportunity to clarify his position. In *The New Music, 1900–1960*, published in 1968, he wrote:

> I have learned, to my discomfiture, that the writing of an autobiographical sketch in mid-career is fraught with peril. Commentators, pleased to be able to quote literally, are convinced that they have pinned the composer down for all time. Thus, the final two paragraphs of my brief memoir have done me considerable harm. The mention of "an imposed simplicity" was taken to mean that I had renounced my more complex and "difficult" music, turned my back on the cultivated audience that understands a sophisticated musical language, and henceforth would write music solely for the "masses." Quoted and requoted, these remarks of mine emphasized a point of view which, although apposite at the time of writing—the end of the '30s—seem to me to constitute an oversimplification of my aims and intentions, especially when applied to a consideration of my subsequent work and of my work as a whole. . . .[16]

The revision also gave Copland the chance to retract his statements on Schoenberg and the Viennese school and to bring up to date the composers who had continued to produce works since *Our New Music*. In the revised version, the section on the media, which had become outdated, was replaced with accounts of musical developments since World War II such as chance operations and electronics. *Our New Music* and *The New Music* are still informative; moreover, they have value as biographical sources on Copland, providing insights and perspectives on his career and the changes in his thinking. If one examines both versions of the book side by side, certain Copland traits are constant; among them: an openness in admitting errors, a gracefulness in correcting them, and a loyal and steady support of modern music as a substantial and worthwhile body of artistic works deserving attention by audiences of all times. Copland's writings on music express vividly and with a sense of immediacy what it meant to be a composer in America during the earlier years of this century.

Copland made his living from writings and lectures during the winter of 1940–41. His carefully kept financial accounts show several fees in 1940 of about $100 each for lecture recitals in Allentown, Pittsburgh, and Philadelphia, at the Town Hall in New York, and at Dartmouth and Colby colleges. Royalties of a few hundred dollars were received from Ballet Caravan for *Billy the Kid,* and over $400 from McGraw-Hill (parent company of Whittlesey House) for *What to Listen For in Music,* and a $250 advance for "Book II." Modest royalties were trickling in from Boosey & Hawkes. The major musical event of the season was the premiere of *Quiet*

City in January in New York and Koussevitzky's conducting of it in Boston on 18 April 1941.

In April a response arrived from the State Department designating Copland a member of the President's Advisory Committee on Music. "The committee is to advise the Department of State through the Division of Cultural Relations regarding musical interchange among the American republics and the coordination of activities in this country which concern inter-American music." When Copland wrote to Clurman that he expected to be sent to South America on a goodwill tour, Clurman replied, "I am impressed! You are coming into your proper field now: diplomacy!" Knowing that Tanglewood, followed by the South American trip, would soon take his full time, Copland again needed a quiet place where he could compose without interruption. He chose Cuba. Only Victor was told of his whereabouts. After checking into the Royal Palm Hotel in Havana, Copland went to work, and returned at the end of May with *Our New Music* ready for the publisher and the *Piano Sonata* almost finished. It was time to pack up for Tanglewood.

One evening early in June 1941 Copland carried two suitcases down the four flights to his car parked outside the loft. When he returned after going back up for the rest of his luggage, the two valises were gone. One was filled with personal belongings; the other with music. Copland went directly to the 20th Precinct police station to report the theft. A reward was offered, and the Department of Sanitation was asked to be on the lookout for odd sheets of music paper. (Copland's fear was that whoever had forced open the window of his car might be so disgusted at finding nothing but papers in one suitcase that he would throw it away.) The newspapers covered the story and even interviewed Mrs. Harris Copland about her son's loss—"His little mother hoped the thief would not destroy the manuscripts, believing them the works of 'just an ordinary' musician." Victor (still waiting to hear from his draft board) volunteered to go around to the neighborhood junk dealers and ragpickers. Before leaving for Lenox, Copland listed his loss for the Great American Insurance Company: "Collected themes for Billy and The City in binding, Sorcery to Science—pencil, Piano Sonata—two movements in ink, 10 pages on thin paper, The Elegies—broad paper, proofs of the Lark; pr rubbers, 4 toothbrushes, Yardley's, "The Critical Composer," mms blank, date-book, article: "Composers Without a Halo," flannel pants, 1 suit, sweaters, some gloves, shoes."

The thief was apprehended. A postcard from Victor to Aaron sent to Stockbridge on 10 June reported: "He's admitted sole guilt, but having a hell of a time getting stuff back. Everything's been dispersed. So far, 3 pr pants and a few other things. . . ." The music manuscripts were not recovered. This was a painful loss, particularly the notebooks of musical ideas collected over several years and the *Piano Sonata*, whose reconstruction had to be undertaken immediately while still fresh in the composer's mind. John Kirkpatrick, for whom Copland had played the *Sonata*, wrote out what themes he could recall and sent them on 7 July 1941.

Copland had rented a very pleasant house in Stockbridge. (He liked it so much that he arranged to rent it again in 1942.) When Bernstein heard about the house, he wrote: "There's a great problem concerning quarters. . . . Is it really impossible to live in your house? You don't work anyway during those six weeks. And think of the fun! We're all feeling rather anti-dormitory. . . ." Copland rejected this idea, recalling the noise and excitement of the students of Cranwell the previous summer, but Bernstein was often at his house in 1941 and guests came every weekend. Rosamond Bernier recalls, "Copland would whisper to me, 'There are *guests* in the house!' as if to say that there were *mice* in the kitchen!"

Again in 1941 Hindemith and Copland divided the duties of the composition department; Olin Downes returned to lecture on early music and to lead public rehearsal discussions on Saturday mornings, supplemented by guests Howard Hanson (who came up to lecture when his *"Romantic" Symphony* [no. 2] was scheduled for performance with the BSO), Putnam Aldrich, and Carleton Sprague Smith. Boris Goldovsky joined Dr. Herbert Graf in the opera program; Gregor Piatigorsky and Jésus María Sanromá were on hand to teach chamber music; and Hugh Ross and G. Wallace Woodworth ran the chorus. A new addition on the scene was the Theater Concert Hall, again designed by Saarinen, with funds donated by Mrs. Mary Curtis Bok. The Doctor's assistant, as in 1940, was Stanley Chapple, and his conducting students were Bernstein, Foss, Thor Johnson, Walter Hendl, Richard Korn, and Robert Whitney. An excellent student orchestra was made up of the best of more than 700 applicants from all over the country. The composition students numbered sixteen. This year it was Harold Shapero who was barred from Hindemith's class, even though he had just won the Rome Prize. Shapero wrote to Copland (16 June 1941): ". . . Hindy doesn't think I ought to be in his class this summer. It is my extremely embarrassing task to ask you if you still have any room, and are prepared or willing to soak up Hindemith's outcasts, particularly me. . . .

Enclosed find a postcard which I hope will make your task easier. Ever since Lenny told me that you get about 75 letters a day, I've considered it a crime to inflict mail upon you." Copland took Shapero into his group, made up of the Mexican-Indian Blas Galindo (sent by Chávez), the Canadian Barbara Pentland, the Hawaiian Dai-Keong Lee, Sam Morgenstern, Gardner Read, Robert Ward, and Arnold Chaitman. In Hindemith's group were Lukas Foss, Norman Dello Joio, John Klein, Herbert Fromm, and newcomers Montague Cantor, Paul Gelrud, and Ulysses Kay.

Copland gave each student a private lesson of an hour and a half and taught two advanced orchestration classes a week. In addition to analyzing major works to be performed in the festival, Copland taught orchestration of contemporary radio and movie music. Gardner Read recalled, "Copland gave us a passage in *Of Mice and Men*, told us to score it in our own style and then showed us *his* score." In summing up the benefits of the summer's study, Read wrote, "Copland and I were at sword's point for some days because he called me a *romanticist.*. . . But it did make me question whether or not my music was a bit too lush, too complex, for contemporaneous expression. It made me sure that if I were standing my own ground, it was with reason. . . ."[17] Hindemith again taught his students in class for over four hours every day. He introduced American students to early music, reading from Zarlino and other theorists in class, and though there were no scores or early instruments at Tanglewood, he would appear at chamber music classes with pages he had copied out himself from the Yale Music Library the previous winter.

During the Music Festival of 1941, proceeds from one concert were designated for British War Relief and for a collection of BSO recordings to be shipped to American musicians in the service. Compositions by American composers were included on Koussevitzky's programs: Samuel Barber's *Violin Concerto* and Copland's *Quiet City*, which was paired with Hindemith's *Concerto for Violoncello and Orchestra*, Piatigorsky as soloist. Olin Downes lectured on the contemporary pieces at the Saturday morning rehearsal. He stated that, in his opinion, "Copland was at his best in the poetic mood of *Quiet City*." Audience and critics were enthusiastic. Immediately following the closing ceremonies of the Music Center, Copland left Tanglewood for Mexico to begin a four-month tour of South America for the State Department—to include Ecuador, Peru, Chile, Argentina, Uruguay, Brazil, and Cuba.

The Early War Years

1941-1942

South America as a whole does not exist. As I was to discover on my first tour in 1941, it is a collection of separate countries, each with different traditions, at different stages of musical development, and with practically no musical contact with each other. Only as I traveled from country to country did I realize that you must be willing to split the continent up in your mind. Also, one could not go south of the border with a critical attitude and the expectation that the level of performance and education would parallel that of North America. Both North and South had experienced a colonial past and had formerly looked to Europe for artistic leadership and inspiration. During the war years the need to reaffirm national characteristics accelerated. The United States government, as part of an effort to improve inter-American relationships, placed leading Americanists in government agencies to promote Pan-Americanism. Carleton Sprague Smith coordinated musical activities for Nelson Rockefeller's Committee of Inter-American Affairs.[1] Rockefeller was only twenty-five. He was determined to set up an ideal model of what inter-cultural relations should be. I had been preceded in Latin America by Kirstein's Ballet Caravan, by Toscanini and the NBC Orchestra, and by a quintet of woodwind performer-composers that included David Van Vactor, Alvin Etler, Jim Barrows, Adolph Weiss, and Robert McBride. Rockefeller's committee seemed more interested in American composers than in virtuoso performers, as was the case later on. When it became clear that a cultural mission to South American countries by a composer who could speak directly with native composers would be useful, I was chosen by the Committee for Inter-American Artistic and Intellectual Relations, an agency set up by the Coordinator of Inter-American Affairs. On the committee was Henry Allen Moe, secretary of the Guggenheim Foundation. Dr. Moe arranged for a grant of $3,100 to cover my four-month tour. He instructed me (14 August 1941): "I want you, please, to come back with a list of composers and musical scholars who in your judgment based on your own knowledge are first-rate and who ought to be given funds to come to the United States for sound music purposes. Among such persons is, in my mind, [Heitor] Villa–Lobos of Brazil; if he is interested in coming to the U.S. please ask him when and for how long and what he would want to do here. . . . In Latin America there has been adopted the word 'goodwillings.' We want no part in 'goodwillings.' We want to assist hard and serious professional work. . . ."

During the summer I wrote to Carleton Sprague Smith to inform him of the lectures I could give in Spanish and the music I wanted to play and conduct. Carleton made the appropriate contacts in each country. I was expected to send detailed reports describing and assessing individual composers, administrators, educational facilities, government attitudes to music, and so forth. Toward this purpose, I made entries in a diary upon leaving each city. Fortunately I kept this diary, and from its seventy-eight pages I can reconstruct the highlights of my journey:

20–28 AUGUST: Meetings with three Mexican composers of the younger generation: Salvador Contreras, Pablo Moncayo, Daniel Ayala. With Blas Galindo they form a group known as "Los Cuatro." Of this group Galindo would seem to be the most gifted. Certainly his technique is the most advanced of the four. All these composers write music very much in the style of the Mexican School, founded by Chávez and Revueltas. Thus far, in their early thirties, the Four have not exceeded their older confreres. They are limited in their use of form which tends always to be sectionally constructed and in types of melodic material which tend always toward the Mexican popular tune. Their forte is orchestration, learned mostly by performing under Chávez in the Orquesta Sinfónica de México. I know Galindo well from Tanglewood where he has just last summer been my student. I visited with musicologists who were mainly Spanish refugees and with Rodolfo Halffter, a refugee Spanish composer. Everywhere I travel the composers are playing their music and showing me their scores. . . .

29 AUGUST: Guatemala City overnight, then Cristobal and Bogotá, Colombia. The attitude of creative musicians in Colombia is pessimistic. The request I heard most often was "send us more records!" I was invited to give two radio programs on the National Radio: for the first, I read a page of greeting in Spanish and played recordings of El Salón México and Music for the Theatre; on the second, I presented works by three Americans—Harris, Piston, and Bowles. Several Colombian composers gathered at the radio station, and following the broadcast, I played some of my own piano pieces, and we talked until the early morning hours. In Quito, Ecuador, I spent a few days before traveling on to Peru. There, I discovered that previous reports were true—no orchestras, no conservatory, and no teachers. "Send us composers," they pleaded, "to teach

harmony, counterpoint, and composition in Spanish." . . .

7 SEPTEMBER: Lima, Peru. I was met by the city's outstanding musical personalities. Preceding me had been successful performances of *Billy the Kid* by Ballet Caravan, and the film version was being shown in local movie houses. The Orquesta Sinfónica Nacional invited me to conduct *Billy* on 10 September. The players left much to be desired technically, but they were lively and enthusiastic. I heard the usual pessimistic story of musical life from the composers. I am spending time with André Sas,[2] a Belgian who has lived in Peru for the past twenty years. . . .

15 SEPTEMBER: Santiago, Chile. I was met by their foremost musical figure, Domingo Santa Cruz, who acted as my host and explained the workings of the Fine Arts Faculty, the official center of all musical life in Chile, of which he is dean. Composers here are highly organized, perhaps because they are not only isolated from the general public, but also from the rest of the Continent, being on the West Coast. Their musical compositions reflect this group tendency. I found Chilean composers definitely behind the times with the romantic and chromatic music they write, and always rather more complex than necessary. Although the music is meticulously written and sensitively handled, all the music seems to have a rather derivative air. Santa Cruz is probably as good a composer as one can find on the West Coast of S.A., and the only young composer-conductor I can recommend for study in the U.S. is twenty-two-year-old Juan Orrego[-Salas], pupil of Santa Cruz. I have been invited to a farewell party by the Chilean composers at the Faculty of Fine Arts. I plan to play my new *Piano Sonata* for the first time. Have been invited to return for a week in October to conduct the orchestra, to lecture, and to preside over a jury to distribute prizes among Chilean composers. Have accepted. . . .

26 SEPTEMBER: Buenos Aires, Argentina. There is a young composer here who is generally looked upon as the "white hope" of Argentine music. He is now twenty-five and is certainly the first candidate for a trip to the States from any standpoint. Alberto Ginastera would profit by contacts outside Argentina. He is looked upon with favor by all groups here, is presentable, modest almost to the timid degree, and will, no doubt, someday be an outstanding figure in Argentine music. Certainly he is far ahead of any of the young men of his age here. The only composer I have met in South America who is using the twelve-tone system is Juan Carlos Paz who seems more like the typical figure of a composer in our modern music movement—serious, learned, literary, and somewhat heroic. One would like to see what his music was before he adopted the twelve-tone system about six years ago . . . an interesting figure, worth watching. . . . I lectured to about 200 people for an organization, La Nueva Musica, headed by Paz.

10 OCTOBER: A night boat to Montevideo. As everywhere, I was treated cordially by the Embassy officials and dignitaries from the local government. The Instituto Interamericano de Musicologia is based in Montevideo, headed by Francisco Curt Lange. I am scheduled to address this group on the subject of modern music in the U.S. There is to be a formal reception and concert includ-

ing Harris' *Trio* which I will play with local musicians, Sessions' two chorale preludes, and a few of my own works. Two of the lectures which I had prepared in advance in Spanish are very much in demand—"The Influence of Jazz" and "Music for Films." American movies are very popular down here. They know *Of Mice and Men*, so my film lecture, punctuated with visual illustrations, has been particularly well-received. South Americans are very sociable; receptions are held after each concert and lecture. I have met Andrés Segovia and the talented young composer Hector Tosar. The nearest parallel I can think of to Tosar is Shostakovitch. Tosar's music has the same easy appeal, and the same dash. . . . The Colon Orchestra, under Juan José Castro, played *An Outdoor Overture*, and for once, I am satisfied with both the orchestra and the conducting—but the audience was small.[3] At a party afterward, I was delighted to see my old friend, Nicolas Slonimsky, who is travelling around South America collecting materials for a book.[4] In José María Castro, brother of Juan José, I found a composer with a fresh style and personality added to an excellent technique. None of the usual Gallicisms or nostalgia or "effect" music so current down here. I should very much like to have him come to New York, and he says he wishes to come. Paz planned a concert of All North American chamber music sponsored by La Nueva Musica for 21 October with works by Sessions, Harris, Gerald Strang, Cowell and myself. It was this concert at which my *Piano Sonata* had its public premiere. The impression was favorable. . . .

24 OCTOBER: Return to Santiago to serve as judge for a contest of Chilean composers. In my absence, a concert had been arranged for 5 November at which I conducted the Orquesta Sinfónica de Chile. The program included *An Outdoor Overture, Quiet City, El Salón México*, and the *Piano Concerto* with myself as soloist. . . .

5 NOVEMBER: Return to Buenos Aires and on to Rio de Janeiro. I have tried to hear as much native music as possible in each country; in Rio, it is the samba band. Brazil's outstanding musical personality, Heitor Villa-Lobos, takes care that I hear the real thing. Villa-Lobos is an independent type. He picks me up in his car and we drive into the mountains around Rio to see the sights. When he heard that I was interested in native music he took me to an "Escola de Samba" up in one of the famous "morros" of Rio.[5] I was struck by the rhythmic similarity to what I had heard in Cuba, but the melodic line is savage and more gutteral than any I have heard anywhere, with no harmony at all—only rhythm and melody. The music was overpowering in the small room where it was performed. Villa-Lobos is rather touchy about coming to America. He is firm on one point—he wishes to come purely as an artist—to be in no way connected with official or governmental authority. I let that pass and explained that a short trip would prepare the way for a real concert tour of imposing proportions later. Finally, he said laughing, "One would think that Copland came here just to get me to come to the U.S.!" His music has one outstanding quality—abundance. He is a kind of de Falla of Brazil in his best works, and a kind of Respighi of Brazil at other times. The works are likely as not to be loosely thrown together in an inextricable melange of authentic Brazilian atmosphere plus a full quota

EXTRA

MARTES 21
DE OCTUBRE
A LAS 21.30

El TEATRO DEL PUEBLO, presenta:

AUDICION XXVIII

LA NUEVA MUSICA

(Antología de las tendencias actuales)

CONSAGRADA A LA MODERNA MUSICA NORTEAMERICANA

y en honor de los maestros

Aaron Coplan y Nicolás Sloninsky

Intervienen: **Anita Sujovolsky** (violín) - **Hilde Heinitz de Weil** (viola) - **Sofia Knoll** (piano) - **Aarón Copland** (piano) - **Nicolás Sloninsky** (piano) - **Esteban Eitler** (flauta) - **Francisco Heltay** (violín) - **German Weil** (violoncelo).

TEATRO DEL PUEBLO
BUENOS AIRES

MINISTERIO DA EDUCAÇÃO E SAÚDE

UNIVERSIDADE DO BRASIL

ESCOLA NACIONAL DE MÚSICA

18.º Concêrto Oficial

Ultimo da Série de 1941

TERÇA-FEIRA, 25 DE NOVEMBRO

ÁS 21 HORAS

MUSICA MODERNA NORTE-AMERICANA

em homenagem ao eminente compositor

AARON COPLAND

Com a colaboração de:

CRISTINA MARISTANY
ALDA BORGERTH
OSCAR BORGERTH
EDMUNDO BLOIS
IBERÊ GOMES GROSSO
MOACYR LISERRA
ANTÃO SOARES
ARNALDO ESTRELLA
FRANCISCO MIGNONE

CONCIERTO

DE

OBRAS CONTEMPORANEAS

NORTEAMERICANAS Y CUBANAS

Presentación de

AARON COPLAND

Compositor, Director y Pianista

ORQUESTA DE CAMARA DE LA HABANA

Dirección: J. ARDEVOL

Con la colaboración de César Pérez Sentenat
y Rafael Morales, pianistas; Alberto Bolet,
violinista, y Alberto Roldán, violoncelista.

LYCEUM

Calzada y 8, VEDADO

JUEVES, 11 DE DICIEMBRE 1941,
5.30 P. M.

Top: Program from Buenos Aires,
21 October 1942.
Middle: Program featuring the world
premiere of the *Piano Sonata*, Brazil, 25 November 1942.
Bottom: Program from Cuba,
11 December 1942.

Copland and Chávez at the piano with (left to right): Domingo Santa Cruz (Chile), Alberto Ginastera (Argentina), and Juan B. Plaza (Venezuela), Caracas, 1957.

of modern French methods of composition. At times it is enormously picturesque. Free of prejudices, full of rhythmic and figured formulas, sometimes cheap and vulgar, sometimes astonishingly original, and full of temperament—a temperament that is profoundly Brazilian. In Brazilian music, folklore informs everything. It is unusually rich—with Negro, Indian, Portuguese, and possibly Spanish influences. Combined with the Brazilian temperament, their music has more "face" than other groups of composers in South America. . . .

8 DECEMBER: Havana, Cuba. Lectures at the Lyceum on modern American composers and meetings with local composers. Gilberto Valdes has his own radio orchestra for which he composes music based on Cuban motifs. He should be the George Gershwin of Cuba, but he lacks both technique and the faculty of self-criticism. José Ardévol is an intelligent musician whose work deserves to be better known up north. Serious music in Cuba has suffered a severe blow with the deaths of its leading figures—Amadeo Roldán in 1939 and Alejandro García Caturla in 1940. In a concert of Cuban and American works, I again played my *Piano Sonata*. I have been away four months. The Japanese at-

tacked Pearl Harbor yesterday. It seems strange to be in Cuba with the United States at war. I am grateful to find American friends, Rosamond and Lew Riley, who are in Havana at this time. . . .

9 DECEMBER: Some thoughts en route to New York: South America is in the process of *becoming*. You can only be interested in these countries if you are interested in growing things. The countries that have developed most rapidly are those with the richest folklore—Mexico and Brazil; whereas, the most interesting thing about Chile is its musical set-up—the Faculty for Fine Arts which is run by and for composers and artists. Argentina's musical creativity is underestimated in North America—composers are better off than we thought. Everywhere, French influence is predominant. Composers work under great difficulties with no opportunity to publish, few orchestras, little contact with live audiences, few radio performances, and little government support (except for Chile). I marvel that there is any creative work done at all, and I am impressed by the good that one energetic man can accomplish—such as Chávez in Mexico, Santa Cruz in Chile and Villa-Lobos in Brazil. It seems remarkable that we have not thought much of South America before! My general recommendations to the Committee for Inter–American Relations are as follows: supply more records for radio stations, and more published music to music centers; establish a distribution center in both North and South America; assist in the publication of South American works; publish a magazine in both languages.

I made my reports to the Committee and to the Guggenheim Foundation, and wrote an article, "The Composers of South America," in which I concluded: "From now on, whatever other result the world crisis may bring, it is a safe bet that musical relations with our southern neighbors will be different."[6] I am told that my 1941 expedition opened the way for many Latin American musicians to make contact with the world of concert music. For me, it was the beginning of friendships and associations that would continue through many years. I realized that such an experience enlarges one's field of vision. It made me feel concern for the provincialism that seemed to be typical of the music scene in New York, where there was a small circle of composers encouraging each other. The tendency to lean back and depend upon that small-circle encouragement seemed to me a lessening rather than an enlarging of one's capacities. While in Rio I wrote to Nadia (24 November 1941): "It was so nice to receive your birthday note—so far from home. I was delighted. . . . My trip through South America has been fascinating. It has been like discovering a new continent. . . . You are well known here. . . . I also had time to complete my *Piano Sonata* which I am anxious for you to hear. . . ." An additional advantage of the South American trip had been the opportunity to test out the *Sonata* before braving it in New York. I felt able to write to Cliff Odets from Rio that I would play "his Sonata" for him soon after my return.

When I originally agreed to compose the *Piano Sonata*, I had asked Odets (2 January 1939): "Is a dedication and a presentation of the manuscript worth $500 to you? It would take me about 2 months to write, I think." Cliff agreed and promptly sent half the commission. One robbery, several interruptions, and almost three years later, the *Sonata* was ready. I have always been grateful to Odets for stimulating me to compose the second of my three major piano works; moreover, he never showed any impatience about delays as the months turned into years. Cliff invited friends and colleagues to his apartment for a first hearing. Clurman and Diamond were in California, but Denby and Blitzstein were present. I never knew how much Cliff really understood about music, but I do know that he felt it deeply. Whatever he thought about the *Sonata*, not an easy work to absorb from a first hearing, he never expressed anything but praise, and after that evening in late December 1941, he wrote to Clurman, "There is a bread-like truth about the *Sonata*." Under an exclusive arrangement with Boosey & Hawkes whereby my compositions were published soon after completion, the *Piano Sonata* appeared in print in 1942. Copies were sent to pianists and teachers. The reactions were favorable. John Kirkpatrick and his wife Hope Miller, a singer, had been performing recitals at various college campuses in the Midwest and the East at which the *Sonata* had been included. "It stands up awfully well with repeated playings," John wrote to me. "Has any pianist trotted out the *Sonata* in public in New York yet?" I had intended to play the premiere myself at a Town Hall Music Forum in February, but I responded that I would be pleased to have John beat me to it. His answer in return was: "Your card with its revelations of your plans of Feb. 17 makes me almost regret our own plans, but the gracious way you put it gives me rather a trusted feeling of responsibility. I'll do my best by you. Would you like to accept a box to decorate? It'll be like old times, back in the twenties—first performances of Copland and Harris, things of Ruggles and Ives, and 'classics.' "[7]

I always connect the *Piano Sonata* with my old teacher, Rubin Goldmark. He thought of sonata form as music's highest goal. It was what a composer aimed for, even more than the fugue. One thinks of the sonata as dramatic—a kind of play being acted out with plenty of time for self-expression. It seems to me that my *Piano Sonata* follows that idea. It is a serious piece that requires careful and repeated study. There is consider-

1/4/39.

Dear Aaron ———

New year's greetings! And everything fine about the sonata. Enclosed first half of the cash. Will send you the second half in six weeks — unless you need it badly before

Love,

Clifford.

P.S. Luise just tells me that she likes you very much.

Above: Letter from Clifford Odets, 1939.
Right: Program including the New York premiere of the *Piano Sonata* by John Kirkpatrick.

able dissonance in it, yet the work is predominantly consonant. Not as spare and bony as the *Piano Variations*, the themes in the *Sonata* are fuller and the chords more protracted than in the earlier piece. But every note was carefully chosen and none included for ornamental reasons. The *Sonata* lies somewhere between the *Variations* and *Our Town*. Its three movements follow a slow, fast, slow sequence and are separate in character, but with subtle relationships between them, so that each seems to grow from the preceding. The first movement is a regular sonata allegro form with two themes, a development section characterized by disjunct rhythms and a playful mood, and a clear recapitulation in which the opening idea is dramatically restated. The second movement scherzo is rhythmically American—I never would have thought of those rhythms if I had not been familiar with jazz. This has to do with a dependence on the eighth note as the basic rhythmic element—very demanding for the pianist because the rhythmic units shift through 5/8, 6/8, 3/4, and 7/8. Leo Smit has reminded me that the instructions in my score for the scherzo read "mezzo piano, delicate and restless." According to Leo, "That's hard to do—even when you're nervous!"[8] The third movement of the *Sonata* is free in form and further from the classic sonata than the previous movements. The British music historian, Wilfrid Mellers, whose writings about American music I have long admired, pointed to the final movement of the *Piano Sonata* as "the essential Copland . . . its relinquishment of the time sense . . . is a phenomenon of quite profound spiritual and cultural implication."[9] Mellers' allusion to a sense of "immobility" in the *Sonata* seems to say in prose what I had in mind when composing the music. The *Sonata* does not end with the usual flash of virtuosic passages: instead, it is rather grand and massive.

John and Hope Kirkpatrick's recital of January 1943, which featured the New York premiere of the *Piano Sonata*, included works by Bach, Purcell, Harris, Beethoven, and Ives. Virgil reviewed the recital in the *Herald Tribune* (10 January 1943): "Superb piano playing. Mr. Kirkpatrick is interesting no matter what he plays." About the *Sonata*: "I was afraid for one whole movement that this piece was not going to get anywhere, and I was still a bit nervous during the second. Happily it got to going along in the finale and became very grand indeed." Reviews were mixed, as I had grown to expect for my more difficult pieces, but Kirkpatrick continued to perform the *Sonata* and Lenny took to it as though it was his own. When in February 1943 I was called back to Hollywood, the Town Hall Music Forum featuring my music took place without me—"Copland Misses His

Own Party," captioned one review. Lenny played the *Sonata* not once, but twice. The second time was unplanned and came after the Forum. Denby reported to me: "Lenny spoke, and then Virgil—brilliant, of course, but in fits . . . and Lenny played the *Sonata* again, this time to absolute perfection. Minna was there and Bill DeKooning with Elaine. . . ." Virgil represented the critics, Israel Citkowitz sat in for me, David Saidenberg and Lenny were the "Interpretive Artists," and Odets represented a "Layman's Viewpoint." Clifford wrote to me that very night: "I would not be your true friend if I did not tell you here how beautiful the *Sonata* sounded on a third and fourth hearing. It has real nobility and so it impressed many varied persons. Modern music aside, in the romantic style I clasp your hand and embrace you!" I responded (10 February 1943): "I'm glad the *Sonata* improves with hearing. I have an inside feeling that I've written something decent there and I continue to have it despite some sourpuss criticisms!"

Judging from the pianists who have performed the *Sonata* through the years, it seems that my feelings were not unfounded. Lenny continued to play the *Sonata*, even in Japan, and Leo Smit, as "a young pianist on his way up," studied and played it in 1945. From then on Leo was closely associated with my piano music.[10] In 1945 Ingolf Dahl introduced the *Sonata* on the West Coast, and in 1948 Andor Foldes played it in Sweden. At about the same time John Kozar and Radu Lupu began playing the work in England. And I had a letter from the twenty-four-year-old pianist William Kapell (3 January 1946):

> I began intensive work on the Sonata once more . . . because all along in my mind was the idea of playing it in Carnegie Hall this season. However, after two weeks I can see that this work needs exactly as much maturing and ripening and mellowing as a Chopin Sonata or a Beethoven Sonata, and I am not willing to take the risk of doing it less than the full justice it deserves. Because, to my mind, this towering work is the one truly great piano composition to come from our country. I adore it, and my great wish was to play it this year. . . . I am going to practice it so that it, and it alone, can be my choice of a great American work when I play in Europe next August. This is a promise I have made to myself. And next year, with your approval of my conception of your work, I will play the Sonata in New York. . . . I have just heard Leo Smit's recording of the Sonata. It is superb. He understands every bar, and the last movement is very moving and powerful in his conception. He is fortunate to have had the benefit of being with you so much. I hope that is a pleasure you'll allow me to enjoy some day. Because, you have a way of playing your own music that is quite unique.

Other pianists who have played the *Piano Sonata* come to mind: Easley

Blackwood, Leon Fleisher, Robert Helps, Noel Lee, William Masselos, and Robert Miller. To my surprise, the choreographer Doris Humphrey chose the *Piano Sonata* for one of her most successful dances, *Day on Earth*, created for the José Limón Company in 1947.[11] Since I could not attend the premiere in Boston, Doris and the dancers came to New York and danced it privately for my approval. I was proud to be part of this beautiful work. As John Martin wrote in *The New York Times* (4 January 1948):

> It is amazing what Miss Humphrey has found in Mr. Copland's *Piano Sonata*. It is difficult music, spare and sinewy, with phrases that use all kinds of rhythmic irregularities to get themselves shaped in their own design. Beneath its surface the choreographer has seen its hardy sweetness, its earth quality, its stalwart, unsentimental statement of beauty. The inherent intricacies of the score have been illuminated by choreographic phrasing that is far less simple than it appears. One is never aware of difficulty, of possible divergence of purpose in score and choreography; it is all one in substance and texture, as if, indeed, the composer had written for this special end.

Leonard Bernstein[12]

The Piano Sonata *is my favorite piece of Aaron's. I adore it. I recorded it for RCA, and they let it drop. But it's been recently reissued. I always thought that the way Aaron played his own music was ideal. Whenever I've heard anybody else play his music, no matter how wonderful—Leo Smit, Noel Lee, even when Willy Kapell played the* Sonata *before he died—I was never really happy with it. But that's a personal thing. Aaron's music just always seemed so natural for me to play or conduct—as though I could have composed it myself, so to speak. (The first piece that I felt I couldn't have composed was the* Piano Fantasy.) *But Aaron's playing, I adored. It was bangy, but that's the way you had to play it. And it was delicate. Delicate is one of his modes, and harsh was another one; he's a great dualist, you know, Aaron, almost in a Manichaean way. He saw everything in terms of good and evil, light and dark, in a dualistic fashion. I think that's because he was always in the middle. So there's something about seeing the world in this dualistic way, and choosing the middle course between the two, in other words, not becoming a biased person in any way. I don't mean bigoted, I mean biased. I don't mean to do any dime-store psychiatry, but when I say "in the middle," I mean able to see both sides. But* not in a Hamlet-like way, in which seeing both sides causes you torture inside. It's not that. It's that there's total good, there's total evil, and Aaron walks a true path of plainness.

That's one of his biggest words—plain. It's plain. That applies to a lot of music of his, as you know, and he used the word above his own music a lot. Sometimes I'd bring him a piece of mine, and he'd say, "I wish it were plainer, it's too chromatic," or, "There are too many notes in that chord," or, "It should be spaced more plainly." It's not Aaron to be either ecstatic or in the depths of despair, or anger, or fear, or guilt, or dancing in the streets, or making a fool of himself by celebrating. I mean, you can't quite picture Aaron in a Mardi Gras parade, can you? Can you imagine Aaron wearing a ring, a jeweled cufflink? It's unheard of! Or wearing some kind of natty leisure suit? Plain, plain, plain! It goes with Appalachian Spring and Our Town, which I think of as a self-portrait of Aaron. No conspicuous consumption. He wasn't miserly, just pinch-penny. It was part of his plainness, it was part of thrift. One of those Puritan virtues like being fair—you're thrifty. It was not easy for Aaron when he was young to be a social success. But if you make those feelings positive as he tended to do, instead of living in dejection with them as negative feelings, the way was to adopt the route of plainness. And make a virtue of that, which then could be, and was, and is, attractive in a very special way.

Aaron was the most moderate man I've ever known. I'll give you an example of what I mean. I came to New York once, and we met for breakfast. Aaron ate either in the Empire or in the Horn & Hardart across the street. But I seem to associate this with an Empire Hotel dining room. Aaron didn't seem his usual bubbly self. I've had a lot of breakfasts with him. He'd take The New York Times, and open it—he'd read the headline first and then, "Who died?" This was very cheerful—a look at the obituaries, and then he felt caught up. It was always in a kind of giggly way, that kind of Aaron we know. But that one breakfast, he was not saying anything and not reacting to what he was reading. I said, "Is something the matter?" And he said, "Well, I have a headache. It's nothing, it'll go away." I found out later that day, or maybe it was the next day, that his father had died the night before. Talk about moderation! And all I could get out of him was, "Well, you know, I have a headache." I think that is a key story about Aaron Copland. It has to do with being a "sober citizen," a "judge-nose," as a friend used to call him. Who, at one point wrote "Into the Streets May First!" and lived to regret it and never wrote anything else like that. At Tanglewood, when we had composers' forums

*every Monday night at the Lenox Public Library, Aaron was the modera-
tor, and he was a perfect moderator. Seeing both sides. But he had very
conclusive opinions of his own. It's just that he was always ready to admit
the possibility that there was a question about the opinion he held. Only
once have I seen Aaron angry. But that is not to say he did not have inner
passions. They seemed to go into his music, a rare combination of spontaneity and care.*

*I never forget a Copland birthday. Two of the most important events of
my life happened on 14 November—the first in 1937 when Aaron and I
met for the first time. Actually it begins before that. When I was a student
at Harvard, Arthur Berger introduced me to Aaron's* Piano Variations *by
taking me in to Briggs & Briggs, our music store, where they had little
booths where you could listen to things, and he said, "I think you ought to
hear this." It was Aaron playing his* Variations *on that old Columbia
record. I went crazy about this piece. Enter David Prall, my great philosophy professor, who was a music fan. David bought me the sheet music because I couldn't afford it, and he also bought himself a little piano, so that
I could play it for him. I wrote a paper in my aesthetics course, which I
took with David, on the* Variations. *There's a third person involved in the
beginning, and that was a graduate student, who was the librarian of Eliot
House, and his name was I. Bernard Cohen. I.B. has been the head of the
History of Science Department at Harvard for years. He became a very
good friend of mine—why, I don't know, because I was this little junior
and he was a fancy graduate student, who knew more about Isaac Newton
and everything else than anyone in the world. He had a great love for
music and poetry. One evening we found ourselves in Jordan Hall in Boston, attending the out-of-town debut of a dancer called Anna Sokolow,
then married to composer Alex North, who wrote all the music for her
dancing and was playing in the wings. We became real fans of this girl,
who was then completely unknown. When we went back for autographs,
she was terribly moved, and said, "Oh, you must come to my debut in
New York," which was on 14 November 1937.*

*In those days for me to go to New York was a whole business. I didn't
have the money or the time—I was a provincial Bostonian, Harvard
Schmarvard, it wasn't so many years since I had discovered there was such
a thing as a world of music and concerts, things you could go to, and that
people could buy a ticket and go to hear Rachmaninoff play a recital in
Symphony Hall. (How amazing. I mean, to think how provincial, and how
restricted I was in the ghetto created by my father.) I.B. called a friend of*

his in New York named Muriel Rukeyser, the poetess. (In those days we said "poetess.") The poet, and a very good one, too. He arranged with her to procure tickets, because she was going to the Sokolow debut. I saved up, and we took the train and went to New York, and found ourselves sitting in the first row of the first balcony at the Guild Theatre. We were old hands, we had seen this in Boston, we were the experts on Anna Sokolow. For everybody else in the front row of that balcony it was news, and so I guess we were looked at with some sort of bemused interest by the others, because we seemed to know so much about Anna's repertoire. I think Muriel was sitting on my left, and I.B. to her left, and on my right sat this unknown person, with buck teeth and a giggle and a big nose, of a charm not to be described, and when I was introduced to him, and found that it was Aaron Copland next to whom I was sitting, I could have been blown away—I was blown away. Because I had become a lover, a fanatic lover, of the Piano Variations, and in fact I had learned them and spoiled many a party by playing them when people'd say, "Oh, come on, Lenny, play something." I could empty the room, guaranteed, in two minutes by playing this wonderful piece I had just learned by Aaron Copland, whom I pictured as a sort of patriarch, Moses or Walt Whitman–like figure, with a beard, because that's what the music says. It's hard as nails, as Moses was hard as nails, with his tablets and prophesying and shattering those two tablets of the Law, and then trying again. I had this kind of connection in my mind between Moses and Aaron. And so I was shocked to meet this young-looking, smiling, giggling fellow, whose birthday it happened to be.

Aaron was giving a party for himself at his loft. He invited everybody in that row, which were all sorts of people like Muriel Rukeyser, Virgil Thomson, Paul Bowles, and Edwin Denby, poets and literary people, musicians, Rudy Burckhardt the photographer, and of course Victor Kraft. He invited all of us in the row to attend this party. It was my real introduction to New York and to the elite sort of artistic community. It was there that, in conversation, Aaron discovered I was his great fan and that I knew the Piano Variations. He said, "You do? A junior at Harvard knows ..." "Yeah." So he said, "I dare you to play it." And I said, "Well, it'll ruin your party, but ..." He said, "Not this party." So I played it, and they were all—he particularly—drop-jawed. And it did not empty the room. I was then learning the Ravel Concerto too, so I played some of that, and I remember distinctly Paul Bowles, sprawled out on some sort of studio-bed that everybody was sitting on, saying in that rather perfumed drawl of his, "Oh, Lenny, ne Ravelons plus (Let's not Ravel any more)."

Copland and Bernstein, 1941.

He was very witty. I don't remember anything more, except I thought Aaron Copland was about the most sensational human being I'd ever come across, and with the passage of many decades, I haven't changed my line. The only trouble is I don't see him enough anymore, because he doesn't go out much, and I don't go out much—I mean that would be an expedition. But I do miss him. I do miss him very much, and I miss his music. We had a personal relationship, of course, that was very strong. He had to come to Boston for something soon after that, and so he came and he stayed in the guest quarters of Eliot House where I lived, and we went to the performance of Saloon, *as we used to call it—"Play the old* Saloon*." Whenever he came to Boston, we saw each other, and the times I came to New York, we always saw each other. We'd take walks in the park, and—I mean, he was a friend. And, after all, he was almost two decades older than I was.*

I graduated from school in '39. I went to New York to look for a job. Didn't find one. Ran out of money. Couldn't pay for a meal. Adolph

Green had sublet an apartment on East 9th Street, which had a Steinway grand in it of all things, and he said if I would chip in with him, we could have it for the summer. So I did. Aaron set up a visit with Davidson Taylor at CBS for me, and he couldn't have been nicer and kinder, but he said, "We just don't have a job at the present time." Aaron called some other people. None of them worked out. I got to the end of that unbearable hot summer in that dirty 9th Street apartment, full of roaches—but there was that Steinway. I remember working on "Lamentation" there.[13] Whatever I wrote, I showed Aaron. And that's the closest I ever came to studying composition with anyone. But Aaron's criticism was as good as years of composition study as far as I was concerned. He wouldn't go into great detail, but he would say, "That note is not fresh, because you've just used it here," or, "All this whole section sounds like warmed-over Scriabin— out! Throw it away, but this is good. Work on that." So it was stylistic more than anything else, with some formal commentary, but he never talked about my sense of harmony or counterpoint or any of the things that I suppose a composition teacher would have done.

When he made a four-hand arrangement of Billy the Kid, I remember playing it with him, which is how I learned the piece, really. I think that was the first time anybody had played it with him. I felt most honored about that. He'd just finished it. I had a similar experience with Rodeo later on at Jacob's Pillow, when he had to play it for Agnes de Mille the first time. There was a party after a performance for the cast backstage, or something like that, while we were playing Rodeo for Agnes, and the people backstage were furious because we were ruining their party with all the noise. (Agnes recalls it somewhat differently in her book.) I wrote about sixteen bars of Rodeo for Aaron where he needed a jazzy barroom piano sequence on one of the tunes.

I finished the summer of '39 with no job, and went back home in defeat with $4 left in my pocket. There I was, twenty-one, a Harvard graduate, and nowhere to go, nothing to do. Aaron had a house in Woodstock that summer, and he invited me to come up in my loneliness and despair. So I went there for a few days to study some scores and get them into my head. I remember sitting on the train to Woodstock with these scores in front of me, trying to memorize them for an upcoming conducting audition with [Fritz] Reiner in Philadelphia and saying, "Oh, my God, this is terrible."

I arrived in Woodstock, and there was Aaron with two or three cats in his house, to which I'm allergic. It was hay fever season, too, around the beginning of September. All the pollens of Woodstock were out, but these *two or three cats—I became so ill with these running eyes and sneezing and swollen—I could barely see the notes of the score I was trying to prepare, and it was in this condition I arrived in Philadelphia for my audition with Reiner. I was accepted at Curtis. My father gave me $40 a month to live on, barely enough to pay my room rent at one of these boardinghouses they had for Curtis students. Also Mitropoulos sent me money. My God, the generosity of that man! Every once in a while he'd just send me a check from Minneapolis. It was that year I got $25 for doing Saloon for piano for Aaron. Then I made the two-piano arrangement, and I think I got $50 for that, or maybe another $25. And then that summer, Koussie opened Tanglewood, and that was—maah!—such an explosion in my life.*

Tanglewood was wonderful. I came in as a student, and Aaron came in as head of the composition department, but we both became so close to Koussevitzky. Aaron and I were close anyway, and that's what that first summer at Tanglewood seems to be about—meeting Koussevitzky, becoming insanely close like his son. He adored Aaron, Aaron adored him, and that summer for me was about them. It was a marvelous summer. Hindemith was one of these guys who just loved music and poured out some that was great, some that was terrible, and some that was everyday. It was always recognizably Hindemith, with masterpieces every once in a while. But Aaron was the exact opposite. Music streams out of him and, God knows, there is fluidity and prolificity, but he is a maniac for "la note choisie," as he always put it. You have to find "the note that costs," I remember him saying after he first came back from Hollywood where he had been paid, really for the first time, a substantial amount to write music for a commercial purpose. We were playing Of Mice and Men, *a score I fell in love with, and I said, "Oh, I love that F sharp in the bass," or whatever it was. And he said, "That's the note that costs." It was a variation on Nadia's "la note choisie."*

Aaron and I have Tanglewood in common ("Tangleberg" or "Tanglefoot," as we jokingly called it). Aaron had a charming house in Stockbridge in 1941 and the same one in '42 where younger composers and performers were almost always welcome. I saw composers come from all over the world to study with Aaron. He used to talk to me about conducting at Tanglewood and would ask me things and say, "I really can't ask Koussie to give me lessons!" Aaron developed his own sort of grinning style, and it was good and got better. Only for one piece, I think it was Appalachian Spring, did Aaron really come to me for advice.

In New York, I often saw Aaron with Clurman. The fact that he and

Harold Clurman were roommates in Paris amazed me. It is one of the most incredible facts about Aaron Copland. And they loved each other so! When I talked to Harold about Aaron, his face would light up. But can you imagine two less likely roommates?

I worried and complained terrifically during the early forties and always took my troubles to Aaron, who would tell me to "stop whining." He seemed to have such complete confidence in me that he didn't show a bit of surprise when on Sunday, 14 November 1943, I made a dramatic success by filling in for the ailing Bruno Walter and conducting the New York Philharmonic. All Aaron's predictions came true. And on his birthday.

I conducted Aaron's Third Symphony in Prague in 1947. The Symphony has become an American monument—like the Washington Monument or the Lincoln Memorial or something. I particularly love the third movement. In 1947, I wrote to Aaron that the last movement needed a cut, and Aaron adopted that cut. His use of Fanfare in the *Symphony is a matter of musical economics and that's Aaron's thrift again. (*Fanfare has *become the world's leading hit tune.) Some of the* Symphony's *last movement is just gorgeous—those high, fleeting, hovering things. And there's a tune there, "Because I'm Leaving Cheyenne" ["Goodbye, Old Paint"], that should be the Tanglewood hymn with words written to it to be sung every year at the closing ceremonies.*

I have conducted at many a Copland event, most recently for several eightieth-birthday celebrations. Conducting Lincoln *with Aaron himself as narrator had a special poignancy and appropriateness. You know, Aaron always had some kind of identification in his mind between plainness and Abraham Lincoln.*

Americans on the home front were gathering their resources. I wrote to Archibald MacLeish, Chief Librarian of Congress, who was serving as Director of War Information, to offer my services, and he referred me to Harold Spivacke, Chief of the Music Division, serving also as Music Chairman for the Army and Navy. But Spivacke responded, "I really cannot advise you about the possibility of getting into the army at the present moment. . . ." Therefore I was delighted to receive a letter from Andre Kostelanetz suggesting I compose a patriotic work: a musical portrait of a great American. He put teeth into the proposal by offering to commission such a piece and to play it extensively. Andre explained (18 December 1941):

Next summer I am conducting a number of concerts with major symphony orchestras. The first part of each program will consist of standard symphonic repertoire, and the second part of the program will be devoted entirely to three new works by American composers. These three works have a correlated idea in that they are to represent a musical portrait gallery of great Americans. . . . Some of the personalities which occur to me are George Washington, Paul Revere, Walt Whitman, Robert Fulton, Henry Ford, Babe Ruth. . . . In addition to approaching you on this matter I am writing to Virgil Thomson and Jerome Kern.

My first choice was Whitman, but when Kern chose Mark Twain, Kostelanetz requested that I pick a statesman rather than another literary figure. Lincoln was a favorite during the war years.[14] Furthermore, I recalled that my old teacher, Rubin Goldmark, had composed an orchestral threnody in 1918, "Requiem Suggested by Lincoln's Gettysburg Address."

Lincoln seemed inevitable. When Virgil and I discussed our choices, he amiably (and wisely) pointed out that no composer could hope to match in musical terms the stature of so eminent a figure as Abraham Lincoln. Virgil, who had been making musical portraits of famous people for years, chose two living subjects: Fiorello LaGuardia and Dorothy Thompson. I had no great love for musical portraiture, and I was skeptical about expressing patriotism in music—it is difficult to achieve without becoming maudlin or bombastic, or both. I was hoping to avoid these pitfalls by using Lincoln's own words. After reading through his speeches and writings, I was able to choose a few excerpts that were particularly apposite to America's situation in 1942. I avoided the temptation to quote only well-known passages, permitting myself the luxury of only one from a world-famous speech. The order and arrangement of selections are my own. The first sketches of *Lincoln Portrait* were ready in February 1942, and the entire work completed by mid-April, the orchestration following a few weeks later. The musical material is original with the exception of two songs: Foster's popular "Camptown Races" and a ballad first published in 1840 under the title "The Pesky Sarpent," but better known as "Springfield Mountain." In neither case is the treatment literal; the tunes are used freely as in *Billy the Kid*.

Lincoln Portrait is a thirteen-minute work for speaker and full orchestra, divided roughly into three sections. In the opening, I hoped to suggest something of the mysterious sense of fatality that surrounds Lincoln's personality, and near the end of the first section, something of his gentleness and simplicity of spirit. I was after the most universal aspects of Lincoln's character, not physical resemblance. The challenge was to compose something simple, yet interesting enough to fit Lincoln—I kept finding myself back at the C-major triad! The first section opens with a somber sound of violins and violas playing a dotted figure that turns into a melodic phrase by the eighth bar; the second subject is a transformed version of "Springfield Mountain." This section ends with a trumpet solo, leading without pause into an unexpected allegro for full orchestra. The second section is an attempt to sketch in the background of the colorful times in which Lincoln lived. Sleigh bells suggest a horse and carriage of nineteenth-century New England, and the lively tune that sounds like a folk song is derived in part from "Camptown Races." In the conclusion, my purpose was to draw a simple but impressive frame around the words of Lincoln himself—in my opinion among the best this nation has ever heard to express patriotism and humanity. The quotations from Lincoln's writings and speeches are bound together by narrative passages, simple enough to mirror the dignity of Lincoln's words. For example, "That is what he said, that is what Lincoln said." And, "He was born in Kentucky, raised in Indiana, and lived in Illinois. And this is what he said. . . ." The background music in the final section, while thematically related to the orchestral introduction, is more modest and unobtrusive, so as not to intrude on the narration. But after Lincoln's final ". . . shall not perish from this earth," the orchestra blazes out in triple forte with a strong and positive C-major statement of the first theme.

After Kostelanetz received the finished score, he wrote (19 April 1942): "I cannot tell you how happy I am about the Lincoln portrait. You have written a magnificent work which I believe, aside from its wonderful musical value, will convey a great message to the American public. I want to thank you again for dedicating it to me." Andre asked only that his exclusive performance rights be extended to spring 1943. As he wrote in his autobiography: "Nineteen forty-two was probably the year when morale was lowest. . . . That spring seemed a good time for the *Lincoln Portrait*."[15] *Time* magazine reported, "Three composers went to work on a job usually reserved for painters. The results, four works for symphony orchestra: Copland's *Lincoln Portrait*, Kern's *Portrait for Orchestra (Mark Twain)*, Thomson's brassy *Mayor LaGuardia Waltzes* and *Canons for Dorothy Thompson*. Kostelanetz commissioned the works for performance during the summer concert rounds he will make with his diminutive wife, coloratura Lily Pons. Next week, three of the portraits will have their premieres in Cincinnati." The premiere took place on 14 May with the Cincinnati Symphony Orchestra, William Adams as speaker. Goddard Lieberson covered the concert the following day for the *New York Herald Tribune*: ". . . Mr. Kostelanetz was able to get from the composers what he wanted, music for large masses of people. And, in the vernacular, he hit the jackpot. . . . I want to record that I have not seen so excited an audience for some years as was this Cincinnati one upon the completion of Copland's *Lincoln.* . . ."

Kostelanetz conducted the piece in several cities; audiences seemed to be moved and critics were kind. "Kosty" had a noncommercial recording made in Toronto with a speaker whose British accent sounded odd for *Lincoln.* I wrote to Ben Britten (16 June 1942): "Reports say that audiences get all excited by it. Moral: you can't go wrong with the Gettysburg Address to end a piece (Why not try Magna Carta?). I hope to hear a live performance in July." In Hollywood Clurman went with Odets and Eisler to hear *Lincoln* performed with Edward G. Robinson narrating—the actor who always played a tough guy in the movies! Harold wrote (15 August 1942): "Odets said he was proud of you, Eisler said, 'a good job.' . . . The audience was held. *I* was held, as nearly always with your music. . . . I wanted to hear it again, was sorry it ended so soon and had a feeling that the audience desired more. I would have wished it more ample in dimension and duration." In Washington the Fourth of July concert of 1942 featured *Lincoln Portrait* and was given on a barge in the Potomac with the Lincoln Memorial in the background. Carl Sandburg agreed to narrate. When it was over and there was no applause at all, Carl said to Andre, "We were a flop." But Kostelanetz soon realized the audience had been moved beyond applause, and he reminded Sandburg that Lincoln himself had heard no applause after delivering his Gettysburg Address. When the concert was repeated in Washington on 15 July, I was in the audience for my first "live" hearing of *Lincoln Portrait.* As Andre mounted the open-air podium not 500 feet from the Lincoln Memorial, he recognized Mrs. Franklin D. Roosevelt, senators, congressmen, and members of the cabinet in the audience. It was seven months after Pearl Harbor; the country was in grave danger. After the concert Andre told me that he felt Lincoln's words "with a terrible new clarity," and we both knew that the audience felt it also.

The first radio broadcast of *Lincoln* took place on Andre's regular CBS Sunday afternoon program, 16 August, again with Sandburg as speaker. I was invited to say a few words of introduction. Sandburg, always a great popular success, added a dimension to the work, being Lincoln's biographer and a famous American poet in his own right. A fine recording was made of *Lincoln* with Kostelanetz and Sandburg that went out of circulation (as did two other early versions featuring Melvyn Douglas and Kenneth Spencer as narrators). Kosty enjoyed telling Sandburg stories. There are two lovely ones about the poet's guest appearances as speaker in the work when he was getting quite old. About to do *Lincoln* again, Kostelanetz invited Sandburg, thinking, "Oh well, if he doesn't read the speaker's part too well, everybody will understand. After all, he is such a distinguished gentleman, and he fits the role." So he invited the poet, and somewhat to his surprise, Sandburg accepted. At the morning rehearsal, during the section of the piece before the speaker stands up to narrate, Sandburg complained about feeling chilly, so someone miraculously found a blanket and put it over him. The rehearsal resumed, and everything proceeded smoothly. On the evening of the concert, Kostelanetz asked his advisers, "Do you think we ought to give him the blanket? He is liable to feel chilly again." "Well," they said, "the audience will understand. After all, he is such an old man, nobody will mind, so let's give him the blanket." They spread it over him and the concert began. During the orchestral introduction the speaker is seated onstage for ten minutes. Kostelanetz was conducting, and the time came for Sandburg to get up. But when the conductor motioned to him, there Sandburg was, fast asleep under the blanket! Kosty, in a stage whisper, called, "Carl, Carl," and the old boy, obviously confused, staggered to his feet, looked around as if to say "Where am I?" Fortunately he recovered his senses just in time to pronounce the opening line: "Fellow Citizens! We cannot escape history."

On another occasion, twenty years after the first memorable Washington concert, Kostelanetz wanted Sandburg for *Lincoln* again—this time for the opening of the Lincoln Center Promenade Concerts of 1962. He went to North Carolina to make the request in person. Sandburg was evasive and would not make a commitment. Finally when it was time to leave, Andre asked Carl's wife, Paula, why Sandburg was reluctant. It seems that the poet did not want to appear in public wearing glasses! Eventually it was worked out: since the concert was being televised, Carl could use the new invention, the Teleprompter, without his glasses. The audience knew nothing about it; in fact, they and the critics marveled at the poet's extraordinary memory. But Sandburg had been warned about the strong television lights, so he closed his eyes during the introduction, this time on purpose. Poor Andre was panic-stricken, thinking Sandburg had fallen asleep again! But all went beautifully.

Koussevitzky conducted *Lincoln Portrait* with the BSO, with Will Geer

as narrator. The program on 3 April 1943 also featured the first performance of Schuman's *A Free Song* for chorus and orchestra. John Burk,
Koussevitzky's assistant, sent reviews of *Lincoln* to me in Hollywood. I
wrote to thank him (23 April): "The advantage of having so large a batch
at one time is that they all cancel each other out. The nicest report you
sent was that of the Doctor's enthusiasm." Elliott Carter heard the BSO
performance and wrote (1 May): "Koussevitzky did not catch the subdued
power and mystery at the beginning, and the scherzo was too brilliant because of K's nervous beat. Geer was a bit too folksy...."

One performance of *Lincoln* I remember vividly was in Caracas, Venezuela. The concert was held in an enormous outdoor stadium with a capacity of I don't know how many thousands of people. I was conducting, and
the speaker in the *Portrait* was a Venezuelan actress, Juana Sujo. She was a
fiery young thing, and very impressive at the rehearsals. Just five minutes
before the concert was to begin, there was an announcement backstage
that the local dictator with his entourage was about to arrive for the concert. This amazed everybody because, as I was told, he had always been
afraid of appearing in public for fear that someone might take a shot at
him. Sure enough, they had to delay the start of the concert until he arrived. He walked into the stadium with a group of ten or twelve hench-
men. They were all seated in the first row. He was much hated,
particularly by my soloist, the fiery actress, and she was out to get him, so
to speak. When she got to the end of the piece, which was also the end of
the concert, she recited with great emphasis the lines: "Government *of* the
people—*Por* el pueblo y *para* el pueblo"—the whole audience of about
6,000 people stood up and started screaming and yelling and applauding.
They told me that six months later that particular dictator was out of
power, deposed! I was given credit for starting that revolution. I am sorry
to add that two years later the dictator was back in power.

A not-so-happy occasion in the history of *Lincoln Portrait* was "the
Busbey incident." This refers to the banning of my piece for performance
at the Eisenhower inauguration. It was scheduled for the Inaugural Concert at Constitution Hall in January 1953, but Representative Fred E.
Busbey, Republican of Illinois, objected on the grounds that I had alleg-
edly associated with Communist front groups. Strange as it seems today
that such a work could come under suspicion, during the McCarthy period
these allegations were not unusual. Busbey said, "There are many patriotic
composers available without the long record of questionable affiliations of
Copland. The Republican Party would have been ridiculed from one end

Photograph by Marc & Evelyne Bernheim.

>: Carl Sandburg narrating
:coln Portrait.

:ddle: Adlai Stevenson narrating,
pland conducting, rehearsal for a
formance of *Lincoln Portrait*,
visohn Stadium, New York City,
nday, 12 July 1964.

:tom: Coretta Scott King, Copland
:ducting.

of the United States to the other if Copland's music had been played at the inaugural of a President elected to fight communism, among other things." Claire Reis was so furious, she fired off a telegram on behalf of the League of Composers. "No American composer, living or dead, has done more for American music and the growth of the reputation of American culture throughout the civilized world than Aaron Copland. To bar from the Inaugural Concert his music, and especially music about Abraham Lincoln, will be the worst kind of blunder and will hold us up as a nation to universal ridicule." But the Inaugural Committee stood by its decision.

When Richard Nixon was Vice President, he attended a concert of my music and during intermission, expressed enthusiasm for *Lincoln* to Mrs. Paul Hume, wife of the well-known critic. He said he had once been asked to narrate it, but hadn't wanted to appear to be aping Lincoln. Nixon explained that he was sorry he hadn't ever heard the piece earlier. Mrs. Hume responded, "Well, you might have, except for a change of plans" (she was, of course, referring to the Busbey incident). Nixon quickly changed the subject. A decade or so after the Busbey incident, the United States Information Agency chose to distribute *Lincoln Portrait* with the narration translated into Arabic, Bengali, Burmese, Cambodian, Chinese, Greek, Hindu, Hungarian, Indonesian, Latvian, Lithuanian, Polish, Portuguese, Spanish, Turkish, Ukrainian, Urdu, and Vietnamese. Times change.

Lincoln Portrait was not intended as a strictly musical work. It is for a large audience and special occasions. *Lincoln* was a piece "made for use"—in this case, Kostelanetz' wartime programs. I never expected it to be performed frequently, but my publisher tells me *Lincoln Portrait* is played even more often than *Appalachian Spring*. During the Bicentennial, when Lenny went on a national and international tour with the New York Philharmonic, William Warfield narrated *Lincoln* in English, German, and French for the appropriate audiences. It was amusing to hear: "Citoyens, nous n'échapperons pas à l'histoire ... c'est ce qu'il disait, Abraham Lincoln." I had never thought of narrating *Lincoln* myself, nor did anyone else until Bill Schuman put together a Copland festival at Juilliard in 1960 and invited me to speak the part. On the occasion of my eightieth birthday at the all-Copland gala at the Kennedy Center, I found myself at the podium again, Lenny conducting. President and Mrs. Carter appeared in their box for the first time in public since Carter's defeat in the election a few weeks earlier. Rosalynn Carter had once spoken the narration, and she was particularly anxious to hear *Lincoln* that evening. When they appeared in the presidential box, a full house stood to cheer them, and my closest friends and relatives sat with President and Mrs. Carter as I spoke Lincoln's words about the country and the presidency. It was a poignant moment.

After the first recordings, others featured Hollywood actors as narrators: Henry Fonda, with myself conducting the London Symphony Orchestra; Charlton Heston, Maurice Abravanel with the Utah Symphony; Gregory Peck, Zubin Mehta and the Los Angeles Philharmonic. These actors adopt understated approaches compared to Sandburg's earlier spunky rendition. Adlai Stevenson's convictions and his stature as U.S. Representative to the United Nations gave his performances and the recording (with Eugene Ormandy and the Philadelphia Orchestra) a special appropriateness.[16]

Two activities became habitual whenever I returned from an extended trip out of New York: first, an appraisal of my financial situation; next, a visit with Claire Reis, who would bring me up to date with everything that was going on. Since it was December, the end of the year, I added up my income for 1941. The "most successful American composer" at age forty-one had earned a total of $4,557.61, made up of small royalty amounts from Boosey, Arrow, Birchard, McGraw-Hill, Ballet Caravan, and Columbia Recordings (for $.48 and $.80). Other fees were culled from occasional lectures, writing and teaching—the mainstay, the Berkshire Music Center's $1,000 for the previous summer. I still had plenty of reason for being "pinch-penny." It was uncomfortable and unnerving to live from one small amount to the next, particularly in wartime when regular sources might become nonexistent at any moment. I was sorely tempted to accept a teaching position (with pension guaranteed) offered me at Brooklyn College, but just then, I received the commission of $1,000 for *Lincoln* from Kostelanetz.

Minutes of the Executive Committee of the League and letters from Claire had trailed me around South America, so I knew that my first obligation was to host the tea in honor of Juan José Castro and to speak informally about my experiences in South America (16 December 1941). Next, Claire let me know (painlessly, over tea in her lovely sitting room) that it was up to me to choose and locate film segments for an event to be held at the Museum of Modern Art on 8 February 1942, billed as "Hollywood Fiction Pictures with Distinguished Musical Scores by Americans and Europeans—Running Comment by Aaron Copland." (It seems that no one at the museum knew anything about the subject.) I chose segments from the following: *The General Died at Dawn,* music by Werner Janssen; *Once in a Blue Moon,* Antheil; *Juarez,* Erich Korngold; *So Ends Our Night,* Gruenberg; *Ladies in Retirement,* Ernst Toch; *Citizen Kane,* Bernard Herrmann; and *Of Mice and Men.* We distributed a questionnaire and a summary of the technical and expressive problems involved in composing music for motion pictures and had a lively discussion after the "concert."

During this period, the League and many other groups were concerned with Russian War Relief. At the request of the Union of Soviet Composers, letters and telegrams were exchanged and music was sent to Russia, but nothing was heard from the Russian group after their country went to war with Germany. We began to hear a great deal of Russian music—Shostakovich was the biggest hero. Interviews with the Russian composer in Moscow about works written while Leningrad was under siege were printed in *The New York Times.* They greatly interested the American people and affected attitudes among composers. Shostakovich said, "I consider every artist who isolates himself from the world as doomed. . . . I think an artist should serve the greatest number of people. I always try to make myself as widely understood as possible, and if I don't succeed I consider it's my own fault. . . . I'm writing about the man in the street. . . ." Dmitri Kabalevsky also became a familiar name. In fact, Kabalevsky seemed to be performed more than any American composer that season.

I finally had a performance of *Statements for Orchestra* in its entirety by the New York Philharmonic, Mitropoulos conducting (7 January 1942). But, as I wrote to Robert Palmer (25 January 1942): "The big success of the winter has been Bill Schuman's *Third Symphony.* . . ." I had felt for some time that here was "a big talent." Bill was typical of young American music of the time—left of center, but more tonal and less experimental than the generation that came of age in the twenties. Schuman's work reflects his personality—full of drive and conviction, not lacking in emotional content, with a love of the grandiose and a wonderful eloquence.

William Schuman [17]

One evening, about a year after Frankie and I were married in 1936, we were invited to a party at the studio of Harry Cumpson, a pianist who was playing new music. I met Aaron for the first time there, and I recall hearing a recording of The Second Hurricane *that evening. We began to see* each other at ACA meetings and other musical events around town, and then Aaron was on the jury (which included Harris, Riegger, and Sessions) for a contest sponsored by the Musicians' Committee to Aid Spanish Democracy for which the prize was a performance and other rewards. My Second Symphony won, and Aaron came to the concert. The WPA orchestra was made up of people who, for the most part, had never played in a symphony orchestra before. They were there because they needed work—not because they could play the music. But Aaron realized what was happening, and he listened to the symphony again when it was selected for broadcast on CBS. (In those days, when you were performed over the radio on a Sunday afternoon, there would be reviews the next day across the entire United States. People paid attention to those radio orchestras.) A few months later, a postcard came from Aaron. To show how long ago that was—it was a penny postcard. On it, he wrote simply: "Please send the score of your symphony to Serge Koussevitzky, 88 Druce Street, Brookline, Mass." So I did, and some weeks later, a letter came saying Koussevitzky would perform the work and wanted to meet me when he was next in New York. Tickets were left at the Carnegie Hall box office, and after the concert, Aaron and Roy Harris took Frankie and me backstage. In bringing my music to Koussevitzky's attention, Aaron once again gave a young composer an incredible boost.

In 1938 Aaron wrote a few sentences about my music in Modern Music, an important endorsement, using the power of his pen as another way of helping a young composer. Aaron is ten years my senior, which doesn't mean anything now, but it was a big difference then—Aaron was already established, and I was just beginning. He was always wonderfully generous with his time when I took him scores, although I was not his pupil in the formal sense. Once when I was very much the neophyte, I showed him fifteen or twenty measures of music for a ballet (later abandoned), and he said: "Well, when you have some music, I really want to see it. It looks like a good beginning." Aaron was always tactful.

As a teacher, Aaron was extraordinary. There have been great teachers—Hindemith, for example. But he taught his pupils how to be little Hindemiths—no mean trick. Copland would look at your music and try to understand what you were after. He didn't want to turn you into another Aaron Copland. He would sit down at the piano, read through a score, and make comments. When he questioned something, it was in a manner that might make you want to question it yourself. Everything he said was helpful in making a younger composer realize the potential of a particular work. On the other hand, Aaron could be strongly critical. And he could become angry if he felt that a composer, through influence, had attained some position that he did not deserve. Because of his agreeable disposition, Aaron is never thought of as being exacting, and this does him an injustice.

From the late thirties on, Aaron came to our home at least a few times a year, I visited his loft often, and Frankie and I drove up to Tanglewood several times. We stayed with him on our first visit in 1941. I was composing my Fourth Symphony, and I brought the score with me to show to Aaron. About the Second Movement, he said: "I want to question the ending." Because he questioned it, I saw some things that I could criticize myself. So I changed it, and the ending worked very well. In the late fall and winter of 1942, we gave Aaron our house in Larchmont for a month or more, where he finished his Piano Sonata.

Through Aaron I became involved with the League of Composers, and I was even on the board for a short time. I thought it a doctrinaire organization, and whereas Aaron was not dictatorial, the satellites around him, especially the boys writing for Modern Music, were. The magazine was important through the distinction of its major contributors. Aaron was powerful there also, but he didn't seek power. His power came because not only was he one of the leading composers, but a natural leader. Aaron's use of power was constructive—he would take things in which he saw merit and promote them.

One evening in his loft, Aaron played a recording of Lincoln Portrait for me. I was very moved by it. After I heard it several times "live," I decided that for me, the popular nature of Lincoln took it out of the class of his other works, which repaid with additional hearings. I wrote to Aaron, who was then in Hollywood, "The best time for Lincoln is the first." His response was: "If it's played only on Lincoln's birthday I'll be happy enough." Many years and many performances later, Aaron accepted my invitation to narrate Lincoln for a special benefit concert at Juilliard. It was the nineteenth of February 1960, and the first time Aaron ever spoke the part. We had marked an "x" on the floor where he was to stand, but when the time came, he forgot to stand on that spot. Consequently, he was out of range of the microphone. But he projected a Lincolnesque aura, so he got away with it.

The year I became president of Juilliard, 1945, we talked about a teaching position for Aaron. We discussed it a lot. One day we took a long walk, and I remember precisely what he said: "You know, I just can't get myself

William Schuman (far right) meeting with composers in Virgil Thomson's apartment at the Chelsea Hotel. Copland (standing right) and (left to right): Samuel Barber, Thomson, and Gian Carlo Menotti.

to take a job. I've never had a regular job, and that's what's bothering me." Aaron came very close that time. Actually, he accepted, and then changed his mind. He just didn't feel right about it.

In 1955 for the fiftieth anniversary of Juilliard, we commissioned Aaron to compose a new composition for the festival of American music. The result was the Piano Fantasy, the third of Aaron's major piano works. It was not finished until 1957, but was well worth the wait. For his sixtieth birthday, we planned an all-Copland week at Juilliard. We showed the film, The City, Aaron gave a public lecture, and many of his compositions were performed, among them, In the Beginning, Nonet, and scenes from the opera The Tender Land. Aaron is a composer with an extraordinarily high percentage of successful works. If his catalogue is not the largest in quantity, it is prodigious in quality. And each work bears his stamp, yet each is special unto itself.

I was to change my thinking about Lincoln Portrait; in it, the Copland

353

sound sets the musical frame which embodies the text and gives fresh and added dimension to Lincoln's compassionate utterances. In compositions such as Rodeo and Billy the Kid, the Copland sound transforms traditional American folk material into the most sophisticated art by discerning potentialities in simple music that could only be perceived by an artist of extraordinary imagination. What an amazing musical world Aaron makes out of songs like "Bury Me Not on the Lone Prairie" and "Sis Joe." Aaron is, of course, no mere populist. His compositions include music of the most esoteric complexities. To the uninitiated it could almost seem as though there were two separate composers at work. Not so, for the same Copland sound that informs the popular music is, in its unique way, heard in the masterworks he has created in every medium.

Aaron has earned the highest regard from his peers. He is the object of our affection and esteem because we recognize his preeminence. Contrary to the ancient wisdom that holds, "two vinegar salesmen can't be friends," composers of serious art music do have a spirit of camaraderie, and nowhere is the letter and spirit of this communal concern so apparent as in the person of Aaron. The core of our appreciation is, of course, for the astonishing scope and diversity of his music. What he has given us is that Copland sound—the unmistakably distinctive personal utterance. In its most popular vein, it can be perceived as national. By now it is hard to imagine anyone who has not been stirred by the noble sound of Fanfare for the Common Man. We've all heard it countless times both in the original and in dilution from legions of imitators. But no second-hand user can ever supplant the master, because the true Copland sound is not a mark of identification that can be divorced from the context in which it is heard.

There have been stretches of time when Aaron and I, because of heavy professional commitments, have not seen each other. But I cannot think of a single occasion or decision in my composer's life that I did not report to Aaron and benefit from his encouragement and friendship. We worked together on more committees and boards than I can even begin to name here, and we have had the satisfaction in our lifetimes of seeing this country change from one that imported virtually all its performing artists and exported all its students, to one that exports the greatest performers all over the world and imports students to study here.

Aaron's birthdays were celebrated with gatherings of distinguished colleagues and friends. My role in each of these events was master of ceremonies. Aaron and I shared these occasions so often that a standard repartee developed. I might say: "Introducing Aaron is my favorite pursuit—not *highly remunerative work, but steady." Aaron would get up and say, "I'm a lucky guy."*

There were other public gatherings that gave me the opportunity to speak seriously and thereby to return a little where I had received so much. It was, after all, in large measure through Aaron that we had the first emergence of a truly indigenous American art music. A whole school of composers came into being in this country while Aaron was at the center as teacher, composer, and critic. If Aaron can say, as he has, that music is "one of the glories of mankind," then we can say, and we do, that Aaron is one of the glories of music.

In the spring of 1942 Bill Schuman invited me to Sarah Lawrence College, where he had been teaching since 1935, to hear his students perform my two choral pieces; I made an occasional visit to Ben Britten and Peter Pears, safely out of Europe and living in Brooklyn; and I took a quick trip to Boston to see Lenny's production of *Hurricane*. But mostly, I stayed home composing. I had to finish a composition commissioned by Hugh Ross, conductor of the Schola Cantorum, to honor the first conductor of the Schola, Kurt Schindler, who had been responsible for bringing to light many unknown and forgotten folk songs.

I chose a "dance-song" from Schindler's final publication, *Folk Music and Poetry of Spain and Portugal.* "Las Agachadas" (no. 202) is a song from Burgos in northern Spain. The words of my song are those in Schindler's book. I had seen and heard groups in South America sing such pieces, and I hoped to give "Las Agachadas" a realistic native feeling. It is written for two groups of singers—solo group and an eight-part mixed chorus. I gave up the idea of instruments when I realized that the larger group could represent a village band, simulating an accompaniment by singing a thrumming refrain. The solo group is instructed to sing "with the freedom of a peasant style."

The Schindler Memorial Concert took place at Carnegie Hall on 25 March 1942. The dancer Paul Draper interpreted some of the "dance-songs," and the Schola Cantorum performed the commissioned pieces. These were by Bernard Wagenaar, Juan José Castro, Chávez, Cowell, Pedro Sanjuán, Deems Taylor, and myself.

One day in April Agnes de Mille phoned. She had an idea for a ballet that she wanted me to hear about.[18] Franz Allers, musical director of the Ballet Russe de Monte Carlo, took me to her studio. When she started to

Oliver Smith, Agnes de Mille, and Copland at Tanglewood, 1942.

tell me about it being a cowboy ballet, I immediately said, "Oh no! I've already composed one of those. I don't want to do *another* cowboy ballet! Can't you write a script about Ellis Island?" But Agnes countered with, "This is going to be different." And then she got up and loped around her studio, showing me some of the steps she was going to use. "Well," I said, "I'll go home and think about it." I came to the conclusion that since De Mille was a very different person from Eugene Loring, it was bound to be a very different ballet. Loring was interested in legendary figures and grandiose effects, while Agnes was after something lighter and more bouncy. So I telephoned her and said, "I'll do it."

She sent me a scenario titled simply: "American Ballet by Agnes de Mille." It began: "This is the story of the Taming of a Shrew—cowboy style. It is not an epic, or the story of pioneer conquest. It builds no empires. It is a pastorale, a lyric joke . . . the quieter and gentler and simpler the style the better. There are never more than a very few people on the stage at a time . . . one must be always conscious of the enormous land on which these people live and of their proud loneliness. . . ." The story was simple—about a cowgirl infatuated with the head wrangler on a ranch. She dresses and acts like a man, hoping to impress him. Agnes also sent a "time-plot" mapping out sequences to the minute. This is a sample of what I had to work with: "Hoe-Down, 4 minutes. Introduction—16–24 measures—girl appears. Pause and silence for about 4 counts while she faces boy. Dance begins on walk—hit a fiddle tune hard. Verse and chorus with brass yells and whoops. Vamps in-between, long tacet toward close for tap cadenza, 8 measures of frenzy. Kiss, tacet or pianissimo. Finale windup—the beginning of the tune again, curtain comes down as the big promenade starts."

The finished ballet did not deviate from Agnes' original script. Agnes sent suggestions for tunes—one with a good "riding rhythm," one called "Ground Hog," and another for the waltz she had heard in Virgil's film, *The Plow That Broke the Plains.*[19] I enjoyed composing the waltz and welcomed "Buckaroo" and "Hoe-Down" as opportunities for some lively rhythmic sections. Agnes was to rehearse the Ballet Russe in July, so she needed the music as soon as possible. By the time I left for Tanglewood in late May of 1942, I had much of *Rodeo* in my head and had only to write it all down.

Agnes de Mille [20]

The title became Rodeo *when [Sol] Hurok wanted something short for advertising, so "The Courting at Burnt Ranch" became a subtitle. It was subsequently dropped altogether. The Ballet Russe had no idea who I was; although it was fourteen years after my first public appearance, I had no reputation, nothing. But it was wartime, and they wanted an American ballet on an American theme by an American. I said, "That would be nice in this country." They didn't know what that meant—nightclubs, probably. I didn't like most of the Ballet Russe pieces, I thought them pretentious. When I made my suggestions for a cowboy ballet, the company manager complained to his colleagues in Russian that I would probably ruin the Ballet Russe.*[21] *Martha Graham advised me, "You be arrogant. If you are not rude, they won't respect you." So I dug in my heels and said I wanted the best American composer for the music, Aaron Copland. Aaron had done Billy, and it was strikingly new and very good. Even earlier than Billy, I had been working on cowboy-style dances and had performed them*

WILLIAM DE MILLE
MANTOLOKING
NEW JERSEY

43 East 9
New York City
Sept. 2, 1942

Dear Aaron—

I showed the management the completed ballet this afternoon and they think they have a smash success. Me, I can only pray and insist on rehearsals up until the opening. But the enthusiasm was terrific.

I'll show you the ballet as soon as you come. It'll be better next week.

back to the beginning of the waltz with first ending, no repeat—then straight on for 9 measures—
i.e. 20 measures of the waltz exactly as it was at the beginning omitting the repeat and the 2nd ending

Then
₮ p. 3 measure 16— (or exactly where he left off) right through as written.

Briefly— on p. 3 of the waltz between measures 25 and 26 we insert measures 1-20 inc. from page 1— (I don't count the upbeat as a measure) So that

now for the musical changes we've made 2 repeats—

1). In the beginning of the ranch house scene with the piano we repeat measures 27— 47—
i.e.— beginning with the 2nd measure after the 2nd ending— it's marked "legato— freely—" where the the theme starts on D.

2) At the end of the waltz. After the 6th measure— "after" the men return"— Tempo I. the key changes— 6 measures as written then

clear?

And is that satisfactory? It was absolutely necessary to me for 3 reasons. costume change Choreographic pattern, drama development.

If there's anything you don't understand for God's sake yell—

Oh Aaron, maybe I've done something good. I can't believe it yet. there's so much that seems crude.

Keep in touch

Agnes

I want to call it "Burnt Ranch Rodeo"

Letter from Agnes de Mille about *Rodeo*.

in London. *I went for my interviews to Ballet Russe in clothes borrowed from my sister. After [Sergei] Denham hired me, Florine Stettheimer was suggested for the scenery, but I didn't want her, so the young unknown Oliver Smith was asked to make some sketches for* Rodeo. *They were brilliant. I said, "Make some more." They weren't so brilliant. He had hit on it the first time. "There's one proviso," I said to Denham and associates, "I dance the lead at the opening night in New York." At that they just fainted. "Take it or leave it," I said. They took it, giving me $500 for the ballet for five months' work. (Later, I got $12.50 and then $8.50 royalties. It was a sliding scale, you see—downward.)*

Aaron finished the score and played it for me up at Jacob's Pillow in Lee, Massachusetts, where I was working for a few weeks with Ted Shawn and Ruth St. Denis when the new theater opened. Aaron was teaching at Tanglewood, and he called when the score was ready and came over with a young friend. I didn't know who he was. They came after an evening's performance, and I told Shawn and the company that I was going to do a new ballet for Ballet Russe, and wouldn't they like to hear the score? While Aaron and his friend were at the piano, I looked around and realized there was nobody there to hear him. Not a soul but my mother and me! I thought, "This is very odd." But Aaron said, "I have got to do it and go. It's getting late." So we started. I got more and more excited and finally I was just screaming, yelling and dancing. He'd written the music on transparent paper that kept slipping, and during the waltz it fell to the ground. The boy with Aaron kept pushing the music back in place. Aaron said to him, "Could you play the treble part? I can't play it." This boy played wonderfully. I said in the waltz part, "Aaron, this section is pretty dull." He giggled, and said, "I think it is, too. I'll do something about it." The friend said, "You'd better!" I remember thinking, "Of all the impudence! To talk to the Maestro like that!" The boy was Leonard Bernstein.

At the end I was yelling and dancing and heard rustlings behind the scenery. I followed the whisperings and went up a stairway, opened a door, and there was Shawn and the entire company in a long line. "For God's sakes," I said, "I asked you to come down. Weren't you interested?" And Ted Shawn said, "Agnes, it's because of music like that that we are having war." "You're joking," I said. And he looked at me and said, "No." And I looked around at the company and asked, "He's making fun of me, isn't he?" The cast said, "Oh no." And all of them dead serious. Shawn said, "I find this the reverse of music. It is a step backwards." I said, "Well, they are downstairs, can they have a drink or something to eat? What shall I do—tell them they've caused a war and reversed civilization?" Shawn said, "I repudiate their music. But I welcome them as human beings." With that he threw open the door, and Aaron and Lenny came in and sat on the floor, giggling and whispering together—in a rather naughty manner, but they had felt very put out by this extraordinary ostracism. I think Shawn must have been just plain jealous of my opportunity to do this ballet. After all, he'd never been asked by Ballet Russe.

As planned, I appeared to rehearse Rodeo in New York in July, but I got more and more nervous and angry with the Ballet Russe management because they didn't schedule rehearsal time. And this dance needed extra work, since the classically trained Russian dancers weren't used to this kind of dance at all. They found my American folk-dance formations unnatural, and the emphasis on comedy and acting was difficult for them to come to terms with. It didn't seem possible that we would open that fall after all. I wrote to Aaron in exasperation, and I wrote an angry and threatening letter to Denham. Well, finally, we got under way. I'd have to talk to the girls about gestures they knew nothing about: "Do you know what a corset is? Do you know what you wore under it? Do you know what the bones are and what they stick into? And how you have to stretch to get it comfortable? You girls haven't got an inch of flesh—no breasts, no hips, no nothing, so you don't know what these girls in Rodeo had to do in order to settle themselves before they were armed for a battle to get a man."

Rodeo has to be performed by very fine actors with real sincerity. If it's done just for easy laughs and quick effects it's cheap as hell and just slides by and doesn't mean a thing. When I was onstage, it mattered to me. That girl was fighting for her happiness. I used to stand there with real tears pouring down my face—I couldn't get the man I wanted and I didn't think I'd ever have any man. You can't imagine some of the letters people have had the idiocy to write me—one said that Women's Lib should take action against this ballet! Well, in 1895 or 1900 a woman had to have a man or she was considered an outcast and became the family drudge.

During rehearsals I realized we needed a little more music in one spot. Aaron was still at Tanglewood; for some reason I couldn't phone him, and you couldn't send a wire because of the war. It had to be an emergency—you couldn't wire and say, "Must have four bars of music." And so I had to write, and Aaron refused. I didn't like it at the time, but he was right; it would have distorted the form. So I put in a tacet.

Aaron and I didn't do any further work on the score again after he played it for me at Jacob's Pillow, and he didn't see Rodeo until a few days

Courtesy Agnes de Mille Dance Collection, The New York Public Library.

Agnes de Mille in the premiere of Rodeo.

before our opening in New York. The cast was scared to death. That opening night—16 October 1942—I gave the performance of my life. I got twenty-two curtain calls. A telegram came afterwards from the Theatre Guild asking me to come talk to them about their new musical show, Green Grow the Lilacs, *with words and music by Rodgers and Hammerstein. (When it opened it had the title* Oklahoma!*) As for* Rodeo, *the business manager of Ballet Russe soon realized that this strange American ballet was their meal ticket; there were seventy-nine performances in 1942* and 1943 alone! When I was traveling with the company in Rodeo they gave me $3 a day expense money, total, to live on. I turned in my Pullman ticket and sat up in coaches with the soldiers, who were all over the place by that time. It was rough going. I carried my clothes in a straw basket so I wouldn't have to pay porters. Out west I stayed with families, but in San Francisco I remember a disreputable place I shouldn't have gone near, as a young woman. Rodeo has stayed in the ballet repertory. In 1976, a year after a severe stroke, I supervised the ballet for the Joffrey company from a wheelchair, and it was a major success.

In the fifties I asked Aaron to compose another ballet for me using sea chanties, but he said he didn't want to repeat himself. Then in the seventies we met at the Harvard Club, and I asked him again for music for a ballet, but he said, "Agnes, I don't think I'm ever going to compose anything else. I'm having such a good time conducting." And I said, "Aaron, that's too bad because there are lots of good conductors and there will be more. There's only one of you as a composer. One. And it's you we need." He asked, "Have you ever conducted?" I looked at him and said, "You know, Aaron, I've been asked a lot of damned fool questions in my life, but this tops them all."

It happens that one of the works I particularly enjoy conducting is Rodeo. After Franz Allers led it in 1942, the Ballet Russe invited me to take the podium at the Metropolitan Opera House in 1948. Years later in 1976, I conducted the American Ballet Theatre production. I am told that Rodeo is one of the most popular of all American ballets. Inevitably it was compared with Billy the Kid. The New York critics, John Martin and Irving Kolodin, praised Rodeo. Kolodin in the Sun wrote: "The Ballet Russe de Monte Carlo awoke to find itself with a genuine American ballet today, and is it surprised! . . . Many curtain calls for Miss de Mille, the performers, Mr. Copland and a believable amount of vocal enthusiasm from the large audience. However, Mr. Copland's bow, a mixture of a lope and a curtsy, seemed also to have been choreographed by Miss de Mille. . . ." Audiences and critics cheered the ballet when the company went on tour. In Chicago Claudia Cassidy wrote in the Daily Tribune (26 December 1942): "Rodeo is a smash hit. What Miss de Mille has turned out in this brilliant skirmish with Americana is a shining little masterpiece." Cassidy praised Kermit Love's costumes and Oliver Smith's settings as well as my score: "Not the least of its wisdoms is asking the orchestra to put down its instruments and clap rhythmic hands in the square dance scene."

It is particularly gratifying that *Rodeo* has stood the test of time. A revival in 1972 by the American Ballet Theatre with Christine Sarry in the leading role was described by Anna Kisselgoff in *The New York Times* (7 January): "*Rodeo* looks new rather than dated. Its interweaving of real and stylized folk steps, unforced humor and unpretentious atmosphere have the mark of virtuosity as well as obvious charm." Personally, I never think of *Rodeo* without Agnes. She gave depth to the role, while still being hilariously funny. It was the De Mille choreography that made *Rodeo* a blend of serious ballet and musical comedy, and the work catapulted Agnes into a fabulous career, one that would change the entire look of the American musical theater.

It seemed fitting to extract an orchestral suite from the ballet—*Four Dance Episodes from Rodeo* was published in 1943. It omits only five minutes of music from the complete ballet, and like the original score, the suite calls for slightly enlarged orchestral forces. The piano takes an important role, as is often the case in my scores. The first section, "Buckaroo Holiday," is the most complex of the four. Included are variations on two folk tunes, "If He Be a Buckaroo by His Trade" and "Sis Joe." I used a rhythmic device to achieve a lilting effect that, together with some unprepared key changes, make for a comic touch, further emphasized by the use of a trombone solo in introducing the "Buckaroo" folk song. Extended pauses further exaggerate the syncopation. "Sis Joe" also undergoes rhythmic transformation before both tunes blend in a canonic treatment for full orchestra. "Corral Nocturne" is characterized by woodwind solos in 5/4 time. I was striving here for a sense of the isolation felt by the heroine. In "Saturday Night Waltz," the third episode, country fiddlers are heard tuning up, followed by hints of the tune "Old Paint." The tempo is a slow 3/4 with the accompaniment of 6/8 as a cross rhythm. The final movement, "Hoe-Down," is the best known and most frequently performed of the four episodes.[22] Two square dance tunes are included: "Bonyparte"[23] and a few measures of "McLeod's Reel" played in folk fiddle style. Pizzicato strings and xylophone add a comic effect to "Bonyparte," and the music winds down like a clock before the tune returns for the last time. Arthur Berger has described "Hoe-Down" (along with *El Salón México*) as "virtually photographic."[24] *Four Dance Episodes from Rodeo* was first performed by the Boston "Pops" under Arthur Fiedler on 28 May 1943.

363

Tanglewood in the summer of 1942 was different from the two previous seasons. The Center began as usual with a ceremony followed by tea in the garden. Viewing the peaceful scene, few would guess the bitter battle fought by Koussevitzky to make possible the opening of the Music Center that year. With wartime gasoline shortages, the Berkshire Music Festival had been canceled. But to close the school as well was *not* possible—at least to Koussevitzky. When his board of trustees stood firm against him, the Maestro threatened to pay for running the Center himself. The Koussevitzky Music Foundation was incorporated in memory of Madame Natalie Koussevitzky, who had died early in 1942. With the Maestro's own funds and contributions from several individuals, the Berkshire Music Center summer of 1942 was saved. A large student orchestra, divided into "first" and "second" groups, worked daily with Koussevitzky and his assistants. To the amazement of all, a series of public concerts was announced in place of the BSO Festival concerts. (Lenny Bernstein and Lukas Foss worked with the second orchestra along with three other specially chosen conducting students, Frederick Fennell, Walter Hendl, and Robert Zeller.) There were many chamber music concerts, Olin Downes' lectures, and a production of Nicolai's *Merry Wives of Windsor* by the opera department. I taught a course in twentieth-century music, and the Composers' Forums were initiated at the Lenox Library and patterned on the popular Town Hall Forums of the Air. We discussed topics such as "What About Opera?", "Government Support of the Arts," "Music Education for Non-Professionals," "Nationalism," and so forth. The subjects seemed new and fresh then, and we even thought they were solvable. But I have seen the same topics up for discussion year after year, right up to the present day.

Koussevitzky had another major disappointment before the opening of the BMC in 1942—Stravinsky, who had agreed to teach, canceled. However, Koussevitzky was fortunate in engaging the noted Czech composer Bohuslav Martinu in his place. Among my student composers were Pablo Moncayo, Allen Sapp, Blas Galindo, Harold Gramatges, Barbara Pentland, and Romeo Cascarino. Martinu's list included Alan Hovhaness, Owen Reed, Spencer Hoffman, Frank Amey, and John Cowell. Once the Center opened, it was a great effort for me to finish *Rodeo*, but I had promised Agnes to have the score ready before the end of the summer. I worked too hard, yet as I wrote to Ben Britten, who had returned to England in June: "It's wonderful being back—so relaxing and peaceful. I'm doing a frothy ballet for the Monte Carlo people on the usual wildwest subject—full of square dances and Scotch tunes and the like. . . ."

Koussevitzky conducted the "first" student orchestra on 12 August in a program that included Howard Hanson's *Third Symphony* to an enthusiastic audience. But it was the concert of 14 August that caused a sensation. The entire day was billed as a Russian War Relief Benefit. Lukas conducted the "second" orchestra in *Billy the Kid* in the afternoon. A supper intermission followed, and in the evening, Koussevitzky conducted the "first" orchestra in the American premiere of Shostakovich's *Seventh Symphony*. This work, composed during the siege of Leningrad, had elicited enormous public interest and much advance speculation in the press as to who would be given permission to conduct the first American performance. Toscanini was granted the first radio broadcast, and Koussevitzky was given permission for the premiere public performance. It was Koussevitzky's courage and skill in proceeding with his student orchestra instead of with the BSO that amazed everyone. But he knew just what he was doing—Koussevitzky was out to show his board of trustees and the world of music what could be accomplished at the Music Center. What better way than by presenting this much-discussed new symphony by the controversial Dmitri Shostakovich? Excitement grew as dignitaries, ambassadors, and newspaper critics arrived in Lenox. We all invited guests—mine were Marc Blitzstein, Robert Palmer, and David Diamond. The reviews for Koussevitzky and the orchestra were unanimous in praise, but divided on Shostakovich—the composer Koussevitzky considered as great as Beethoven. Following the concert, Olin Downes wrote in *The New York Times*:

> In a neighboring box sat Princess Juliana of the Netherlands. The occasion was brilliant and imposing, like the finale of the symphony, which at the close of a highly dramatic interpretation, received an ovation, which lasted for a good ten minutes, of a shouting, cheering audience which rose to its feet as it extended this homage to the distant composer, to the land and the cause which his symphony symbolized, and to the conductor and the student orchestra, which had carried out his wishes with a spirit and technical proficiency that elicited the highest praise. . . . Aside from the question of the actual value of the score, the performance tonight could be summarized in terms of unsparing praise of all that Koussevitzky and his American boys and girls did in proclaiming Shostakovich's message. Not a point in the score was missed. . . . the conductor more than vindicated his vivid comprehension of the symphony, the prowess of the young players whom he had assembled and drilled, in the short space of five weeks, for a really heroic task.[25]

The closing ceremony of the Berkshire Music Center in 1942 was conducted in an atmosphere of apprehension. The future of the school was in danger, and we all knew it. Worse, we recognized that many of the talented young artists we saw that day were facing futures far different from what Dr. Koussevitzky's Music Center had prepared them for. Within a year's time Koussevitzky had lost his wife and his great dream. The school and the festivals became war casualties in spite of the successes of 1942; neither would resume in full force until 1946.

A brief return to New York convinced me to make a change from the Hotel Empire to a place in the country. I rented a small cottage, Dellbrook Farm, from Mary and Bill Lescaze for $30 a month, caretaker included. Located in Oakland, New Jersey, it was not far from New York. I set to work reviewing my film scores; it struck me that a suite might successfully mirror in musical terms the wide range of American scenes in the three films for which I had written music, *The City*, *Of Mice and Men*, and *Our Town*. The result was *Music for Movies*, a suite in five movements for small orchestra. None of the music was transcribed literally from the films. The greatest modifications come in the opening and closing sections. All were reorchestrated from full orchestra to small ensemble. "New England Countryside" is based largely on the title music of *The City*; "Barley Wagons" originally accompanied an outdoor landscape in *Of Mice and Men*; "Sunday Traffic," also derived from *The City*, serves the purpose of a scherzo in the suite; "The Story of Grover's Corners" was developed from *Our Town*—it was a kind of theme song in the film; and "Threshing Machines" was compiled from several dramatic scenes in Steinbeck's story. *Music for Movies* is dedicated to Darius Milhaud, whom I considered a pioneer in the field of film music. The first performance was at the Town Hall Forum concert of 17 February 1943.

Claire Reis had invited several composers to write pieces for the League's twentieth anniversary, to be celebrated at a concert sponsored by Town Hall on 9 December 1942. I felt that Claire and the League deserved a big vote of thanks from composers, and I was pleased to be included. Also, her request gave me the incentive needed to put to paper some musical ideas that had been in my mind since my earlier trips to Cuba. *Danzón Cubano* was composed for two pianos in the fall of 1942 while I was staying at Dellbrook Farm. It is based on Cuban dance rhythms, particularly the *danzón*, a stately dance, quite different from the rhumba, congo, and tango, and one that fulfills a function rather similar to that of the waltz in our own music, providing contrast to some of the more animated dances. The special charm of the *danzón* is a certain naive sophistication. Its mood alternates between passages of rhythmic precision and a kind of nonsentimental sweetness under a nonchalant guise. Its success depends on being executed with precise rhythmic articulation. *Danzón Cubano*, six minutes in length in two contrasting sections, makes use of four simple Cuban dances—simple from a melodic standpoint, but with polyrhythms and the syncopated beat typical of the Cuban *danzón*. I did not attempt to reproduce an authentic Cuban sound, but felt free to add my own touches of displaced accents and unexpected silent beats. In fact, I arranged one of the tunes in the traditional "blues rhythm," giving the final product something of an inter-American flavor. At the premiere, the work was called *Birthday Piece (On Cuban Themes)*. As commentator for the program, I explained to the audience that *Danzón Cubano* was "a genuine tourist souvenir."

Lenny played the premiere of *Danzón* with me. This was not the usual League of Composers audience, but a subscription concert of the Town Hall Endowments Series. It seemed that everything, including *Danzón Cubano*, was too "moderne" for them—until the final piece by Louis Gruenberg, which incorporates the familiar "Man on the Flying Trapeze." Claire and I agreed that it was a good thing Schoenberg's contribution had not been ready in time to be included.

Danzón Cubano was soon picked up by duo piano teams wanting to expand their repertoire, and it is often paired with *El Salón México*. I was pleased when requests for the music came from Mexico and Latin America. In the forties Leo Smit made an arrangement of *Danzón* for solo piano; I prepared an orchestral version in 1946, taking full advantage of the Cuban rhythms to make use of an interesting battery of percussion. It has become better known than the original two-piano version. The Baltimore Symphony under Reginald Steward gave the premiere of the orchestral version on 17 February 1946, and Lenny conducted it soon afterward with the BSO as well as for its New York premiere with the Rochester Philharmonic at a Gershwin Memorial concert on 16 March. The choreographer Eliot Feld used my music for a dance also called *Danzón Cubano*, pairing it with another of his works, *La Vida*, to my *El Salón México*. Feld and I participated in a "Dance in America" television program at which we discussed various aspects of the choreographer's relationship to music. Eliot asked me why my *El Salón* is longer than *Danzón Cubano*, and I replied jokingly that it was probably because I had spent so much more time in Mexico than in Cuba. In a more serious mood, Feld remarked that he related to certain jazz phrases and to the reconciliation of the classical traditions with the present day in my music.

Eugene Goossens, conductor of the Cincinnati Symphony Orchestra, had written to me at the end of August about an idea he wanted to put into action for the 1942–43 concert season. During World War I he had asked British composers for a fanfare to begin each orchestral concert. It had been so successful that he thought to repeat the procedure in World War II with American composers.[26] Goossens wrote: "It is my idea to make these fanfares stirring and significant contributions to the war effort, so I suggest you give your fanfare a title, as for instance, 'A Fanfare for Soldiers, or for Airmen or Sailors.' I am asking this favour in a spirit of friendly comradeship, and I ask you to do it for the cause we all have at heart. . . ." As with *Lincoln Portrait*, I was gratified to participate in a patriotic activity. Goossens, a composer himself, suggested the instrumentation of brass and percussion and a length of about two minutes. He intended to open the concert season in October with my fanfare, so I had no time to lose. I composed an introduction for the percussion, followed by the theme announced by trumpets, and then expanding to include groups of brass. The challenge was to compose a traditional fanfare, direct and powerful, yet with a contemporary sound. To this end, I used bichordal harmonies that added "bite" to the brass and some irregular rhythms. The music was not terribly difficult to compose, but working slowly as was my custom, I did not have the fanfare ready to send to Goossens until November. I had some difficulty with the title. The piece has been *Fanfare for the Common Man* for so long that it is surprising to see on my sketches that other titles were considered: *Fanfare for a Solemn Ceremony, for the Day of Victory, for Our Heroes, for the Rebirth of Lidice, for the Spirit of Democracy, for the Paratroops, for Four Freedoms.* . . . After I decided on *Fanfare for the Common Man* and sent the score to Goossens, I think he was rather puzzled by the title. He wrote, "Its title is as original as its music, and I think it is so telling that it deserves a special occasion for its performance. If it is agreeable to you, we will premiere it 12 March 1943 at income tax time. . . ."

I was all for honoring the common man at income tax time. Since that occasion, *Fanfare* has been played by many and varied ensembles, ranging from the U.S. Air Force Band to high school groups who transpose the piece because their trumpets cannot quite manage the high C. A band arrangement of *Fanfare* has been made, but the instrumentation often is

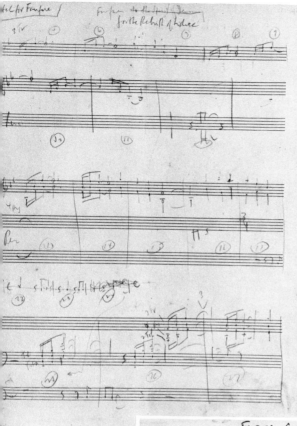

Sketch page of *Fanfare for the
[Comm]on Man* with early provi-
[sional] titles.

Manuscript, first page of the
[sco]re of *Fanfare for the Common
[Man]*.

Copland composing *Danzón Cubano* for the League of Composers 20th Anniversary Concert.

adapted to particular needs—in 1983, Notre Dame's band performed the piece with one hundred clarinets! *Fanfare* was played at the ground-breaking ceremony for Lincoln Center with President Eisenhower in attendance and for the Nixon presidential inauguration. It was used to introduce the "Omnibus" television series in the fifties, for the Olympics, and by John Curry, who skated to *Fanfare* at the 13th Winter Olympiad. *Fanfare* is often played at events that have to do with outer space. Recently it was used to announce the television celebration of the Centennial of the Brooklyn Bridge. To my amazement, several "popular" musicians also have taken up *Fanfare*. Woody Herman asked to arrange it in something called "boogaloo style." I must admit that my initial response was, "What's that?" The popular Emerson, Lake, and Palmer group made two versions of *Fanfare*—one was so similar to my own that I wondered why they wanted to do it at all. After that, Keith Emerson felt more comfortable about showing me his more original version. They took *Fanfare* on

370

tour, as did Mick Jagger with a version by the Rolling Stones. While I have listened with interest to these arrangements, I confess that I prefer *Fanfare* in the original version and as I used it later in the final movement of my *Third Symphony*. At the the time I composed *Fanfare for the Common Man* I was becoming anxious about my financial situation, since *Danzón Cubano* and *Fanfare* were both contributions to causes I wanted to support. Little did I think in the fall of 1942 that these works, composed for particular occasions, would be used so frequently.

To mark the twentieth anniversary of the League of Composers, *Modern Music's* first issue of 1943 was to be a special edition titled "Two Decades in Review." Minna invited me to prepare an article summing up the period.[27] I wrote about the recognition of the American composer at home and abroad, and about the composer's entry into the world of business in order to take responsibility for his own affairs. I pointed to the startling differences resulting from radio broadcasting and phonograph recording. Finally, I chastised critics and historians for "the lack of serious, critical, full-length studies of compositions by American composers." (No one had followed Paul Rosenfeld's early lead; nothing similar to *An Hour with American Music* had been published since 1929.)[28] In conclusion, I wrote: "It is true that nobody wants to write 'modern music' any more. Yet the modern movement has been historically sound and musically fruitful. . . . it was an exciting time for musical ideas and works. We can consider ourselves lucky if we produce as vital a progeny in the next twenty years."

Notes

Various lists will be included in the Appendix to the second volume, among them: a chrono-logical listing of musical works with first performance information; literary writings; and bib-liography. In the following notes, the reader is asked to assume that when a music publisher is not cited, that publisher is Boosey & Hawkes. Similarly, when the location of autograph material (drafts, scores) is not given, the source is the Library of Congress. Interviews are noted in two ways: one for those in the Yale Oral History, American Music project; the other for interviews conducted specifically for this book. The footnotes were prepared by Vivian Perlis.

INTRODUCTION, THE MITTENTHALS AND THE COPLANDS

1. The reason was probably anti-Semitic in origin. Nicholas I was rigorous in attempts to secularize the Jewish population.

2. Vishtinets (Polish, Wisztyniec), a small border town in what was East Prussia, now the Russian part of the Soviet Union, east of Kaliningrad (formerly Königsberg). The town is not indicated on modern maps. According to the family, half of the house in Vishtinets was in Germany, the other half in Russia.

3. They were Jessie, Pauline, Hannah, Philip Nathan, Jacob, and Max.

4. Only a trickle of several thousand came before 1870, about 40,000 in the 1870s, and approximately 2 million in the 1880s. See Irving Howe, *World of Our Fathers*, Chapter I, "Toward America" (New York: Harcourt Brace Jovanovich, 1976), pp. 5–25.

5. The family has had a long and successful merchandising history in Dallas. Ephraim's daughter, Hattie, married Meyer Lichtenstein; their daughter, Minnie, married Herbert Marcus, one of the original founders (with Al Neiman) of the Neiman-Marcus store.

6. They were named Jacob and Abraham. Copland's "Uncle Abe" became the family historian, an unofficial position assumed after Abe's death in 1954 by his son, Arnold Mittenthal.

7. Since family opinions varied on Aaron Mittenthal's death date, a search was made at the Bureau of Vital Statistics, establishing the fact that he died 12 March 1896 at age fifty-nine.

8. Interview, Selma Gordon Furman with Vivian Perlis, 13 December 1979, New York City.

9. Interview, Felice Copland Marlin with Perlis, 12 April 1981, New York City. The song was the sixth verse of "Glory! Glory! Hallelujah!" The first line is, "They will hang Jeff Davis to a tree." See *Grand Army War Songs*, ed. Wilson Smith (Cleveland: Brainard's Sons, 1886), pp. 54–56.

10. Shavli (Lithuanian, Siauliai), a town in Lithuania, now part of the Soviet Union, still has the same name.

11. Several theories have been put forth concerning Copland's name. See Edward T. Cone, "Conversation with Aaron Copland," *Perspectives of New Music*, VI:2 (Spring-

Summer 1968), pp. 57–72; repr. in *Perspectives on American Composers*, ed. Benjamin Boretz and Edward T. Cone (New York: W. W. Norton, 1971), pp. 131–46.

12. Copland's grandparents, Frieda and Sussman Kaplan, lived the rest of their lives in Brooklyn and died in their late seventies only a few months apart in 1918. They had eight sons and daughters, twenty-six grandchildren, thirty-one great-grandchildren, and eighteen great-great-grandchildren.

13. This and all following data pertaining to Harris M. Copland's real estate interests were obtained from the City Register of Kings County, Brooklyn.

14. H. M. Copland bought a style 1 walnut upright with stool on 4 November 1905 for $625 (special price because previous piano was defective). Later, on 23 April 1919, he bought an O ebony grand for Aaron: 5' 10½" long, for $1,050 with a $250 trade for the upright. (Information from Steinway & Sons, New York.) The grand piano was sold in 1921 when Copland was in Paris and the family left Washington Avenue.

15. For Uris information, see interview, Harold Uris with Perlis, 25 November 1980, New York City.

16. Irving Copeland, Fanny and Arthur Abrams' son, took the name Copeland as a youngster after his father died. Interview, Irving Copeland with Perlis, 7 April 1981, New York City.

17. Harris had invested in a silk business in addition to the store, probably in Manhattan, that suffered losses in the early twenties.

18. Interview, Madeleine Uris Friedman with Perlis, 4 May 1981, New York City.

Brooklyn, 1900–1921

1. Aaron Copland, "Composer from Brooklyn," *Magazine of Art*, 32 (September 1939), pp. 522, 523, 548, 549, 555. Repr. in Aaron Copland, *Our New Music* (New York: Whittlesey House, 1941), pp. 212–30; and in rev. edn., *The New Music 1900–1960* (New York: W. W. Norton, 1968), pp. 151–68.

2. Founded in 1855, Baith Israel Anshei-Emes was known as Brooklyn's "Mother Synagogue."

3. Israel Goldfarb (1880–1967) founded the School of Sacred Music of the Hebrew Union College–Jewish Institute of Religion. He is known as the father of congregational singing in synagogues.

4. Charles-Louis Hanon, *The Virtuoso Pianist in Sixty Exercises for the Piano for the Acquirement of Agility, Independence, Strength and Perfect Evenness in the Fingers as Well as Suppleness of the Wrist*, translated from the French by T. Baker (New York: G. Schirmer; Boston: Boston Music Co., 1900). Copland has identified some exercises in his Juvenilia file as "probably by Wolfsohn."

5. Also described in an interview, Martha Dreiblatt with Perlis, March 1981, New York City.

6. Correspondence from Copland to John Kober was provided by Kober. Seeing these letters in 1980, Copland commented, "I must have been trying to look artistic!"

7. "Auf Flügeln des Gesanges."

8. Kober admits that he did not understand Copland's harmonies, but he valued their piano sessions and missed them when his friend went to France. Interview, Kober with William Owen for Perlis, 22 April 1981, Garden City, New York.

9. Ernst Friedrich Eduard Richter, *Manual of Harmony*, translated from the German by John Morgan (New York: G. Schirmer, 1867); Arthur Foote and Walter Spalding, *Modern Harmony in Its Theory and Practice* (Boston & New York: Arthur Schmidt, 1905).

10. Ives compiled a list of prominent musicians, Goldmark among them, to whom he sent free copies of his *Second Piano Sonata* ("Concord, Mass., 1840–1860") in January 1921. See Ives Collection, Yale Music Library, New Haven, Connecticut.

11. "I had my lesson right after his, and Goldmark would tell me, 'Here's this very talented fellow, really extremely musical and gifted, so I give him fugues to write and look what he brings me!' And Goldmark would show me these advanced things of Copland. . . ." For Leopold Godowsky II's memoir of Goldmark's comments on Copland, see interview with Perlis, Oral History, American Music, Yale, September 1970, Westport, Connecticut. Godowsky died 18 February 1983.

12. In Copland's Juvenilia file are six books (undated) of studies with Goldmark. In book two Goldmark wrote: "Avoid parallel fourths. Do not let voices be more than one octave apart. . . . The above is not good. Avoid unisons and octaves as much as possible." Also included are a fugue for four voices and a movement of a piano sonata.

13. Aaron Schaffer, *Selected Poems* (Boston: The Poet Lore Company; The Gorham Press, 1916).

14. *The Call* was published daily in New York from 1908 to 1923.

15. In Copland's Juvenilia file: *Poème* (December 1918) and *Lament* (circa 1919) for cello and piano (incomplete). *Lament* makes use of a traditional Hebrew melody. Also dating from this period are a trio and arrangements of several Chopin *Preludes* for cello and piano.

16. Aaron Schaffer died 24 February 1957, Austin, Texas.

17. "Melancholy" (4 September 1917), subtitled "à la Debussy," text by Jeffrey Farnol; "Simone" (16 September 1919), text by Remy de Gourmont; "Music I Heard" (7 April 1920), text by Conrad Aiken.

18. Early piano pieces include *Moment Musicale*, subtitled "a tone poem" (28 May 1917); *Waltz Caprice* (March 1918); *Danse Characteristique* for four-hands (1917 or 1918); and *Sonnets I, II, III: Sonnet I*, "GF" (Gus Feldman); *II*, "A.V." (Arne Vainio) with a quotation from Aiken at the head of the page; *III*, also "A.V." with a quotation from Sandburg. The first of these was removed from this series by Copland to become the second of *Three Sonnets*.

19. Phillip Ramey gave the first performance of No. 1, "Amertume," 22 November 1980 at "Wall-to-Wall Copland," Symphony Space, New York City; the complete *Trois Esquisses* were performed and recorded in 1981 by Leo Smit to whom they are dedicated. The pieces were published as *Three Moods* (I. "Embittered"; II. "Wistful"; III. "Jazzy") in 1981. Sketches reveal that the group was originally planned as "four moods." Copland labeled the third of the four, "Petit Portrait," a "supplement." The subject was a school friend, Abe Ginsburg, who, according to Copland, was "rather moody and unhappy with himself." The first three notes—A-B-E—spell his name and are heard as a motive throughout. "Petit Portrait" is published in *Aaron Copland Piano Album*, ed. Leo Smit (New York: Boosey & Hawkes, 1981).

Fontainebleau, Summer 1921

1. Copland played the Beethoven *Sonata*, op. 90.

2. For some reason, Copland did not study with Philipp after all.

3. Among Copland's manuscripts are the pieces mentioned here as well as several exercise books from Fontainebleau with markings in pencil, probably by Vidal or Bloch.

4. This must have been "Jazzy."

5. The concert was at the Salle Gaveau for the benefit of l'Association Nationale des Anciens Élèves du Conservatoire de Musique et de Déclamation.

6. Interview, Harold Clurman with Perlis, 20 May 1979, New York City. Clurman died 9 September 1980.

7. According to a review by E. Gilles from the Paris newspaper *La Seine et Marnais* of 3 September 1921, which Copland sent to his family with a note that it was "the best" of the reviews, the pieces were *Le Chat et la Souris, Ce qu'a vu le vent d'ouest, Le Rêveur*, and "Jazzy" from *Trois Esquisses*. Copland accompanied a "Miss Mac Alister" in his "Melodie Chinoise" and in songs by Alexandre Brackocki, who had been "called home suddenly." M.

Gilles described Copland as "having the fine temperament of an artist. . . ." No piece with the title *Le Rêveur* has survived. According to Copland: "It probably became something else, since I never threw anything away!" No information has been found about Miss MacAllister (Copland's spelling) or "Mac Alister" (the newspaper review).

Paris, 1921–1924

1. Clurman interview.
2. Aaron Copland, *Copland on Music* (Garden City, New York: Doubleday, 1960; repr. New York: W. W. Norton, 1963).
3. Harold Clurman, *All People Are Famous* (New York: Harcourt Brace Jovanovich, 1974).
4. 7.0400 cents to the franc; in 1921, 500 francs was worth $32.50.
5. The name was later changed to 3 Place Lili Boulanger in memory of Nadia Boulanger's sister.
6. Included in Copland's writings on Boulanger are "A Note on Nadia Boulanger," *Fontainebleau Alumni Bulletin*, 5 (May 1930); and "An Affectionate Portrait," *Harper's Magazine*, 221 (October 1960), pp. 49–51.
7. Léonie Rosenstiel, *Nadia Boulanger; a Life in Music* (New York: W. W. Norton, 1982), p. 198.
8. Nadia Boulanger died 22 October 1979 at the age of ninety-two.
9. Marcelle de Manziarly described Copland as she first knew him and during their continuing friendship. Interview with Perlis, 29 August 1979, Paris.
10. Founded in 1909 by Gabriel Fauré.
11. Interview, Nadia Boulanger with Perlis, Oral History, American Music, Yale, 2 June 1976, Paris.
12. For Copland on Milhaud, see "The Lyricism of Milhaud," *Modern Music*, VI:2 (January-February 1929), pp. 14–19, repr. in *Our New Music* and *The New Music 1900–1960*; and "The Art of Darius Milhaud," *Saturday Review of Literature*, 31:26 (26 June 1948), p. 43.
13. Emile Vuillermoz, an influential critic, was particularly angered by the group's contempt for Debussy and Ravel.
14. Virgil Thomson, *Virgil Thomson* (New York: Alfred A. Knopf, 1967), p. 64.
15. Aaron Copland, "Stravinsky's 'Oedipus Rex,' " *New Republic*, LIV (29 February 1928), pp. 68–69.
16. For the entire letter from Copland to Berger, see Dorothy Norman, *Letters of Composers* (New York: Alfred A. Knopf, 1946), pp. 402–03.
17. The pianists were Samuel Barber, Aaron Copland, Lukas Foss, and Roger Sessions, with the American Concert Choir and The Columbia Percussion Ensemble.
18. Interview, Virgil Thomson with Perlis, 6 June 1979, New York City.
19. Copland's first contribution to *The League of Composers' Review* (later called *Modern Music*) was on George Antheil, in "Forecast and Review," II:1 (January 1925), pp. 26–28.
20. Rough sketches toward a string quartet, dated 1921, are in Copland's files, but the completed score has been lost.
21. On 26 January in a concert with works by Boulanger's students—among them Lennox Berkeley, Igor Markevitch, Marcelle de Manziarly, and Jean Françaix. The program lists Copland's piece as: "*Trois Motets*, a first performance."
22. Jack Beeson, composer and friend of Douglas Moore, found pages of a Copland score among Moore's papers left to Columbia University after his death; Beeson identified it as the *Four Motets* and was responsible for a performance and publication in 1979.
23. On 3 April 1934 one Motet was included in a program at the Euclid Avenue Temple on East 82nd Street and Euclid Avenue, Brooklyn. "An Evening of Hebrew Sacred

and Folk Music" concluded with "Modern Compositions" by Ernest Bloch and Aaron Copland. On the program Copland's work is called "Prayer (Motet)" and Copland is identified as "a brilliant young Jewish composer."

24. This manuscript is in Copland's files.

25. In Copland's files are: a sketch for a ballet in one act, *Longchamp* (undated, but probably from this period); and a "Plan for Longchamp: Intro, Dance I, Interlude, Dance II, Interlude, Dance III, and Finale," with timings for each section.

26. Lillian Coombs stayed with Sarah and Harris Copland until both died—she in 1944, he in 1945.

27. Copland's letters to Boulanger were sent to Copland by Annette Dieudonné in 1981, after Boulanger's death.

28. A sketch in Copland's files shows streetwalker written as "street girl" in Copland's hand.

29. From Clurman interview: "You can imagine that we had some hilarious times, Aaron and I, acting out those parts!"

30. The score of *Cortège macabre* was donated by Copland in 1925 to the Sibley Library, Eastman School of Music, Rochester, New York.

31. Also extracted from *Grohg* was *Dance of the Adolescent* in a two-piano arrangement.

32. Three versions are in Copland's unpublished Juvenilia.

33. *Two Pieces for String Quartet* was arranged for string orchestra and is published in both versions; Copland's files contain an undated sketch toward the orchestration.

34. The article appeared in *Musical Quarterly*, X:4 (October 1924), pp. 573–86.

35. It was first published in *New Music Quarterly*, II:4 (July 1929).

36. It is not clear whether Koussevitzky or Boulanger originated the idea for the piece.

INTERLUDE I

1. Pitts Sanborn, "Honors of the Season," *The League of Composers' Review*, I:2 (June 1924), p. 3.

2. For a history, description, and list of performances, see R. Allen Lott, " 'New Music for New Ears,' " *Journal of the American Musicological Society*, XXXVI:2 (Summer 1983), pp. 266–86.

3. See Louise Varèse, *Varèse: A Looking-Glass Diary* (New York: W. W. Norton, 1972), pp. 169–91; and Claire R. Reis, "Twenty-five Years with The League of Composers," *Musical Quarterly*, XXXIV:1 (January 1948), pp. 1–14. Also, for a description of the ICG board meetings before the break, see Claire R. Reis, *Composers Conductors and Critics* (New York: Oxford University Press, 1955; repr. Detroit, Michigan: Information Coordinators, 1974), pp. 13–15.

4. See Rita H. Mead, *Henry Cowell's New Music, 1925–1936: The Society, the Music Editions, and the Recordings* (Ann Arbor, Michigan: UMI Research Press, 1981).

New York: 1924–1926

1. See Aaron Copland, "Memorial to Paul Rosenfeld," *Music Library Association Notes*, 4:2 (March 1947); repr. as "A Verdict," *Paul Rosenfeld, Voyager in the Arts* (New York: Creative Age Press, 1948), pp. 166–69.

2. Paul Rosenfeld, "The Newest American Composers," *Modern Music*, XV:3 (March–April 1938), p. 153.

3. The Scherzo was arranged for two pianos by John Kirkpatrick. The unpublished manuscript is in Kirkpatrick's private collection.

4. Thomson interview, and "Notes on Copland's Organ Symphony," unpublished

typescript, which, according to Thomson, was probably meant as an article for the *Boston Transcript*; copy sent to Perlis, 1980.

5. The score for Copland's *Prelude* for chamber orchestra was donated to the Sibley Library, Eastman School of Music, by David Diamond, November 1943.

6. See Aaron Copland, "Serge Koussevitzky and the American Composer," *Musical Quarterly*, XXX:3 (July 1944), pp. 255–69.

7. Allan Kozinn, "Is There Life After Premieres for New Music?" *The New York Times*, Arts and Leisure Section (29 December 1981), pp. 19–20.

8. See minutes of the Koussevitzky Foundation meetings, in Copland's files.

9. Interview, Minna Lederman with Perlis, 17 September 1980, New York City.

10. Aaron Copland, "What Europe Means to the Aspiring Composer," *Musical America*, XLI:11 (3 January 1925), pp. 15, 27.

11. Aaron Copland, "Defends the Music of Mahler," *The New York Times* (5 April 1925), Sec. IX, p. 6.

12. Ink autograph manuscript at Lincoln Center Library, Museum of the Performing Arts, New York City.

13. The Guggenheim Foundation was founded by Senator and Mrs. Simon Guggenheim in the memory of their son, John Simon Guggenheim, who died in 1922.

14. A copy of Damrosch's letter is in Copland's files; see also a letter from Koussevitzky to Copland (17 April 1925): "It will be a pleasure to help you gain a scholarship from the Guggenheim Foundation."

15. Virgil Thomson, "Aaron Copland (American Composers VII)," *Modern Music*, IX:2 (January–February 1932), pp. 67–73.

16. Aaron Copland, "Jazz Structure and Influence," *Modern Music*, IV:2 (January–February 1927), pp. 9–14.

17. Clarence Adler, as quoted by M.L.S. (Mary L. Stoltzfus, assoc. ed.), *Musical Courier*, CXXXIV:3 (September 1946), p. 40.

18. "The Sidewalks of New York," by Charles B. Lawlor and James W. Blake (New York: Herman Darewski Music Publishing Co., August 1904).

19. Olin Downes, *The New York Times* (26 April 1933), p. 11.

20. In 1942 Lincoln Kirstein used the score for *Time Table* by Ballet Theatre, choreography Anthony Tudor, first presented under the title of *Despedida* by American Ballet Caravan for a South American tour in 1941; in 1943 the "Prologue" was used by Doris Humphrey and Jerome Weidman for *Decade*; in 1966 *Music for the Theatre* was combined with *Danzón Cubano* by Peter Darrel for *Lessons in Love*; and in 1979 Eliot Feld used the score for his ballet *Scenes for the Theatre*.

21. *The Seven Arts*, 1–2 (November 1916–October 1917), New York: The Seven Arts Publishing Company, 1916–17.

22. Waldo Frank, *Our America* (New York: Boni and Liveright, 1919).

23. Stieglitz's galleries were considered the most important centers for advanced art in the U.S.: The Little Galleries (also called "291") until 1917; The Intimate Gallery, from 1925 to 1929; and An American Place, from 1929 to 1946.

24. Aaron Copland, "America's Young Men of Promise," *Modern Music*, III:3 (March–April 1926), pp. 13–20. Copland would write three similar articles at about ten-year intervals: (1936) "America's Young Men—Ten Years Later"; (1949) "The New 'School' of American Composers"; and (1959) "Postscript for the Generation of the Fifties." All repr. in *Copland on Music*.

25. *Ballet mécanique* had its U.S. premiere in Carnegie Hall on 10 April 1927. Composed in 1924 to a scenario by Fernand Léger, it was originally planned for sixteen mechanical pianos and percussion. Reports vary on the instrumentation for the Paris and New York premieres. See George Antheil, *Bad Boy of Music* (Garden City, N.Y.: Doubleday, Doran, 1945), pp. 190–96, and Thomson, *Virgil Thomson*, p. 81.

26. Aaron Copland, "Playing Safe at Zurich," *Modern Music*, IV:1 (November–December 1926), pp. 28–31.

27. See also Clurman, *The Fervent Years* (New York: Alfred A. Knopf, 1950), pp. 13–14.

28. Later, when a sequence, *Four Blues*, evolved, the original "Blues 1" was removed and renamed "Sentimental Melody, Slow Dance." The original "Blues 2" became "Blues 4." Copland recorded "Sentimental Melody" on a piano roll for the Ampico Company in 1927, and Schott included it in Volume III of an album, *Piano Pieces by Contemporary Composers.* On the cover appeared some of the composers' names—Bartók, Stravinsky, Milhaud, Hindemith, Bornshein, H. K. Schmid, Schulthess, Windsperger, and H. Zilcher. Copland's name did not appear. Evidently, in 1929 he was not as well known as Zilcher.

29. Copland continued to point out the limitations of jazz. See "Aaron Copland Finds Flaws in Jazz," *Down Beat*, 25 (1 May 1958), pp. 16, 39–40; and "Modern Music: 'Fresh and Different,' " *The New York Times Magazine* (13 March 1955), pp. 15, 60, 62. The *Times* article was a dialogue with Henry Pleasants, "Modern Music: 'A Dead Art,' " which appeared in the same issue, pp. 14, 57, 59.

INTERLUDE II

1. Aaron Copland, "Baden-Baden, 1927," *Modern Music*, V:1 (November–December 1927), pp. 31–34; repr. in *Copland on Music*, pp. 183–88.

2. Interview, Ross Lee Finney with Perlis, 20 March 1982, Ann Arbor, Michigan.

3. Copland's lecture notes are preserved in his files.

4. According to the printed program, the works were: Krenek's *Concerto for Violin and Piano* (Barbara Lull and Copland); Stravinsky's *Serenade for Piano* (Carl Buchman); Hindemith's "Eight Songs from 'Das Marienleben' " (Greta Torpadie and Copland); Cowell's *Aeolian Harp*, *Advertisement*, *The Banshee*, and *Antinomy* (Cowell as pianist); and a *Group of Pieces for Violin and Piano*—Ravel's *Berceuse*, Webern's *Four Pieces*, op. 7, and Copland's *Nocturne* and *Serenade* (all performed by Barbara Lull and Copland).

5. Blitzstein Collection, State Historical Society of Wisconsin, Madison, Wisconsin.

6. *Répertoire Moderne de Vocalises-Etudes*, publiées sous la direction de A. L. Hettich, Vol. 8 (Paris: Alphonse Leduc et Cie, 1929). The collection contains over 100 vocalises: no. 1 is by Fauré; no. 71 by Copland. The first volume appeared in 1907 (Copland's piece is in volume 8).

7. Heinsheimer's attempts to interest ballet companies failed; the work was never published in this version. Interview, Hans Heinsheimer with Perlis, 21 May 1981, New York City.

8. Interview, Gerald Sykes with Perlis, 24 October 1980, New York City.

9. Marc Blitzstein admired Copland's *Lento Molto* and arranged it for two pianos. Unpublished manuscript in Blitzstein Collection, Wisconsin Historical Society.

10. In April 1983 the string quartet movement was played for Copland by the Alexander String Quartet at the composer's home in Peekskill, New York.

11. Sessions sent "An American Evening Abroad" to Minna Lederman for *Modern Music* (November–December 1926), followed in the twenties by "Ernst Bloch" (November–December 1927) and "On Oedipus Rex" (March–April 1928).

12. See Carol Oja, "The Copland-Sessions Concerts and Their Reception in the Contemporary Press," *Musical Quarterly*, LXV:2 (April 1979), p. 214. See Oja also for a complete listing of Copland-Sessions Concerts programs, pp. 227–29.

13. At the close of 1928, Sessions sent Copland an ink score, *Largo* from *Symphony in E Minor*, with the inscription: "For Aaron, Affectionately, Roger. Rome, Dec 4, 1928." Also in Copland's files is Sessions' score for *Chorale Prelude No. 2 for Two Manuals and Pedal*, inscribed: "For Aaron Copland, most cordially, Roger H. Sessions, June 30, 1926." This must have been sent to Copland soon after he and Sessions met in the spring of 1926 in Paris.

14. Interview, John Duke with Richard Miratti for Perlis, 8 December 1982, Northampton, Massachusetts. In the thirties Duke played the entire *Sonata* at a League concert in

New York and at a Yaddo Festival concert. An autograph manuscript of Sessions' complete *Piano Sonata* is in John Duke's possession.

15. Interview, Roger Sessions with Perlis, 4 May 1983, New York City.

16. Sessions addressed the issue of nationalism in several publications, among them: "Music and Nationalism," *Modern Music*, IX: 1 (November–December 1933), pp. 3–12; "On the American Future," *Modern Music*, XVII: 2 (January–February 1940), pp. 71–75; and *Reflections on the Musical Life in the United States* (New York: W. W. Norton, 1963), pp. 146–53.

Music for Musicians, 1928–1930

1. Together with Varèse, Copland arranged a series of six concerts at the New School, beginning with a song recital by Greta Torpadie on 13 January 1928. For 17 December 1928, Copland would produce another "Concert of Modern Music" with works by Chávez, Schoenberg, Szymanowski, Poulenc, Stravinsky, and Ravel.

2. It is unclear exactly where and when Copland and Chávez met. At a party given for them in the late seventies by Claire Reis in New York, a toast was made to the two old friends, and surrounded by a group of friends and colleagues, they reminisced: "We met in Paris," said Chávez none too certainly. "In Paris? No, in New York—I *think!*" said Copland. "In '26," offered Chávez. "*Really?*" said Copland.

3. *The New York Times* (29 May 1928), p. 16: "*Victor Company Offers $40,000 in 3 Prizes for Native Symphonic and Jazz Compositions.* The plan and the rules governing the competition were announced by John Erskine, author . . . at a dinner last night at the Plaza. . . . 'Recognizing a clear division among the ideals of American composers . . . the awards are offered for two distinct classes of compositions. Twenty-five thousand dollars is to be awarded for the best work of symphonic type, in any form which the composer may employ or develop, within the playing scope of the full symphony orchestra. . . . The closing date is May 27, 1929. The award will be announced on Oct. 3, 1929. . . . The Board of Judges . . . will comprise Mme. Olga Samaroff . . . Rudolph Ganz . . . Leopold Stokowski . . . Serge Koussevitsky . . . and Frederick Stock. . . .' It was said that the prize of $25,000 in the symphony competition is the largest amount yet offered for a single composition. The hope was expressed by speakers that out of the competition would come a great symphonic work which would be truly American in conception."

4. This piece had its first performance in New York in 1935 for a *New Music Quarterly* recording, with Ethel Codd Luening, soprano, Copland, piano. It was arranged for flute for Doriot Anthony Dwyer in 1972 and is published in both versions.

5. See Léonie Rosenstiel, *Nadia Boulanger*, and reviews of Rosenstiel: Ned Rorem (*The New York Times Book Review*, 23 May 1982, p. 28); Robert Craft (*The New York Review of Books*, XXIX: 9, 27 May 1982, pp. 8–12); Allen Hughes (*The New York Times*, 18 June 1982, p. C29).

6. The lectures were titled as follows: The Realism of Moussorgsky's *Boris Godunov*; the Impressionism of Debussy's *Pelléas et Mélisande*; the Post-Romanticism of Mahler's *Das Lied von der Erde*; the Post-Impressionism of Ravel's *Daphnis et Chloé*; the Expressionism of Schoenberg's *Pierrot Lunaire*; the Dynamism of Stravinsky's *Le Sacre du printemps*; the Mysticism of Scriabin's *Prometheus*; the Lyricism of Milhaud's *Création du monde*; the Neo-Classicism of Hindemith's *Das Marienleben*; the Objectivism of Stravinsky's *Oedipus Rex*; and a Summary of Lesser Masterworks.

7. Olin Downes, "Music: Young Composers Heard," *The New York Times* (31 December 1929), p. 8.

8. Thomson's response to a telephone inquiry of 14 October 1982 concerning the title was: "At first, Gertrude's title was *Capitals, Capitals*—two s's, one comma—later, she preferred *Capital Capitals*." On the concert program of 1929, the title appears as *Capital, Capitals*.

9. Thomson, *Virgil Thomson*, p. 136.

10. Copland must have been referring to Harris' *Concerto for Piano, Clarinet and String Quartet* of 1927, first performed at a League of Composers concert on 12 February 1928.

11. Several incomplete short pieces in Copland's Juvenilia use traditional Jewish melodies.

12. "Hora," arranged by Copland, was published in Series I—"Dances of Palestine," *Folk Songs of the New Palestine* (New York: Nigun, 1938). Some other contributors were Dessau, Weill, Milhaud, Toch, Wolpe, Saminsky, Jacobi, and Honegger.

13. Roger Sessions, "An American Evening Abroad," *Modern Music*, IV:1 (November–December 1926), p. 34; and Virgil Thomson, "Aaron Copland (American Composers VII)," *Modern Music*, IX:2 (January–February 1932), pp. 67–73.

14. S. Ansky, pseudonym for Solomon Rappaport (1863–1920), *The Dybbuk*, a play in four acts translated from the Yiddish by Henry G. Alsberg and Winifred Katzin (New York: Liveright, c. 1926).

15. Interview, Lehman Engel with Perlis, 4 June 1981, New York City. Engel died 29 August 1982.

16. In the program notes of early performances of the *Symphonic Ode*, the source of this quotation is given as Gide's book, *Préludes*, and the error was reprinted in several newspaper articles and reviews. The correct source is André Gide, *Paludes* (Paris: Gallimard, 1920); the quotation is from the preface page, translated by Copland for his own use.

17. No score survives. Copland had played this piece for John Kirkpatrick. See Interview, John Kirkpatrick with Perlis, 24 February 1983, New Haven, Connecticut.

18. The unpublished manuscript is in Kirkpatrick's private collection.

19. Kirkpatrick interview.

20. Sykes interview.

Yaddo and Mexico, 1930–1932

1. See Rudy Shackelford, "The Yaddo Festivals of American Music, 1932–1952," *Perspectives of New Music*, XVII:1 (Fall–Winter 1978), pp. 92–125; and Marjorie Peabody Waite, *Yaddo Yesterday and Today* (Saratoga Springs, New York: The Argus Press, 1933).

2. Interview, Arthur Berger with Perlis, 13 November 1981, Cambridge, Massachusetts.

3. Paul Rosenfeld, *Discoveries of a Music Critic* (New York: Harcourt, Brace, 1936), p. 358.

4. Arthur Berger, *Aaron Copland* (New York: Oxford University Press, 1953. Repr. Westport, Connecticut: Greenwood Press, 1971), p. 43.

5. After publication, John Kirkpatrick wrote to Copland with mostly favorable reactions and Copland responded from Mexico (7 October 1932): ". . . Your remarks about the published Variations amused me. You *did* find one mistake—the ties that are missing after Var. 20. But I can't agree about your strictures about the new A flat in meas. 1 of Var. 19 or the E flat in m. 19 of V. 20. That latter E flat is necessary because there has been too much A flat. It comes as a surprise and therefore needs a reiteration in order to really establish it. Therefore to have it twice doesn't in this case, 'spoil the effect.' . . ."

6. For correspondence from Copland to Koussevitzky, see Koussevitzky Collection, Library of Congress.

7. Gertrude Stein, *The Autobiography of Alice B. Toklas* (New York: Harcourt, Brace, 1933), p. 309.

8. From a memoir sent by Paul Bowles from Tangier, Morocco, 19 March 1979.

9. Interview, Vivian Fine with Frances Harmeyer for Oral History, American Music, Yale, 28 June 1975, Bennington, Vermont.

10. Engel interview. See also Berger and Siegmeister interviews.

11. Interview, Henry Brant with Vincent Plush for Oral History, American Music, Yale, 11 May 1983, Santa Barbara, California.

12. Arthur Berger, "The Young Composers' Group," *Trend* (April–May–June 1933), pp. 26–28.

13. The line reads: "He [Copland] is not walking with god or talking with men or seducing house-maids or tickling duchesses. He is crying aloud to Israel. And very much as if no one could hear him." Virgil Thomson, "Aaron Copland (American Composers VIII)," *Modern Music.*

14. Aaron Copland, "Thomson's Musical State," *Modern Music*, XVII:1 (October–November 1939), pp. 63–65.

15. Thomson interview.

16. Levant felt out of place at Yaddo. He called it a "closed shop" and left before the end of the festival. Oscar Levant, *A Smattering of Ignorance* (Garden City, N.Y.: Country Life Press, 1942), pp. 222–30.

17. Composers included were Robert Russell Bennett, Nicolai Berezowsky, Paul Bowles, Henry Brant, Carlos Chávez, Israel Citkowitz, Aaron Copland, Vivian Fine, Louis Gruenberg, Roy Harris, Charles Ives, Oscar Levant, Walter Piston, Silvestre Revueltas, Wallingford Riegger, Roger Sessions, and Virgil Thomson. For full programs, see Shackelford, "The Yaddo Festivals . . . ," *Perspectives.*

18. A.V.B. (Arthur V. Berger), "Yaddo Music Festival," *Daily Mirror* (New York), 3 May 1932 (final edition), p. 18.

19. See interview, Bernard Herrmann with Perlis, Ives Project, Oral History, American Music, Yale, 12 November 1969, New York City. Herrmann died 24 December 1975.

20. Copland's copy of *114 Songs* was donated to the Ives Collection, Yale Music Library. Ives would occasionally cut pages from copies of *114 Songs* when preparing smaller groups of songs for publication.

21. The seven Ives songs chosen were "The Indians," "Walking," "Serenity," "Maple Leaves," "The See'r," "Evening," and "Charlie Rutlage."

22. Aaron Copland, "One Hundred and Fourteen Songs," *Modern Music*, XI:2 (January–February 1934), pp. 59–64; rev. and repr. as "The Ives Case," in *Our New Music*, pp. 149–61; and with additional comment in *The New Music 1900–1960*, pp. 116–17.

23. Correspondence at Ives Collection, Yale Music Library, and in Copland's files.

24. Paul Rosenfeld, *Discoveries of a Music Critic*, pp. 352–60.

25. Alfred H. Meyer, "Yaddo—A May Festival," *Modern Music*, IX:4 (May–June 1932), pp. 172–76. The performers were Ada MacLeish, Jesús María Sanromá, Hubert Linscott, and John Kirkpatrick; Hans Lange Quartet; League of Composers Quartet; and composer-pianists Vivian Fine, Aaron Copland, and Oscar Levant.

26. Aaron Copland, "The Composer and His Critic," *Modern Music*, IX:4 (May–June 1932), pp. 143–47.

27. The composers repeated at Yaddo from 1932 were Israel Citkowitz, Roy Harris, Charles Ives, Walter Piston, and Roger Sessions. Those performed for the first time in 1933 were George Antheil, Theodore Chanler, Henry Cowell, Richard Donovan, Ross Lee Finney, Charles Martin Loeffler, Otto Luening, Quincy Porter, and Carl Ruggles.

28. Randall Thompson, "The Second Year at Yaddo," *Modern Music*, XI:1 (November–December 1933), p. 41.

29. The *Short Symphony* was reorchestrated for chamber ensemble by Dennis Russell Davies, who conducted the first performance of his version with the Saint Paul Chamber Orchestra on 17 February 1979 in Minneapolis.

30. An ink score of *Elegies* dated 1932 includes pencil indications for orchestration and a note from the composer on the first page: "Part I arranged for str orch and used in Statements (movt 4-Subjective)." Pencil sketches are also with the composer's manuscripts.

INTERLUDE III

1. George Orwell, "Inside the Whale," *The Collected Essays, Journalism and Letters of George Orwell, I: An Age Like This, 1920–1940* (London: Secker & Warburg, 1968), p. 510.

2. Interview, Mary Lescaze with Perlis, 25 April 1980, New York City.

3. Tom Wolfe, *The Painted Word* (New York: Farrar, Straus & Giroux, 1975), pp. 40–41.

4. Irving Howe, *A Margin of Hope* (New York: Harcourt Brace Jovanovich, 1982), pp. 11, 9, 59.

5. For more on the history of the Group Theatre, see Clurman, *The Fervent Years* and Margaret Brenman-Gibson, *Clifford Odets, American Playwright* (New York: Atheneum, 1981).

6. Clurman, *The Fervent Years*, p. 34.

7. Interview, Robert Lewis with William Owen for Perlis, 12 May 1981, Irvington, New York.

8. Lewis interview.

9. Brenman-Gibson, *Clifford Odets*, p. 412.

10. Clurman, *The Fervent Years*, p. 247.

11. Lewis interview.

12. Copland to Perlis, December 1976.

13. Carl Sands, "Copeland's [sic] Music Recital at Pierre Degeyter Club," in Sands' column *The World of Music, Daily Worker* (New York), 22 March 1934.

14. See correspondence and notebooks of Marc Blitzstein (Marcus Samuel Blitzstein) and bylaws and minutes of the Executive Committee meetings, State Historical Society of Wisconsin, Madison; David King Dunaway, "Unsung Songs of Protest: The Composers Collective of New York," *New York Folklore*, V:1 (Summer 1979), pp. 1–19; Barbara Zuck, *A History of Musical Americanism* (Ann Arbor, Michigan: UMI Research Press, 1980); Steven E. Gilbert, " 'In Seventy-Six the Sky Was Red': A Profile of Earl Robinson," lecture delivered to the American Musicological Society, November 1976, Washington, D.C.; and in response to the above, Henry Leland Clarke, "The Composers Collective" (Gilbert and Clarke unpublished).

15. See Blitzstein Collection.

16. In *Unison, The Organ of the American Music League*, I:2 (June 1936).

17. Interview, Charles Seeger with Perlis, Oral History, American Music, Yale, 16 March 1970, Bridgewater, Connecticut.

18. Interviews, Henry Leland Clarke with Perlis, by telephone, 14 May 1982 and 15 September 1983.

19. Interview, Elie Siegmeister with Perlis, by telephone, 10 November 1982.

20. In a letter from George Maynard to Vivian Perlis on 10 June 1982: "He [Copland] was a delightful chap then, slightly Communized as we all were in those days when we were young and Soviet Russia was idealized."

21. Interviews, Earl Robinson with Perlis, by telephone, 12 November 1982 and 16 February 1984. (Robinson became famous for his "Ballad for Americans," as sung by Paul Robeson.)

22. Aaron Copland, "Workers Sing!", *New Masses*, XI:9 (5 June 1934), pp. 28–29.

23. Seeger interview.

24. *New Masses*, XI:5 (1 May 1934), pp. 16–17.

25. Ashley Pettis, "Marching With a Song," *New Masses*, XI:5 (1 May 1934), p. 5.

26. Robinson interview.

27. Aaron Copland, "A Note on Young Composers," *Music Vanguard*, I:1 (March–April 1935), pp. 14–16.

28. Aaron Copland, "The American Composer Gets a Break," *The American Mercury*, XXXIV:136 (April 1935), pp. 488–92.

29. As announced in *Unison, The Organ of the American Music League*, I:2 (June 1936).

30. Aaron Copland, "1936: America's Young Men—Ten Years Later," *Modern Music*. Repr. in *Copland On Music*, p. 160.

Music for the People, 1934–1937

1. Interview, Ruth Page with Perlis, by telephone, 29 November 1982.

2. A two-piano arrangement was donated to Lincoln Center Library by Ruth Page. In Copland's files are a rough pencil score, a small orchestral one made in 1935, and an incomplete ink score of three cabaret dances. At Library of Congress are conductors' scores.

3. For a stage design by Remisoff for Hear Ye!, see Modern Music, XII:1 (November–December 1934), p. 18.

4. Cecil Michener Smith, "Copland's 'Hear Ye! Hear Ye!,'" Modern Music, XII:2 (January–February 1935), pp. 86–89.

5. Masters of Our Day, ed. Lazare Saminsky and Isadore Freed (New York: Carl Fischer, 1943). The album includes pieces by Copland, Cowell, Freed, Hanson, Milhaud, Moore, Sessions, Taylor, Thompson, and Thomson. Copland's two works are also published individually.

6. Lehman Engel, "New Laboratories and Gebrauchsmusik," Modern Music, XIII:3 (March–April 1936), p. 53.

7. Interview, David Diamond with Perlis, 10 November 1980, New York City.

8. Saminsky severely criticized Copland, and also Paul Rosenfeld for his support of the young composer. Saminsky called Copland "precocious and over-ripe, designing and altklug . . . the well-known ghetto-type is recognizable. One could accuse Copland of being too clever, too deliberate and too cerebral an observer and exploiter of modern European ways. His neurotic drive and stringent intellectualism are typically Jewish, but of the worst sort." Lazare Saminsky, Music of Our Day (New York: Thomas Y. Crowell, 1932), p. 154.

9. Copland and Odets discussed the adaptation of Odets' play Rocket to the Moon as an opera. A draft libretto is in Copland's files.

10. For descriptions of this incident, see interviews, Betty Bean with William Owen for Perlis, September 1983, New York City; and Leonard Bernstein with Perlis, 22 September 1983, Fairfield, Connecticut.

11. Thomson, Virgil Thomson, p. 254.

12. Copland's copy, given him by Toor in Mexico City in 1932, is with Copland's manuscripts at the Library of Congress. Cancionero Mexicano de Mexican Folkways, ed. by Frances Toor, illustrations by Rufino Tamayo (Mexico: c. Toor, 1931).

13. Rubén M. Campos, El Folklore y la Música Mexicana, Publicaciones de la secretaria de education publica (Mexico: Talleres graficos de la nacion, 1928).

14. Hans Heinsheimer, Best Regards to Aida (New York: Alfred A. Knopf, 1968), pp. 170–72, and interview with Perlis, 21 May 1981, New York City.

15. Copland wrote about El Salón México after it was recorded: Aaron Copland, "The Story Behind 'El Salón México,'" Victor Record Review, I:12 (1939), pp. 4–5.

16. Heinsheimer, Best Regards to Aida, p. 172.

17. Kirkpatrick's earlier two-piano version is in his private collection. Bernstein was invited by Boosey & Hawkes to adapt his solo piano arrangement for the published two-piano version.

18. See Robert Charles Marsh, Toscanini and the Art of Orchestral Performance (Philadelphia: J. B. Lippincott, 1956), Appendix. This was the only performance of a piece by Copland conducted by Toscanini.

19. A search in Grosse Pointe and the Detroit area has failed to locate Ruth Leonhardt. An ink holograph of the score on transparent paper is at Library of Congress with a memo at the end by Copland: "May–July 1937; New York, Hollywood, Mexico." Also at Library of Congress is a piano sketch, "for study only," and other pencil sketches of the orchestral score (incomplete).

20. Edwin Denby, "A Good Libretto," Modern Music, XIII:3 (March–April 1936), pp. 14–21.

21. Interview, Edwin Denby with Perlis, 6 May 1980, New York City. Denby died 12 July 1983.

22. Virgil Thomson, "In the Theatre," *Modern Music*, XIV:4 (May–June 1937), p. 235.

23. Interview, Rosamond Bernier with Perlis, 3 February 1983, New York City.

24. George Antheil, "Breaking into the Movies," and "On the Hollywood Front," *Modern Music*, XIV:1 (January–February 1937), pp. 82–86, 105–08.

25. George Antheil, "On the Hollywood Front," *Modern Music*, XIV:1 (November–December 1936), p. 47 footnote.

Music for Use, 1937–1939

1. "The Composers Organize. A Proclamation," *Modern Music*, XV:2 (January–February 1938), pp. 92–95. See also *ACA Bulletin*, XI:2–4 (December 1963), 25th Anniversary Issue.

2. Otto Luening, *The Odyssey of an American Composer* (New York: Charles Scribner's Sons, 1980), p. 434.

3. See David Hall, "CRI: A Sonic Showcase for the American Composer," *ACA Bulletin*, XI:2–4 (December 1963), pp. 21–29.

4. *Study Outline for Use with Aaron Copland's What to Listen For in Music*. Ninth book in the course of study prepared by the National Federation of Music Clubs (New York: Whittlesey House, McGraw-Hill, 1939).

5. For reproductions of three Jared French designs for *Billy the Kid*, see *Modern Music* XVI:4 (May–June 1939), p. 244.

6. See Walter Noble Burns, *The Saga of Billy the Kid* (Garden City, New York: Doubleday, Page & Company, 1926).

7. Interview, Eugene Loring with Perlis, by telephone, 14 December 1981. Loring died 30 August 1982.

8. Pencil sketches, typescript of poem, and ink score at Library of Congress. "Lark" was published by E. C. Schirmer, Boston, 1941.

9. Michael Kidd is listed in the original cast as Michael Forest. In 1943 he danced the title role in *Billy the Kid*, Ballet Theatre production.

10. See the Dance Collection, Lincoln Center Library, for a CBS-TV film of *Billy the Kid*, broadcast 8 November 1953, with John Kriza, artists of the Ballet Theatre, and Loring as narrator.

11. Interview, Lincoln Kirstein with Perlis, 11 May 1980, New York City.

12. *Time Table* choreographed by Anthony Tudor to Copland's *Music for the Theatre* was premiered 27 June 1941 in Rio de Janeiro, Brazil, and revived 13 January 1949 at the City Center in New York. By 1949 *Time Table* was viewed as a pale predecessor of more important ballets.

13. In the published score, "The Open Prairie" and "Street in a Frontier Town" are the only sections in which titles appear.

14. Elliott Carter, "Once Again Swing; Also 'American Music,'" *Modern Music*, XVI:2 (January–February 1939), pp. 102–103.

15. Lincoln Center Library holds the autograph ink score of *Five Kings* with notes by the composer in pencil. Library of Congress Collection includes original sketches, forty pages of cue sheets, and orchestral parts by copyist (unidentified)—the last bought from Max Marlin 2 September 1965 (Marlin was orchestra director and organist for the production). Cue sheets reveal that recorded music was called for in some places.

16. The score is at Library of Congress.

17. At Lincoln Center Library: an eleven-page autograph ink score of *From Sorcery to Science* on transparencies with revisions and indications toward a fuller instrumentation penciled in, signed and dated "May 4–8 '38;" and instructions, probably by the director or conductor of the production.

18. The scenario of *The City* was by Henwar Rodakiewicz, the production was supervised by Oscar Serlin, and the musical conductor was Max Goberman.

19. In addition to piano sketches, a typescript of the scenario of *The City*, with cues showing the placement of musical sequences in the film, is at Library of Congress.

20. At Library of Congress: pencil sketch of original verson (complete); ink score (bound); and ink score of revised version with parts.

21. See Aaron Copland, "A Visit to Snape," *Tribute to Benjamin Britten on His Fiftieth Birthday* (London: Faber & Faber, 1938).

22. Britten's *Concerto for Piano and Orchestra* in D major, op. 13, was composed in 1938 and revised in 1946.

Hollywood, 1939–1940

1. Aaron Copland, "Second Thoughts on Hollywood," *Modern Music*, XVII:3 (March–April 1940), pp. 141–47; and Aaron Copland, "The Aims of Music for Films," *The New York Times* (10 March 1940), Sec. 2, p. 7.

2. Lawrence Morton, "About Aaron," *Ron Wagner's Script*, 15 June 1940, pp. 18–19.

3. When Carl Van Vechten set up a George Gershwin Memorial Collection at Fisk University Library in Nashville, Tennessee, and asked for a manuscript, Copland donated the score of the piano pieces from *Our Town*. The original piano score of the orchestral suite was donated to the Motion Picture and Television Museum in Hollywood. In Copland's files is an unpublished arrangement of "Story of Our Town" for violin and piano, signed and dated "1940."

INTERLUDE IV

1. From Koussevitzky's statement to the trustees of the Boston Symphony Orchestra, 1939. Quoted in "A Tanglewood Dream," *25th Anniversary Album*, ed. Daniel Selznick, 1965.

2. For collections relating to Tanglewood, see Lenox Library Association, Tanglewood minutes from 1934 to 1944, Lenox, Massachusetts; Stockbridge Library, papers of George Edmos, first clerk of the Berkshire Music Festival, Stockbridge, Massachusetts; and Boston Symphony Orchestra, inactive and active records of the Berkshire Music Center and the administrative files of Tanglewood, Symphony Hall, Boston, Massachusetts. The above cited in Susan Kaufman, "Archival Resources for the Arts in Berkshire County, Massachusetts," 30 April 1983, unpublished research paper, Spaulding Library, New England Conservatory of Music, Boston, Massachusetts. See also Koussevitzky Collection, Music Division, Library of Congress. For histories of Tanglewood, see James R. Holland, *Tanglewood* (Barre, Massachusetts: Barre Publishers, 1973), and Moses Smith, *Koussevitzky* (New York: Allen, Towne & Heath, 1941), pp. 274–95.

3. This information and other background material about Hindemith from Luther Noss, Dean Emeritus and Curator of the Paul Hindemith Collection, Yale School of Music and former colleague of Hindemith at Yale.

4. The chorus sang Bach's *B Minor Mass* conducted by Koussevitzky on 15 August, and the orchestra played Hindemith's *Concerto for Strings and Wind Choirs*, Copland's *Music for the Theatre*, and Stravinsky's *Histoire du soldat*.

5. Quotations from Hindemith's letters to Gertrud Hindemith and to Herbert Fromm, courtesy Hindemith Collection, Yale.

6. Interview, John Colman with Caitriona Bolster, Oral History, American Music, Hindemith Project, Yale, 21 November 1976, New York City.

7. For interviews with other Hindemith students, see Oral History, American Music, Hindemith Project, Yale School of Music.

8. Interviews, Harold Shapero with Bolster, Oral History, American Music, Hindemith Project, Yale, 24 April 1976, and with Perlis, 9 October 1980, Natick, Massachusettts.

9. Interview, Robert Palmer with Perlis, by telephone, 12 May 1983.

10. See Howard Boatwright, "Paul Hindemith as a Teacher," *Musical Quarterly*, L:3 (July 1964), p. 282. Boatwright states, "His [Hindemith] ideas of what ought to be accomplished at a summer school such as Tanglewood did not coincide with those of Koussevitzky." Boatwright recalls, "Hindemith once told his class at Yale ... that Copland complained to him about the morale of his [Hindemith's] composition students." Hindemith tells this story in *A Composer's World*, deleting Copland's name: "Once I had a discussion on this subject with a well-known composer. He said, 'I think your system of teaching composers is all wrong. It discourages young people....'" Paul Hindemith, *A Composer's World* (Gloucester, Massachusetts: Peter Smith, 1969), p. 215. As the anecdote continues, Boatwright and Hindemith both refer to Boulanger's supportive methods with students; Hindemith again deletes the name and refers to Boulanger as "a famous teacher in Europe." *A Composer's World*, p. 216.

11. Interview, Lukas Foss with Bolster, Oral History, American Music, Hindemith Project, Yale, 11 November 1976, New York.

12. Nicolas Slonimsky recounts the incident in *Music Since 1900*, p. 486: "Charles Naginski, 31-year-old Egyptian-born American-Jewish composer of brilliant eclectic gifts, drowns in the Housatonic River by accident, or, more likely, by design." The following September (1940) Naginski's *Sinfonietta* was performed at Yaddo.

13. Belwin Mills holds the copyright for *Episode*. An incomplete score at the Library of Congress bears the following inscription on the title page: "Episode/Improvisation/Piece for Organ."

14. Roger Sessions, "American Music and the Crisis," *Modern Music*, XVIII:4 (May–June 1941), pp. 211–17.

15. Theodore Chanler, "The New Romanticism," *Modern Music*, XIX:1 (November–December 1941), pp. 65–67.

16. Aaron Copland, *The New Music 1900–1960*, p. 161.

17. Gardner Read, "Tanglewood: Investment in Musical Futures," *The Music News*, XXXII:20 (18 December 1941), pp. 6–7, 22.

The Early War Years, 1941–1942

1. Gilbert Chase was Latin American Music Specialist at the Library of Congress, 1940–43, and Charles Seeger was chief of the Music Division of the Pan American Union.

2. Sas wrote after Copland returned to the States (2 February 1942): "Just as you have to practice your Spanish, I must rehearse my English ... it was a very great pleasure to meet you in Lima, where I am living almost as an anchor in a desert. The bad is that you came and disappeared just as a comet. I remember your piano Sonata that you played unfinished here...."

3. This report to Dr. Moe had direct results. By the end of the year Juan José Castro was in New York. Copland alerted Claire Reis to the idea of the League paying more attention to South American music. "An Evening for Juan José Castro" was held 7 December 1941 at the Museum of Modern Art.

4. Nicolas Slonimsky, *Music of Latin America* (New York: Thomas Y. Crowell, 1945).

5. "Escola de Samba" ... in the "morros" refers to a popular kind of social club located in the hills above Rio.

6. Aaron Copland "The Composers of South America," *Modern Music*, XIX:2 (January–February 1942), pp. 75–82.

7. See John Kirkpatrick, "Aaron Copland's Piano Sonata," *Modern Music*, XIX:4 (April–May 1942), pp. 246–50.

8. Interview, Leo Smit with Perlis, 29 January 1981, New York City.

9. Wilfrid Mellers, *Music in a New Found Land* (New York: Stonehill Publishing

Company, 1964), pp. 81–101. Mellers and Copland corresponded from 1942 on, after Copland read Mellers' article, "Language and Function in American Music," *Scrutiny*, X (1942), pp. 346–57.

10. See *Aaron Copland, The Complete Music for Solo Piano*, performed by Leo Smit, produced by CBS Masterworks in 1979, released in honor of Copland's eightieth birthday.

11. See the Dance Collection, Lincoln Center Library for two films of *Day on Earth*: one, filmed in 1959 by Helen Priest Rogers at Connecticut College, as part of the Film Notation Project, with José Limón and others; another, filmed in 1972 by Dwight Godwin at the Juilliard School for the Jerome Robbins Film Archive, performed by members of the Juilliard Dance Ensemble.

12. Bernstein interview.

13. "Lamentation," movement III of "Jeremiah," *Symphony No. 1*.

14. See Charles C. Alexander, *Here the Country Lies* (Bloomington, Indiana: Indiana University Press, 1980), p. 194: "The favorite American historical personage in the Front years was Abraham Lincoln. The cresting Lincoln vogue dated from the 'twenties, when John Drinkwater's successful Broadway dramatization of Lincoln's life, Stephen Vincent Benet's epic poem 'John Brown's Body,' and Carl Sandburg's two volumes on Lincoln through his election to the presidency had all made the Civil War leader the personification of the innate, democratic goodness of America."

15. Andre Kostelanetz, *Echoes: Memoirs of Andre Kostelanetz* (New York: Harcourt Brace Jovanovich, 1981), p. 101.

16. Among the many who have narrated *Lincoln Portrait* are: Walter Abel, William Adams, Marian Anderson, Edward Arnold, Leonard Bernstein, Kingman Brewster, Myron Bush, Jorge del Campo, Rosalynn Carter, Jerome P. Cavanaugh, William Conrad, Aaron Copland, Walter Cronkite, Melvyn Douglas, Hugh Downs, Dan Evans, Jose Ferrer, Henry Fonda, Seamus Forde, Barry Foster, Will Geer, Arthur Godfrey, Robert Goheen, Lorne Green, June Havoc, Roland Hayes, Edward Heath, Charlton Heston, Jacob Javits, James Earl Jones, Edward Kennedy, Otto Kerner, Eartha Kitt, Canada Lee, Max Lerner, John V. Lindsay, Eugene McCarthy, Raymond Massey, Adolph Menjou, Burgess Meredith, Zero Mostel, Frank D. O'Connor, Fess Parker, Gregory Peck, Walter Pidgeon, Thomas Pulaski, Claude Rains, Basil Rathbone, Edward G. Robinson, Eleanor Roosevelt, Robert Ryan, Luis Salazar, Carl Sandburg, Willie Stargell, Adlai Stevenson, Kenneth Spencer, Juana Sujo, John Charles Thomas, Franchot Tone, Charles Del Vecchio, Sam Wanamaker, William Warfield, and Andre Watts.

17. The Schuman material is derived from: interviews with Perlis on 2 June 1983 and 29 December 1983 at Greenwich, Connecticut, and New York City; the program book for the Kennedy Center Honors of 7 December 1979; and an address delivered on the occasion of the dedication of the Copland School of Music, Queens College, 29 April 1981. It has been edited by William Schuman.

18. See Agnes de Mille, *Dance to the Piper* (Boston: Little, Brown, 1951), pp. 271–302, and *Speak to Me, Dance with Me* (Boston: Little, Brown, 1973), p. 337.

19. The tune in Copland's "Saturday Night Waltz" from *Rodeo* is a version of "Old Paint." It was used by Thomson in the film, *The Plow That Broke the Plains*, and in the suite derived from the film, section three, "Cattle."

20. Interview, Agnes de Mille with Perlis, 25 June 1980, New York City.

21. Sergei J. Denham was director of the Ballet Russe de Monte Carlo, Inc.

22. "Hoe-Down" is also published in a string orchestra version, for solo piano, and for violin and piano. The complete ballet is available for solo piano. "Hoe-Down" and "Saturday Night Waltz" have been arranged for two-pianos by Arthur Gold and Robert Fizdale.

23. "Bonyparte," a Kentucky variant of the tune "Bonyparte's Retreat Across the Rocky Mountains," was taken by Copland from John and Alan Lomax, *Our Singing Country* (New York: MacMillan, 1941), pp. 54–55.

24. Berger, *Aaron Copland*, p. 57.

25. See Olin Downes, "Shostakovich Seventh Receives First U.S. Concert Performance," *The New York Times* (15 August 1942), p. 12.

26. Titles of fanfares by other composers commissioned by Goossens: *Fanfare for the American Soldier,* Felix Borowski; *Fanfare for Paratroopers,* Paul Creston; *Fanfare de la Liberté,* Darius Milhaud; *Fanfare for American Heroes,* William Grant Still; *Fanfare for the Fighting French,* Walter Piston; *Fanfare to the Forces of Our Latin American Allies,* Henry Cowell; *Fanfare for Russia,* Deems Taylor; *Fanfare for France,* Virgil Thomson; *Fanfare for Freedom,* Morton Gould; *Fanfare for Airmen,* Bernard Wagenaar; *Fanfare for the Medical Corps,* Anis Fuleihan; and *Fanfare for Poland,* Harl McDonald. *Fanfare for the Common Man* was published in *Ten Fanfares by Ten Composers for Brass and Percussion* (New York: Boosey & Hawkes, 1944).

27. Aaron Copland, "From the '20's to the '40's and Beyond," *Modern Music,* XX: 2 (January–February 1943), pp. 78–82.

28. Paul Rosenfeld, *An Hour With American Music* (Philadelphia: J. B. Lippincott Company, 1929).

Index

Page references in boldface indicate illustrative material.